Adults in Higher Education
International Perspectives on Access and Participation

of related interest

Assessing Quality in Further and Higher Education
Allan Ashworth and Roger Harvey
ISBN 1 85302 539 9

Transition to Work
The Experiences of Former ERASMUS Students
Ulrich Teichler and Friedhelm Maiworm
ISBN 1 85302 543 7

Students, Courses and Jobs
The Relationship Between Higher Education
and the Labour Market
J L Brennan, E S Lyon, P A McGeevor and K Murray
ISBN 1 85302 538 0

Academic Community
Discourse or Discord?
Edited by Ronald Barnett
ISBN 1 85302 534 8

Adults in Higher Education
International Perspectives on Access and Participation

Edited by Pat Davies

Jessica Kingsley Publishers
London and Bristol, Pennsylvania

All rights reserved. No paragraph of this publication may be reproduced, copied or transmitted save with written permission or in accordance with the provisions of the Copyright Act 1956 (as amended), or under the terms of any licence permitting limited copying issued by the Copyright Licensing Agency, 33-34 Alfred Place, London WC1E 7DP. Any person who does any unauthorised act in relation to this publication may be liable to criminal prosecution and civil claims for damages.

The right of the contributors to be identified as author of this work has been asserted by them in accordance with the Copyright, Designs and Patents Act 1988.

First published in the United Kingdom in 1995 by
Jessica Kingsley Publishers Ltd
116 Pentonville Road
London N1 9JB, England
and
1900 Frost Road, Suite 101
Bristol, PA 19007, U S A

Copyright © 1995 The contributors and the publisher

Library of Congress Cataloging in Publication Data
A CIP catalogue record for this book is available
from the Library of Congress

British Library Cataloguing in Publication Data
A CIP catalogue record for this book is available from the British Library

ISBN 1-85302-286-1

Printed and Bound in Great Britain by
Biddles Ltd, Guildford and King's Lynn

Contents

	Introduction *Pat Davies*	1
1.	Australia *Glen Postle*	6
2.	Austria *Roseanne Benn*	38
3.	Belgium *Etienne Bourgeois and Jean-Luc Guyot*	61
4.	Denmark *Anthony Cooke*	84
5.	England, Wales and Northern Ireland *Gareth Parry*	102
6.	France *Pat Davies*	134
7.	Germany *Pat Davies and Evelyn Reisinger*	159
8.	Italy *Stella Parker*	181
9.	The Netherlands *Anna Spackman and Marleen Owen*	203
10.	Scotland *Michael Osborne and Jim Gallacher*	224
11.	Spain *Michael Osborne*	252
12.	Themes and trends *Pat Davies*	278
	Index	293

Introduction

Pat Davies

The origins of this book lie in a network of interests and activities. Of considerable importance has been funding for research in continuing education, which was made available to universities in the UK in 1990–93 by the then Universities Funding Council (UFC). A number of the chapters in this book – France, Germany, The Netherlands and Denmark – are direct outcomes of that funding, and a further three – Austria, Italy and Spain – were at least in part inspired by the growing interest provoked by that work. Four – Australia, Belgium, Scotland, and England, Wales and Northern Ireland – are the result of long standing involvement and interest and of links, through the growing international network, with some of the comparative work taking place. In this sense, the book is evidence of the effectiveness of the funding both as a source of research activity and a means of promoting interest in the field of study.

The choice of countries for inclusion has therefore been somewhat eclectic, based on research activities and comparative studies which were being undertaken at the time; it does not represent, as is the case with other publications of this sort (such as Gellert 1993, Goedegebuure *et al*. 1994), the outcome of collective action planned as a single coherent study from the beginning. Rather the studies take different approaches to their subject – historical, policy-oriented, practice-oriented – depending on their particular perspectives. Thus each author emphasises slightly different aspects of the question.

Access to and participation in higher education was one of the four main areas of action recently addressed by the European Commission (Task Force on Human Resources, Education, Training and Youth 1991), encouraging new and further development. However, this question was also a reflection of past and current development, evidenced by the growth in international links and in mutual interest and curiosity, and of the need to develop better understanding of our partners in order to move forward. It is not surprising, then, that the main focus of the book is Europe. It is not, however, a comprehensive study – there are some notable omissions – but complete coverage is not possible within a single volume. Neither is it restricted to the existing boundary of the European Union – Austria is included; in addition, there is one contribution from beyond Europe – Australia – which arose partly from collaboration with the author on comparative studies, but also, and more significantly, because that country has undergone 'sudden and dramatic change' (Meek 1994 p.36) in both structural and policy terms and is thus an interesting case study of the impact of such changes on the position of adults in higher education.

With some exceptions and cases of ambiguity (Australia, Belgium, England, Wales and Northern Ireland, and Scotland), the chapters are not written by natives or by insiders of the system under discussion, but by UK academics looking in from the outside. While we may therefore stand accused of a certain Anglo-centrism, there are nevertheless some strengths in the questions, perceptions and interpretations of the outsider, the anthropological 'other'. Despite a conscious attempt to set aside one's own cultural assumptions and frameworks, and to see the world as others see it in order to understand and make sense of what one sees, there is inevitably an undercurrent of comparison in such research. While there is a danger of asking the 'wrong' questions, there is also a greater likelihood that the outsider will ask questions which challenge many of the assumptions of the native and will thus reveal the layers beneath. In addition, some found that the need to grapple with language, which at times has a spurious similarity and at others a genuine unfamiliarity, forced insights which might not otherwise have surfaced. The writers have not therefore been merely observers of other systems but have engaged in dialogue with those closely involved to develop understandings which make sense in their own context as well as resonating with the concerns of the researcher. Thus, although our perceptions and interpretations perhaps inevitably reflect our own experience, as one of the authors has pointed out elsewhere (Bourgeois *et al*. 1994 p.ii), they are also enhanced by a dialogue in which those involved see 'anew what was familiar'. Such an approach allows ethnocentric assumptions on both sides 'to be identified and challenged by the existence of alternative, and equally deep-rooted, practices' (Broadfoot and Osborn 1992 p.71); it contributes to mutual knowledge; and it helps to 'situate' policies and practices in relation to our neighbours in an increasingly inter-dependent situation (Jallade 1992 p.35).

While this comparative approach has been a feature of many of the studies reported here, each chapter focuses primarily on the country in question. They are therefore essentially descriptive rather than analytical, although this varies somewhat depending on the author. Since, as Goedegebuure *et al*. point out (1994 p.xii), policy and practice in higher education is 'not a static phenomenon (but)...as dynamic as the society' in which it is located, this book runs the risk, particularly in a period of rapid change, of being 'at best an adequate picture at a given moment in time' and of quickly going out of date. However, as Gellert notes (1993 p.242), by focusing on the 'classifications of overall systems of higher education in the first place, one obstructs a meaningful insight into what those structures really are'. 'In the first place' is the key phrase in explaining the purpose of this book; there is a prior stage, that of setting out the key features of policy and practice in relation to a particular set of concerns, 'what is happening and what is being done' (p.241). Certainly, if only classifications are available, criticism is inhibited or restricted to those who are familiar with a range of national systems and who operate at this international level. This book attempts to extend the understanding of other structures and to make them more 'transparent' (to use a good European word) to our partners and counterparts. Thus within the constraints of space it offers more detail than most collections of this sort, in order to support an appropriate interpretation of practice which growing numbers in higher education need in order to take advantage of the opportunities for mobility now available.

The book also takes a theme – access to and participation in higher education for adults – which differs from that of most other international collections, which tend to focus on the systems level. Others have adopted this approach, notably CERI (1987); however, that report was structured around themes rather than countries, and most of the data on which it was based related to the early 1980s. Most commentators agree that there have been significant changes since then. It is useful, therefore, to take some of the trends identified at that time, and the future scenarios suggested, and to examine the extent to which they have continued or changed direction. Has the concept of 'adult' changed? Has mature student participation actually resulted in 'increasing inequalities amongst different sections of the population rather than making for a decrease in such differences' (CERI 1987 p.38), as was feared? Is the typical adult in higher education still 'more likely to be there because of previous educational advantages rather than disadvantages' (p.37)?

Other analyses have identified a number of significant changes at the systems level in recent times. Halsey (1993 p.135) points out that in universities 'control is now much more in the hands of politicians and budgetary administrators' than teachers; and others (Goedegebuure *et al*. 1994) have identified shifts in the relationship between government and institutions in a number of countries. The increase in diversity is a recurring theme: 'horizontal diversity' (Rasmussen 1992 p.91) or 'external diversity' (Jallade 1992 p.36) (the growth of non-university institutions of higher education) and 'vertical diversity' (Rasmussen 1992) (the availability of courses of different length with different exit points) have been identified as factors which make an impact on access and participation (de Weert 1994). In the English context, Wright (1991) has referred to such developments as changes in the 'accessibility' of higher education. Expansion, and in particular the transition from what Trow (1974) defined as elite to mass systems, affects public and academic perceptions about access and standards and brings to the surface tensions and conflicts in the debates. Halsey (1992 p.15) hypothesised that expansion leads to credentialist inflation and that therefore 'access becomes an arena of status struggle between social groups', that although access expands it 'is socially shaped to yield absolute but not relative gains in educational chances for traditionally disadvantaged groups', and that it is 'socially controlled by institutional differentiation'. One of the purposes of this book is to examine the extent to which these changes and developments have affected adults.

Despite the different sources of the chapters presented here, in order to provide a means of addressing these questions across the range of countries involved and to permit some trends, patterns and comparative themes to be developed, authors were asked to construct their contribution around a common framework of issues and concepts. These were: the structure, organisation and size of higher education; admissions procedures and norms; patterns of participation; political and policy frameworks and stakeholders; the concept of the adult; alternative entry routes; alternative provision and institutional arrangements for adults, and resources and funding. The final chapter seeks to draw together the various contributions under these themes and to identify current trends in relation to adults in the academy within the wider context of change in higher education.

References

Bourgeois, E., Duke, C., Guyot, J.L., Merrill, B., and de Saint Georges, P. (1994) *Comparing Access Internationally. The Context of the Belgian and English Higher Education Systems.* Coventry: University of Warwick.

Broadfoot, P. and Osborn, M. (1992) French Lessons: comparative perspectives on what it means to be a teacher. In D. Phillips (ed) *Lessons of Cross-national Comparison in Education.* Wallingford: Triangle Books.

Centre for Educational Research and Innovation (CERI) (1987) *Adults in Higher Education.* Paris: OECD.

Gellert, C. (ed) (1993) *Higher Education in Europe*. London: Jessica Kingsley Publishers.

Goedegebuure, L., Kaiser, F., Maassen, P., Meek, L., van Vught, F., and de Weert, E. (eds) (1994) *Higher Education Policy. An International Comparative Perspective*. Oxford: Pergamon Press.

Halsey, A.H. (1992) An International Comparison of Access to Higher Education. In D. Phillips (ed) *Lessons of Cross-national Comparison in Education*. Wallingford: Triangle Books.

Halsey, A.H. (1993) Trends in Access and Equity in Higher Education: Britain in international perspective. *Oxford Review of Education 19*, 2, 129–140.

Jallade, J.P. (1992) Access to Higher Education In Europe: Problems and Perspectives. In B. Marchione and M. Giuberti (eds) *Proceedings of the Conference on Access to Higher Education in Europe, Parma 13–16 October 1992*. Parma: Università degli Studi di Parma.

Meek, L. (1994) Higher Education Policy in Australia. In L. Goedegebuure, F. Kaiser, P. Maassen, L. Meek, F. van Vught and E. de Weert (eds) *Higher Education Policy. An International Comparative Perspective*. Oxford: Pergamon Press.

Rasmussen, T.K. (1992) Equality. In B. Marchione and M. Giuberti (eds) *Proceedings of the Conference on Access to Higher Education in Europe, Parma 13–16 October 1992*. Parma: Università degli Studi di Parma.

Task Force on Human Resources, Education, Training and Youth (1991) *Memorandum on Higher Education in the European Community*. Brussels: European Commission.

Trow, M. (1974) Problems in the Transition from Elite to Mass Higher Education. In OECD (1974) *Policies for Higher Education from the General Report on the Conference on Further Structures of Post-Secondary Education*. Paris: OECD.

de Weert, E. (1994) *Access to Higher Education and Labour Market Needs*. An international review of policy instruments. Paper presented at the European East/West Convention on Access to Higher Education, March 1994, Berlin (unpublished).

Wright, P (1991) Access or accessibility? *Journal of Access Studies 6*, 1, 6–15.

Chapter 1

Australia

Glen Postle

General Context

Australia is a sparsely settled continent (18 million approximately) comprising six states (Queensland, New South Wales, Victoria, Tasmania, South Australia, Western Australia) and two territories (Northern Territory and Australian Capital Territory). Most of the population is located on the eastern coastline with a heavy concentration of people living near the capital cities of Brisbane, Sydney and Melbourne.

There are two levels of government with interests in education in Australia. The Commonwealth (national) government provides funds for tertiary education and significant supplementary funding for schools. The state and territory governments provide funding for schools (government and non-government) and for technical and further education.

Tertiary education includes higher education institutions (universities) and technical and further education institutions (TAFE colleges). This chapter focuses on access and participation of adults in higher education – universities. However reference will be made to adults in technical and further education to illustrate particular points of comparison.

There have been a number of clearly defined phases in the development of universities in Australia. For the first half of this century, they were a state and not a federal responsibility and adopted structural models derived from the best traditions of the British university. They enjoyed significant autonomy over their officers and were relatively small institutions – prior to 1945 none exceeded 4000 students.

The postwar period (1945–1960) marked an increase in Commonwealth involvement. A number of factors accounted for this: '...national needs, university poverty...the commitment of the Prime Minister, Robert Menzies...the influx of returned servicemen...'

(Smart 1990a p.255). This period also saw the start of an increase in numbers entering higher education and the university sector grew rapidly, so rapidly in fact that it was recommended (Committee on the Future of Tertiary Education in Australia 1965) that a number of Colleges of Advanced Education (CAEs) be established. These were, at least in the first instance, more technologically oriented, and were perceived by staff and students as being a useful alternative to, but not having quite the same status and prestige as, universities. The funding for these institutions and for the universities was established on a shared Commonwealth and state basis. Hence, the binary system was established.

In 1972 a Labor government took office and began making significant changes in tertiary education. It assumed total control over funding and thus the seeds were sown for future government intervention, although direct intervention in planning and policy was not evident until the late 1980s.

While the 1980s marked a continuation of considerable autonomy over internal affairs, the tertiary sector was not being adequately funded. Smart points to the Commonwealth Tertiary Education Commission (CTEC) report of 1986 which '...detailed the shortage of student places and the deteriorating conditions in both teaching and research...(and) many of the CAEs...were increasingly unhappy with the binary system and its restriction of federal research funding to the university sector' (1990a p.258).

With the appointment of John Dawkins to the new Labor government Ministry of Employment, Education and Training in 1987, the stage was set for a major overhaul of tertiary education. It was clear that this new Ministry was concerned to create a link between what universities and colleges do and the process of economic adjustment, and to force the pace of change (Smart 1990b).

Dawkins abolished the CTEC and replaced it with a small, statutory National Board of Employment, Education and Training (NBEET). As Smart maintains, Dawkins '...deliberately crafted a weak, understaffed and tokenistic NBEET in order to enhance his capacity for swift ministerial and bureaucratic intervention in higher education' (1990a p.259).

The release of the Commonwealth government's White Paper (*Higher Education: A Policy Statement*) in 1988 heralded the beginning of a major overhaul of tertiary education. One of the most noteworthy statements contained in this document described the requirement that higher education institutions annually develop an 'institutional profile' on which their funding levels would be established, providing the Commonwealth government with significant potential to influence teaching and research in universities. As 'access and equity' was an educational priority for this government, particularly in higher education, it became a significant element in 'institutional profiles' of universities across the country. The Commonwealth government forced higher education to embrace access and equity and to focus resources on the provision of programmes that would enable under-represented groups to access higher education.

The White Paper also recommended the establishment of a unified national system and set out clear conditions for membership, some of which were that:

- institutions have a minimum sustainable level of at least 2000 equivalent full-time student units (EFTSU)
- all institutions develop an education profile detailing their 'particular areas of activity and specified goals'
- institutions follow a national framework for course length and nomenclature
- institutions be responsible for the accreditation of their courses within a framework agreed by the federal and state governments
- institutions develop clear and consistent guidelines to allow credit transfer to occur. (1988 pp.27–38)

Those institutions that could not meet the condition of minimum size were required to merge with a larger institution. Institutions that shared common or adjacent sites were also required to combine under a single management structure.

In the final analysis, the major outcomes of the 1988 document were that:

- all institutions (not TAFE colleges) were classified as universities
- a number of institutions were amalgamated
- funding was allocated on a triennial basis with all institutions able to compete for funds directly from the federal government. (Castles 1992)

As well as having access to universities, students wishing to pursue tertiary education also had access to Technical and Further Education (TAFE). This sector began to emerge in 1974 with the release of the Kangan Committee Report which suggested that these institutions should meet '…individual and community needs as well as industry requirements' (Castles 1992 p.16). They are responsible for a wide range of vocational courses (literacy, numeracy, pre-vocational training, para-professional training) as well as recreational courses, and are the responsibility of the state (or territory) governments. They are administered by a Director, who is responsible to the state Minister for Education. While the bulk of their funding is from the state government, some additional funding is provided by the federal government.

Admissions procedures, practices and norms

School leavers wishing to enter courses in TAFE colleges may do so following completion of compulsory secondary education. School leavers wishing to enter courses in universities may do so following completion of Year 12. However, access to universities is by no means automatic on successful completion of Year 12. Every state has adopted a different process for selecting school leavers for universities, ranging from the radical approaches of Queensland and Victoria which use a combination of school assessment and a range of different assessment tasks to arrive at a score or rating, to the conservative process used by New South Wales which employs a moderated school component in university entry subjects based on a continued use of public examinations.

The last decade has seen significant changes in the entry pathways of students to universities in Australia. There are three clearly identifiable models of entry to universities involving two groups of students – school leavers seeking direct entry and mature students seeking non-direct entry.

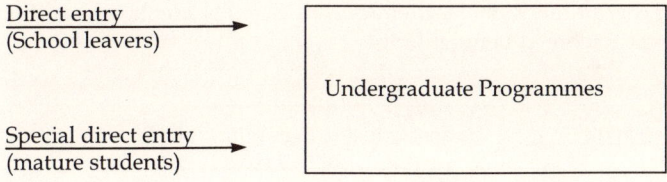

Figure 1.1: Entry to higher education – model 1

This first model describes a situation where most students gain entry to the university through school matriculation, with some (mature students) gaining special direct entry often on the basis of age, for example 23 or over. Some institutions continue to employ this procedure. However, this is not widespread. When this model was popular demand did not exceed supply and sufficient places were available for most school leavers who both wanted a place and had attained the necessary score.

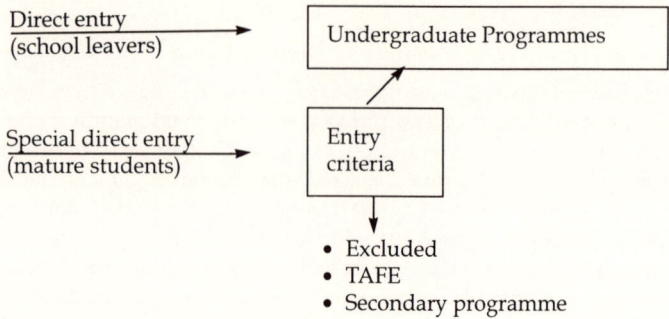

Figure 1.2: Entry to higher education – model 2

The second model involves the imposition, either by the state or the institution, of entry criteria for students seeking special entry. Its adoption had much to do with an increase in the number of school leavers wanting to enter higher education. In order to control mature age entry, several issues were raised: some of the students were deemed not to possess the necessary skills and abilities to commence the programme; some academics considered students who did not possess a score as being inferior.

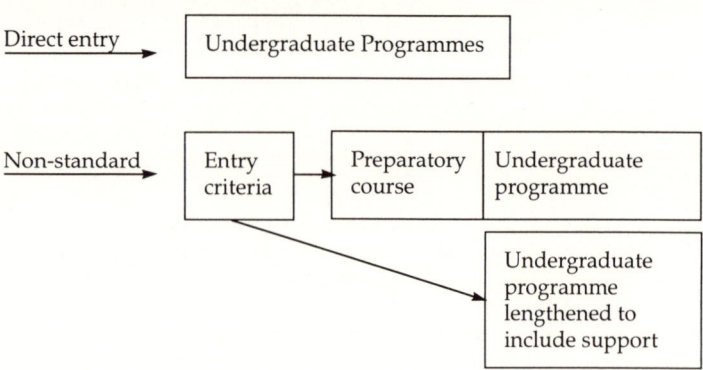

Figure 1.3: Entry to higher education – model 3

The third model acknowledges the fact that some mature students, after meeting the special entry criteria, require different levels and types of support. It has become popular in those institutions which have adopted a profile which includes access and equity for under-represented groups. Support may take the form of preparatory programmes (communication skills, study skills, maths skills) or ongoing support during the course. Adoption of this model results in different rates of progress by students through their courses.

The development of different models of entry to universities by higher education institutions must be viewed in the light of changing participation rates in higher education. For example, in 1946, 3.5 per cent of students aged 17–22 were undertaking undergraduate studies in universities; in 1977 this figure had risen to 9.5 per cent.

At the same time, higher education had become more accessible to the wider community. West explains the situation at the end of the 1970s thus:

> We contend that the flood of mature age students into higher education grew out of the complex interaction between these three systems. The discontinuity of growth in the institutions provided the places, the demands of the employment sector provided the pressures and motives for some mature age students, while the change in community values provided them for others. (1980 p.162)

Size of the system

The abolition of the binary system caused substantial changes in higher education. For example, in 1986 there were some 70 tertiary institutions in Australia. In 1991 there were 35. This was the result of mergers and amalgamations forced on some institutions where minimum size could not be sustained. As would be expected with a decrease in the number of institutions and an increase in the number of students (336,702 in 1981 and 534,538 in 1991) the average number of students per tertiary institution rose from 5400 in 1986 to 15,000 in 1992 (Castles 1992 p.22), although there is still considerable variation. Table 1.1 details the growth in the number of students enrolled in higher education over the decade from 1981 to 1991.

Table 1.1: Students enrolled in higher education, 1981–1991

1981	1983	1985	1987	1989	1991
336 702	348 577	370 016	393 734	441 076	534 538

Source: Australian Bureau of Statistics 1992

Substantial growth has also occurred in the TAFE system, from 692,014 students in 1981 to 985, 942 in 1991. This growth can be attributed mainly to direct government intervention, based on a perceived link between this type of education and the development of skills necessary for economic recovery. Growth has not been as dramatic as the rate of growth in universities (40% increase in TAFE, 60% in universities). One of the reasons for this may be a widely held belief that a university education was vastly superior to a TAFE education and that the rewards were greater in terms of better paid jobs on completion. However, it is difficult to compare enrolments between the two sectors as many TAFE courses are of a shorter duration than other higher education courses and can include '...basic education courses in areas such as literacy and numeracy; Year 12 certificates; courses for those returning to the workforce after a long absence; pre-vocational training; trainee apprenticeship; technician and para-professional training [as well as] recreational and non award courses...' (Castles 1992 p.16).

Table 1.2 details the number of tertiary institutions by state in 1991.

Table 1.2: Tertiary institutions by state in 1991

	New South Wales	Victoria	Queensland	South Australia	Western Australia	Tasmania	Northern Territory	Australian Capital Territory	TOTAL
TAFE	243	279	37	21	86	7	10	1	684
University	9	7	7	3	4	1	1	2	35

Source: Castles 1992 p.30

Patterns of participation

Table 1.3 provides some information on higher education student demographics. There was an increase of 59 per cent in total enrolments between 1981 and 1991. The number of females in higher education now exceeds the number of males, a reverse of the situation in 1981. Higher education students are mainly young, with some 62 per cent in 1991 aged under 24 years. It is interesting to note that older students (over 30) comprised 26 per cent of the student body in 1991. Even though older students now make up a substantial component of the student body, it is noted that there has been an increase of 4 per cent in the proportion of students aged under 20 while the proportion of students aged 25–29 decreased by 3 per cent. This is largely due to increased demand for higher education from school leavers (Castles 1992 p.82).

Table 1.3: Higher education students by age and sex, 1981–1991

Age group (years)	1981	1983	1985	1987	1989	1991
19 and under						
Males	46 687	47 220	49 617	56 099	66 531	74 820
Females	46 460	49 062	54 223	65 741	81 892	96 617
Persons	*93 147*	*96 282*	*13 840*	*121 840*	*148 423*	*171 437*
20–24						
Males	59 698	61 120	61 377	60 759	65 482	80 304
Females	43 007	45 009	47 956	52 558	61 182	79 967
Persons	*102 705*	*106 129*	*109 333*	*113 317*	*126 664*	*160 271*
25–29						
Males	31 227	30 644	30 669	29 251	28 630	32 334
Females	20 159	20 530	21 999	23 088	25 321	30 693
Persons	*51 386*	*51 174*	*52 668*	*52 339*	*53 951*	*63 027*
30 and over						
Males	44 558	47 753	51 970	50 022	50 642	62 218
Females	41 296	45 894	51 478	55 733	61 396	77 585
Persons	*85 854*	*93 647*	*103 448*	*105 755*	*112 038*	*139 803*
Age not listed						
Males	1 253	580	421	253	–	–
Females	2 357	765	306	230	–	–
Persons	*3 610*	*1 345*	*737*	*483*	–	–
Total						
Males	**183 423**	**187 317**	**194 054**	**196 384**	**211 285**	**249 676**
Females	**153 279**	**161 260**	**175 962**	**197 350**	**299 791**	**284 863**
Persons	**336 702**	**348 577**	**370 016**	**393 734**	**441 076**	**534 538**

Source: Castles 1992 p.109

The Concept of Adult

Little in the way of policy can be uncovered which might clarify the commonly held view by universities of the concept of an adult as being a student over 25 years of age. In the early 1970s, a predominant view held by many was that an adult was a person over the age of 23, although 25 was a cut-off point used in some universities. This absence of policy has been largely responsible for the random nature of decision-making concerning the entry procedures used by universities for adults.

Table 1.4 shows how the percentage of students enrolled as full-time students has increased from 49 per cent in 1981 to 61 per cent of total higher education enrolments in 1991. However, the proportion of students undertaking courses externally has remained constant at approximately 11 per cent of the total number of students, a somewhat surprising statistic given the growth of interest in distance education and open learning.

Table 1.4: Higher education students by enrolment status, 1981–1991

Enrolment status	1981	1983	1985	1987	1989	1991
Males						
Internal	162 911	166 314	170 683	174 214	189 105	224 862
Full-time	93 649	98 623	204 276	114 739	129 437	153 210
Part-time	69 262	67 691	66 407	59 475	59 668	71 652
External	20 512	21 003	23 371	22 170	22 180	24 814
Total	183 423	187 317	194 054	196 384	211 285	249 676
Females						
Internal	134 320	141 147	153 737	173 789	203 562	252 754
Full-time	85 177	89 884	100 063	119 415	142 664	175 197
Part-time	49 143	51 263	53 674	54 374	60 898	77 557
External	18 959	20 113	22 225	23 561	26 229	32 108
Total	153 279	161 260	175 962	197 350	229 791	284 862
Persons						
Internal	297 231	307 461	324 420	348 003	392 667	477 616
Full-time	178 826	188 507	204 339	234 154	272 101	328 407
Part-time	118 405	118 954	120 081	113 849	120 566	149 209
External	39 471	41 116	45 596	45 731	48 409	56 922
Total	**366 702**	**348 577**	**370 016**	**393 734**	**441 076**	**534 538**

Source: Castles 1992 p.119

The data contained in Table 1.5 are from 1988, and are the most recently published statistics in the area. Participation rates of people in remote areas is approximately half that of urban dwellers. Of some interest is the fact that female participation rates are higher than male participation rates in each location.

Table 1.5: Participation rates of higher education students by home location (per 100 of relevant population cohort)

	Urban	Rural	Remote	Total
Males	4.0	2.4	1.9	3.4
Females	4.2	2.9	2.5	3.8
All	4.1	2.6	2.2	3.6

Source: Castles 1992 p.83

A framework for classifying mature students

Hore and West (1980) provide a useful framework for understanding the nature of the mature student in Australia. They suggest that mature students fall into two broad groups. One group is representative of those people who had little opportunity to pursue higher education when they were younger. The second group are those people involved in recertification or requalification such as teachers, nurses and librarians and other professions could now be included as the notion of retraining has become more urgent, widespread and institutionalised since 1980. This group is more likely, but not exclusively, to be involved in graduate studies.

Government responses to adults

A close analysis of federal government statements about mature students over a period of time extending from the mid 1970s to the late 1980s provides some evidence that enrolment of adults has been allowed by governments to bolster student numbers in times when participation rates of young people were low. For example, in 1975 the proportion of students who were 'mature/older' was 40 per cent. At this time the proportion of 'young' students began to decline while the proportion of mature students increased to 46 per cent of the total in 1980. This pattern was repeated in CAEs (pre-amalgamation times) with a mature age level of 37 per cent in 1975 increasing to 47 per cent in 1979 and documented in a Commonwealth Tertiary Education Commission report which stated that 'A decline of one fifth in the participation of young people in higher education is surely a matter for community concern...' (CTEC 1984 p.8). CTEC was also sympathetic to preserving and in some instances increasing the numbers of mature students as a way to achieve access and equity by suggesting that: '…although our emphasis is on growth in youth participation, it is essential to maintain, at least at present levels, the opportunities which now exist for older people to undertake a course of tertiary education' (CTEC 1984 p.8).

The government, however, was more concerned about the position of young people and stated that it 'would be particularly concerned at the longer term economic and social implications of the situation where young school leavers were unable to obtain tertiary places and where entrance requirements were becoming more restrictive. The Government considers that the emphasis in the coming triennium must be on creating more opportunities for young people…' (Ryan 1984 p.3).

Currie, Baldock and Bossinga point out that the federal government at that time showed little concern for those students who might have stepped out of the educational system in the period from 1976 to 1981 to undertake a short period of work experience. These students could be classed as mature students but would now be denied entrance to tertiary education. They also point out that the government ignored a mounting body of evidence (see, for example, Hore and West 1980) which suggested that mature age students do extremely well in tertiary studies and that school leavers who take one or two years off between secondary school and tertiary studies seem to return to their studies with a higher degree of motivation (Currie et al. 1984 p.176).

In addition, the kind of changes that have taken place in student composition have been instrumental. As Toyne states, 'the very pressures for institutional survival have tended to lead to instrumental changes and many of these changes have tended to be product-led based on perceived assumptions about customer needs rather than on direct evidence of those needs or aspirations' (1990 p.135). The reason behind the adoption of wider access by many Australian universities, particularly the former CAEs, can be linked to institutional survival and increased numbers rather than meeting the needs of all capable students who wish to access higher education. Now that the demand for places exceeds supply it seems to be more convenient to concentrate on mainstream activities and to place the issue of increasing access at the margins of institutional portfolios. The 'new' universities now have little difficulty in filling their quotas, so the pressure to attract non-traditional students is not an issue. These universities are also keen to demonstrate that they are at least equal to some of the longer established universities, and the enrolment of students who cannot produce an entry score which can be equated with the more traditional tertiary entrance scores does not relate to the elite and rationalised system of higher education which they are trying to embrace (Parry and Wake 1990).

Policy Relating to Adults in Higher Education
Influence of federal government
In February 1990 the federal government's Department of Employment, Education and Training published its *Fair Chance for All* with the aim of providing 'higher education that's within everyone's reach'. The general thrust of this policy was to provide opportunities for those groups who have been typically under-represented in higher education, namely those from socio-economically disadvantaged backgrounds: Aboriginal and Torres Strait Islander people, women, those from non-English-speaking backgrounds, those with disabilities and those from rural and isolated areas. The document also made reference to specific targets to be reached by higher education across the country. These were:

- all institutions to develop special entry arrangements for socio-economically disadvantaged groups by 1992;
- an increase of 50 per cent in Aboriginal enrolments in higher education and an improvement in the graduation rate of Aboriginal students to a level comparable to the total student population by 1995;
- an increase in the proportion of women in non-traditional courses to at least 40 per cent and in engineering courses from 7 per cent to 15 per cent, by 1995; and an increase in the number of women in postgraduate study, particularly in research, relative to the proportion of female undergraduates in each field by 1995;
- all institutions with a significant number of people from non-English-speaking backgrounds in their catchment area to provide tertiary awareness programmes and adequate support programmes by 1992;
- double the present initial enrolments of people with disabilities by 1995, including an improvement in professional and vocationally-oriented courses of 30 per cent by the same date;
- all institutions in rural and regional areas to provide information programmes on opportunities in higher education directed at rural schools and communities by 1992;

- institutions with designated Distance Education Centres to improve student support for isolated and rural students by 1992 to increase graduation rates.

Specific funding was available for higher education institutions through the government's Equity Programme, to provide incentives to those institutions with a commitment to equity; thus it became a significant element in the institutional profiles of universities across the country. However, guidelines for the development of these profiles were difficult to implement. Higher education institutions were required to assess the levels of under-represented groups in their catchment areas, to compare these levels with the actual enrolments of students in these groups and to develop strategies to reduce differences. For example, if an institution had ascertained that in their catchment area 5 per cent of the population were Aboriginal and Torres Strait Islanders, and that the actual Aboriginal and Torres Strait Islander enrolment was 1 per cent of the student body, then it was required to indicate the strategies it would employ to close the gap in its triennium plan. The *Fair Chance for All* document (DEET 1990 p.21) suggested some of the strategies that might be used in this context:

- establishing negotiation mechanisms between Aboriginal people and higher education institutions
- developing special entry arrangements
- developing bridging courses linked specifically to entry to award courses
- promoting off campus and alternate study modes
- establishing Aboriginal support units in higher education institutions
- developing supplementary study units concurrent with award courses
- reviewing the higher education curriculum.

Several difficulties have been identified in implementing this programme. For example, many institutions have had considerable difficulty in defining what is meant by the catchment area since they have large numbers of distance education enrolments drawing students from every state in Australia and even overseas in some institutions. The second problem concerns defining some of the categories mentioned in the document. For example, it has been difficult to gather data which would assist in defining socio-economically disadvantaged students and in finding ways of identifying them. A further problem concerns the difficulty some institutions are now experiencing in continuing the programme once the initial three year funding from federal government ceased.

There are also more fundamental problems with this policy. Many of the documents issued by the federal government over the last few years concerning mature students convey a clear ideological framework which stresses the notion of unequal treatment of under-represented individuals and groups to achieve equal outcomes. However, it is also clear that some higher education institutions are reluctant to adopt this ideology and instead concentrate almost entirely on equality of opportunity, focusing on the single criterion of academic attainment or performance so that disadvantaged groups have the same access to higher education as any other group in the community. There is sufficient evidence now to suggest that in this approach such students become part of a vicious circle: many will not gain entry if performance or scores are the criterion for entry, nor will they stay the distance if they are not given support on entrance and, for some, during the course.

It is clear from many of the documents produced by the federal government that there is tension between those advocates of a higher education system that needs to be more efficient and those who support the view that greater opportunities for under-represented groups are necessary.

Healy (1993), quoting Professor Michael Osborne, points out that the government's new quality assurance committee was using criteria such as 'placement in employment', 'cost effectiveness of institutions in graduating students in various fields of study', and 'time taken to complete courses' to set the scene for further intervention in institutions, which might take the form of transfer of funds from ineffective and inefficient universities. 'This will mean that 'institutions...will lose funded load...and thus...be punished for investing their efforts in students whose circumstances make it unlikely that they will complete courses in the minimum time... The hollowness of earlier protestations of interest in equity and in a much vaunted Fair Chance for All is thereby manifest.'

The federal government has also linked courses in higher education with national objectives. It has been argued in government circles that the provision of access and equity programmes for adults would contribute to economic recovery, as it would limit the potential loss of human resources; universities and TAFE colleges in particular were seen as the conduit to the work force. For example, it has been argued that while women represent approximately 50 per cent of the population they do not represent 50 per cent of the student body in some faculties; engineering has been singled out in this respect. They are also under-represented in postgraduate studies. The argument made by supporters of access and equity programmes is that the national economy can ill-afford to ignore the human resource potential contained within these groups.

Influence of state governments

State governments represent another source of policy in this field. First, by virtue of the fact that they administer the norm-referenced screening procedures at the end of Year 12 used by universities for selecting entrants to particular courses, they exert influence over tertiary selection. That higher education institutions embrace such screening procedures as 'the single most important criterion' on which to make decisions about entry is not a requirement or a mandate of state governments. However, the fact that it is there and state governments allocate significant resources to maintaining such a procedure provides evidence of tacit approval by governments for higher education institutions to continue with such a practice. This indirectly affects the prospects and numbers of mature students entering universities. Second, both federal and state governments are also currently sympathetic to the view that more places should be provided for Year 12 graduates. This has a great deal to do with the current economic situation and the fact that young people represent a major proportion of the unemployed. Third, state governments can influence policy through the imposition of suggested quotas on particular courses offered by higher education. Teaching and nursing are two areas where this occurs. Currently, there is an over-supply of teachers, and as state governments employ the majority of graduates from teacher education programmes, they can influence intake by allocating fewer employment opportunities. In the past when more teachers have been needed, state governments have encouraged teacher educators to enrol more students in these areas and encouraged 'alternative' entry by supporting the enrolment of mature students. Finally, they also control the TAFE sector which provides vocational and retraining programmes. Their policy in relation to mature students, therefore, tends to be concerned primarily with providing places for such students in such programmes. Currently state governments are being encouraged by federal funding to offer more places in such institutions for school leavers *and* mature students, although there is again more tangible support for school leavers given the government's commitment to reducing youth unemployment. However, there are no generally recognised pathways between TAFE colleges and universities so that progression to higher education through this route is limited. Nevertheless, some useful pilot projects involving some TAFE and higher education institutions are under way.

Influence of employer and employee organisations

In response to the federal government initiative concerning the need to develop a set of 'key competencies' around which national curriculum frameworks may be developed, several reports (Australian Education Council Mayer Committee 1992, Australian Education Council Review Committee 1991, Employment and Skills Formation Council Australia 1992) have been released detailing the nature and range of competencies which might be expected of people who would be able to contribute positively to the future workforce. Membership of the groups who compiled these reports was strongly representative of employer and employee organisations. While there has been considerable debate on these reports in a range of forums they have not been adopted by governments at any level or in any state, due, no doubt, to the collapse of discussions between the states on the adoption of a national curriculum framework. Nevertheless, the emergence of 'competencies' and the adoption in several higher education institutions of the general principle of recognition of prior learning may lead to the development of entrance requirements that are more favourably disposed to the plight of mature students than the current arrangements.

Influence of higher education institutions

The higher education institutions represent the final link in the chain of those who contribute to existing policy and are generally supportive of adult access. However, in some instances this has more to do with available funding than a desire to see adult enrolments become a significant and continuing feature of admissions and thus may change as the numbers of school leavers wishing to access higher education exert more pressure on student numbers. Many also support the view that adults should compete on an equal basis with traditional students which, as already indicated, conflicts with government policy approaches. The equality of opportunity stance is popular particularly in those institutions which believe that mature students lower standards. Some university departments have actively sought the high scoring Year 12 graduates to fill their courses since these students bring status to the department.

The adoption of a 'unified national system' as recommended by the federal government would suggest a need to strive for a more cohesive and comprehensive policy statement on adults in higher education than currently exists. However, the influences detailed above, both supportive and non-supportive of adult access to higher education, paint a picture which goes some way towards explaining the general absence of policies which are coherent and consistent across the higher education system. A generalised set of policies may not be wanted by higher education institutions that have been accustomed to a degree of autonomy in the past, particularly in reference to the nature of enrolments.

Alternative Entry Routes for Adults

One of the most favourable outcomes of the federal government's access and equity policy has been the internal reviews concerning entry procedures that have been forced upon many higher education institutions. Some of these reviews have begun to challenge the dominant model of admissions which focuses on a single score or rating. Whilst it is still widely used, there are some signs of questioning the conventional academic selection as the only way to admit students. Higher education institutions are now more informed by research which is showing that '...very rarely can aggregate marks...account for even half of the variation which occurs within the scholastic attainments of our students in universities' (Anderson 1992 p.4).

Some of the more common alternative entry routes for adults include preparatory programmes, recognition of prior learning and positive action strategies.

Preparatory programmes

A number of higher education institutions have opted for 'preparatory programmes' to provide disadvantaged groups with an alternative entry route to higher education. Some of the most innovative programmes of this type in Australia include the Access and Equity programme at the University of Southern Queensland and the Open Foundation Course at the University of Newcastle. These programmes teach and test the qualities associated with potential university students and also develop other qualities (self-esteem, confidence) that will enhance success in tertiary studies. Courses such as communication skills, advanced learning skills and mathematics skills are common elements of such programmes and precede entry into the 'course proper'. Some of these courses even go so far as to provide bridges for students into selected courses. For example, at the University of Southern Queensland, students are provided with opportunities to enter the Mathematics Skills preparatory course at their level of proficiency and to exit at whatever level provides them with the necessary prerequisites for entry to their selected course. Such approaches are promising, as universities engaged in these sorts of programmes are being forced to reconsider the wisdom of using norm-referenced measurement procedures as the most appropriate way to select students for entry. As well as this, they are being asked to think more carefully about the design of instruction, particularly in respect of how they assess student progress. Specifying learning outcomes is a prerequisite for criterion-referenced assessment, an assessment model that has not been widely used in higher education up to now.

At the University of Newcastle another type of preparatory programme is offered: the Open Foundation Course, which targets late-start adults from socio-economic groups not traditionally well represented in student cohorts. It is different in that it does not focus on skills such as essay writing, basic numeracy, study skills, time management and library techniques. Instead it offers a wide range of subject, time, location and mode options. In 1992, 17 subjects were available from which the mature students could select two, chosen from academic disciplines rather than professional areas. The rationale for this course is based on the following:

- the prospective student learns the skills associated with particular disciplines in a safe and supportive environment
- teaching and learning academic writing techniques is best done when the student has something academic to communicate
- late-start students are more likely to foreclose on their options when professional subjects are offered too early in their study programme (Collins 1992 pp.1–8).

While preparatory programmes constitute the major alternative entry route for adults, there are still objections to be overcome. The problem of standards continues to be a major issue. Many faculties remain unconvinced that satisfactory completion of preparatory programmes is any substitution for the conventional tertiary entrance score. Several have even attempted to equate the completion of preparatory programmes with a comparable score; an administratively convenient way to deal with this complex matter. Another issue concerns a general lack of support for the student after the completion of the preparatory programme. There is a widely held view that these students must compete on the same basis as students who have gained entry through more traditional paths. It disregards the argument that many of these students may require to be treated unequally at the beginning of their award programme.

Recognition of prior learning

It is the 'new' universities and TAFE colleges which have tended to make the running in this area. The most prevalent method used in Australian higher education institutions is recognition of learning undertaken by students in formal award courses, and of the equivalence of academic qualifications. This provides little assistance for the majority of disadvantaged adult students as most of them have no prior tertiary qualifications and often have not completed secondary school. The TAFE colleges are more likely to recognise experiential or work-based learning, and some useful work has been done in this area. The most widely used techniques for assessing prior learning include:

- portfolio preparation where a student may provide documentation which can be used to demonstrate prior learning
- the provision of dedicated units which identify learning outcomes with strategies to provide opportunities for demonstration of claims.

Although the universities have been reluctant to embrace any concept of recognition of prior learning which includes experiential or work-based learning, some have established close links with TAFE colleges and interesting pathways have been established for adults. For example, some certificate or diploma level TAFE courses have been recognised by universities and in some cases substantial credit has been given to students wishing to proceed to undergraduate studies at universities. While this obviously provides a pathway for adults, there is a concern that adults with highly instrumental views of the value of education may fail to appreciate the full range of possibilities that higher education may be able to provide.

The main issues surrounding recognition of prior learning include:

- the concern relating to quality assurance based on the belief that to demonstrate mastery, students must have covered the whole course and satisfactorily completed all of the assessment;
- the reluctance by many faculties to accept that course coherence might in any way be in the hands of students rather than staff;
- the absence of pathways that will allow students to move between institutions (although links between TAFE colleges and some universities are promising).

Positive action strategies

The major impetus for this type of programme was *A Fair Chance For All* which identified specific areas where participation was low (e.g. women, aboriginals) and detailed strategies that institutions might adopt to redress imbalances in student composition.

Many of the positive action programmes offered by higher education institutions target secondary schools and school leavers. For example, the Maths and Science Summer School for Girls offered by the University of Southern Queensland is a programme for Year 10 girls, designed to influence their subject choice in mathematics and science areas for the last two years of secondary school. Monash University tackles the problem of the reluctance of girls to enter engineering courses by encouraging discussion between the Faculty of Engineering and the secondary school community. The major positive action programmes for adults are those which target Aboriginal and Torres Strait Islander students since research has shown that these students experience loneliness and identity problems in higher education. For example, the Monash Orientation Scheme for Aborigines is a programme based on ideas put forward by the Koori people. It offers a full academic year of preparation for university study but focuses on activities aimed at bridging the educational and cultural gap between the Koori people and first year university students by providing an 'enclave' through the provision of specific staff, rooms and support mechanisms for candidates during their orientation year and throughout their time at Monash (Barwood 1992). The University of Southern Queensland provides a similar 'enclave' through a programme offered by the Office of Aboriginal and Torres Strait Islander Education (OATSIE), with a preparatory programme focusing on bridging the educational and cultural gap and ongoing support for students for their entire study programme.

The main issue arising from positive action programs stems from a view which is still widely held by both the academic community and the general community that students in these programmes receive special privileges and are advantaged over other students. This perception is difficult to dispel for it is clear that these students are treated differently. If they were not then there would be even greater attrition and failure rates than there are now. None of these programmes suggests a lowering of standards; all students are expected to achieve the course objectives. They are treated differently in order to ensure they have similar chances of success as other students.

Alternative, Accessible Programmes in Higher Education

It is necessary here to revisit the classification which Hore and West (1980) proposed concerning mature students in Australia: it has a bearing on the range and type of alternative programmes available in higher education. Hore and West indicated that mature students can be represented by two broad groups. The first group involves those with a recertification or requalification need, in professions where pressure exist to update qualifications: for example, teachers, nurses and librarians. They also identified women as a special subgroup and predicted, quite accurately, that this group would constitute '...an index of what is to come in the workforce in general' (1980 p.164). Since 1980 many more professions can be considered in this way. For example, accounting and engineering now have mandatory professional development requirements set by representative professional associations which must be undertaken in order to retain current membership. The other mature age group they identified was one they labelled as disadvantaged. While they linked disadvantage to year of birth, this group could now include those who are geographically isolated, financially disadvantaged or belong to an ethnic minority group.

To meet the needs of these students, tertiary institutions in Australia have responded positively and extensively. Some have had external studies departments in place for some time: the University of New England in Armidale, New South Wales has a considerable reputation in the area of external studies with a range of external study opportunities across a number of faculties; others have developed expertise in particular areas such as the University of Queensland's external studies opportunities for teachers.

Over the last decade the interest in external studies has expanded as professional development and retraining has gathered momentum. A number of universities have also restructured their external studies department around the concept of distance education. This often involved the elevation of distance education within the institution as a disciplined form of study and the acquisition of specialist staff to work in areas such as instructional design, educational technology and open learning.

In its 1988 White Paper the federal government aimed to rationalise distance education provision, improve its quality and increase the efficiency of delivery. The major thrust of this policy was to limit the number of institutions responsible for the production of distance education course materials since quality in this field requires an expensive infrastructure. Action arising from the White Paper saw the establishment of eight distance education centres (DECs) across

Australia. These were selected on the basis that they could demonstrate
- a broadly-based educational profile
- the ability to meet national as well as state needs
- a strong distance education infrastructure
- a broad range of courses available or able to be developed
- a demonstrated capacity to develop and deliver high quality materials. (Department of Employment, Education and Training 1988 p.51)

The eight DECs were established at University of Southern Queensland, University of Central Queensland, Deakin University, University of New England, Murdoch University, Monash University, Charles Sturt University, and University of South Australia and were encouraged to work collaboratively with other universities in order to service the needs of students across Australia. In the first instance the main mode of delivery was by way of printed materials. Since the eight institutions selected had already demonstrated a strong distance education infrastructure (instructional design, print and non-print production facilities, printing facilities, distribution facilities) the materials produced were usually well designed and provided a high quality service to students. Some of the services provided by these universities include:
- strategically placed study centres equipped with supplementary print and non-print materials
- outreach programmes where academic staff visit study centres to conduct tutorials with students
- residential schools where students attend short on-campus programmes
- teleconference facilities for staff/student contact.

Some state governments have given their support to the establishment of a statewide structure. For example, in Queensland, the state government provided financial support for the development of the Open Learning Network consisting of approximately forty-five centres strategically located across the state to provide information and support services for students, particularly adults. Information about the courses offered by all universities and TAFE colleges is available at these centres through access to staff in some centres and/or extensive databases in others. These centres also provide careers information, information about enrolments, credit transfer and articulation between courses and institutions. The Open Learning Network was also involved in the development of a Preparatory

Studies Programme for use by a number of universities in Queensland and now available for all universities to use as an alternative entry programme for adults.

The designation of the eight DECs has not been accepted by all universities, particularly those which previously offered external studies. Some have tried to continue offering their own programmes but, with a lack of funding, have found this to be a difficult task. Others have grappled with this problem in other ways. It was obviously the intention of the federal government to rationalise the offering of distance education courses throughout the country; clearly they envisaged clusters around the DECs in order to provide a full range of offerings for all students regardless of their situation or circumstance. By and large this has occurred.

However, recent developments in communications technology have put a different emphasis on the nature of these university clusters, and the federal government has given support to the further development of open learning. The Open Learning Agency, a consortium of higher education institutions (Deakin University, Monash University, Griffith University, Charles Sturt University, Curtin University, University of Central Queensland, University of Southern Queensland and University of New England) has been established to offer open learning programmes through national television and radio with the Australian Broadcasting Commission (ABC). The programme has some striking similarities to Open University provision in the United Kingdom. Television is the main delivery mode although supplementary printed material is available. Students can use the courses studied in this way to enter formal award courses in any of the participating universities. Currently the Agency offers mainstream professional courses at graduate certificate, graduate diploma and masters levels in areas including gerontology, public health, race relations, linguistics, environmental management, education, cultural studies and accounting (Healy 1994). The chief rival to the Agency is the University of Wollongong's Graduate Consortium, which offers a similar range of courses.

This development heralds a shift in focus for distance education in Australia. The discussion surrounding the courses available for adults wishing to access tertiary education is being dominated by the term 'open learning', and universities and TAFE colleges are now keen to portray access to their courses for adults in terms of flexibility and choice, demonstrating that adults wishing to study in this way need not be geographically isolated. This shift in focus is also beginning to influence the way courses are designed and offered in tertiary institutions. Where academics have been involved in designing distance education material, it has been reported that they have become more aware of the elements of sound instruction. Some tertiary institutions are using distance education materials for all students and have adopted a form of mixed-mode teaching with some face-to-face instruction and some distance education materials often within a single course. Some have seen the potential of communications technology in designing instructional programmes for all students. The current interest in interactive multimedia technology is a case in point. The potential now available through computer software development based on the CD ROM format is significant, particularly for students engaged in upgrading or updating of qualifications who are usually engaged in full-time work and need access to materials which can be used at a time and place that is convenient for them and which have a direct application to the work situation through case studies or simulations.

Credit accumulation and transfer

A by-product of this greater flexibility in the way in which adults, particularly those updating or upgrading qualifications, can access programmes in higher education has been a renewed interest in credit transfer arrangements within and between higher education and TAFE sectors. In 1989, the Department of Employment, Education and Training (DEET) and the National Board of Employment, Education and Training (NBEET) agreed to fund a joint study relating to credit transfer practices in the two sectors with a view to using its findings to develop a strategy for the improvement of credit transfer arrangements.

The study revealed that there were some promising developments in the direction of consistency and facilitation:

> '...Griffith and Wollongong Universities have policies on credit for TAFE awards and for awards of recognised institutions, which include all Australian higher education institutions. In Western Australia, a quarter of places is reserved in higher education institutions for students transferring from TAFE. The tertiary institutions in South Australia are working towards a state-wide system of credit transfer between institutions, courses and sectors. Some institutions are granting credit for in-house courses provided in industry and more are looking at this issue'. (NBEET 1989 p.6)

However, most of the activity was described as random and it was pointed out that much of the goodwill and energy in higher education would amount to nought if there were 'no agency to sustain it' and to 'press for coordination to fit with a national system'.

The report also indicated that TAFE systems throughout Australia had developed policies towards credit transfer and articulation, but there was little evidence that these policies were being implemented. Doubts were also expressed about the depth of understanding of the key issues surrounding credit transfer and articulation in the TAFE sector: '...staff in all parts of TAFE systems need to understand systemic policies on articulation and credit transfer. Otherwise, there is little prospect of long-term and lasting progress' (NBEET 1989 p.18).

The report was distributed to all institutions for comment and responses were invited, which were to form the basis of the Higher Education Council's recommendations for a strategy for the improvement of credit transfer arrangements to be submitted to the National Board of Employment, Education and Training, and the Department of Employment, Education and Training. At the time of writing, no such strategy is available, even though there would seem to be a general acceptance for the need for some national framework.

Resources and Funding

As pointed out earlier in this chapter, funding for programmes for adults aimed at improving participation rates of particular disadvantaged groups was made available through the federal government's access and equity strategy. Institutions wishing to access such funding needed to indicate in their profile the groups being targeted and the strategies which would be used to improve participation rates of those groups. Following the acceptance of the profile statement, an institution was funded for three years in order to establish the programmes. At the end of this three-year period, specific funding would cease but an institution was expected to continue the programmes until targets were attained and it was also expected that access and equity would continue to be a component of the institution's profile. However, 'it appears that the shift of funding totally to institutions, has been premature' (Anderson 1992 p.5).

Anderson suggests that although specific funding had made it possible for institutions to provide entry for some disadvantaged groups, the fact that the institution was required to continue the programme at the end of the three year period can place the future of such institutions in jeopardy. Access and equity programmes are more likely to persist where institutions have developed special infrastructures to deal with such programmes, and less likely to do so where the funds have been used to employ part-time staff and where access and equity programmes have been accorded the status of a marginal activity. The criteria adopted by the committee on quality assurance such as 'cost effectiveness of institutions in graduating students in various fields of study' and 'time taken to complete courses' also make it extremely attractive for some unsympathetic academic managers to relegate access and equity programmes to tokenistic proportions.

While the total resources for higher education have increased substantially, the resources per student have declined by approximately one third over the last ten years. The increase in student numbers has been largely responsible for this. To fund the increase in numbers the government has reintroduced tuition fees. Under the provisions of the Commonwealth government's Higher Education Funding Act, all students are required to contribute to the cost of their tertiary education through the Higher Education Contribution Scheme (HECS). The amount of contribution in 1992 for an equivalent full-time study was $1125 per semester. The HECS liability can be met by up-front payment (a 25% discount then applies) or by deferred payment through the taxation system following the attainment of full-time work. By and large the HECS has not inhibited under-represented groups of students from applying as the fees are regarded as a loan to be repaid when the student is gainfully employed.

While distance education has been used with considerable success in meeting the demands created by an increasing number of adults engaged in updating and upgrading of qualifications, the federal government has argued that students undertaking such courses are worth considerably less (0.5 equivalent full time student) in determining the allocation of funds to higher education institutions. While this formula has now been altered to more accurately reflect enrolment differences between full-time students and students undertaking their courses part-time (a student undertaking 2 units of an 8 unit course in any one year now attracts a level of funding which is .25 that accorded a full-time student in that course) it would seem to be the government's way of ensuring more students have access to higher education. However, it also, in one respect, draws clear distinctions between full-time and part-time students and fails to acknowledge the demands made upon staff in the design and delivery of distance education materials. It also gives some weight to the argument that distance education is a 'second best way' of accessing higher education and that a real tertiary education demands a face-to-face situation.

The federal government has actively encouraged institutions to market their courses as a way of funding their programmes. Institutions have responded by creating Continuing Education Units which offer a range of award and non-award units to adults who are

·prepared to pay for the privilege. This has been particularly productive for institutions which have some distance education capacity. Courses offered in this mode can be offered in ways that provide maximum flexibility and are therefore very attractive to students who have both family and work commitments.

Many higher education institutions in Australia have also become involved in marketing their courses to overseas students, offering courses off-shore with access through distance education. Others offer full-time places for overseas students to attend courses on campus. While this activity has been a lucrative source of income for many institutions, in recent times it has become extremely competitive, not only between Australian universities but between universities from other overseas countries.

Institutional Arrangements

The sections or departments in universities which are usually involved in the design, development and delivery of programmes for adults in higher education include special access and equity units, continuing education units, distance education or open learning units and student services units. The access and equity units target students who are disadvantaged or under-represented. Continuing education units provide, for a fee, courses for adults that might range from general interest courses to professional development and training courses. Distance education units offer adults upgrading and retraining opportunities while student services units provide access to guidance and counselling. Distance education units and student services units are also heavily involved in programmes and services for students entering university after completion of secondary school.

In the majority of universities in Australia most of these units are centrally administered, rather than attached to particular faculties or departments. In many cases, they report directly to a Deputy Vice Chancellor or equivalent. A structure which is centrally administered obviously has some advantages, not the least being a strong possibility that the work of these units will be more likely to be valued and to find a place in the institution's mission statement and strategic plan, and less likely to be considered dispensable when demand for places is high and resources are scarce.

Where these units are centrally administered it is common for them to be led by senior staff and staffed with permanent members of staff. However, many of the access and equity units are staffed by a majority of part-time staff, a situation which can be linked to the way these units were established by the federal government's 'three year establishment grant'. The message that such a staffing structure conveys to students and staff is that the unit and its courses are relatively unimportant and a rather marginal operation.

Although there was a requirement from the federal government that institutions should continue to incorporate clear principles and procedures about access and equity into their profile after the funding had ceased, there was no mechanism put in place to assess institutional performance in the area. In fact, the government's quality assurance committee seems to have embarked on a path that may actively discourage involvement in access and equity programmes.

The four types of units detailed above are usually set up as semi-autonomous units. The fact that distance education units and student services units are also heavily involved with school leavers often results in limited support being available for adults. Many adults take some time to adjust to the tertiary environment and have other demands on their time such as families and work. Many take longer to complete their course of study and may need guidance and counselling support for the duration of the course. They have quite different needs which often do not relate to the way support services are structured or offered. Suggestions that adults require different treatment are not looked upon favourably, and while many institutions provide a range of services, few are prepared to provide the necessary extra resources to address the special needs of adults, particularly those who have entered via preparatory or positive action programmes. The exceptions are the 'enclaves' previously described that have been established at some universities for aboriginal students.

Research in the Field

The Hore and West (1980) study referred to earlier was a most significant study of mature students and covered such issues as policies and practices of tertiary institutions, academic performance, profiles of mature students, reasons for mature entry and attitudes of staff towards such students. Prior to this, very little research had been undertaken although valuable opportunities had existed when 'The Commonwealth Reconstruction Training Scheme for ex-service personnel introduced new sorts of students to universities (and the) Education Department's studentships (approximately 1955–75) also brought new groups into university' (Anderson 1992 p.11).

Nothing as comprehensive as that study has followed since, apart from isolated studies on specific issues. With the recent emphasis given to adults through the government's *A Fair Chance for All* and the growth of demand for recertification and upgrading programmes, there has been some renewed interest in research in the area. In general, however, surveys have dominated, emanating from a need for those who work in the area to demonstrate that adults in these special programmes perform at a level which is at least the equal of traditional tertiary students. The overall aim seems to be to justify the continuation of these programmes. One can understand this, but there are other areas in which research is urgently needed.

While there is obviously a need to develop comprehensive and informative databases on numbers of adults enrolled in courses at universities so that further work can be done on ensuring that under-represented groups gain access, there is very little research undertaken that can be described as longitudinal. There are far too many snapshots which provide limited data on which to gather information to assist in the development of appropriate programmes and services for adults. This has much to do with the way research funding is allocated, usually for a one year period. Very little funding is available for studies which extend over a period of time. In fact, in comparison with other areas, very little funding is available for research particularly in respect of adults who are members of under-represented groups in higher education.

Before the national symposium at the University of Southern Queensland in 1992, no professional body existed in Australia which could provide a focus for those who work in the area. At the symposium it was argued that there was a need for an association and suggested that one of the roles for such an association was the '…importance of basing the professional service on a scientific basis and on principles which are research tested' (Anderson 1992 p.5).

Since then, a small interest group has formed and some interesting research has emerged, particularly action research, interventionist in nature, and aimed at improving present practice. Some of the studies which will contribute considerably to future work in the area deal with curriculum design, teaching strategies, cross-cultural issues and the use of technologies.

The Future

In his address, Anderson (1992) suggested that Australia was 'in the middle of the revolution'. He indicated that there would be greater diversity in university courses, curriculum and structures and suggested we would see the emergence of 'something like a foundation year'. To some extent this is happening, and in some of the most conservative faculties. The University of Queensland is looking at offering a compulsory foundation year (liberal studies) for medical students. Should this pattern gain momentum it could have significant implications for the adults wishing to access higher education, as there would be some formal recognition of the concept of 'intervention studies'.

Anderson also predicted an expansion of the use of communications technology particularly 'in the more routine parts of courses' and the developments that have occurred in interactive multimedia software development should provide greater opportunities for adults through the provision of greater flexibility and greater choice.

While these comments express a certain optimism about the future, there are particular developments which suggest an element of caution. The adoption of a unified national system was the federal government's response to 'rationalising' higher education. Prior to this, colleges of advanced education had filled the most important role of offering a 'different type' of higher education to that offered by the traditional university. Teaching was valued and greater emphasis, in many instances, was given to the development of 'professional' courses. They also tended to be more innovative and more readily adopted issues such as access and equity. It would be unfortunate should the 'new universities' relegate such activity to marginal status in an attempt to gain full 'university status'. The access and participation of adults in higher education in Australia would suffer immeasurably.

References

Anderson, D. (1992) 'Access and Equity in Australian Universities'. In *Proceedings of the Access and Equity Symposium*. Toowoomba: University of Southern Queensland (unpublished).

Australian Education Council Review Committee (1991) *Young People's Participation in Post-compulsory Education and Training Report of the Australian Education Council Review Committe*. Canberra: Australian Government Printing Service.

Australian Education Council Mayer Committee (1992) *Report of the Committee to advise the Australian Education Council and Ministers of Vocational Education, Employment and Training on Employment-related Key Competencies for Post-compulsory Education and Training*. Melbourne: Australian Education Council.

Barwood, B. (1992) Strategies for Improving Access and Equity: An Approach in Secondary Schools. Paper presented at *Proceedings of the Access and Equity Symposium*. Toowoomba: University of Southern Queensland (unpublished).

Castles, I. (1992) *Education and Training in Australia.* Canberra: Australian Bureau of Statistics, Australian Government Publishing Service.

Collins, J. (1992) Late Start Matriculants as Non-Traditional Students – Curriculum Design for Their Encouragement. *Proceedings of the Access and Equity Symposium.* Toowoomba: University of Southern Queensland (unpublished).

Committee on the Future of Tertiary Education in Australia (1965) *Tertiary education in Australia: report of the Committee on the Future of Tertiary Education in Australia to the Australian Universities Commission.* Canberra: Australian Government Publishing Service.

Commonwealth Tertiary Education Commission (1984) *Report for 1985–87 Triennium, Vol. 1, Part 1: Recommendations on Guidelines.* Canberra: Australian Government Publishing Service.

Commonwealth Tertiary Education Commission (1986) *Efficiency and Effectiveness Review.* Canberra: Australian Government Publishing Service.

Currie, J., Baldock, C. and Bossinga, G. (1984) Access to Tertiary Studies: The Case of Mature Age Students and the Federal Government's Participation and Equity Policy. In *Research and Educational Futures; Technology, Development and Educational Futures.* Collected Papers Vols. 1 and 2. Perth: Australian Association for Research in Education National Conference.

Department of Employment, Education and Training (1990) *A Fair Chance for All: Higher Education That's Within Everyone's Reach.* Canberra: Australian Government Publishing Service.

Department of Employment, Education and Training (1988) *Higher Education: A Policy Statement* (White Paper). Canberra: Australian Government Publishing Service.

Employment and Skills Formation Council Australia (1992) *The Australian Vocation Certificate Training System Employment and Skills Formation Council.* Canberra: National Board of Employment, Education and Training.

Healy, G. (1993) Quality Committee 'given too much power. In *Higher Education Supplement, The Australian,* 15 December.

Healy, G. (1994) Open learning meets demand. In *The Weekend Australian,* January 15–16.

Hore, T. and West, L.H.T. (eds) (1980) *Mature Age Students in Australian Higher Education.* Blackburn: Acacia Press.

National Board of Employment, Education and Training (1989) *Credit Transfer: A Discussion Paper.* Canberra: Australian Government Publishing Service.

Parry, G. and Wake, C. (eds) (1990) *Access and Alternative Futures for Higher Education.* London: Hodder and Stoughton.

Ryan, S. (1984) *Guidelines to the Commonwealth Tertiary Education Commission for the 1985–87 Triennium.* Department of Education and Youth Affairs.

Smart, D. (1990a) Who should control universities and colleges? In J.V. D'Cruz and P.E. Langford (eds) *Issues in Australian Education*. Sydney: Longmans Cheshire.

Smart, D. (1990b) The Dawkins Reconstruction of Australian Higher Education. In *Education Research and Perspectives, 17*, 2 pp.11–22.

Toyne, P. (1990) Achieving Wider Access. In G. Parry and C. Wake (eds) *Access and Alternative Futures for Higher Education*. London:Hodder and Stoughton.

West, L.H.T. (1980) Toward a theoretical perspective of the phenomenon of mature age students in higher education. In T. Hore and L.H.T. West (eds) *Mature Age Students in Australian Higher Education*. Blackburn: Acacia Press.

Chapter 2

Austria

Roseanne Benn

General Context

Austria is a small country covering an area of 83,850 km^2. Its geography is varied with most of the country being highlands and mountains; the lowlands and the hilly areas around the Danube are the main residential and commercial areas. The population in 1991 was 7,812,100 (Europa World Year Book 1993). A high proportion live in Vienna and the regional capitals of Graz, Linz, Salzburg, and Innsbruck. Ninety-eight per cent of the population speak German with the minority groups being Serbs, Turks, Polish, Rumanians, Croats, Slovenians, Hungarians and Czechs. There are nine federal districts: Burgenland, Carinthia, Lower Austria, Salzburg, Steiermark, Tirol, Upper Austria, Vorarlberg and Vienna.

The Austrian Education System

In Austria, the most important selection in education takes place at the transition from primary to secondary school at the age of ten. At this stage pupils and their parents have to choose between the 'academic' higher level secondary general schools which provide entrance qualifications to universities, and 'lower' secondary schools which are typically followed by a vocational training at 14 to 15. The curriculum of the vocational schools offers far fewer opportunities than the higher secondary vocational schools but entry is controlled by the same examination. This selection process can mean that the vocational schools are seen as a route for underachievers (BMWF and BMUK 1992). The percentage of the 16-year-old population in education is very high – 96.3 per cent (in 1990), but approximately 60 per cent of these are in vocational schools or apprenticeships. The selective system produces only 12.8 per cent of 18-year-olds graduating with the *Matura* from higher secondary schools and 14.9 per cent from higher secondary/vocational schools (BMWF and BMUK 1992).

The Structure and Organisation of Higher Education

The higher education institutions include the Universities and Colleges of Art and Music which offer first and second degrees together with Teacher Training Colleges, Colleges of Social Work, Technical Colleges and Schools for Para-Medical Professions which offer qualifications at a level between the secondary school final examination and the first university degree. Passing the final examination of a higher secondary school (*Matura*) or its equivalent is the entrance requirement to these institutions. Any *Maturand* has right of entry to a higher education institution. Some courses in higher education have prerequisites; those for certain subjects such as medicine must be completed before registration, others may be taken whilst at university.

The university sector comprises the Universities of Vienna, Graz, Innsbruck, Salzburg, Linz and Klagenfurt; the Technical universities of Vienna and Graz; the four specialist universities (Mountain Engineering, Agriculture, Veterinary Studies and Economics) and the Colleges of Art and Music. The universities are federal institutions and charters, location, organisation and, to a large extent, funding, are federal matters. The General Universities Studies Act which came into effect in 1966, and the various subsequent University Study Acts and other Acts of Parliament contain regulations governing all aspects of university study: enrolment, registration, curriculum matters, examination matters, duration of studies and subject matter to be taught in given universities. Within this legislation, the Study Boards of individual universities decide their own study plans. The volume, extent and complexity of the legal regulations has been criticised as obstructing efficient university management, and recent legislation (the Amendment of the General Universities Studies Act 1990) will give more autonomy to the institution. Owing to the lack of non-university alternatives, most entrants into the tertiary sector of education choose university studies. Little short-term change is expected in the overcrowding of universities and total enrolment is still increasing.

The non-university sector (NUS), which comprises Teacher Training Colleges, Colleges of Social Work, Technical Colleges and Schools for Para-medical Professions, leads to a qualification between the Matura and the first university degree (MA or equivalent). Entry is by the Matura. The organisation of studies and examinations is similar to that of the universities. In contrast with many other countries, no broad non-university tertiary education sector has developed in Austria. However, since the late 1980s, pressure has been increasing to develop the vocational system by creating special institutions, the *Fachhochschulen*. These would complement and relieve the university sector and would be institutions of training and continuing education for various vocational areas. They are intended for ongoing professional development rather than for career change or school leavers. For example, a potential student who has been working in the car industry for several years would be able to continue studying at a *Fachhochschulen*.

Admission and Participation

The *Matura* is a passport to higher education for life: entry is guaranteed. It is also used as a passport to a career, but rising unemployment has restricted this route and has led to an increase in the proportion of *Maturands* entering higher education. The universities are now very stretched with large class sizes and consequently there is no policy to increase participation; indeed rather the reverse is true. There is also concern at the implications of Austria entering the EU. Many other EU countries limit entry, particularly in high demand subjects, for example Germany with its *numerus clausus*, and this has led to fears of an influx of students across the borders, burdening an already overburdened system. It is possible that some form of quota system may have to be introduced.

There is provision for applicants who did not take or did not pass the *Matura* whilst at school. The *Matura* may be taken at any age and preparatory courses are provided, or applicants may be accepted on the basis of an aptitude test, the *Studienberechtigungsprüfung*.

The development of the *Fachhochschulen* may lead to a wider acceptance of prior-experiential learning, with non-*Maturands* being able to top up their experience with, for example, maths and/or languages at a college. If *Fachhochschulen* are introduced, there are likely to be three routes into higher education:

(1) *Matura* and its adult version
(2) *Studienberechtigungsprüfung* (access examination) for university entrance
(3) *Studienberechtigungsprüfung* (access examination) for *Fachhochschulen* entrance.

The proportion of the resident population with a university degree or a certificate of post-secondary education is 5 per cent (for women, the figure is 3.8% of the female population). The percentage of new entrants to Universities and Colleges of Art and Music of the 18–21 age group is 18.5 per cent overall and 18.4 per cent for females (BMWF and BMUK 1992). The number of students in higher education for 1990–1 is shown in Table 2.1.

Table 2.1: Students in higher education 1990–1

	New entrants	Students	Graduates
Universities	19,688	170,718	10,239
Colleges of Art and Music	525	4,683	403
Teacher Training Colleges	2417	6281	1951
Colleges of Social Work	366	933	215
Technical Colleges	3246	5012	2141
Schools for Para-Medical Professions	737	1618	583
Total	**26,979**	**189,245**	**15,532**

Source: BMWF and BMUK 1992 p.18

A comparison of participation rates in OECD countries in 1991 showed Austria placed 15 out of 20 in the annual participation rate (APR) in full-time tertiary education and 19th in the ratio of university graduation to the population at graduation age (OECD 1993). Approximately a third of 18–19 year olds obtain the *Matura*, and about 80 per cent of these progress to post-secondary education; 20.8 per cent of all 19–26 year olds enter university.

The average age of students is increasing: the proportion of students older than 25 years is now approximately 35 per cent in contrast to 25 per cent in the early 1980s. This is partly explained by increases in the length of courses, but new entrants are also getting older (see Table 2.2).

Table 2.2: Age of entrants to higher education

	1980–81	1989–90	1992–93
17–19	66.7%	59.1%	56.3%
20–24	27.5%	34.4%	36.3%
25–29	2.1%	3.5%	4.0%
over 30	2.8%	3.1%	3.4%

Source: BMWF 1993 p.150

Entry to post secondary education is 51 per cent female, 49 per cent male; but on exit the proportions are 40 per cent female, 60 per cent male (BMWF 1993). The higher non-completion rates for women may be explained by both the lack of a universal grant system and the fact that the average completion time for a degree is 14 to 15 semesters with some courses being considerably longer. The social background of students has remained relatively unchanged since the early 1980s with approximately 20 per cent of fathers self-employed, 66 per cent white collar and 13 per cent blue-collar (BMWF and BMUK 1992).

There are certain features of the Austrian education system that affect participation in higher education. First, the system is highly segmented with a developed system of secondary technical and vocational schools and great importance attached to apprenticeship training. The non-university sector is small, existing in only selected areas (compulsory-school teacher training, social work, para-medical occupations). Second, there is no limit on entry (no *numerus clausus*). The *Matura*, the higher secondary-school graduation certificate, or its alternative the *Studienberechtigungsprüfung* is the only condition of entry to higher education. Third, there is a high degree of detailed legal regulation ensuring extensive nationwide uniformity and control.

In addition to undergraduate and postgraduate degree programmes, adults may participate in continuing vocational education and occasional or regular provision for the community (Federal Ministry of Education and Arts 1991). These options can be taken up by deferrers or those from second chance routes, those who wish to re-enter to update their professional knowledge or who require an additional qualification to change or advance their career. The purpose can be personal fulfilment, career development or both (OECD 1987).

Participation by adults in higher education is low compared to some other countries. Reasons might include the existence of a well-developed non-academic adult education sector but this is non credit bearing and hence may not provide all the outcomes required by participants.

Policy Relating to Adults and Higher Education
Labour market trends
Most firms in Austria are small or medium-sized. Two consequences of this are a well-structured vocational system but, by international standards, a low proportion of the population with degrees. However a study on *fachhochschulen* commissioned for the OECD Background

Report (BMWF and BMUK 1992) found that Austria has, and will continue to have, increased qualification requirements. If these are not met there will be major obstacles to necessary innovation due to a shortage of highly qualified staff. The position in engineering and technology is particularly serious as there is a shortage of engineers with tertiary qualifications due to the very extended periods of study and consequent high drop-out rates. There is a linked fear that technical-school technicians, who dominate the staff-profiles of many Austrian enterprises, received a highly applications-orientated training which will not be adequate for future needs (BMWF and BMUK 1992). Vocational qualifications are held in high esteem in Austria but vocationally-orientated studies tend not to lead to the highest levels of management. It is hoped that the *Fachhochschulen*, by providing a more general education alongside technical training, will allow practical people to rise above middle management. These labour market trends have led to government support for increased access to vocational training at both undergraduate and post-experience level by the proposed introduction of *Fachhochschulen* and the further development of continuing professional training by the higher education sector. The situation in the non-vocationally orientated disciplines is more complex. Here there is a less clear manpower requirement, heavily overcrowded universities and a lack of ideological commitment to widening access.

Targeting for higher education provision

Because of the system of guaranteed entry for those with Matura or its equivalent and the resultant pressure on the university system, there is little evidence that the universities or the government are seeking to increase the numbers in the present system or to widen the range of applicants. Equal opportunities, in the British sense, for example, is not on the agenda. The traditionally under-represented groups in higher education are adults, women, ethnic minorities and those from a working class background. As has been shown, the proportion of students in higher education over the age of 21 is more than one third. However this is mainly due to the length of courses and the large increase in entrants in the 21–24 age range. The number of adults over this age attracted into higher education is low with the percentage of new entrants over 24 in 1992–3 being 7.4 per cent, with only 3.4 per cent over 30 (BMWF 1993). Women profited by the expansion of the 1970s and now enter higher education in equal numbers but they suffer a higher drop-out rate. The situation with regards to ethnic minorities is complex. Numbers are relatively small with 400,000 *Ausländer* (foreign nationals; this is only 5% of the population) and there is little evidence of a commitment to integration through education. However, *Volkshochschulen* and other providers are becoming involved in multicultural education both for adults and for children through community education. This may filter up through the system to affect either access course provision or university policy. Again there is no evidence of a systematic policy to make higher education more accessible to those from working class backgrounds.

However, the discussions around the introduction of *Fachhochschulen* have raised various issues relating to targeting. The background report to the OECD (1987), whilst concentrating on issues of manpower requirements, also highlights wider opportunities. In questioning whether *Fachhochschulen* should concentrate on those with traditional study qualifications or should deliberately make efforts to attract graduates of vocational apprenticeship, the report may open up a path into higher education for a sizeable group traditionally under-represented (BMWF and BMUK 1992). It notes that the introduction of *Fachhochschulen* or polytechnics in other countries led to socially disadvantaged groups being represented to more than a proportionate degree and that thus post-secondary programmes could become open to persons who otherwise might not have found any access (BMWF and BMUK 1992). In the discussions about those people without traditional university entry rights, there have been conflicting opinions. Many proposals insist that entry should be through the existing, but modified, study access examination and some argue that certain curricula should be compulsory for entry to the *Fachhochschulen*. However, there are more liberal proposals such as credit for relevant vocational practice. This could lead to the separating of entry rights to the *Fachhochschulen* from those to the universities. The obverse of this coin could be a perception that education at *Fachhochschulen* will be second-best to that at a university, a familiar issue in the development of non-university sectors. Discussion is also taking place on issues that would underpin wider access such as educational leave, part-time study and distance study but with little in the way of proposals for concrete implementation (BMWF and BMUK 1992). There are current regional disparities in the university sector with half of all students studying in Vienna and no universities in Lower Austria, Burgenland and Vorarlberg. The locally-based *Fachhochschulen* would contribute towards a more regionally balanced distribution of post-secondary education and make this resource more available to rural communities and those who are unable to move due to domestic or employment situations.

These new institutions are conceived as a major source for the continuing education of adults and hence as a contribution to the need for a well-trained workforce. They are also seen as a route to a change in career for young adults who missed earlier opportunities. The proposed short duration of the courses together with their work and practice-based curricula and their geographic proximity may lead to sponsorship by employers. However the development of *Fachhochschulen* could also lead to the mobilisation of the talent reserves of population groups previously under-represented in the tertiary sector (adults, women, the working classes and the rural population), the expansion of higher education outside of university towns, and the facilitation of part-time study by employed persons (BMWF and BMUK 1992).

If the higher education system is to attract more under-represented groups then there may need to be more emphasis on learning needs. At present, within the university system, the concept of special learning needs of adults or other groups does not arise. As all entrants must have gained the *Matura* or its equivalent and as these are considered to be designed to prepare students for the Austrian university approach, undergraduates are assumed to have the requisite skills. The large class sizes inevitably lead to a didactic approach, with little or no opportunity for participation or study skill support. At present university lecturers are not trained in the learning needs of their students, although there are moves to change this through continuing education and the introduction of an appraisal system.

Alternative Entry Routes for Adults

There are two main routes for adults who do not have the Matura but who wish to enter higher education: the adult *Matura* or the *Studienberechtigungsprüfung*.

Adult Matura

Adults who wish to pass the *Matura* for either career enhancement or progression to higher education may attend part-time evening provision in either federal or private institutions (here private includes bodies such as the state supported *Volkshochschulen*). Approximately fifteen to twenty thousand students embark annually on this route. There is also a small provision by truly private institutions (two to three thousand students). School and adult *Matura* are directly comparable to ensure standards. There is no day-time provision.

The Ministries of Education and Arts, Social Security and the Federation of Employers funded a three-and-a-half year project to investigate the problems and needs of these second chance students from 1989 to 1993. The study found that the motivating factors for students were: to obtain a more general education, realise potential, be more competitive in work, facilitate a career or job change, compensate for what had been missed first time round and improve finances. A sizeable 62 per cent wished to enter university (Feldner 1992).

In federal schools the course takes four years but in a *Volkshochschule* it may be shorter and previous experience and learning may be rewarded with advanced standing. However, the survey showed that choice between institutions was made on the grounds of geographical location not quality. Provision is predominantly in the urban areas and even then accessibility is an issue for students in terms of personal safety or availability of transport. In federal institutions attendance is two hours per evening, five evenings a week for four years; in the *Volkshochschulen*, times and attendance are more flexible. Federal courses are free while fees at a *Volkshochschule* vary. The survey found that 20 per cent of students have financial problems. The student group is mixed: three-quarters are between 20 and 30 years of age, with a half between 21 and 25. There are no statistics on ethnic minorities.

The men are mostly in full-time work with wives carrying the childcare and domestic responsibilties. The women are also working full-time but they tend to be single. The number of single parents is very small, of the order of two to three per cent. In the non-technical disciplines, 60 per cent were women. All the women had more practical difficulties than men, carrying the main responsibility for both child and household care and having, in general, lower income levels. Students did not wish for study centre creches but for help in obtaining appropriate independent solutions.

Two-thirds of students worked full-time, a fifth worked half-time and a sixth were unemployed. The unemployed in the group have usually been so for one year or less. The majority of the students are white collar workers in the middle or higher levels. Usually the employer and colleagues were told of the studies but nine per cent kept it secret. Half of the group obtained the agreement and support of their employer, seven per cent received active opposition and, for the rest, their study was ignored; 60 per cent reported problems in getting free time for examinations. A half reported less than one hour a day for themselves. There was an increased strain on personal relationships with partner, family, and friends and an increase in health and mental problems with 30–40 per cent being more nervy, aggressive and less sociable. This was especially true of the women. However there was a substantial increase in self-confidence reported by over 90 per cent of the students surveyed.

The difficulties of fitting in study with work and domestic commitments were not the only problems facing this group of second-chancers. There was considerable criticism of teaching approaches and styles and a perception that their problems and needs were being ignored by teachers and the institution. When asked for suggestions for change, the most commonly expressed were for increased, or sometimes any, use of infrastructure such as a library or study rooms, appropriate adult-orientated texts, self-study materials, counselling in the early stages and on-going counselling and guidance. Despite all this, a sizeable 80 per cent of students said they would choose this way again.

The survey raises serious issues for the institutions providing these second chance opportunities for adults. There is a clear need for staff development for tutors and in particular those who mainly teach the young. Though all tutors said that teaching adults and children was different, half of them felt that training for adult teachers was not necessary. Students were critical of the level of information given in pre-course publicity and a very high proportion wanted improved educational guidance (Feldner and Heinz 1992).

On completion, this route allows unrestricted and guaranteed entry to all branches of higher education, and improved career opportunities. It does, however, seem a long and arduous journey with, particularly for those studying in federal institutions, little regard given to the adults' previous experiences or to their needs as adult learners.

Studienberechtigungsprüfung

The other main route to higher education for adults without the *Matura* is the *Berufsreifeprüfung* or *Studienberechtigungsprüfung*. In 1946, the *Berufsreifeprüfung*, an alternative vocational examination enabling entry to higher education for adults, was introduced for the postwar situation and the returning armed forces. The quantative impact of this route was minimal: from 1945 to 1979 the total number of applicants was 1292 of which only 311 were women (OECD 1987). Requirements for admission to the test, which was administered by the universities, were a minimum age of 25, Austrian citizenship, existence of obstacles which prevented the applicant from taking the *Matura*, work experience or successful private study in the field which the candidate wished to study and expert certification of the candidate's specialist knowledge. The mode of preparation was not regulated. The test was composed of a general and a subject-specific examination and, if successful, the applicant was accepted onto degree courses in the field of his or her specialisation. Because of the very limited impact of this route, an alternative method of entry to degree courses for mature students was introduced in 1976. A new law, the *Bundesgesetz Über die Vorbereitungslehrgänge für die Studienberechtigungsprüfung*, provided for the organisation of preparatory courses for mature students without the *Matura*. These courses could be provided by any institution – the universities themselves or adult education institutions – but the universities had control over the examination. In December 1991 further legislation was passed setting out the new arrangements. From 1993, four of the five examinations could be set by the providing institution and the students may sit them at the centres. Applicants may still sit all their examinations at the university without formal preparation and the examination retained by the university is intended to ensure standards. The effects of this new legislation are as yet unknown. In 1986–7 the age of entry was reduced from 25 to 22 and in 1990 from 22 to 20 for those with appropriate vocational or academic backgrounds.

The *Studienberechtigungsprüfung* courses usually involve one or two years study for several evenings per week. A pass only confers the right to entry to higher education in an appropriate area of study. Consequently if a potential student is committed to a path of study then the *Studienberechtigungsprüfung* provides a shorter route into higher education. Otherwise the longer Matura, which allows entry to all higher education and is a valuable qualification for work, may be the most appropriate choice.

Students must enrol for the *Studienberechtigungsprüfung*, but thereafter they may either prepare for the examinations through a formal route, or independently. They must attend the university before or during the *Studienberechtigungsprüfung* to check that their experience and curriculum is appropriate for their future study, and to register. This is not a selection but a checking process to ensure that all requirements are met. If the applicant has no background or experience in the designated area of study, he or she may be required to attend relevant lecture courses for a semester, either before the *Studienberechtigungsprüfung* or more usually in parallel. This checking process must be completed before the examination. Those who fail may resit the failed papers in March, June or September. This examination process is easier than the Matura but students must know what they wish to do before they start. If a student wishes to change direction, additional papers may be required.

There are grants to support attendance at *Studienberechtigungsprüfung* courses but this is not a right and most are bound by conditions. Common criteria for eligibility include a previous period of four to five years in work; current work must be for less than 21 hours per week; and all money earned is deducted from the grant.

The Ministry for Science and Research produces annual higher education statistics for and regular analyses of aspects of higher education of current interest. In 1990 these pre-entry courses were examined (BMWF 1990a, 1990b) and the findings give a flavour of the kind of people on the *Studienberechtigungsprüfung*. In the period 1986–9, 4173 people enrolled, of whom 2537 were men and 1636 were women. On application, 72 per cent were in employment, 23 per cent were unemployed and two per cent were retired. Of those in employment, 78 per cent were white collar workers or civil servants, 12 per cent were working class (men 16% and women 6%). Less than 1 per cent of the women were housewives. When the family backgrounds were investigated, applicants had less educated fathers than *Maturands*: only six per cent of their fathers had degrees. For the 1989 entrants, on average half of both men and women had relevant qualifications and 28 per cent were given credit for prior learning for past qualifications such as associate student qualifications or language certificates. The largest number of applicants were to the University of Vienna (over one third) and Linz (over one fifth) and the most popular areas of study were humanities (17%), law (25%), and science and engineering (23%). Women make up 69 per cent of the applicants to medicine and 67 per cent of those to humanities.

Only a small number of entrants to higher education use this route: in 1988–9, 482 (48.6% of whom were women) or 2.3 per cent of all entrants (21,423) had the *Berufsreifeprüfung* or *Studienberechtigungsprüfung*.

In 1988–9 the applications to register for the *Studienberechtigungsprüfung* and the pass rate were as shown in Table 2.3.

Table 2.3: Applications to register for the *Studienberechtigungsprüfung* 1988–9

	registered	passed
Men	727	115
Women	546	106
All	1273	221

Source: BMWF 1990a p.158

Most students who are unsuccessful do not fail the examination but leave the course. Since pursuing the pre-entrance courses takes a considerable commitment in time and energy, it is little wonder that many mature students with multiple responsibilities cannot cope with the commitment.

For later years pass rates are not shown in the statistics but registrations were as shown in Table 2.4; they indicate a steady growth in numbers; particularly of women for whom there was a 44 per cent increase in registration from 1988–9, and 1991–2.

Table 2.4: Applications to register for the *Studienberechtigungsprüfung* 1990–2

	1990–1	1991–2
Men	814	929
Women	705	785
All	1519	1714

Source: BMWF 1993 p.146

The figures above are from the only national survey but a more illuminating review of this provision can be gained by briefly examining the position at two *Volkshochschulen*.

Experiences of Studienberechtigungsprüfung at Volkshochschule Margareten and Ottakring

Margareten is a dynamic and forward-looking institution that has well-developed provision in this area. About 500 people start the course annually, 400 in October and 100 in February, and of these about a third drop-out during the year. Recruitment is mainly by word of mouth and all applicants are interviewed for half an hour or more either individually or in groups. Student motivation is mixed. For many the goal is work-related, for example those studying law, economics, or medicine, but some are looking for increased status and personal development. Students are mainly in the 22–28 age range followed by the 28–35 year-olds, and about two thirds are women. They are mainly white-collar workers with a small group of working class and a few unemployed among them. Margareten has a commitment to attract people from educationally disadvantaged backgrounds. The most popular subjects are medicine and psychology with a substantial number of the women coming from the health service (for example, nursing).

Most work and study, so most courses are in the evening. However, some work part-time or are at home with child care responsibilities, so daytime and twilight sessions are also run. For people who cannot make weekdays, who live outside Vienna or who are 'self-didactics', Margareten also runs weekend courses, one weekend a month. The limited availability of *Studienberechtigungsprüfung* courses elsewhere makes these courses particularly valuable.

The programme can be completed in one to two years of intensive work. Assessment is by five examinations. Law, for example, involves core examinations in German, history and Latin plus two optional examinations, perhaps Roman law and philosophy. This would involve three to four days a week, although other subjects may only take two days a week. Approximately 90 per cent pass the examinations at Margareten.

Courses are subsidised by the state, with a maximum fee to the student of 3800 AS. Margareten does not see this as a problem since students who are not working are entitled to a state grant, but very few students apply. If a student has financial problems, then concessions are given. There is a belief, at least in the *Volkshochschulen*, that lack of money should not be a bar to education.

Another *Volkshochschule* in Vienna that offers the *Studienberechtigungsprüfung* is Ottakring, held to be the oldest adult education institution in Europe. One hundred and twenty students are enrolled there annually. The main motivating factors are either entry to a profession such as law or medicine or a serious hobby such as languages or history. Most take a year to a year-and-a-half to complete, with about two-thirds completing, and about half of these enter university. Provision involves about eight to twelve hours attendance a week and is mostly in the evening with some morning classes. The majority of students are either in work or are housewives with children over ten years of age. Only 10 to 15 per cent do not work. Ottakring has not found this course particularly suitable for unemployed people who enroll simply because they see no prospect of work. They record a high drop-out rate for this group. The fee is 3500 AS per annum and concessions are given.

Evaluation of the Studienberechtigungsprüfung

There is little formal evaluation or research into either the *Studienberechtigungsprüfung* or the student experience at university. There is no funding for research in this area and hence very little theoretical work has been carried out. Although there are academics specialising in adult education, there seems to be a communication gap between theoreticians and practitioners. This, combined with the practitioner perception that they are funded to run courses, not to reflect and evaluate, has led to a lack of a reflective theoretical underpinning to developments such as the Studienberechtigungsprüfung.

The 1990 report (BMWF 1990a) does however discuss the effect of increasing the number of adult entrants to higher education. It questions the ethics of giving people education with little chance of commensurate employment and suggests that this could have a destabilising effect. It balances this by commenting that not all adult students expect to follow a career or, indeed, are studying for career reasons at all. It notes also that expectations and motivations vary with disciplines but the three main reasons for university study for this group are career, personal interest and self-development. The report found five motives for study: fulfillment of potential, delayed career choice, social purpose, high status and 'compensation' (part/time study to compensate for work).

The thoughtful evaluations of the *Studienberechtigungsprüfung* by the two *Volkshochschulen* considered above agreed that this route was providing a valuable service for adult returners. Students are highly motivated, usually succeeding if personal problems are not too great. Courses are grounded, as is appropriate in adult education provision, on the learning-to-learn principle. As elsewhere, the quality of the courses varies with the dedication of the tutors, most of whom are part-time. Informal research has shown that the *Volkshochschule* is seen as a supportive stepping stone particularly in contrast to the high numbers and anonymity of the universities. There are also indications that at university *Studienberechtigungsprüfung* students tend to work part-time, they need one more year than *Maturands* to complete their studies, and few drop-out.

Courses are not targeted and so should perhaps not be judged on that criterion. However the *Volkshochschulen* do have an underlying commitment to widening opportunities for traditionally disadvantaged groups and, in reality, it is those groups that attend. Unemployment is now seven per cent: if this rises, more unemployed may enrol but this is not an aim of the programme.

It is, important however, to remember that this provision is not large or wide spread. There are only six state providers, three of the 16 *Volkshochschulen* in Vienna, a *Volkshochschule* in Salzburg, a vocational adult school in Tyrol and a university in Klagenfurt. The course is therefore not available in all cities and certainly not in the rural areas. Providers meet every two years but this is not seen as a network. It is an institutional choice as to whether to run the *Studienberechtigungsprüfung*.

The impact on higher education is limited by the small numbers involved. Recent estimates show entry to universities is now 97 per cent *Matura*, three per cent *Studienberechtigungsprüfung* (BMWF 1993). However, it could be argued that this provision does widen the social and cultural base of universities because graduates of the *Studienberechtigungsprüfung* bring with them work and life experiences. For example, a popular route into medicine is nursing and one into psychology is teaching. Sadly the knowledge and experience which is brought into the university system is not always well received. One of the consequences of the mass higher education system is that the professors are not perceived to be interested in teaching or in students. It can be a cultural shock for adults not to have their past experiences valued when they move to university. The change of teaching styles can also be disturbing. Group sizes of 100 compared to 20 at the *Studienberechtigungsprüfung* require considerable independence and self-motivation.

The current pressures on the higher education system have led to discussions about restricting higher education courses. Ideas mooted include restricting any extension to a student's period of study, the introduction of minimum grades for university entrance, and the limiting of grants to a specific period. The major aim of these changes would be to reduce the numbers in universities and a result might be a backlash against *Studienberechtigungsprüfung* courses, where grades would have to be introduced. The present size of the *Studienberechtigungsprüfung* might be its main protection; if it grows, it might become vulnerable.

Proposed Centre for Distance Education

At the end of October 1993, the Minister of Education and Arts confirmed the financial support for a new Centre for Distance Education to be based in Vienna but to cover all Austria. The Centre, conceived on the same lines as the National Extension College in the United Kingdom, is founded in the belief that there is a substantial unsatisfied demand for increased access to educational opportunities. The objective is to establish distance learning for adults in employment at *Matura* level but, unlike present provision, accessible to the whole population and with less contact time. An Austrian distance learning university may eventually be developed. There will be active cooperation in this venture with the *Volkshochschulen* and other adult education providers. As an example of this and in order to pave the way for this development the Ministry organised, in collaboration with the unions, a programme of study circles to form a recruitment base for the Centre. Students registered with the Centre will receive independent study materials with tutorial backup. As there is no existing pool of teachers trained to write distance learning materials, the intention is to use existing materials and books.

The Ministry wishes to develop an alternative approach which is both cost effective and an appropriate form of learning and assessment for adults. It is hoped that adults will learn and be tested in a new and different culture which will develop powers of critical analysis and thought rather than memory and rote learning. This thinking springs from a wish in some Government circles to stimulate change in what is seen as a conservative educational system. The goal is to create a learning society with a consequent democratisation of the adult education system even though this may well clash with the present authoritarian system. There is strong support from the Ministry for alternative, more accessible programmes of study with the aim of developing styles of teaching and learning which will engender new styles of thinking, and hence democracy.

Vocational routes into higher education

Part-time attendance at higher secondary vocational schools leads to a qualification which guarantees the right to attend university. Progression is to middle management or to university. Courses typically last four years for those with professional experience and five otherwise. Working specialists can register for the examination without attending any course of instruction and, provided they pass, can enter university. The option of attending courses in the first year to make up any shortfall in their knowledge is rarely used.

Approximate numbers attending these schools per year are not large being of the order of 5000 for technical engineering and trade, 4000 for domestic science, and 1000 for commercial studies. Most firms are small or medium sized and are not interested in giving time for study so there is no system of paid educational leave although fees are paid by the state. Nevertheless five hours every weekday evening for four years makes this a hard struggle for students. The drop-out rate is 50 per cent with failure due to domestic rather than academic reasons. Distance learning techniques are sometimes introduced to reduce attendance to three evenings a week. The examination is the same for 19-year-olds as for adults but the laws governing the adult examination are looser allowing resits and some absence. The qualification is valued by industry, and graduates of industrial or agricultural higher secondary schools are awarded the legally regulated title of engineer after three years practical work at the appropriate level. Universities are not attractive to many of this group, being seen as providing an excessively lengthy and irrelevant curriculum where the average length of study in a technical field is 15 semesters with a minimum of 10 semesters. It is perhaps not surprising that less than ten per cent progress to university.

Alternative, Accessible Programmes in Higher Education

Although in many ways the Austrian system is very inflexible, the centralised structure and rigid legislation does allow credit accumulation and transfer across the system. The augmented autonomy and the introduction of the *Fachhochschulen* may also increase flexibility and accessibility. The issue of part-time/full-time has little meaning in the Austrian higher education system. There are no tuition fees but the very limited maintenance grant system means that many students support themselves by working. Students enrol at the beginning of their studies and then register subsequently and at the time for each semester. Many take a semester off either to earn money or cope with external work or domestic pressures whilst others extend their programme out of interest. There is no evening or weekend provision by the universities. The study plan for each course is controlled by legislation but within these constraints it is possible to negotiate individual programmes. There is no outreach, franchising or similar. One small but interesting development has been the successful introduction of two foreign distance learning universities into Austria.

Distance learning higher education

The University of Hagen opened study centres in Bregenz and Vienna (and later Linz) in the early 1980s which were the first of their kind anywhere (Palank 1993). This trans-national periphery of the German education system offers distance learning leading to an award from the German University. Foreign study centres of a similar kind are spreading over Europe. The role of the Austrian centres is counselling and tutoring, but in addition there are tasks regarding integration into the foreign university system and the provision of a focus for the student's study. Their aim is, as with all distance learning provision, to satisfy needs not met by the traditional university system. Education is part-time at times to suit the student and to fit in with jobs. There is positive targeting at women, the handicapped, prisoners, people alienated from the traditional system and Austrians who, for whatever reason, need a portable qualification. Qualifications offered are degrees at Bachelor, Masters and PhD level and provision is also made for Associate (Guest) students. For the latter group, there is open entry but those reading for a degree need the *Matura* or its equivalent. Less than ten per cent transfer across into the Austrian system during their studies. Qualifications gained are German but it is possible to convert these to Austrian with little or no extra study. Students encounter all the traditional problems of mature students and distance learners but additionally they have the difficult task of assimilation into a foreign system and of acquiring a sense of identity and belonging. This means that guidance and counselling are of crucial importance. There is a strong emphasis on study skills in the first semester, and pre-start courses are provided in mathematics. Courses are not multi-media but mainly face-to-face supported by written materials. The satellite links are used mainly for cultural transmissions. Considerable autonomy is given to study centres in the design and delivery of courses and this builds up a strong sense of group identity. Courses are usually at the weekend and are offered in the social sciences, humanities, economics, business studies, mathematics and informatics. The centres are fully paid for by the Ministry of Science and Research and students pay only a nominal amount for language tuition and a small fee for materials (for example, 10 DM for a course unit of 20 hours of study). The study requirement is 20 hours per week. In the first three to four years, tutorials are organised and students can always ask for extra help. The Masters course takes eight years to complete.

The centres have found the prime motivating factor to be the acquisition of a degree, usually as a way of planning for the future but not necessarily for a career. There were more than 700 students in 1993 and of these, about 25% were women. The centres have found the courses not suitable for those with a weak educational background, and too long for many mothers at home with their children. However, it is hoped that this provision will be made available to a wider group by the extension of the study centres into other institutions on the lines of the British Open University. Numbers are expanding rapidly; the 700 students in 1993 rising to 1000 in 1994. This expansion has helped raise the profile of the University and publicity is friendly and welcoming with surely the ultimate in international cooperation, a German university in Austria and a cartoon in English on the cover of the brochure!

Because centre costs are high, there is talk of restricting grants, reducing the length of time for study or introducing a student contribution to tuition. Palank (1993) emphasises, however, that with distance learning the cost per student per year is a fifth of the cost of traditional higher education although the set up costs may be high. Hagen is nevertheless looking to reduce costs, perhaps by providing only written materials. A newcomer to the Austrian scene is the British Open University (OU) now running a limited range of its courses in Austria with its headquarters in Vienna. Courses offered are BA degree studies in arts, mathematics, social sciences, science and technology; Certificate, Diploma, MBA and individual courses from the Open Business School and professional training courses in computing, manufacturing management and technology, health and social welfare, and professional training in education. As in Britain, students must be over 18 but there are no entry qualifications required for first degrees. The OU started in Austria in April 1992 and the first students started in February 1993; 120 enrolled in 1993 and a similar number will begin in 1994. Half the students enrolled on business courses. In 1993, 70 per cent were British but in 1994 this reduced to 50 per cent. The age range is 18–60 but the average is 35–40 about 60 per cent of those being women. Most of the students do not have the *Matura*, although since all courses are in English, they must have a good grasp of the English language. The courses are identical to the British ones and pre-study packs are provided. There have been language problems but the small tutorial group sizes (maximum 10) have helped and have probably also contributed to the low drop-out rate. Unlike the University of Hagen, the OU is not subsidised and must be self-financing. At the present a full credit costs £700. The OU has no sense that this fee is too high or is acting as a barrier. There is no targeting, nor is equal opportunities on the agenda.

There is considerable cooperation between the OU and the University of Hagen with the main differences being the language of study and the OU's multi-media approach. Together they form the part-time arm of the Austrian higher education system although there is interest in the establishment of an Austrian distance learning university. However, any effective distance learning system must have strengths in the areas of curriculum, course management, distribution and assessment and considerable development work is needed in all these areas.

Vocational courses

In recent years, the universities have developed a range of continuing education provision for those in employment who wish to acquire vocationally orientated or specialist knowledge and skills (BMWF and BMUK 1992). These are open to graduates and non-graduates alike with some courses leading to qualifications. The legislation governing this provision is now in place. These classes may be held in the evenings or in blocks to accommodate employed students. Approximately 1000 students are attending two to three year courses in business, languages, export, tourism and management, and their tuition is paid by the state; larger numbers of the order of 10,000 are attending short courses of between one and four weeks. The Open Institute of the Technical University of Vienna runs between 12 and 20 such courses every year for people sponsored by their companies. This provision is increasing slowly with about 20 companies using the scheme. Although the government wishes to expand this cooperation between universities and companies, it is usually only the large businesses that take advantage of this scheme and these are very limited in number in Austria.

Research in the Field

With notable exceptions, there is no large body of research and publications in the area of access to higher education. There are Departments of Continuing Education within the Institutes of Pedagogics whose remit is to research into adult education and educate future adult educators. However the absence of a group of academics who are also adult education organisers and practitioners may contribute to the lack of a substantial body of advocates for adults in the university system; and practitioners themselves are too busy organising and teaching to have time to underpin their work with a theoretical foundation. Individual institutions have records of their own courses and students but there is little national collaboration. There has been some research funded at national level into second chance courses, but little is written on adult students within the higher education system.

However there is one inter-university institute whose prime purpose is to develop action research into the area of professional continuing education. This Institute for Interdisciplinary Research and Continuing Education (IFF) of the Universities of Innsbruck, Klagenfurt and Vienna is financed partly by the Austrian Ministry of Science and Research for the secondment of professors from the three universities and a small group of senior researchers. In addition IFF must attract 'soft' money (from a variety of other sources) to pay its teams of junior researchers. The constituent sections are Health and Organisational Development, Social Ecology, Space, Economy and Regional Development, School and Social Learning, the Theory, Organisation and Teaching of Science, and Technical and Scientific Research. IFF was set up in 1979 with the remit to develop alternative higher education systems, to develop new forms of study and new forms of teaching and research, and all research projects are interdisciplinary. IFF undertakes traditional basic research. Sometimes the theory is developed first, then disseminated through continuing education programmes. Otherwise, the theory is developed through the continuing education work itself. The aim is to provide research with practical outcomes where the research itself comes from practice. Some examples of its work are continuing education for farmers in marketing for the EU; staff development, organisation, and management theory and the reflective practitioner; and courses in health systems and organisations for doctors and nurses.

The objective is to combine the process whereby individuals gain knowledge and qualifications with organisational change and interdisciplinary cooperation. These objectives are fulfilled through interdisciplinary research, scientific continuing education and public relations work. An example of IFF's work is its approach to health promotion as a process of organisational development. It develops and implements health promotion projects and activities, such as training programmes, workshops, research projects, seminars and conferences in a national and international context. Out of these experiences and in cooperation with international experts in the field of health promotion and organisational development, the department develops a specific health promotion approach. These interventions are aimed not so much at modifying individual behaviour but at changing the settings and developing innovative social systems (IFF 1993).

The Institute is a platform for problem areas in the professions and a forum for professional and university teachers/researchers, and either group may instigate a project. To summarise, IFF researches collaboratively with the professions, initiates courses and then attempts to implement the results in the traditional university system. This approach is an interesting innovation in the area of professional development and a substantial contribution to the provision of higher education for adults.

Conclusion

The basic picture that emerges in Austria is an exclusive system of education with selection early in the school system deciding higher education opportunities later; the *Matura* and its equivalents provide a guaranteed path into higher education for life for those able and lucky enough to obtain it, but a long uphill struggle for second-chancers. An over-crowded, heavily legislated higher education system gives excellent opportunities for those with adequate support mechanisms, but the high drop-out rate, particularly among women, indicates the problems for those without such support. Innovative developments to encourage more adults into higher education such as the *Studienberechtigungsprüfung*, the distance learning centre, the distance learning universities and IFF have as yet had little impact on the system. The picture for adults in vocational higher education may be improved by the introduction of the *Fachhochschulen*; indeed, it may be that the introduction of this new sector will transform the whole higher education system, as it has so notably done elsewhere in Europe.

Note

This chapter arises from a study visit to Austria and thanks are due to all those who supported that visit in particular Mag. Andrea Waxenegger, IFF. I should also like to thank the Ministry of Education and Arts and IFF for their practical support and Mag. Andrea Waxenegger and Dr.Ada Pellert for their comments on this chapter.

References

Bundesministerium für Wissenschaft und Forschung und Bundesministerium für Unterricht und Kunst (BMWF and BMUK) (1992) *Diversification of higher education in Austria: Background report submitted to the OECD*. Vienna: BMWF and BMUK.

Bundesministerium für Wissenschaft und Forschung (BMWF) (1990a) *Hochschul Bericht 1990: Band 1 Text*. Vienna: BMWF.

Bundesministerium für Wissenschaft und Forschung (BMWF) (1990b) *Hochschul Bericht 1990: Band 1 Anhang*. Vienna: BMWF.

Bundesministerium für Wissenschaft und Forschung (BMWF) (1993) *Hochschul Bericht 1993: Band 1 Statistisches Porträt*. Vienna: BMWF.

Europa World Year Book 1993, Vol.1. London: Europa Publications Ltd.

Federal Ministry of Education and Arts (1991) *OECD Country Report: Further Education and Training of the Labour Force in Austria*. Vienna: Federal Ministry of Education and Arts.

Feldner, E. (1992) *Probleme und Bedürfnisse der Studierenden im Zweiten Bildungsweg*. Vienna: IKUS.

Feldner, E. and Heinz, G. (1992) *Kurzstudie zur Infrastruktur und Serviceleistungen der Einrichtungen des 2. Bildungsweges in Österreich*. Vienna: IKUS.

IFF (1993) *WHO-Collaborating Centre for Health promotion, Training and Organisational Development*. Vienna: IFF-Institute für interdisziplinäre Forschung und Fortbildung und Abteilung Gesundheit und Organisationsentwicklung.

OECD (1987) *Adults in Higher Education*. Paris: OECD.

OECD (1993) *Education at a glance. OECD indicators*. Paris: OECD.

Palank, F. (1993) Distance Learning on an International Basis: the Case of Austria. *Open Learning*, 8, No.1, pp.44–46.

Chapter 3

Belgium

Etienne Bourgeois and Jean-Luc Guyot

The Structure and Organisation of Higher Education

As a general rule, higher education in Belgium is open to students with a secondary school diploma, which they obtain normally at the age of 18 after having completed 12 years of schooling (six years of primary schooling and six years of secondary schooling). The higher education system is organised into two institutional sectors (see Figure 3.1), namely, non-university higher education (*enseignement supérieur non-universitaire*) and university higher education (*enseignement supérieur universitaire*).

'Non-university' higher education

This sectors consists of two types of programme. The short-cycle non-university higher education programme (*enseignement supérieur non-universitaire de type court*) consist of two to three years of study and offer vocational training in seven occupational fields: technical, economic, agricultural, artistic, paramedical, social and pedagogical. Long-cycle higher education programmes (*enseignement supérieur non-universitaire de type long*) consist typically of four years of study providing more advanced qualifications in the same occupational fields as the short-cycle programmes. They are not open to people with a vocational secondary school diploma. Institutions providing either long-cycle or short cycle non-university higher education courses are called higher education schools (*écoles d'enseignement supérieur*).

University higher education

University higher education is provided by universities (*universités*) or university centres (*centres universitaires*). The former provide the whole range of university degrees in most fields of the arts, sciences and professions (theology, philosophy, law, economics, political and

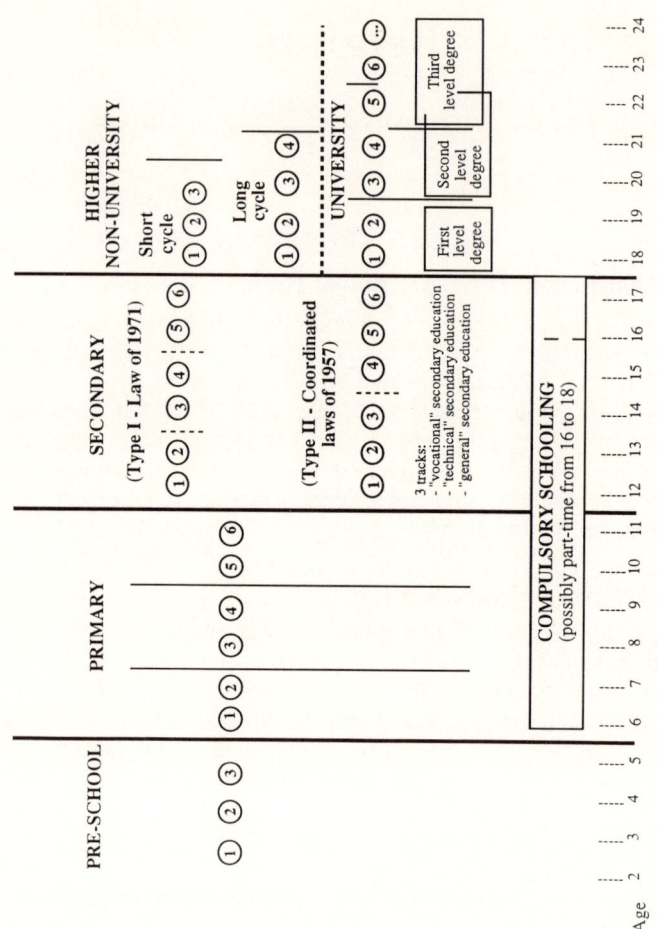

Figure 3.1 Structure of the Belgian education system

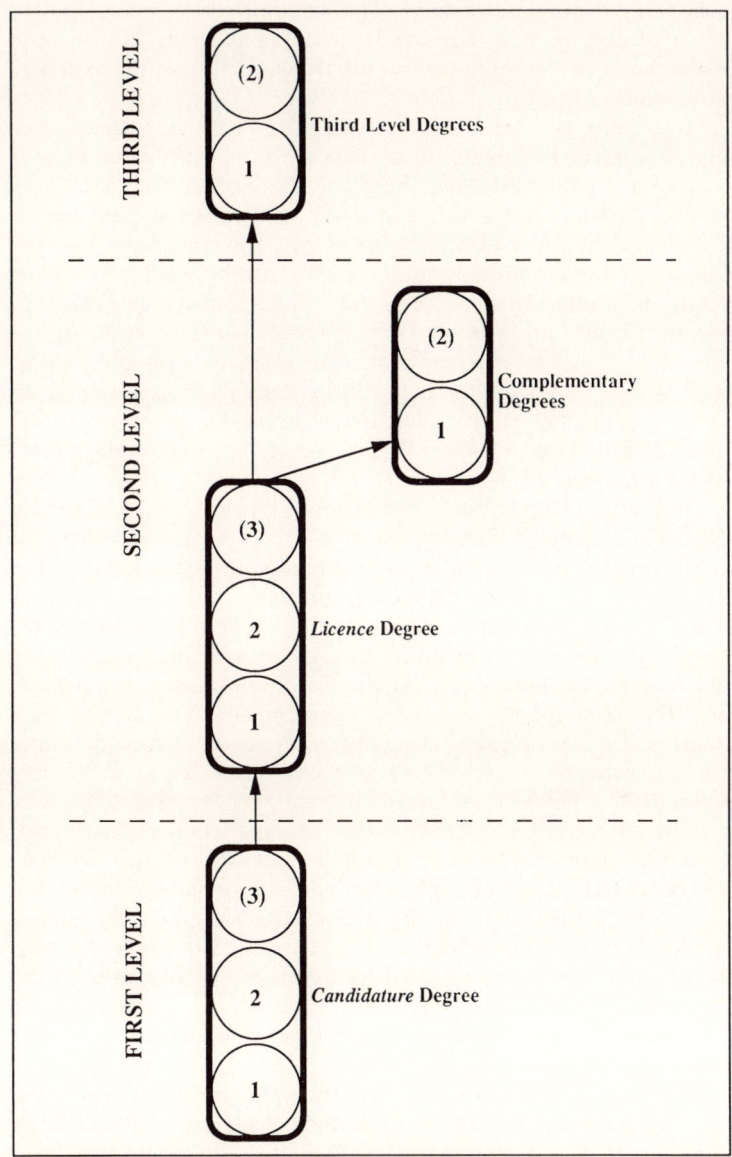

Figure 3.2 Structure of the Belgian university education system

social sciences, humanities, psychology, education, medicine, science, engineering, agronomy). The latter provide a more limited range of degrees in a more restricted range of fields. However, to make the presentation clearer we use the word 'university' to denote both kinds of institutions here.

University education is organised into three degree levels (see Figure 3.2). The first degree level is known as the *Candidature* degree. It is normally the first stage of the university curriculum consisting of two years of study, except in a few fields, such as medicine or veterinary studies, which take three years. The *Candidature* curriculum is intended to provide students with core knowledge in a given disciplinary or professional field and is broad in coverage. For example, the *Candidature* leading to an advanced degree in psychology or education consists of foundation courses in biology, philosophy, statistics, sociology, as well as psychology and education. The *Candidature* is not a final degree. It has virtually no value on the job market but is designed and used mainly as a preparatory stage giving access to a second level degree.

The second degree level consists of two types of degree. The main degree of this type is the *Licence* degree (except for medicine where it is known as the *Doctorat*). As a general rule, its access is limited to holders of a *Candidature* degree or equivalent. It consists of two or three years of study, depending on the field. Whereas the *Candidature* curriculum focuses on breadth, the *Licence* curriculum emphasises depth and specialisation in the field. Besides the *Licence* degree there are other second-level degrees called complementary second-level degrees (*Diplômes d'études complémentaires de second cycle* or sometimes *Licence spéciale, diplôme d'études complémentaires*, or *licence complémentaire*). They generally take one year of study, sometimes two, and are intended to provide graduates in one discipline with second-level education in another discipline. To that extent, access is generally restricted to holders of a *Licence* degree in another discipline. The *Agrégation* degree is a particular type of second-level complementary degree. It provides a theoretical and pedagogical training that prepares graduates in a given field for teaching their discipline at the (higher) secondary school level, and generally takes one year. The second-level degrees are the most commonly found and sought after university degrees on the job market.

The third degree level consists of two types of degree: that is, the PhD (*Doctorat*) and the advanced study degree (*Diplômes d'études approfondies*). The doctorate consists mainly of a dissertation, with no specific course provision. Advanced study degree programmes generally take one year of study and provide holders of a *Licence* degree with specialised training in their discipline. They have different names according to the field of study (*Maîtrise, Licence complémentaire, Diplôme de…, Certificat de spécialisation, Licence spéciale*, etc.).

Thus far, we have considered the award bearing educational provision. In addition it should be pointed out that most higher education institutions (the universities as well as the others) provide a wide range of non-award bearing continuing education programmes.

Admissions Procedures, Practices and Norms

One major characteristic of the Belgian higher education system is that, in accordance with the laws regulating higher education, admissions at any level are based on formal qualifications only. Table 3.1 shows the standard formal qualifications required for admission to the different types of higher education programme. There is no such a thing as a national or local standardised entrance examination, or admissions officers with the authority to decide which candidates will be admitted to a given programme in a given institution. Neither is there any consideration of the academic grades of a candidate applying to a given programme, with some minor exceptions at third level where a portfolio and previous academic marks are considered. Similarly, there is absolutely no formal limitation on the number of students that can be admitted to a given institution or programme. In other words, the necessary and sufficient condition for admission to a given higher education programme at any level is to have the proper formal qualifications.

Table 3.1: Formal qualifications required for admission to different types of higher education programmes

Standard Formal Qualifications Required…	…for Admission to a:
Secondary School Degree	Non-University Short-Cycle Programme
Secondary School Degree (from Non-Vocational Tracks Only)	Non-University Long-Cycle Programme University Candidature Programme
Candidature Degree	University Licence Programme
Licence Degree	University Second-Level Complementary Degree Programme in Another Field
Licence Degree	University Third-Level Advanced Degree Programme in the Same Field

Such a policy makes the Belgian higher education system both highly open and selective. It is highly open in the sense that the candidates with the proper qualifications cannot be denied admission to the institutions and programmes of their choice, regardless of their prior academic performance, the schools from which they have graduated, or the actual or projected enrolment figures of the programme or institution to which they apply. On the other hand, it is highly selective in the sense that it is quite difficult for people without the formal qualifications required ('non-traditional' students) to gain access, especially to non-university long-cycle and university education. As a result, the major feature of efforts to facilitate the access and participation of adults in higher education has been the attempt to increase the flexibility of the admissions policy at different degree levels. We shall enlarge on this point at a later stage.

Another consequence of the formal qualification-based admissions policy is the fact that selection occurs within the system rather than at entry. An enormous number of students enters the first *Candidature* year and it is not rare to find several hundred of them attending the same course in the first year. It is therefore not surprising that selection occurs later on, especially at the end of the first *Candidature* year: between 50 and 60 per cent of students enrolled in the first year of *Candidature* do not pass the final exams (either they fail or they drop out).

Size of the System

For the whole country, there are 19 universities or university centres. The number of non-university higher education schools is much higher: 113 in the French-speaking community and 162 in the Flemish.

Despite a fall in the number of young people in the relevant age group, the student population in higher education is increasing, especially in the non-university sector. This trend is related to several factors: the feminisation of the higher education student population, the growing demand from the labour market for highly qualified workers and increasing unemployment. Table 3.2 presents the statistics for 1984–90 for both Communities. It is obvious that the market share of the non-university system is increasing, in the Flemish-speaking community as well as in the French-speaking community. Table 3.3 shows the expansion of higher education from 1961 to 1990. Enrolments in non-university higher education in 1989–90 are five times as high as in 1961–62.

Table 3.2: Enrolments in Belgian higher education by community 1984–90

Flemish Community

Years	University		Non-university H.E.		Total
	N	%	N	%	N
1984–85	53,756	43.65	69,402	56.35	123,158
1985–86	54,159	43.54	70,242	56.46	124,401
1986–87	53,838	41.87	74,759	58.13	128,597
1987–88	54,275	41.27	77,247	58.73	131,522
1989–90	55,452	40.40	81,807	59.60	137,259

French Community

Years	University		Non-university H.E.		Total
	N	%	N	%	N
1984–85	50,387	56.20	39,231	43.80	89,618
1985–86	50,472	55.80	40,033	44.20	90,505
1986–87	50,702	55.20	41,070	44.80	91,772
1987–88	50,111	55.10	40,872	44.90	90,983
1989–90	53,845	54.80	44,520	45.20	98,365

Source: OECD 1992

Table 3.3: Enrolments in Belgian higher education since 1961

	1961–62	1989–90	Variation (n)	Variation (%)
Non-University H.E	24,734	126,327	+101,593	+411
University	31,312	109,297	+77,985	+249
Total	**56,046**	**235,624**	**+ 179,578**	**+ 320**

Sources: Fondation Universitaire 1962–1992; Ministère de l'Education Nationale 1961–1971; Ministère de l'Education, de la Recherche et de la Formation de la Communauté Française de Belgique 1972–1992; Ministère de l'Education Néerlandophone 1972–1988

Pattern of Participation and Availability of Data

The above figures indicate that, from a strictly quantitative point of view, more and more people enter higher education. However, there are problems in the available data. Due to federalisation, national statistics agencies have management problems and the agencies of the two Communities are not yet able to supply reliable data. In addition there is strong competition between higher education institutions and they are opposed to the publication of data which would permit comparisons between them. (For further discussion of this issue, see Guyot 1992.) It is therefore difficult to give an accurate description of the characteristics of the intake of the higher education system. Nevertheless, we can point out two features from a number of sources (see for example Dal and Guyot 1992, OECD 1992):

(1) Women are entering in increasing numbers: 48.53 per cent of new entrants to the first year in the French-speaking universities in 1989 compared to only 40.91 per cent in 1974.

(2) Most students enter higher education via the first year of the first level: every year more than 90 per cent of the (Belgian) students entering the French speaking university system for the first time enter via the first *Candidature*.

Table 3.4: Social inequalities in non-university higher education in 1983–84 (French and German speaking communities)

Social class (from high to low)	Primary schools (for comparison)	Non-university higher education	
		Short cycle	Long cycle
Class I (upper management, legal and medical professions, teachers, middle management)	16.3%	29.6%	36.9%
Class II (lower management, farmers, retailers, craftmen and the arts)	24.6%	34.4%	32.7%
Class III (blue-collar workers, unemployed)	59.1%	36.0%	30.4%
Total	100.0%	100.0%	100.0%

Source: Liénard, G. 1991

However, nothing can be said with any accuracy about the origin (social or economic background) and the characteristics (gender, nationality) of the students in higher education. Nonetheless, we know that there are some differences between the university and the non-university higher education student populations. It seems that the latter is a little older than the former (a difference of one or two years on average in a comparable level of study) and some previous studies give information about social inequalities in higher education. Tables 3.4 and 3.5 show some figures concerning the social origin of students in the late 1970s and early 1980s, and it is clear that there was enormous under-representation of lower socio-economic groups in both university and non-university sectors. This information is not recent but it can reasonably be assumed that the situation has not changed significantly since these studies were conducted.

Table 3.5: Example of social inequalities in university education parents' occupational status of students enrolled in the first candidature year at the Catholic University of Louvain (UCH) in 1979–80

Categories	*U.C.L. students*	*Wallonia and Brussels population*
Professional classes and executives	48.9%	24.0%
Employees	18.6%	17.5%
Traders	13.5%	10.1%
Workers	6.2%	42.3%
Farmers and rural workers	6.1%	3.0%
Others	6.7%	3.1%
Total	**100%**	**100%**

Source: Liénard, G. 1991

Adult entrance is quite marginal, especially in universities: for the academic year 1990–91, only 8.2 per cent of the Belgian students enrolled in Belgian universities were 30 and over, and the proportion in 1989–90 was 7.96 per cent (Fondation Universitaire 1962–1991). These figures include students who enrolled at a younger age and are continuing their studies, and is not therefore a good indicator of access for adults. We do not have any recent figures for the non-university higher education sector and there is no information about adult entrants in higher education.

The Concept of Adult

In Belgium there is no legal or official definition of an adult student and this lack of standardisation makes it difficult for researchers and academic managers to have a clear idea of the evolution of adult access to higher education.

We were ourselves confronted with this problem in a study we recently conducted on adult access and participation in the Catholic University of Louvain. The adult student is clearly older than the young student; the question is how much older must he or she be? It is clear that the answer should vary as a function of the level of study being considered. In our study, we set up the following age criteria to define the adult student with regard to each level of study:

- First year of the first level *Candidature* degree programmes: 23 years old and over

- First year of the second level *Licence* degree: 26 years old and over (increased to 27 and over for medical studies, as the first level is one year longer than in other fields)

- First year of the second level complementary degrees, and first year of the third level degrees (except for the PhD): 29 years old and over (increased to 35 and over for medical studies).

Another approach to the notion of the adult student is to consider the period of time elapsed between the time when the student left the formal education system and the time of his or her re-entry to the system, regardless of age. This is the notion of adult students as 'returning' students, an approach which has been widely adopted in the literature (Marchand 1983). This criterion deserves to be considered independently of the age criterion, although they partly overlap. A 23-year-old student who has been out of the system for several years and is entering the higher education system for the first time has specific needs, expectations and perspectives that may differ significantly from those of another student of the same age who has never left the system since primary school.

A third possible approach to the concept of adult student is to look at the student's occupational status. From this angle, a student can be viewed as an adult to the extent that he or she works alongside his or her study. In other words, studying is not the main activity in his or her life. This is the notion of adult student as a 'part-time' student. Again, this variable overlaps with the first two, but not completely, so that it also deserves independent consideration.

Ideally, it seems to us that these three approaches should be combined in order to identify the adult student, because each of them highlights a specific set of characteristics which should be taken into consideration, whether in conducting research or in making policies regarding access and participation of adults in higher education. Unfortunately, the latter two criteria are virtually impossible to take into consideration in the Belgian context, given the current state of the statistical system at both the national and the institutional levels.

Policy Relating to Adults and Higher Education

At the risk of oversimplification, it can be said that most of the effort to promote equality of educational opportunity in Belgium has traditionally been concentrated outside the formal education system. Since World War II labour organisations have been very active in the development of lifelong education provision for young and adult workers. Trade unions and other organisations have developed a wide variety of both formal and informal educational activities, specifically geared to the social and cultural development of workers. With only a few exceptions, these educational programmes have always been non-award bearing activities so that they could not be used as entry routes to the formal schooling system (Bourgeois 1990).

Another source of development in continuing education of workers is the 'vocational training' sector (*formation professionnelle*). This sector consists of a network of state and private institutions dedicated to the vocational training of workers, structurally independent from the formal education system and the responsibility of the Ministry of Employment (*Ministère de l'emploi et du travail*) rather than the Ministry of Education. These institutions have generally open admissions policies (no entry requirements in terms of prior qualifications) and provide short skill-updating programmes in a wide variety of vocational fields. This educational sector has considerably grown over the last fifteen years. One of the reasons for such a growth is the economic crisis and the rise of unemployment in particular. Again, the 'vocational training' network has very little connection with the formal higher education system, and is little help as an entry route to the higher education system (Maroy 1984).

In general, the formal higher education system has never been very responsive to the concern for equal opportunity, in either theory or practice. This is particularly true of the university system. Yet, in the late 1960s, many voices from various segments of society accused the university of elitism and deplored its lack of commitment to equal opportunities. It is in this ideological context that the idea to create an Open University in Wallonia, based on the British model, emerged in the late 1960s. This ambitious project was to involve different stakeholders: the State, most of the French-speaking universities of the country, the major labour organisations and the national broadcasting network. After about three years of multilateral negotiations, the different partners could not reach an agreement and the project collapsed. No project of this kind has been initiated since that time, and initiatives for promoting the access and participation of non-traditional groups in higher education have been few. Moreover, most of them have been driven from inside the higher education system, by the institutions themselves. This is due to both ideological and institutional reasons.

As in most Western countries, the economic crisis that has developed over the last two decades hit the higher education system quite badly. Institutions had to face a severe reduction of their income and pressure to decrease their expenditure. In the late 1980s and early 1990s the economic position of higher education institutions improved somewhat; however, another external pressure replaced it when Belgium became a federal state and education was one of the responsibilities transferred from national government to the two community governments. The budget of the community governments is such that this move has again resulted in reduced income for higher education institutions. The situation is not likely to improve in the near future, given the current economic depression and the particularly poor shape of public finances in Belgium.

In such an economically depressed context, the higher education system has adopted a withdrawal position with respect to the issues of equal opportunity and openness to non-traditional student groups that were among the foremost preoccupations of some political and academic leaders in the late 1960s. These issues gradually gave way to a concern for more efficiency in the achievement of the traditional goals of the higher education system: namely, the advancement of scientific research and the education of its traditional student clientèle. Such a response from higher education was driven from both inside and outside the system.

The external stakeholders – governments and employers – have never exerted any real pressure upon the higher education system to develop access policies. For example, there have never been any governmental regulations to encourage the development of affirmative action policies and there have been no policies to stimulate research on access and participation of non-traditional students. In fact, as will be explained below, the existing governmental regulations concerning the funding of universities and their admission procedures actually discourage rather than encourage the development of any form of curriculum modularisation or more flexible admission policies. Another indicator of the relative lack of interest of government in the equality of opportunity issue is the absence of national statistics on the socio-economic background of pupils and students enrolled at any level of the education system. In this respect, it should also be emphasised that Belgian social scientists do not seem to have exerted any pressure on the government to systematically collected that kind of data; it was an issue for them in the 1960s and 1970s, but it since seems to have lost their attention.

To say that the government has completely neglected the equal opportunities issue with regard to higher education would be unfair, however. Two measures have been taken by the government that may have contributed to facilitating the access and participation of adults in higher education. The first one is a law passed in the early 1970s (which has been revised several times since then), which allows employees to take a fixed amount of time off for study without any salary loss. The other measure is the provision of financial support to low income students enrolled in a higher education degree (except for complementary second level degrees or third level degrees) in the form of tuition fee reductions.

Employers themselves have some impact on the higher education system, because of the growing demand for highly skilled workers. However, this has not fundamentally affected the organisational behaviour of higher education institutions in terms of access and participation. At most, it has encouraged the development of highly specialised training programmes in some fields. To some extent, it may have also affected the curriculum in more professionally oriented fields (such as education or business), but it has not stimulated the development of policies for encouraging the admission of non-traditional groups.

Just as equality of opportunity in higher education has not been, or is no longer, a key issue in Belgian society at large for the last two decades, neither has it appeared to be among the foremost preoccupations of academic leaders. In times of scant resources, academic leaders in some other Western countries have seen the development of access opportunities for non-traditional students as an effective way to reach new student markets and hence to compensate for the expected loss of income. In Belgium, however, academic leaders have not taken this approach. On the contrary, they have tended to see the development of access policies primarily as a source of additional expense. They reason that, in times of economic difficultly their priority goals of research and initial education of the young leave no extra money to spend in the development of access policies. Several reasons explain such an attitude. First, as pointed out above, the higher education system did not have to face any significant pressure from the outside to increase participation of non-traditional students.

Second, equal opportunity has never been a key concern in the dominant culture, either inside or outside the system. Widening and increasing access is therefore seen as something novel, if not alien to the system. Third, given the formal qualification-based admissions policy, the priority concern of academic leaders is how to manage the massive student intake at entry rather than how to bring more students (or different students) into the system. Given the increase in numbers, the big issue now for academic leaders is clearly quality – quality of process and quality of output.

This overview might lead the reader to think that virtually nothing has been done in Belgium to facilitate the access and participation of adults in higher education for the last two decades. Even though the ideological and economic context did not encourage the development of adult access policies, some effort has been made in this direction by some institutions in particular. Two basic types of initiatives have been taken, namely, increasing the flexibility of admissions conditions and procedures and making some programmes more suited to the specific needs of adult students. This will be explained in more detail in the following sections.

Alternative Entry Routes for Adults

For non-university higher education it should be noted that there is no possibility to gain entry other than through the first year of the programme. In universities, three types of programmes can be distinguished as far as admissions are concerned. The first type has what we would call a *conventional admissions policy*. The majority of university programmes fall into this category. Access to these programmes is restricted to the people who have the standard entry qualifications (see Table 3.1). Some of them even have additional entry requirements (for example, an entry examination or extra courses). It should be noted that some of the programmes in this category are specifically aimed at adults. For example, admission to some university complementary second level degree programmes, such as business or educational administration, is restricted to people who have the standard qualifications (that is, a *Licence* in another discipline), are at least 25 years old, and have at least five years of work experience in the field.

The second type of programme has what we call a bridging admissions policy (*passerelles*). The programmes of this type are far less numerous and most of them are *Licence* programmes. They are accessible not only to holders of the standard qualifications (that is, a *Candidature* degree in the discipline), but also to holders of a non-university higher education degree in the field. In other words, their non-university degree is somehow treated as equivalent to a *Candidature* degree in the field. In some cases, such students have direct access to the programme. In other cases, they have to fulfil some additional requirements. For example, they may be required to take a few additional courses (sometimes up to the equivalent of one full-time year of study), or they may be required to have obtained good grades in their non-university final degree, or both.

The third type of university programme has an open admissions policy. Programmes of this kind are very rare and most of them are *Licence* degree programmes. Admission to this type of programme is open in the sense that it not based on formal qualifications. However, it is typically restricted to the people who meet the following conditions: 25 years old or over, having at least five years of relevant experience in the field, having passed an entry examination that is aimed to test the basic competencies defined as prerequisites, and being able to demonstrate motivation that fits the objectives and goals of the programme.

Besides these arrangements, there are virtually no opportunities for accreditation of experiential learning and there are few opportunities for transferring vocational qualifications obtained outside the higher education system, for example, in the 'vocational training' system, into higher education. Even the opportunities of credit transfer from one university to another are also fairly restricted, although the situation is currently improving. As mentioned above, there are no affirmative action strategies towards any social groups in the Belgian higher education system. The only form of positive action is the provision of degree programmes whose access is limited to adults (age and work experience requirements).

In conclusion, the Belgian higher education system is relatively open to the extent that there is virtually no selection of students at entry other than formal qualifications. However, access opportunities for those people who do not have the formal entry qualifications are fairly scarce. So, as far as the admissions policy is concerned, the major problem with this system is not so much that it is not open to returning adults (in fact, as mentioned above, several programmes are open to adults exclusively), but that it is open to anyone, including adults, insofar as he or she has the formal qualifications to enter the system. The admissions policy therefore discriminates more against the socio-economically disadvantaged than against adults per se.

Alternative Accessible Programmes in Higher Education

The most frequent pattern remains the conventional one: daytime, weekday, on-campus courses; lectures; large classes; very limited possibilities of credit transfer and accumulation.

Unquestionably, some efforts have been undertaken recently by certain higher education institutions to make their educational provision more suited to the specific needs and characteristics of adults students. However, these efforts remain rather limited on the whole.

Evening and weekend course provision

Some higher education degree programmes are delivered entirely on an evening and weekend basis. In universities, most evening/weekend programmes are second level degree programmes. There is no available data on the precise number or proportion of such programmes in the whole higher education system but at the Catholic University of Louvain, evening/weekend programmes represent nearly 11 per cent of the total number of degree programmes delivered (Guyot *et al.* 1993). Another type of arrangement is the concentration of courses in one or two weekdays.

Decentralised, franchised, outreach programmes

There is virtually no franchising system of any kind in Belgian higher education apart from one example in Flanders. Since the early 1980s, the degree programmes of the Open University of the Netherlands have been accessible to students enrolled in several accredited Flemish universities. The students are officially enrolled in a given programme of the Dutch Open University; they receive the television courses at home via the cable network and they get tutoring support in one of the Flemish universities accredited by the Dutch Open University. Their final degree is from the Dutch Open University.

De-centralisation is another arrangement which appears to be more widely spread. Students enrolled in such a programme have the possibility to attend the courses either on campus or in one of the different off-campus locations proposed by the institution. Sometimes they have to take all the coursework in the same location. In other cases, the courseload is split into two or more locations, so that all the students attend several locations. Although there is no national data, this type of arrangement appears to remain quite marginal. For example, less than 2 per cent of the degree programmes at the Catholic University of Louvain are decentralised (Guyot *et al.* 1993). One of the reasons for this is certainly the small size of the country

(Belgium is 18 times smaller than France and 8 times smaller than UK).

Multi-media, distance and open learning

The small size of the country has always been a major obstacle to the development of distance learning systems on a large scale. On the one hand, the national student market is so small that it would be virtually impossible to secure the financial viability of such system, which generally involves considerable investment in broadcasting and multi-media technologies. On the other hand, the country is so small that geographical distances have probably never been a major obstacle to participation in higher education anyway. Another problem is the high degree of institutional, political, linguistic and ideological segmentation of Belgian society, which increases the difficulty faced by the many institutional partners that would have to be involved in reaching an agreement. The failure of the Open University project in the early 1970s referred to above provides a striking illustration of this and has remained in the memories of political and academic leaders.

There are however a few local initiatives, most of them developed by universities. For example, the University of Mons has a Master's degree in educational technology in collaboration with French and Portuguese universities, which is partly delivered in a distance learning format. Similarly, the University of Namur has developed a course in computer programming delivered in a distance learning format, via a local television cable network. Very recently, representatives of all the French-speaking universities and the Ministry of Education (Department of Distance and Open Learning) have been meeting in order to explore the possibility of jointly developing a set of courses (probably *Candidature* degree level courses) to be delivered in a distance learning format. This course package could be taken by students enrolled in any of the French-speaking universities, and would be duly accredited by all of them. Non-university higher education institutions are also collaborating with the Ministry of Education (but not the universities!) on a similar project. (For a detailed report on the current state of affairs of distance learning, see Fransen and Waterschoot 1993.)

In addition, educational technology research laboratories in most universities have been very active for years in the development of various kinds of multi-media educational support materials in different subjects. Most of this activity is taking place within the framework of European networks such as COMETT or DELTA.

Modularisation, credit accumulation and transfer

The concept of modularisation of the curriculum in higher education is characterised by three distinct aspects. First, modularisation implies the possibility of individualising the curriculum taken by each student in the programme with courses chosen from a wide range available. Second, it implies the possibility of credit accumulation whereby each student has the possibility to decide which and how many credits (courses) he or she is going to take in a given period of time (say in a given semester or year) and the total amount of time he or she will take to complete all the degree requirements. The third aspect is the possibility of credit transfer whereby the student has the possibility to obtain accreditation of academic or non-academic qualifications obtained elsewhere; it may also imply the accreditation of work experience.

How does the Belgian higher education system stand with regard to those three aspects of modularisation? First, curriculum individualisation is generally very limited both in non-university higher education and in university higher education. The curriculum is largely standard. All students enrolled in a given programme are required to take the same courses, in the same order and few electives are available. Such a standardisation characterises most *Candidature* degree curricula but more flexibility can be found in second-level degree, although it varies from field to field. In most *Licence* programmes, for example, the students have to take compulsory courses and electives from within the programme; in some cases, they may also take a few electives outside of the programme, but this possibility is not common.

Second, the Belgian higher education system offers little flexibility in terms of credit accumulation. This is due mainly to the funding system that has prevailed for years. As will be explained below, the funding of higher education institutions is largely based on enrolments, and students must meet certain conditions to be able to receive funding. One of these is that they must be registered in an accredited programme for a complete, full-time year (the legal annual minimum courseload is 300 hours). Such a requirement is not likely to encourage the development of credit accumulation policies in higher education. There is however one major exception to this general rule. Students with a job are allowed to spread the 300 hours over two years and are funded as a half unit in each year. Such a measure is potentially very useful for students who seek to study on a part-time basis and for those institutions which seek to encourage part-time study. However, in practice it is not common. One of the reasons is that credit accumulation – and modularisation in general – is quite alien to the dominant culture, in terms of philosophy and practice, of the Belgian higher education system. Another reason is the lack of information. Many students, and sometimes programme leaders, simply ignore this opportunity and it is not well publicised. In some programmes, students are not allowed or encouraged to use this opportunity, mainly for pedagogical reasons. Another obstacle to the development of credit accumulation policies is the fact that tuition fee reductions are granted by the state to students with low incomes only if they successfully complete a full-time courseload in the year.

Third, the possibility of credit transfer across institutions is very limited. This is certainly the case of credit transfer from an educational institution outside the formal higher education system to a higher education institution, or from non-university to university institutions, although some flexibility exists in the so-called 'bridging' university programmes. Credit transfer is also fairly limited across universities, for political and ideological reasons. Higher education institutions belong to different institutional networks. There is a first split between the 'State' institutions (directly governed by the Ministry of Education) and the 'Free' institutions (with their own governing board). Moreover, there is also a split within the 'Free' institutions network between the Catholic and the lay institutions. Traditionally, the mobility of both students and faculty members across these different institutional networks have been very limited.

To complete the picture, we should also mention the possibility for a student to register for one, two or more courses offered by a given programme and to sit the examination. These students are called 'free' students. However, if at some point such a student decides to graduate from that programme, he or she cannot count the courses taken previously as a 'free' student but has to sit for the full courseload, including those already passed. Free students are not taken into account in the funding formula.

In conclusion, it can be said that there is little flexibility in terms of curriculum modularisation. On the one hand, the funding system has not encouraged higher education institutions to develop that kind of practice and on the other, modularisation is quite alien to the culture of the higher education system. Things are gradually changing, though. Modularisation is gradually taking root in the mind of both political and academic leaders. For example, the Ministry of Education of the French-speaking community is currently working on a major reform of the non-university higher education system. In a very recent document presenting the guidelines of the proposed reform (Ministère de l'Enseignement supérieur de la Communauté française de Belgique 1993), modularisation of the curriculum appears as one of the priorities. The same trend can be observed within universities, at least in some fields (such as education), as demonstrated by recent programme reform proposals.

Pedagogy

Some pedagogical arrangements specifically designed to facilitate access and achievement of adults can be found in higher education. These arrangements emphasise:

- feedback in the teacher/student relationship (formative evaluation)
- relatively small classes (typically 20–25 students per class)
- experiential learning and theory-practice interactions
- peer learning
- student supervision and services
- group dynamics in the learning process
- student participation in the course design and evaluation
- independent study
- faculty pedagogical development.

These pedagogical arrangements are generally concentrated in those programmes that are open to adult students exclusively. In all of the other programmes (that is, in about 95 per cent of the programmes), little has been done in terms of pedagogy to facilitate the participation of adults specifically. This does not mean that no pedagogical innovations have been developed in these programmes. However, such innovations are rather scarce on the whole and have not been motivated primarily by a concern for adult participation. As explained above, most of the pedagogical innovations that have been implemented recently at the university were motivated primarily by the need to manage expansion and drop-out in the *Candidature*. Their rationale is not *a priori* to reduce the selection that occurs within the *Candidature* level but rather to make it fairer and more effective and has led to innovative practices such as small group exercises, formative evaluation devices, independent study devices, individualised student guidance and orientation. It is clear that all these innovations could also be profitable to adult students but to date, such developments are rare. The pedagogical practices that prevail in the largest part of the higher education programmes are little suited to adult students. It is therefore not surprising that so few adult students are actually found in those programmes.

Resources and Funding

Funding of courses

The University funding system is regulated by the law of 27 July 1971 (published in the national Official Journal *Moniteur Belge* 17 July 1971). The system is based on the concept of 'cost per student' and has four parameters which define the funding formulae and the amount of funding but do not affect the effective use of the funding by universities. The four parameters are: fields of study, guaranteed numbers, staff/student ratios, and quotas.

For each field of study – social sciences, sciences, applied sciences and medicine, agriculture – and for each type of expenditure – academic and scientific staff, auxiliary staff, and running costs – the cost per student is fixed by order each year. Fundable students (those counted in the formula) are those that are enrolled in an accredited programme on a full-time basis (300 hours or 150 hours for two years for working students), and comply with the legal entry requirements (in term of prior qualifications). For a year, the total funding of a university is the product of the funding fixed for each field of study and the number of fundable students.

A guaranteed minimum number of students for each field of study is set by law. If a university has less than the minimum number of students it is guaranteed to receive funding corresponding to the minimum number. A maximum number is also fixed by law. If a university has more students enrolled than the maximum number it will get no more than the funding corresponding to the maximum number.

For each field of study, the application of staff/student ratios defined by the law will determine the amount of spending for academic and scientific staff cost. However, universities are not required to apply the ratios in their internal allocation of resources; thus these ratios do not affect the effective use of the funding. There is also a quota of two members of academic staff to three scientific.

It should be noted that the funding system of the non-university sector is similar to that outlined here for universities. Several remarks must be made with regard to the funding system. First, this system does not favour the credit system since only full-time students are taken into account for funding. Second, the access of non-traditional students is not favoured since the students must meet the legal conditions of accessibility to be taken into account for funding. Third, for three years, and in spite of the increasing number of enrolments, the Community governments have limited funding at a fixed level, irrespective of the number of enrolments. Fourth, there is no special funding for developing adult-oriented programmes.

Student financial support

Students are entitled to means-tested financial support from the State in the form of tuition fee reductions. There is no particular provision for part-time students, and people in receipt of unemployment benefit are not allowed to enrol in higher education for daytime programmes since they are supposed to be available for any job offer. If they do enrol in such programmes they may lose their unemployment benefit.

Research in the Field

Except for a few recent research projects, including those that have been conducted by the authors (Guyot *et al.* 1993), research on access and participation of adults in higher education has never been developed as such in Belgium. This also applies to research on access to education in general. As mentioned above, social scientists as well as political leaders seems to have diverted their attention from the access issue for years (as attested by the discontinuation of the collection of statistics directly related to the issue in the early 1980s). However, some research has been conducted in related fields. A lot of work has been done recently on continuing education in firms and other non-educational organisations. For example, a great deal of attention has been devoted to various forms of staff training practices as means of socialisation in organisations and some researchers are concentrating on the current development of 'non-formal training' practices in firms. Others are studying the staff training strategies in relation to various characteristics of the organisation. The research and development effort in this area also concerns the methodology of continuing education programme evaluation and development in various organisational contexts. These research themes are developed mainly in education departments, business schools, labour studies departments, and to a lesser extent in either sociology or organisational studies departments. Another research theme concerns the relationship between employment and vocational training, from both an applied and a fundamental perspective, and this is an area which is mostly studied in sociology and labour studies departments. Some research is also conducted on adult teaching and learning. Usually, this is basic research and developed mainly by psychologists and educationalists. Although a lot of research work is currently being done on university teaching and learning, it does not concern adult students specifically.

References

Bourgeois, E. (1990) *University Politics: Adult Education in a Belgian University.* Chicago: The University of Chicago. (PhD Dissertation, unpublished).

Dal, L. and Guyot, J.L. (1992) *Recherche prospective sur l'évolution du nombre d'étudiants dans les universités francophones belges (rapport intermédiaire de recherche),* polycopié, Louvain-la-Neuve, Institut de Démographie de l'Université Catholique de Louvain.

Fondation Universitaire (1962–1992) *Rapports Annuels du Bureau de Statistiques.* Bruxelles: Fondation Universitaire.

Fransen, J. and Waterschoot, V. (1993) *L'enseignement à distance en Communauté Française de Belgique. Rapport de recherche.* Bruxelles: Ministère de l'Education, de la recherche et de la Formation de la Communauté Française de Belgique.

Guyot, J.L. (1992) Le système éducatif en Belgique: trous noirs et nébuleuses, in *News Letter du Point d'appui Women Studies* (U.L.B.-U.I.A.), 4, 16–21.

Guyot, J.L., Bourgeois, E. and de Saint George, P. (1993) *Adult Access and participation in Higher Education in Belgium. An overview.* Louvain-la-Neuve: Université Catholique de Louvain, FOPES-FORG.

Liénard, G. (1991) Formation et culture: démocratie inachevée ou rêve dépassés, *Pédagogies,* 3, 11–29.

Marchand, L. (1983) *Introduction à l'éducation des adultes.* Montréal: Préfontaine.

Maroy, C. (1984) *Institutions de formation et crises. Les indices de la restructuration actuelle des champs de formation en Belgique francophone.* Namur: Cahiers de la faculté des sciences économiques et sociales de Namur (FNDP).

Ministère de l'Education, de la Recherche et de la Formation de la Communauté Française de Belgique (1972–1992) *Etudes et Documents.* Bruxelles: Ministère l'Education, de la recherche et de la Formation de la Communauté Français de Belgique.

Ministère de l'Education Nationale (1961–1971) Annuaires Statistiques de l'Enseignement. Bruxelles: Ministère de l'Education Nationale.

Ministère de l'Education Néerlandophone (1972–1988) *Statistische Jaarboeken van het Onderwijs.* Bruxelles: Ministère l'Education Néerlandophone (1972–1982).

Ministère de l'Enseignement Supérieur de la Communauté Française de Belgique (1993) *Enseignement supérieur. Type long et type court. Réformer pour mieux former. Propositions de Réforme de Michel Lebrun, Ministre de l'Enseignement supérieur.* Bruxelles: Ministère de l'Enseignement Supérieur de la Communauté française de Belgique.

OECD (1992) *Les systèmes éducatifs en Belgique: similitudes et divergences.* Paris: OECD.

Chapter 4

Denmark

Anthony Cooke

Denmark has a population of 5.2 million of which some 2 million live in Copenhagen. It is one of the most prosperous countries in the European Union and spends a larger proportion of GDP on public education (6.8% in 1988) than any other country in the EU (Ministry of Education and Research 1993). Compared with many other Western European countries, it has an unusually homogenous population without large religious or ethnic divisions. In 1992, 3.3% of the population were foreign nationals of whom approximately one third were from Scandinavian countries or the EU, others being from Turkey, Iran, Pakistan and Sri Lanka. There are few religious divisions as 89.3 per cent of the population are members of the Lutheran Church.

The country does share a number of features with its Western European neighbours. It has an ageing population with a low birth-rate, and an increasing proportion of elderly people in the population. There is growing concern about unemployment, which reached 10.6 per cent in 1991, and a strong emphasis on keeping Danish industry competitive in international terms. These trends are reflected in the reforms currently being carried out in the education system.

Denmark has a long and honourable tradition of adult education and high participation rates at all levels of education. Like other Western European countries, it is making the transition to a system of mass higher education. The themes of the recent Danish reforms in higher education are 'deregulation and decentralisation', although it seems likely that this rhetoric cloaks growing demands for accountability leading to 'increasing centralisation of planning, policy making and supervision' (Nielsen and Webb 1992).

The Structure and Organisation of Higher Education

The higher education system is traditionally divided between the university and the non-university sector with a further division between long, medium and short-term courses. 'Horizontal diversity' (Rasmussen 1992) exists in the different types of institutions and courses – universities (academic courses of five years or more), non-university (professional, vocational courses of 3–4 years), and vocational institutions (2 year courses). 'Vertical diversity', defined as creating more flexible exit points in the system, is being developed through the introduction of a three year bachelor's degree in the universities in addition to the traditional five year master's degree. A further distinction exists between those institutions which award degrees and where staff are required to carry out research (five universities and 19 other institutions), and a much larger group of smaller institutions which award diplomas or certificates and where there is no requirement that staff carry out research (Nielsen and Webb 1992). Bache (1993) too makes the distinction between universities and university-level institutions (*hjere laereanstalter*) which offer courses for *kandidat* and PhD degrees and undertake research, and the 90 or so smaller institutions which offer shorter courses in a narrower range of subjects.

Institutions vary in size between the University of Copenhagen with 27,000 students and the four other universities with enrolments between 14,800 (Aarhus) and 4000 (Roskilde). Non-university institutions tend to be smaller – for example the nine engineering colleges have a total enrolment of 8500, the 18 teacher training colleges a total enrolment of 7000 and the 34 colleges for social educators (pre-school, recreation centre teachers) a total enrolment of 9000.

The system has expanded rapidly in the last thirty years from an annual admission of 7920 in 1960 to 39,995 in 1992. Nevertheless this expansion has not kept pace with the demand for places which rose from 26,200 in 1982 to approximately 60,000 in 1991. The 1992 reform of higher education called for 41,000 study places a year and this has already been revised upward by the new Centre/Left coalition government. Some 40 per cent of an age cohort now enters higher education in Denmark with approximately equal numbers of men and women.

The expansion of numbers in higher education should be seen in the context of very high participation rates in all forms of education. In 1992, it was estimated that some 1.5 million people were receiving some form of adult education. Of these, about 500,000 were taking part in vocationally orientated continuing education, some 100,000 were in programmes for disadvantaged groups, another 100,000 were taking general qualifying courses for adults and the remainder were taking part in leisure-time education, folk high schools etc. If adult education courses are excluded, about a third of all 15–34 year olds were enrolled in education in 1990–91. Amongst 15–19 year olds 78 per cent were enrolled, compared with 30 per cent of 20–24 year olds, 13 per cent of 25–29 year olds and 5 per cent of 30–34 year olds (Ministry of Education and Research 1993).

Admissions Procedures, Practices, Norms

In common with many other Western European countries, Denmark displayed until recently a 'dual monopoly' of entry to higher education: through an academic kind of school (the gymnasium) or through the state examination (*Studentereksamen*) which provided an automatic right of entry to higher education (Neave 1987). The first significant modification to this system was the introduction of the Higher Preparatory Examination, *Hojere Forberedelseseksamen* (HF), in 1967. It mimicked the *Studentereksamen* by offering a broad-based nationally designed curriculum, but one that could be completed in two years full-time study rather than three. The HF rapidly developed into an alternative but parallel method of entry into higher education. Since 1978, it has been possible to prepare for the HF examination on a single-subject basis by part-time study and this has proved particularly popular for adults. This programme is discussed in more detail below.

With increasing pressure of numbers and demands for more flexibility, the admissions system has continued to diversify. The Higher Commercial Examination, *Hojere handelseksamen*, (HHX) and the Higher Technical Examination, *Hojeretekniskeksamen*, (HTX) which were introduced in the 1960s primarily as vocational qualifications are now recognised as another route into higher education. This increase in the number of pathways into higher education finds parallels in other European countries: 'in place of the broad path for the few arose the narrow paths for the many' (Neave 1987 p.17).

Table 4.1: Number of students gaining higher education entry qualifications 1990

Studentereksamen (three years in gymnasium)	18,600
HF (Higher preparatory exam)	5000
HHX (Higher commercial exam)	7100
HTX (Higher technical exam)	1000
Total	**31,700**
Percentage of age cohort leaving upper secondary and vocational education	44%

Source: Bache, 1993

The relative significance of these routes is indicated in Table 4.1, which shows that while the *Studentereksamen* is clearly the most important, the three other routes together contributed 41 per cent of the total who qualified to enter higher education in 1990.

A major issue in the development of admissions policy has been the balance between demand for and supply of places in higher education. Until the late 1970s, there was open admission to all courses of higher education with some exceptions such as dentistry and midwifery. Due to increasing pressure on places, restricted admission, *numerus clausus*, was introduced for courses such as medicine, architecture and librarianship, in an attempt to tie the number of graduates to labour market requirements. From 1993 onwards, the intention has been to delegate more responsibility for admissions from the Ministry of Education and Research to the institutions themselves. Restricted admission will continue to apply to long and expensive programmes such as medicine and dentistry but in other subjects each institution will decide how many students it admits to each programme, and if the number of qualified applicants exceeds capacity, it will then decide selection criteria. This represents a shift from a system with a considerable degree of central regulation where the selection of students for higher education was the responsibility of the Ministry of Education and Research towards a more Anglo-Saxon model where selection and admission become more a matter for the institutions themselves. It remains to be seen how quickly it is possible to move from a dominant culture of central regulation towards a more autonomous system; and the impact it will have on patterns of admission and participation.

The Ministry of Education publishes a good deal of data on Danish education, although there are gaps. For example, it is difficult to track progression through the system. A number of educationalists interviewed believed that one of the reasons for seemingly high drop-out rates was that students who transferred courses were counted as drop-outs. It is also difficult to track the progress and performance of adult students transferring from HF courses to higher education, or indeed to establish the numbers of adults in the higher education system or what courses they are studying. In part, this reflects the fact that there is no general agreement as to what constitutes an 'adult student'.

The Concept of Adult

There is no generally agreed definition of adulthood as applied to education in Denmark. The Formal Adult Education (AVU) Act of May 1989 defines adults as 'all citizens above the age of 18' (Ministry of Culture 1993 p.15) whereas the regulations for the HF or Higher Preparatory Examination stress the idea of a break between compulsory full-time education and resuming study. Although it is possible to attend an HF course directly after the tenth year of the *Folkeskole*, the guide to HF points out that it is 'above all directed at young people and adults who have left the education system and wish to return'(Ministry of Education and Research 1992b). In another area, the *Jysk Aabent Universitet* (Open University of Jutland) is open to 'all students over 25 and not registered at another institution of higher education'. By contrast, the Open Education Act which came into force in January 1990 and is aimed at encouraging adults to take vocationally-orientated qualifying part-time education courses does not specify a lower age limit for entry. Financially, there is no discrimination either in favour of, or against adults in higher education. They are entitled to the same student grants and loans as school leavers, and to free tuition. Only the Open Education Act, which is aimed at those in work, requires students to pay significant fees and even here it is limited to 20 per cent of the cost.

Participation

Because of high participation rates among adults in all forms of education it is considered 'normal' for adults to study in Denmark. Consequently, the concept of the 'mature' or 'non-traditional' student who has special needs and requirements is seen as less of a problem than in the UK, for example. The average student enters higher education later than in the UK, often taking a year out after school and entering at 20 or 21, and stays longer in the system. In the university system, the average age of the undergraduate population tends to be in the mid to late twenties. It remains to be seen how far the recent reforms aimed at cutting the length of degree programmes will reduce the average age of the Danish undergraduate population.

Although participation rates in higher education in Denmark are high in general by European standards, research has shown that equality in terms of access to higher education is still some way off. A survey of 1000 school leavers who graduated from secondary school in 1989 showed that those from higher socio-economic groups had higher grade averages than those from lower groups, and tended to apply more often for the longer university courses (Bredo, Foersom and Laursen 1993). Interviews conducted in May 1993 with Rectors of *gymnasiums* and regional adult education centres (VUCs) revealed that both young people and adults from working class backgrounds often viewed academic education with suspicion and typically aimed for the shorter and more vocationally-orientated higher education courses. The head of the Higher Education Division in the Ministry of Education has recently argued that the increase in the participation rates in higher education is largely due to more enrolment by women rather than to increased social mobility (Rasmussen 1992).

However, although women and men now enter in approximately equal numbers, the increased participation by women masks a gender division whereby women outnumber men in medium cycle higher education, but men outnumber women in long cycle higher education. In 1989–90, of the women leaving general upper secondary education, 43 per cent entered medium cycle higher education and 14 per cent long cycle higher education. The comparable figures for men were 34 per cent entering medium cycle higher education, and 24 per cent, long cycle (Ministry of Education and Research 1993). To this extent, it can be argued that the introduction of a three year Bachelor degree at Danish universities may 'improve accessibility to non-traditional higher education students' (Rasmussen 1992 p.91).

A combination of generally high participation rates and a homogenous population means that there is little targeting of groups such as adults, women and ethnic minorities. However, special provision is made for students with disabilities in many areas, for example the Act on Higher Preparatory Examination Courses of June 1990 lays down that 'Handicapped students shall be offered special instruction or other special educational assistance' (Ministry of Education and Research 1991 p.3).

Policy Relating to Adults and Higher Education

Denmark is a country 'distinguished in the provision of adult education' (Nielsen and Webb 1992 p.20). The distinctively Danish concept of *folkeoplysning* or popular enlightenment, derived from the ideas of Grundtvig in the nineteenth century, has influenced all parts of the education system. Grundtvig's ideas grew out of his disillusionment with an over-academic education in the grammar school which he referred to as the 'black school' or 'school for death' (Thaning 1972 p.94). He stressed the importance of the 'living word' or the spoken word in the Danish mother tongue as opposed to the type of education based on Latin or German which alienated children from real life. His ideas had their roots in the assertion of Danish national identity in the light of a military threat from the south, in growing demands for democracy and in economic pressures facing the farming population. Popular enlightenment places strong emphasis on popular or grassroots movements and on people's right to decide for themselves what they want to learn in their own organisations with financial support from the state.

These ideas are seen at their fullest expression in the Folk High Schools and the area of general adult education, but have also had an influence on higher education. For example, the concept of state support for voluntary educational organisations is seen in the teacher training colleges. Of the 18 colleges, 6 are public and 12 are private but with full state funding. Of the 34 colleges for social educators, 4 are state colleges and the remaining 30 are private but with full state funding. Teaching and learning styles are also influenced by these ideas. In both the main examinations which prepare for higher education – the *Studentereksamen* and the HF – teachers are expected to consult students in planning the study programme for each subject. Some adult education colleges or VUCs make extensive use of study circles to prepare people for the HF, and find this method very successful. A similar emphasis on the autonomy of the learner informs the group project methods widely used by the Roskilde University Centre. Even within vocational education, general education is seen as having an important part to play, as it is felt that too narrow a training for a particular job is counter-productive.

In addition to the concept of popular enlightenment, higher education in Denmark has been influenced by two alternative and parallel traditions – the academic and the vocational. The academic tradition has survived both in the *gymnasium* which prepares school leavers for higher education, and in the universities themselves. The older universities, such as Copenhagen, or Aarhus, operated on the Humboldt model with a strong emphasis on basic research, a close association between teaching and research, longer degree courses based on research, a high degree of formal autonomy and no external representation on governing bodies. More recent university foundations such as Aalborg or Roskilde have established basic introductory programmes (one year at Aalborg, two years at Roskilde) with an interdisciplinary element, and in the case of Roskilde have introduced a large element of groupwork and group assessment into their learning programmes.

The vocational tradition has been strengthened in recent years by rising unemployment and by the concern to keep Danish industry competitive on the international stage. In the field of higher education, the Open Education Act of 1990 is designed to encourage adults in the workforce to take part-time qualifications with a view to vocational updating. However, a concern for high quality education for the professions goes back a long way in Denmark, as shown, for example, by the establishment in the nineteenth century of the Technical University of Denmark, the Royal Danish School of Pharmacy and others.

From 1982 to the beginning of 1993, Denmark was governed by a Centre-Right coalition government, replacing a long period of Social Democratic rule. Like governments throughout most of Western Europe, this government was influenced by the philosophy of the market place, a diminishing enthusiasm for state intervention and a belief in the virtues of competition. Under the Liberal Minister for Education, Bertel Harder, who was in office for the whole of these ten years, attempts were made to apply these ideas to the higher education system.

In 1992, the government published its 'Education Reform 92 – A Danish Open Market in Higher Education' (Ministry of Education and Research 1992a). The reform was based on 'a diminishing belief in the value of central planning and a strengthened belief in self-regulating mechanisms, in decentralized responsibility and in adaptation to market conditions' (Ministry of Education and Research 1992a p.7). Key elements of the reform were: a better balance between the supply of and demand for places; free intake to as many programmes as possible; a new uniform study structure (3 years for Bachelor's, additional 2 years for Master's, additional 3 years for PhD); an improvement in the quality of the PhD programme; a financial reform to reward institutions with high pass rates; measures to improve educational quality; and a reform of university government.

In an interview in May 1993 with the author, the former Education Minister Bertel Harder said that his vision behind the education reforms was 'to combine the mobility and effectiveness of the private sector…with equality of opportunity which we in this country have a tradition of'. He added that he wanted to see 'more choice and a more competitive environment in the whole of our public sector, especially in the education sector, but at the same time, I want to secure people their rights, and I don't want young people to be dependent on money from their parents'.

If this was the philosophy of the market place, it was a distinctly Danish market. Bertel Harder was greatly influenced by the concept of *Folkeoplysning* – he was actually born in a Folk High School (his father was the Principal), and wrote his university thesis on Grundtvig. In keeping with Danish tradition, the reforms had been agreed by all the major parties in the *Folketing* (Parliament). They had been planned on a four year cycle and the general feeling was that the incoming government was unlikely to make major changes.

The majority of institutions of higher and further education come under the remit of the Ministry of Education and Research (with the exception of a few such as the four Music Academies, the Royal School of Librarianship, the Royal Academy of Fine Arts in Copenhagen and the School of Architecture in Aarhus, which come under the Ministry of Cultural Affairs). The Ministry of Education lays down regulations for: admission to studies, study programmes, the award of doctorates and PhD degrees, employment of teachers and research staff, and the expulsion of students. It is also responsible for the planning and development of higher education. The Danish Conference of Rectors is an informal body consisting of the heads of all higher education institutions which carries out research and provides a forum for cooperation.

Since 1970, the administration of higher education has been reorganised. Students and administrative and technical staff have been given representation on boards and committees along with academic staff. One of the stated aims of the 1992 reforms was to devolve more autonomy to institutions, although it seems likely that central control will continue to be exerted through financial means.

The concerns of the 1990s appear to be focusing increasingly on labour market needs and the growing problem of unemployment. A senior official has recently claimed that 'The goal of equality of opportunity has not been as widely pursued in the 80s as in the 60s and 70s – at least not explicitly so. Issues related to employment of graduates, finance, labour market needs and not least quality have been given higher priority' (Rasmussen 1992 p.89).

Within the labour market in Denmark, the most striking trends are the high overall participation rate (83.8% in 1988, the highest in the OECD) and the high rate of participation by women – at 77.6 per cent in 1988, it was only exceeded by Sweden amongst OECD countries (OECD 1992). High female participation rates in the labour force are shared by all the Scandinavian countries and are linked with a high level of nursery provision (in Denmark 73% of 3–6 year olds are in nursery care). With unemployment over 10 per cent, concern is currently focusing on the older members of the workforce who are being de-skilled by changing technology; and on the 10% of the school leaving population who leave school without going on to some form of further education.

From 1977 onwards, restricted intakes, *numerus clausus*, were introduced into many subject areas of higher education in response to the rapid growth of the higher education system and rising graduate unemployment. Maximum numbers of entrants or quotas were fixed for each area of admission and criteria were laid down for selection by the Ministry of Education. The aim of the policy was 'to move a substantial part of the student body from long liberal arts studies (with presumed bad employment outlook) to studies in the technical, natural and social science field' (Personal communication from Ministry of Education, 17 August 1992). At the same time, shorter courses, typically of two years, were established in the non-university sector, aimed at employment in the private sector through focusing on computer science, international trade and so on. However, graduate unemployment continued to pose problems not only in the humanities subjects, but also in areas such as engineering, the natural sciences and biochemistry, and the 1992 reforms have resulted in the abandonment of this system (except in some of the longer disciplines such as medicine and dentistry) in favour of greater institutional autonomy.

Alternative Entry Routes for Adults

The Higher Preparatory Examination *Hojerefoberdelseseksamen* (HF) was set up in 1967. It was originally designed in a period of teacher shortage for adults who wished to enter teacher training college, but soon diversified into an entry examination for higher education in general. It is an examination and not a form of schooling, anyone over the age of 18 has the right to sit the examination and, if they pass, to enter higher education. Most people follow courses to prepare for the examination but every year people exercise their right to prepare for the examination by private study only. Two year full-time courses to prepare for the examination are held in *gymnasia*, adult education colleges (VUCs), and teacher training colleges, and there has been a major growth in part-time single subject courses in the VUC sector.

The system has expanded rapidly. In 1967, 500 students started HF courses, in 1988–89, 11,896 full-time and 48,221 part-time students were enrolled. The courses are designed particularly for people who have had a break from full-time study, and have thus become 'a very important example of recurrent education in Denmark' (Ministry of Education and Research 1992d p.40). In 1992, 39,995 people entered Danish higher education (18,256 men, 21,739 women). Of these, 6,372 (16%) entered via HF of whom 4,417 (69%) were women.

The HF curriculum is laid down by the Ministry of Education and Research and consists of a common core with optional subjects. It mimics the Upper Secondary School Leaving Examination (*Studentereksamen*) in many ways, with its broad academic curriculum, and only university graduates are allowed to teach courses leading to the two examinations. Some flexibility is built into the system in that specific planning and organisation of each subject is carried out between teacher and students within the guidelines of the national curriculum. Guidance and counselling are an important part of all HF courses and subject teachers who are appointed guidance counsellors after training are allocated some 30 per cent of their time for counselling. Assessment is by written and oral examinations: there is no element of continuous assessment.

HF in the *gymnasium* is largely taken by a younger age group – students coming from the tenth year of *Folkeskole* or young people who have taken a year out since leaving school. In the VUCs (adult education colleges) the age range is more mixed, – a higher proportion of older students take up the part-time courses particularly – and women outnumber men, forming 60–70 per cent of the intake. Many of these older students are aiming at shorter programmes of higher education – teacher training, nursery education and so on, for which they need a smaller range of subjects than the complete HF examination. There is a dilemma here in that HF runs the risk of being seen as second class education and of not reaching the standards required for the longer higher education courses, particularly in the sciences.

HF courses are open 'to anyone considered sufficiently capable of studying at this level' (Ministry of Education and Research 1992d p.40); capabilities taken into account may include work experience as well as prior learning or experience, for example residence in a foreign country if the student is studying the language of that country. In practice, most HF students have passed the leaving examination of the *Folkeskole* or its equivalent. Those adults without this have to take formal adult education courses (AVU) in general subjects which are run in the same adult education centres as the HF courses. The 1989 Act on Formal Adult Education states that AVU is a competence-based education for adults, aiming to improve their general knowledge and skills and enabling them to take an active part in community life and to understand and influence their own life situation. It will give adults the possibility of obtaining general qualifications for further education and knowledge and skills relevant for working life.

AVU is seen by employers and trade unions as more flexible than HF. It is becoming common for it to be planned by VUCs in co-operation with local employers, and this includes making provision for some courses based in the workplace. The curriculum consists of six main subjects which are available at all centres, with additional subjects and locally-organised subjects which vary from one centre to another. In 1990–91, some 50,000 adults were enrolled in AVU programmes and the target group for this and also certain kinds of non-formal adult education is seen as the eight to nine hundred thousand unskilled workers in the population (Ministry of Culture 1993).

Information on progression in the system is hard to find, but Principals of VUCs have reported that only a minority of adults progress from AVU to HF programmes, and certainly the length of time required to gain entry to longer courses in higher education for those with few formal qualifications must act as a disincentive. Many of the reforms in the last few years have attempted to ease this problem by making it easier to move from one sector of the education system to another. This is the declared aim of the Report which formed the basis of the 1992 reforms: it tried to avoid 'educational compartmentalisation' by creating 'well-defined levels for leaving and entering courses' (Ministry of Education and Research 1992a p.12). This is one of the reasons given for the introduction of the three year Bachelor degree at universities and of more two year courses in the non-university sector. Open education is seen as an important part of the network by making it possible for students to receive their education on a part-time basis, to piece together different parts according to individual needs and to move from one institution to another.

Recognition of prior experience and prior learning including work-based learning is gradually creeping into the system. The 1990 Act on Open Education stipulates that 'special allowances should be made for real qualifications acquired by the applicants in working life or in any other way' (Ministry of Education and Research 1992d p.79). Similarly, the regulations for the HF course state that 'the principal may exclude a student from instruction in a subject if the student has sufficient previous knowledge to be able to take the examination in the subject' (Ministry of Education and Research 1991 p.16). Available places in higher education are divided into two quotas, the first based on examination marks, the second based on an assessment by the admitting institution. According to the Registrar's Office at Copenhagen University, if students apply for admission under Quota 2, 'most institutions of HE will credit them in some way for their work experience' (Personal communication, 3 March 1993). Indeed, the Handbook of Copenhagen University states that under the second option or quota, students are admitted on their average marks plus other qualifications such as courses of study, stays at a Folk High School, work experience or periods abroad.

Alternative, Accessible Programmes in Higher Education

There is a declared intention in Denmark to move towards a more accessible system of higher education by the introduction of measures such as modularisation and credit transfer. As already indicated, diversity, both vertical and horizontal, is seen as a key strength of the Danish system, and such measures are in keeping with that strength. Modularisation is more advanced in some institutions than in others. The Technical University of Denmark, for example, has a modular system based on a two semester year with two fourteen week teaching periods from late August to early December and from early February to mid-May, plus time for examinations and a three week period in each semester for whole day work such as laboratory work. Student progress is measured by credit points based on the number of hours worked, and assessment is based on written and oral examinations supplemented by assignments.

It is felt (or hoped) in official circles that the 1990 Act on Open Education will eventually play a major role in opening up the Danish higher education system. The purpose of the Act is to give educational opportunities to adults in the form of 'vocationally-orientated qualifying part-time education courses and single subject courses' (Ministry of Education and Research 1992d p.78). Courses are offered in the field of vocational education (at commercial and technical colleges) and in higher education (at universities, business schools, engineering colleges). The teaching must be organised in such a way that it can be followed outside working hours by those in employment, and the unemployed must be able to use the scheme without losing their entitlement to unemployment benefit. For the academic year 1990–91, some 45 full-time or part-time courses were endorsed by the Ministry of Education as eligible for state subsidy under the open education scheme. Students have to pay 20 per cent of the cost of the course and are not entitled to maintenance grants.

Another more flexible alternative to conventional higher education is the *Jysk Aabent Universitet* or Open University of Jutland which was founded in 1982. This was established as a joint venture between the Universities of Aarhus and Aalborg and the South Jutland University Centre at Esbjerg, which is a research institution supported by the local authorities. The aim was to provide access to university-level education for people with no formal entry qualifications, along the lines of the British Open University. Access was open to all students over the age of 25 who were not registered at another higher education institution. Initially, only degrees in the Humanities were offered but from 1990 courses in Chemistry and Psychology were also offered.

Open University courses are heavily orientated towards distance teaching, with printed material replacing weekly face-to-face teaching. Students are, however, in contact with tutors by post and telephone, and week-end seminars are an integral part of each course. In 1990, some 700 students were enrolled with an average age of 40. Of this total, 75 per cent were in employment and 20 per cent were unemployed. The female/male ratio was 60:40. Originally the students paid no fees but since the Act on Open Education of 1989, they are subject to the same regulations as other part-time students and must pay 20 per cent of the cost of their courses.

Teaching in the Open University is by members of staff of the partner universities who typically will do half their teaching with the OU and half in their own faculty. Admission requirements are now similar to those of the parent university: that is a *Studentereksamen* or equivalent examination or qualification is required. This and the imposition of fees marks a significant narrowing of access in this area, although it is too soon to measure the impact of these measures. In addition to study centres in Aarhus, Aalborg and Esbjerg, course premises have been established at Holstebro in mid-west Jutland with the support of the municipality. Experiments have been tried with computer conferencing in the delivery of OU courses both at Aarhus and Aalborg universities. However, as the Act on Open Education makes no distinction between distance education and other types of part-time education, it remains difficult to find the finance for this type of development.

Resources and Funding

Traditionally Denmark has been a country with a highly developed social welfare system and a network of social, labour, educational and health activities, all publicly run and financed through the tax system. In 1989, total public spending in Denmark amounted to 59.4 per cent of Gross Domestic Product, the highest in the OECD countries apart from Sweden. In the same year, public spending on education in Denmark amounted to 6.8 per cent of GDP, tying with Finland as the highest proportion amongst OECD countries. Spending on higher education in Denmark amounts to some 30 per cent of the total education budget, the highest proportion amongst OECD countries, with only the Netherlands spending a comparable proportion (Ministry of Education and Research 1993). This high level of spending is accounted for by high participation rates, by state payment of student fees and by relatively generous student support systems.

Throughout the 1980s, rising student numbers in higher education and the rising cost of higher education caused anxiety for the Centre-Right coalition government. One symbol of the pressures to reduce spending was the worsening student/teacher ratio in higher education from 13:1 to 20.6:1 in the humanities between 1982 and 1991, from 13:1 to 17:1 in medicine and from 7.5:1 to 12.2:1 in engineering in the same period (Bache 1993). The introduction of a three year university degree to replace the previous standard five year course was one attempt to keep costs under control. Another was the introduction of a voucher system in 1988. Under this system, the student receives a certain number of monthly grants that corresponds to the stated length of their course. They are entitled to vouchers for an additional year of study in each voucher group under certain conditions but the general intention is to cut down on the average length of time each student spends in higher education.

A major concern has been high drop-out rates, particularly in the longer degree courses, which have been as high as 60 per cent in some cases.

The 1992 Reform Act on Higher Education attempted to reward institutions with low drop-out rates and penalise those with high ones by the introduction of a new funding system based on the 'taximeter' principle. This tied funding to the number of students passing their exams and was linked to growing government interest in quality in higher education. It was planned that institutions would receive their allocations as block grants as opposed to the previous system of allocation by faculties.

Student support in Denmark remains generous by comparison with many other Western European countries. Fees for virtually all full-time higher education courses are paid by the state. Student support grants are also generous. In 1992, students living away from home were entitled to a grant of DKK 38,376 a year plus a state loan of up to DKK 17,268. For students over the age of 19, grants are not dependent on parental income. Older students are entitled to the same grant and loan conditions as everyone else. Full-time students at a *gymnasium* or HF institution are also eligible for state grants or loans depending on financial circumstances.

The system is expensive to resource. In 1990, the total expenditure on higher education by the Ministry of Education and Research amounted to DKK 6.3 billion, excluding student grants. In 1989–90, 90,000 students received DKK 2.8 billion in grants, and 60,000 took out loans amounting to approximately DKK 910 million. Nonetheless, there seems no widespread pressure to switch support for higher education costs from the state to students or employers other than in areas such as open education. Even Centre-Right politicians, when interviewed, felt that it would be difficult to move away from the principle of full state support for student fees.

Conclusion

It seems likely that continuing education will play a more central role in the higher education system in the future, moving from the margins to play a key part in a more flexible and responsive system. Continuing education is seen as having a vital role to play in opening up the higher education system and making it more responsive to the needs of the Danish economy, particularly the export-orientated private sector. This is the stated aim of the 1987 Act on Further Training which aims to provide training 'specifically designed for Danish exporters and import-competing firms' (Ministry of Education 1987 p.4). It targets three areas – adaptation to new technology, enlargement of market opportunity and improvement of productivity and quality. Development funds are available for either public or private educational institutions to design new vocational and occupational courses. The target groups for this training are seen as skilled and semi-skilled workers, supervisors and the self-employed without an academic education. Provision is by regional and local authorities and private training companies, and the emphasis is on local response to local needs: courses do not require the approval of the Ministry of Education.

Although the Act on Further Training applies to the further education sector, similar concerns with competitiveness and responding to market needs underlie the Act on Open Education of 1989 which seeks to encourage vocationally-orientated part-time education for adults in both further and higher education. Similarly, the adult education colleges are being encouraged to forge closer links with employers and take their courses out to the workplace.

For a country with such an outstanding tradition of adult participation in education at all levels, there is a surprisingly small amount of research being carried out on adult participation in higher education. Laursen (Bredo, Foersom and Laursen 1993) of the Education Department at Copenhagen University has carried out work on admission to higher education in relation to social equity, and Jacobsen (Jacobsen 1992) of the same department has written on popular enlightenment, on life experience in adult education and on changing conceptions of adulthood. In addition, the Danish Research and Development Centre for Adult Education (DRDCAE 1988) has carried out research and development work on AVU and HF courses for adults; and recent initiatives on quality assessment of higher education have called for institutions to carry out self-evaluation exercises on a wide range of topics including the social structure of the student body and involvement in continuing education/training activities. External evaluations will also examine areas such as admission, drop-out rates and qualification profiles (Ministry of Education and Research 1992c).

Nevertheless, there are wide-ranging opportunities for future research. It would be particularly fruitful to trace progression of adult students within the system and to compare destinations, drop-out rates and employment outcomes with those of younger students. Another long term project might be the effect of shortening the university degree programme on the age profile of the student population and whether it had the effect of opening up the universities to a wider profile by age, gender or social class. The much vaunted development of open education and the growth of distance learning are also valuable areas for research.

Note

This chapter arises from a UFC/SHEFC-funded research project 'Policy Frameworks for Access in Three European Educational Systems (Denmark, the Netherlands and Scotland)' carried out in 1992–4.

References

Bache, P. (1993) Reform and Differentiation in the Danish System of Higher Education. In C. Gellert (ed) *Higher Education in Europe*. London: Jessica Kingsley Publishers.

Bredo, O., Foersom, T. and Laursen, P. (1993) A Model of Students' Choice of Higher Education in Relation to the Danish Policy of Admission, *Higher Education Review*, 26, 1, 64–73.

Danish Research and Development Centre for Adult Education (DRDCAE) (1988) *New Approaches to Adult Education in Denmark*. Copenhagen: DRDCAE.

Jacobsen, B. (1992) Denmark. In P. Jarvis (ed) *Perspectives on Adult Education and Training in Europe*. Leicester: National Institute of Adult Continuing Education.

Ministry of Culture (1993) *Act on Formal Adult Education*. Copenhagen: Ministry of Culture.

Ministry of Education and Research (1987) *A Guide to the Act on Further Training*. Copenhagen: Ministry of Education and Research.

Ministry of Education and Research (1991) *The Danish Higher Preparatory Examination*. Copenhagen: Ministry of Education and Research.

Ministry of Education and Research (1992a) *Education Reform 92 – A Danish Open Market in Higher Education*. Copenhagen: Ministry of Education and Research.

Ministry of Education and Research (1992b) *General Upper Secondary Education*. Copenhagen: Ministry of Education and Research.

Ministry of Education and Research (1992c) *Quality Assessment of Higher Education in Denmark*. Copenhagen: Ministry of Education and Research.

Ministry of Education and Research (1992d) *The Education System*. Copenhagen: Ministry of Education and Research.

Ministry of Education and Research (1993) *Facts and Figures. Education Indicators, Denmark*. Copenhagen: Ministry of Education and Research.

Neave, G. (1987) Interfaces between Secondary and Tertiary Education, *Higher Education in Europe*, 12, 2, 5–19.

Nielsen, J. L. and Webb, T. (1992) *Higher Education in Denmark*. Roskilde: Roskilde University Centre.

OECD (1992) *Education at a Glance. OECD Indicators*. Paris: OECD.

Rasmussen, T.K. (1992) Equality. In B. Marchione and M. Giuberti (eds) *Proceedings of the conference on Access to higher education in Europe, Parma 13-16th October 1992*. Parma: Università degli studi di Parma.

Thaning, K. (1972) *N.F.S. Grundtvig*. Copenhagen: Danish Cultural Institute.

Chapter 5

England, Wales and Northern Ireland

Gareth Parry

Although for long the main audience for part-time and distance forms of higher education and for short course and short cycle types of provision, it has only been in recent years that adults have been discovered as a significant presence in British higher education. This discovery has coincided with the movement, or rather a complex pattern of movements and currents, in the second half of the 1980s, which nudged and then propelled higher education in the direction of a mass system. In a situation in which reform of the traditional entry qualification for higher education was rejected by central government, it was arrangements aimed at adults rather than young people, and relationships forged with further education rather than school education, which were to provide much of the impetus for this transition and transformation.

The focus of this chapter is on the policies, patterns and practices which accompanied this shift, together with the ways in which adults are constructed in official statistics and framed by regulatory procedures. While much of the discussion and most of the data presented in this paper is referenced to the United Kingdom (or Great Britain) as a whole[1], arrangements and approaches in Scotland are somewhat different and are the subject of a separate chapter.

By far the largest numbers of students and establishments within the sector of higher education are located in England where 71 universities, 48 colleges of higher education and ten regions of the Open University account for about four out every five students enrolled in the United Kingdom. Thirty-three of these universities were formerly polytechnics (now referred to as 'new' universities) and the remainder are established or 'old' universities, the largest (excluding the Open University) being the University of London with eight separately funded schools and colleges. Nearly half of the colleges of higher education are 'specialist' institutions, generally small in size and with most students in one academic area, such as art and design, education or music.

Higher education in Wales – accounting for some 5 per cent of the student population in the United Kingdom – is provided by the six federated colleges of the University of Wales, the University of Glamorgan (previously the Polytechnic of Wales) and eight colleges of higher education. Wales, like Northern Ireland, is a separate region of the Open University. In Northern Ireland there are only two universities, Queen's University Belfast and the University of Ulster, the latter formed in 1984 by the merger of the New University of Ulster and the Ulster Polytechnic. These exist alongside two colleges responsible for teacher education, and together they account for about 3 per cent of the student population (Department of Education and Science 1991).

With the exception of the University of Buckingham (in England), all of these establishments, together with a small number of higher education courses provided in colleges of further education, are publicly funded. Following the Further and Higher Education Act of 1992, which abolished the binary system and permitted the polytechnics (and other major institutions) to award their own degrees and adopt university titles, a single funding structure was established for higher education with separate funding councils for England and Wales to distribute public funds for teaching and research. Arrangements in Northern Ireland remained largely unchanged, with higher education funded through the Secretary of State for Northern Ireland on the advice of a special committee for the province.

The same legislation created separate funding councils in England and Wales for a new sector of further education composed of a variety of institutions, the majority of which are colleges of further education offering a mixture of general, academic and vocational courses for young people and adults. Also included in this sector are sixth form colleges aimed mainly at young people (formerly under schools regulations) and colleges designated for adults, such as the adult residential colleges (previously funded directly by government). Unlike their newly independent counterparts in England and Wales, the colleges of further education in Northern Ireland are still under the control of the local authorities.

Trends, Terms and Territories

Mass higher education has come late to the United Kingdom, and without the addition of new institutions to achieve this goal. Despite the expansion of provision in the 1960s – the establishment of new universities, the promotion of the colleges of advanced technology to university status, the creation of the polytechnics, and the foundation of the Open University – it was not until 20 years or so later that levels and patterns of participation began to approach those associated with a mass system. One of the distinctive features of the British experience, and a central theme in this chapter, was that adults were to play a key role in the 'breakthrough' to a mass phase: not just as the focus for many of the debates and developments which paved the way for this passage, but as the 'new' majority of entrants who were to shape and share in this expansion.

In the same year – 1988 – that those styled 'mature' students began to outnumber young entrants to higher education for the first time, the full-time participation rate for eighteen- and nineteen-year-olds was to reach the modest but important level of 15 per cent (Department for Education 1992, 1993). This was the figure which Trow (1974, 1989) had suggested as the point beyond which the core characteristics of an élite model might no longer be able to be sustained across the system as a whole. By 1993 this figure had doubled to around 30 per cent and the number of students in higher education had increased by more than 40 per cent over the same period. The dual nature of this expansion – with older as well as younger students contributing to this growth – together with the late but rapid character of this transition, were to invest the British case with considerable complexity and much instability; an episode which has still to be properly analysed and understood.

Table 5.1: Home students in higher education (including the Open University) in the United Kingdom by age and mode of study (Thousands: column percentages in brackets)

	1976–7	1981–2	1986–7	1991–2
20 and under	287 (38%)	360 (45%)	371 (40%)	463 (39%)
21–24	231 (31%)	200 (25%)	228 (25%)	278 (23%)
25 and over	235 (31%)	244 (30%)	311 (34%)	448 (38%)
Total	753 (100%)	805 (100%)	910 (100%)	1190 (100%)

Source: Education Statistics for the United Kingdom (Department of Education and Science)

Although the movement away from an élite tradition has increased the visibility of older students, their participation in higher education, both in terms of numbers and proportions, is not a new or sudden phenomenon. As early as the mid-1970s, some three out of ten students were aged 25 and over, and this proportion had expanded to one in three by the mid-1980s (Table 5.1). Nonetheless, the most conspicuous growth in this category has been in the recent period, with numbers increasing by 44 per cent between 1986–7 and 1991–2 (compared to 25% for those aged 20 and under, and 22% for those in their early twenties) and their share rising to nearly two in five of the student population at the beginning of the 1990s (roughly equal to that for young people aged 20 and under).

In order to consider the meaning and significance in the United Kingdom of adults in the academy, a number of definitional questions need to be addressed at the outset, both with respect to the identity of the learners involved and the educational territories they inhabit. The distinction drawn in the British system between adults or mature students on the one side, and young people or recent school leavers on the other, is a familiar (if confused) one in this context, being found in the regulations governing admission to institutions and courses, in the rules applying to the administration of student awards and grants, and in the categories used in the collection of official statistics. In each of these activities, the need to distinguish between different categories of student has served to highlight many of the key attributes and arrangements which continue to set this system apart from other structures and styles of higher education.

Higher education in England, Wales and Northern Ireland is formally defined in terms of courses which lead to qualifications at a standard above the Advanced Level of the General Certificate of Education (the GCE A-level). Above this line are courses or programmes at three main levels: short cycle or two year courses leading to 'sub-degree' qualifications, mainly in vocational and professional subjects; first degree courses extending over three or four years (or longer if part-time) in discipline-based and professional fields; and postgraduate programmes of some variety, both taught (as in most masters courses) and by research (as with doctoral studies).

In addition to study at these formal levels, and either articulated with them or deliberately detached, are opportunities for continuing education and training, embracing short courses as well as more individualised forms of flexible and open learning. Programmes differ in their liberal or vocational emphasis, their ability to offer credit and progression, and their degree of openness. As with the Open University, these remain parts of higher education where adults are the target or exclusive audience.

Not all these levels and types of activity are to be found in every university and college of higher education. Indeed, courses leading to qualifications below the level of the first degree, whether part-time (the majority) or full-time, are almost exclusively a feature of provision in the (former) polytechnics and the (present) colleges of higher education. The majority of postgraduate education, on the other hand, is concentrated in the established universities, reflecting their traditional role as research as well as teaching institutions. For courses at first degree level, widely regarded as the core of the system and mostly studied on a full-time basis, the pattern of provision is more evenly spread, with all the major institutions of higher education offering undergraduate programmes, but with the majority of places now offered outside the 'old' universities.

Although the binary organisation of higher education inherited from the 1960s was finally abandoned in 1992, and the 'academic drift' of the 1970s moved the local authority controlled polytechnics closer to the 'autonomous' universities (Burgess and Platt 1974), there remain important differences in mission and provision between the 'old' universities and the 'new' universities in the present unified system. During the 1980s many of the polytechnics were to recover some of the objectives originally set for them as 'socially responsive' institutions – more open and local access, part-time and all-through provision, vocational and regional relevance – and it was this category of institutions, along with certain of the colleges of higher education, which were to lead in the expansion of numbers and in the recruitment of adults to each of the three main levels in the system. The established universities, which recruited predominantly from the schools and from the most highly qualified of their A-level candidates, were to join in this growth rather later than their non-university counterparts.

The decision about which individual students to admit to these levels, including discretion to modify or waive the formal entry requirements for mature applicants, has remained the responsibility of individual institutions, or rather of the departments which offered the particular courses. This freedom was however a qualified one for the institutions whose courses were approved, and degrees awarded, by the Council for National Academic Awards (CNAA). In addition to regulations governing the admission of students, these institutions were subject to periodic advice and guidance on matters relating to entry qualifications and selection procedures, including an early injunction to limit the percentage of mature students who might be admitted to a course without the conventional qualifications for entry (Council for National Academic Awards 1983).

Admission to first degree courses is selective (often highly so), and the possession of the minimum qualifications for entry – two GCE A-levels (or their equivalent) – is only a basis for eligibility, not a right to admission. Over and above these general requirements (what used to be termed 'matriculation') are course entry requirements which stipulate further conditions which normally need to be satisfied: passes in a specified range and number of subjects and, more critically, passes to be achieved at particular grades.

Entry to sub-degree courses is generally less competitive but more complicated, given the variety of programmes and qualifications offered at this level. Qualifications like the Diploma of Higher Education and some professional courses have the same entry requirements as degree courses whereas other programmes, such as the Higher National Diploma (HND) and Certificate (HNC) offered by the Business and Technology Education Council (BTEC), specify a minimum of one A-level or an 'appropriate' BTEC National Diploma or Certificate. Until quite recently, BTEC courses were not available in schools and it was the colleges of further education which provided an 'alternative route'[2] to higher education – always for a small minority – through their 'ladder' of vocational qualifications.

For taught postgraduate courses, the possession of a relevant first degree or an equivalent professional qualification is the normal entry requirement; and in some fields, such as business and management, experience gained over a reasonable period and at a relevant level can qualify a candidate for admission. For registration for a research degree, the possession of a 'good' class of first degree is a usual requirement.

Unlike at postgraduate level where courses build on initial forms of higher education and expertise acquired in the world of work, the regulations which relate to first degree and sub-degree courses employ the notion of 'mature' age or status to distinguish between those who enter direct from school or college of further education, and those who experienced a 'break' between their school education and their later return to formal study. The construction of the mature student as a 'returner' – as someone who 'missed out' on earlier educational opportunities – is a dominant motif in the discourse of higher education, summarising a variety of experiences, identities and intentions on the part of older entrants (Edwards 1993, Pascall and Cox 1993, Weil 1989) but pointing also to acknowledged deficiencies and inequities in the system of compulsory and post-compulsory education; in short, a history of low levels of participation, achievement and progression, and corresponding high levels of failure, rejection and disaffection (Ball 1991, National Commission on Education 1993).

Put another way, the high level of attainment (at A-level) reached by the minority who continued their schooling beyond the minimum school leaving age (at sixteen) has made possible a system of higher education which can educate undergraduate students in a short time and with relatively low drop-out rates (Smithers and Robinson 1991)[3]. Given this front-end and intensive model of higher education, in which an entrant from school at the age of 18 or 19 would normally graduate and leave the system at 21 or 22, the notion of mature student was able to be established and maintained as a separate and discrete category, even under mass conditions.

The reference to full-time in the British system is a key to the perceived efficiency and status of the first degree, and its early identification with conventionally qualified young entrants. Following the Anderson Report (Ministry of Education 1960), all those accepted for entry to a full-time first degree course on the basis of two A-levels were entitled to a mandatory award paid by the local education authority which covered the fees to the institution, and a means-tested grant towards maintenance. The assumption here was that young students would be able to study away from home and that only during the long vacations might they need to consider paid employment. Although the value of the maintenance grant has been eroded in recent years and a system of student loans introduced to supplement and augment the payment of grants, many of the advantages which attach to full-time study have remained; and few of the disadvantages associated with part-time study – the main preserve of adult students – have been reduced.

Part-time higher education has traditionally provided an important means of access for those who are unable or unwilling, for whatever reason, to study full-time (Bourner *et al.* 1991, Tight 1987, 1991). This it has continued to do, despite the need for students (or employers) to pay their own fees, and in the absence of a national policy to support paid educational leave. Sometimes the local education authority was able offer a 'discretionary' award to help cover fees but these have since become a casualty of controls on the expenditure of local government.

For these and other reasons, not least the idea of a 'real' or 'proper' higher education, the pull of the full-time first degree has been strong for many adults. Although the mandatory principle was extended to a range of short cycle courses in 1976, the narrower vocational focus of many of these programmes has appealed more to a young population, especially male students and including some in their early twenties with recent experience of study in further education. Access to full-time undergraduate study was also made more of a possibility, though not immediately, through the removal in 1975 of the necessity of prior educational qualifications for mandatory awards. Amid the complexity of the regulations governing the awards system were special provisions for mature students whereby an entrant aged 26 or over (another definitional datum) might be entitled to an additional allowance, alongside other benefits payable through the social security system.

It was therefore in relation to first degree education on a full-time basis that the distinction between 'mature' and 'young' students was to occupy a special place in the admissions process, even if expected – in the early days – to be applied only occasionally or exceptionally. Although the CNAA had adopted 21 years and over as the qualification for 'maturity' in its regulations, it was not until the end of the 1980s that the established universities agreed to move to this common definition. Up to this point, individual universities had identified minimum ages for mature entry ranging from 19 to 26, with 23 being the most frequently adopted (Liggett 1982). More significant for the intending student was the disposition of the department and, more particularly, the attitude of the admissions tutor to applications from mature students who may or may not hold the formal qualifications for entry.

Mature students compete for full-time places with school-leavers, each applying through a central admissions system for courses at up to eight establishments. One of the many irrationalities in this system is that a decision about whether (or not) to offer an individual a place, sometimes involving an interview, is usually taken in advance of the results of qualifying examinations and assessments. The difficulties confronting the mature student in this process are profound, especially if he or she does not hold the normal or recognised qualifications for entry – the so-called 'non-standard entrant'. For the older person who might be using a return to study or access-type course to inform a judgement about their interests and abilities, the need to select and apply for specific courses in higher education some ten months ahead of admission, and to detail their experience and learning on an application form designed mainly with A-level and BTEC candidates in mind, has posed an additional set of problems. Some of these hurdles are avoided by intending part-time students who are able to apply direct to the courses and institutions of their choice, and where entry requirements are generally less stringent than for full-time programmes.

In the largest institution of higher education in the United Kingdom, the Open University, there are no entry qualifications for undergraduate programmes: foundation courses are designed so that they can be studied by adults with little prior knowledge; and admission is on a first-come, first-served basis, subject to ability to pay and availability of places (which might mean a waiting list in some subjects). As in the rest of the system, admission is normally on an annual cycle, but with the academic year for the Open University beginning in February rather than October.

The other main source for the designation of mature and young students are the various data collection systems operated by government and other national agencies. As in previous attempts to survey the access and participation of adults[4] in British higher education (Jones and Williams 1979, McIntosh 1978, Percy 1985, Slowey 1987, Squires 1981, Woodley 1981, Wynne 1979), commentators have struggled with a multiplicity of definitions, categories and conventions; along with late publication and national and sectoral variation in the case of government statistics.

The definition used in recent statistical bulletins published by the Department of Education and Science (now the Department for Education) is based on a different minimum age on entry for sub-degree and first degree education – 21 years and over – and for postgraduate education – 25 years and over. This simple but nonetheless convenient formulation is adopted in the remainder of this chapter. Comprehensive data is only available for the period up to 1991–92 and is presented in terms of the (then) two sectors of higher education: the universities on the one side, and the polytechnics and colleges on the other.

Numbers, Patterns and Policies

Despite sometimes marked differences within the university and the non-university sectors, it was the binary pattern of development which was to exercise a decisive influence on how and where older students were able to secure access to sub-degree, first degree and postgraduate education. During the 1970s this pattern was reflected in steady growth in the public sector of higher education, and little change in the small numbers and proportions of mature students who entered the universities (Squires 1981). However, in the 1980s and into the 1990s all levels, modes and sectors of higher education were to experience greatly increased numbers and larger proportions of older entrants.

Between 1981 and 1991 the number of mature first year students on undergraduate courses almost tripled, from 26,000 to over 70,000, such that nearly one in three entrants were aged 21 and over by the end of this period (Table 5.2). The expansion was nearly as large in postgraduate education, while the numbers who entered sub-degree courses – the location of the majority of mature students – increased by some two-thirds.

Table 5.2: Young and mature home first year entrants to higher education (excluding the Open University) in Great Britain by level of study (Thousands: percentage mature in brackets)

	1981	1985	1991
Postgraduate			
Young	22.9	22.7	31.1
Mature	24.6 (52%)	33.0 (59%)	58.8 (65%)
Total	47.5	55.7	89.9
First degree			
Young	109.5	111.0	162.0
Mature	25.8 (19%)	28.7 (20%)	71.6 (31%)
Total	135.3	139.7	233.6
Sub-degree			
Young	57.5	58.2	66.4
Mature	89.2 (61%)	124.6 (68%)	147.6 (69%)
Total	146.7	182.8	214.0
All students			
Young	189.9	191.9	259.5
Mature	139.6 (42%)	186.3 (49%)	278.0 (52%)
Total	329.6	378.2	537.5

Source: Statistical Bulletin 18/92 and private communication (Department for Education)

This represented a faster rate of growth for undergraduate rather than sub-degree education – even though the expansion of short cycle vocational education had featured at various times as a particular concern of government policy. Of those mature students who secured entry in 1991, just over half were in sub-degree education, just over a quarter were enrolled on first degree courses, and one in five were engaged in postgraduate studies.

Within these levels of higher education, the distribution of mature entrants was differentiated by sector and by mode of attendance, with eight out of ten mature students enrolled in the polytechnics and colleges, and six out of ten engaged in part-time study (Table 5.3).

Table 5.3: Young and mature home first year entrants to higher education (excluding the Open University) in Great Britain by mode of attendance, type of institution and level of study, 1991 (Thousands: percentage mature in brackets)

	Young	Mature	Total
Full-time			
Postgraduate			
Universities	18.3	12.7 (41%)	31.0
Polytechnics and colleges	8.0	9.1 (53%)	17.1
Total	26.3	21.8 (45%)	48.1
First degree			
Universities	79.4	12.6 (14%)	92.0
Polytechnics and colleges	80.9	37.8 (32%)	118.7
Total	160.3	50.4 (24%)	210.7
Sub-degree			
Universities	0.5	0.9 (64%)	1.4
Polytechnics and colleges	36.2	32.8 (48%)	69.0
Total	36.7	33.7 (48%)	70.4
Part-time			
Postgraduate			
Universities	2.5	18.7 (88%)	21.2
Polytechnics and colleges	2.3	18.3 (89%)	20.6
Total	4.8	37.0 (89%)	41.8
First degree			
Universities	0.1	2.3 (96%)	2.4
Polytechnics and colleges	1.6	18.9 (92%)	20.5
Total	1.7	21.2 (93%)	22.9
Sub-degree			
Universities	0.5	1.9 (79%)	2.4
Polytechnics and colleges	29.2	112.0 (79%)	141.2
Total	29.7	113.9 (79%)	143.6
Total	259.5	278.0 (52%)	537.5

Source: Private communication (Department for Education)

At the all-important level of the first degree, where institutions in both sectors were major providers of full-time and sandwich courses, the proportion of mature entrants on these programmes remained relatively unchanged in the first half of the 1980s; but expansion in the second half of the decade raised this proportion from 11 per cent in 1986 to 14 per cent in 1991 in the case of the universities, and – more spectacularly – from 21 per cent to 32 per cent over the same short period in the polytechnics and colleges.

Women in particular were to benefit from this growth in numbers, becoming the majority of mature student entrants to both full-time and part-time first degree courses by the end of the 1980s, and commanding a much larger share of places on postgraduate and sub-degree courses than at the beginning of the decade (Table 5.4).

Table 5.4: Mature home first year entrants to higher education (excluding the Open University) in Great Britain by sex, mode of attendance and level of study
(Thousands: percentage women in brackets)

	1980		1985		1990	
	M	W	M	W	M	W
Postgraduate	15.3	7.6 (33%)	18.8	10.8 (36%)	26.5	22.8 (46%)
First degree	14.0	10.3 (42%)	14.8	12.9 (47%)	24.3	25.0 (51%)
Sub-degree	60.2	26.7 (31%)	66.8	44.1 (40%)	74.1	62.6 (46%)
Total	89.5	44.7 (33%)	100.4	67.8 (40%)	124.8	110.3 (47%)

Source: Statistical Bulletin 18/92 and private communication (Department for Education)

Expansion, if at a slower and more uneven rate, has also been a feature of recent enrolments in the Open University, both for first degree and for associate students. In 1991 there were over 18,000 new undergraduate students registered with the Open University, who joined a total continuing undergraduate population of 80,000 (compared to 14,000 and 60,000 respectively in 1981). Those registered in England accounted for some 83 per cent of this population, followed by Wales at 4 per cent and Northern Ireland at 2 per cent. The average age of this population was 34, the majority being in the 25–45 age group, and around three-quarters remaining in employment throughout their studies. While the proportion of women has generally increased year by year, they were still a minority (48%) of the undergraduate population in 1991 (Open University 1993).

Associate students in the Open University are registered on a range of long or short courses at advanced, professional and postgraduate levels, as well as courses taken from the undergraduate programme. Some of these short courses resemble those offered as continuing education programmes in other institutions of higher education, except that within the Open University they carry academic credit and they operate at a distance.

Programmes of short courses in several of the former polytechnics were also accredited, and some were integrated into the modular structure of their undergraduate and postgraduate provision. This was less common in the established universities where the liberal tradition of extra-mural education and the organisation of cost-recovery post-experience vocational education represented separate spheres of activity, even if coordinated through a single centre or department of continuing education. Most of these courses do not at present lead to certification, but to be eligible for future funding many of these programmes will need to demonstrate that they contribute to higher education awards. Extra-mural courses are virtually all part-time, averaging about 25 hours in contact time and most lasting for one term or less. In contrast, most post-experience courses are organised on a one-off basis, often outside of institutions of higher education and sometimes involving a short period of full-time study (mostly three days or less). The numbers of associate students registered at the Open University and continuing education students enrolled elsewhere in higher education are calculated using different bases, but an indication of the scale of participation is given in Table 5.5.

The promotion of continuing education in its widest sense was one of the ways in which broader access for adults was pursued as a policy objective at national level. The early focus for this policy effort was not national government as such but the new National Advisory Board for Local Authority Education (NAB) which was established in 1982 to provide a machinery for the management and planning of higher education in the public sector, a body parallel to the University Grants Committee (UGC) on the other side of the binary line. As the owners of the polytechnics and colleges in the public sector, the local authorities were given a strong role in policy-making and resource allocation in the national body, and it was through their involvement that wider access was brought to the centre of the policy stage, 'as the central unresolved policy issue for the government' (Fulton 1991).

Table 5.5: Associate students in the Open University (United Kingdom) and continuing education students on short courses in the universities (Great Britain) and the polytechnics and colleges (England) (Thousands)

	1987	1988	1989	1990	1991
Open University associate students					
Degree and diploma level	11.7	12.0	10.7	11.6	13.4
Short course	8.4	10.4	11.7	15.9	19.6
Continuing education students					
Universities	481.4	520.8	574.0	594.6	691.3
Polytechnics and colleges	255.5	232.7	248.0	235.9	249.4

Source: Open University Statistics (Open University) and Statistical Bulletin 17/93 (Department for Education)

The local authorities, many of which were Labour-controlled during the 1980s, were also among the main sources of opposition to the market-led policies and approaches advanced by the incoming Conservative government in 1979. Through their control of the colleges of further education as well as the polytechnics, some of the larger metropolitan authorities – London and Manchester in particular – sought to integrate their provision of adult, further and higher education, experimenting with early forms of 'open college' collaboration (Browning 1991) and targeting their discretionary awards at the unwaged and 'disadvantaged' groups in the local community.

Whilst the universities responded to financial cutbacks at the beginning of the 1980s by reducing sharply their intake of students, and civil servants planned for contraction ahead of a steep demographic decline in the school leaver population, the polytechnics and colleges were able to take up the extra students, reduce further their unit costs, and embark on a phase of expansion. Part of this growth was to come from school leavers, but another substantial part began to be derived from the recruitment of new clienteles, including those attracted to part-time study and others from groups which were traditionally under-represented at this level of education: women and members of black and minority ethnic groups in particular.

Not all the polytechnics and colleges, and not all their departments, sought actively to recruit from these constituencies but, led by the NAB, the sector was to become increasingly identified with an access mission: one based on the assumption, already demonstrated, that demand for higher education was a managed phenomenon and not fixed by the size of the pool of qualified eighteen year olds. The principle laid down in the Robbins Report (Committee on Higher Education 1963) – that courses of higher education should be available for all those who are qualified by ability and attainment to pursue them and who wish to do so – had encouraged a restrictive interpretation of the word 'qualified' (a minimum pass in two GCE A-levels), and in 1984 a reformulation of this axiom was jointly proposed by the NAB and the UGC in terms of 'ability to benefit' (National Advisory Body 1984, University Grants Committee 1984):

> The principle of access, which we have reaffirmed and re-formulated...is concerned with providing places for students from different backgrounds and attempting to compensate for previous inequalities. We would broaden it and include students not only from different social classes, but also from different ethnic groups. Moreover, opportunities for women must be as good as opportunities for men. The principle is also concerned with the relationship between each institution and its locality. It is as important as ever that institutions should contribute to the cultural life of their communities. In the world of the 1980s, it is equally important to contribute to the economic, industrial and commercial life of the locality. (National Advisory Body 1984 p.6)

Rather than endorse the sentiments and priorities elaborated in this statement, the government qualified its acceptance of this reformulation with the insertion of two caveats: that the benefit had to be 'sufficient to justify the cost'; and that the test of ability to benefit be 'applied as stringently to those with formal qualifications as those without' (Department of Education and Science 1985b).

In the same joint statement, the NAB and the UGC suggested that a fifth objective for higher education be added to the four set out by Robbins some twenty years earlier, namely: 'the provision of continuing education in order to facilitate adjustment to technological, economic and social change and to meet individual needs for personal development' (National Advisory Body 1984, University Grants Committee 1984). The concepts of lifelong education and recurrent education which international agencies like UNESCO and OECD developed in the 1970s attracted little attention in official policy circles, but they were to be among a number of 'discoveries' made by government in the course of the 1980s.

In 1985 a Green Paper on higher education affirmed that educational opportunities should be 'available throughout life' and that continuing education should be one of the 'principal parts' of the work of higher education (Department of Education and Science

1985b). This was one of the earliest official pronouncements in support of lifelong education in the British context, and was to be followed by a string of similar statements in the field of education and training, as various government departments sought to recover lost ground in the creation of a skilled and qualified workforce (Parry 1993).

The subsequent White Paper on higher education (Department of Education and Science 1987) was a different kind of document, outlining a 'revised' policy on access to higher education and a modest expansion in numbers based on increased and widened participation for both young and mature entrants. At a time of improved economic conditions and better employment prospects for graduates, and with an eye to the popular appeal of expanded opportunities in this sector, the government planned for a steady growth in student numbers up to 1990, followed by a return to current intake levels in the mid-1990s.

In acknowledgement of their achievement in stimulating and meeting increased demand, and to reflect their maturity as national institutions, the polytechnics and the larger colleges of higher education were incorporated in 1988 as free-standing institutions outside local authority control. At the same time, the NAB and the UGC were abolished and replaced by separate funding councils for the two sectors. This removal of the local authorities from higher education, both at the national planning and policy level and at the institutional level, was seen by some to put at risk the achievements gained in access up to that time, especially their role in forging relationships between colleges of further education and establishments of higher education. Mindful of this inheritance and in consultation with the sector, the new funding council for the polytechnics and colleges adopted a commitment to widening access as one of its three aims, and made this a specific objective for the sector.

Outside government and its agencies, much of the policy debate about the issue of access to higher education was being conducted under the auspices of learned societies and other independent bodies. Their intervention reflected a shared frustration among leading industrialists and educationalists about the scope and pace of official policy on education and training, and one of the most influential of these forums, the Royal Society of Arts, published three major reports on the theme of widening access to higher education (Ball 1989, 1990; Royal Society of Arts 1988), each concerned to make the case for expansion, to identify the impediments to progress, and to contribute to an agenda for action. The need for higher education to anticipate and adjust to a more diverse and adult population ('more means different') was a central theme in these enquiries, although it was left to the national bodies in adult and continuing education to translate these arguments into the vision of 'an adult higher education' (National Institute of Adult Continuing Education 1989, 1993).

One of the central concerns in these enquiries was the dominance of the A-level examination in the preparation and selection of students for entry to higher education. Although the narrow and specialist nature of the A-level curriculum had been the subject of mounting criticism from inside and outside education, the government in 1988 rejected the major recommendations of the committee[5] it had established to review the examination (Department of Education and Science 1988). It was largely because of this reluctance to reform the main entry examination for higher education – in the interest of maintaining high academic standards – that debates and developments around the future shape of a mass system tended to be directed towards the needs and demands of adults, whether they were initial entrants or engaged in recurrent or more intermittent forms of study. The delay in the reform of A-levels has also helped to preserve the division, deep-rooted in British culture, between academic and vocational education: the former associated with what in the past was taught in the schools and the universities, and the latter identified with what was offered in further education.

Rather than look to a unified system of education and training which would bridge or dissolve this divide (Institute of Public Policy Research 1990), the government has sought instead to establish a national framework of competence-based vocational qualifications and to introduce the General National Vocational Qualification (GNVQ) as a separate but equal track to the GCE A-level. Although intended as a broad preparation for employment as well as a route to higher qualifications (Department of Education and Science, Department of Employment and Welsh Office 1991), GNVQs have been dubbed 'vocational A-levels' and establishments of higher education have recognised them in principle as a suitable basis for entry to undergraduate courses, but have yet to encounter them in practice.

Although GNVQs have been identified mainly with the needs of young people, key responsibility for the delivery of these qualifications has been given to the colleges of further education. Following a history on the margin of educational policy, this sector has recently been recovered by government as a strategic site for future education and training, and as a key component in any move to a mass or lifelong model of higher and post-secondary education, as Trow (1987) had argued some years earlier.

Both the idea of 'mass' higher education and the notion of 'further' education were to enter into the language and mainstream of official policy towards the end of the 1980s. In two keynote speeches in 1989, the Secretary of State for Education offered a 'new' and 'bold' vision of higher education and a 'new strategy' for further education. The first envisaged a doubling of the participation rate and a movement to mass higher education 'accompanied by greater institutional differentiation and diversification in a market-led and multi-funded setting' (Baker 1989a). The second promised 'the most radical set of proposals for the reform of further education for many years' (Baker 1989b). Both of these statements were to be the subject of legislation in 1992, but the relationship between these sectors – a critical dimension in access and participation for adults – was left unaddressed.

Table 5.6: Highest qualification of home first year entrants to first degree courses in universities (excluding the Open University) in Great Britain by age and mode of attendance, 1990 (Percentages)

	Under 21	21–24	25+	Total
Full-time first degree				
2 or more GCE A-level passes (including Scottish Highers)	94.3%	40.2%	33.8%	87.3%
1 A-level pass	0.3%	4.9%	9.2%	1.3%
BTEC HND/HNC/OND/ONC passes	2.3%	15.7%	7.5%	3.5%
Other	2.9%	29.3%	49.4%	7.9%
Total (thousands)	**74.6** (100%)	**5.2** (100%)	**6.2** (100%)	**86.0** (100%)
Part-time first degree				
2 or more GCE A-level passes (including Scottish Highers)	1.0%	2.2%	5.2%	4.1%
1 A-level pass	0.0%	0.3%	1.4%	1.1%
BTEC HND/HNC/OND/ONC passes	0.2%	0.6%	1.0%	0.9%
Other	98.8%	96.9%	92.3%	93.8%
Total (thousands)	**0.5** (100%)	**0.8** (100%)	**3.1** (100%)	**4.3** (100%)

Source: Statistical Bulletin 18/92 (Department for Education)

Pathways, Programmes and Credits

In their White Paper on higher education in 1987, the government formally identified for the first time the main routes which were to govern entry to higher education in future years. Two of these pathways were identified mainly with adults, and two were offered largely in colleges of further education. As already noted, principal among these, and the basis of 'standard' or 'normal' entry, has been the channel of GCE A-levels: an examination designed essentially for young people studying full-time over a period of two years.

Yet, as Tables 5.6 and 5.7 suggest, a large number of adults have also used these qualifications as a basis for admission to first degree higher education, either inherited from school or gained later in the context of part-time courses (usually evening and often one year) in colleges of further education. In 1990 over a third of older adults (those aged 25 and over) who entered full-time undergraduate courses in the universities and one in five in the polytechnics and colleges held the standard requirements for entry. These were also important for a minority of mature entrants to part-time undergraduate education where they outnumbered those who achieved admission with one pass at A-level.

Table 5.7: Highest qualification of home first year entrants to first degree courses in polytechnics and colleges in England by age and mode of attendance, 1990 (Percentages)

	Under 21	21–24	25+	Total
Full-time first degree				
2 or more GCE A-level passes	76.8%	35.6%	19.7%	63.4%
1 GCE A-level pass	2.0%	6.4%	7.6%	3.4%
BTEC and other vocational and professional qualifications	10.7%	23.8%	14.3%	12.9%
GCE O-level/CSE/GCSE	1.5%	4.3%	6.5%	2.6%
Access and conversion courses	0.2%	5.5%	20.6%	3.8%
Other qualifications	8.2%	19.3%	22.3%	11.7%
No formal qualifications	0.6%	5.1%	8.9%	2.4%
Total (thousands)	**58.8** (100%)	**10.0** (100%)	**11.6** (100%)	**80.3** (100%)

	Under 21	21–24	25+	Total
Part-time first degree				
2 or more GCE A-level passes	27.3%	13.6%	8.2%	12.3%
1 GCE A-level pass	1.9%	2.9%	3.3%	3.1%
BTEC and other vocational and professional qualifications	34.0%	49.3%	27.3%	32.6%
GCE O-level/CSE/GCSE	2.0%	4.2%	5.3%	4.8%
Access and conversion courses	0.7%	0.7%	2.3%	1.8%
Other qualifications	19.3%	21.6%	38.7%	33.1%
No formal qualifications	4.7%	7.6%	14.9%	12.3%
Total (thousands)	**1.3** (100%)	**2.8** (100%)	**8.9** (100%)	**13.0** (100%)

Source: Statistical Bulletin 18/92 (Department for Education)

The second recognised pathway is associated with 'staged access' from further education to vocational higher education, through BTEC and related qualifications at intermediate and higher levels. These qualifications are a normal means of entry to vocationally-based sub-degree courses, but they also describe the highest qualification achieved by a good proportion of mature entrants to first degree courses, especially young adults (those aged 21 to 24) in the polytechnics and colleges where they feature strongly in entry to both full-time and part-time programmes. For a number of candidates whose vocational qualifications did not meet the requirements for entry to first degree studies, successful completion of a HND (or HNC) might offer the possibility of transfer to an undergraduate programme.

In the polytechnics, HNDs are commonly offered alongside first degree courses, with transfer possible in both directions, with admission usually into year two of a degree, and with the short cycle pathway providing a 'safety valve for doubtful candidates' (Fulton and Ellwood 1989). In the universities sector where courses are not generally provided at this level, transfer to the second year of an undergraduate degree is frequently discouraged. Across both sectors, it would appear that admissions tutors for first degree courses display a clear preference for A-level qualifications rather than their vocational equivalents, whether offered at intermediate or higher levels. According to Smithers (1991), their experience of vocational qualifications was one of variable standards and deficiencies of content, and a general run of performance in higher education which was below that of A-level entrants.

Notwithstanding these long-standing and familiar criticisms, the White Paper emphasised the importance of the vocational route in meeting current shortages and future needs for highly qualified personnel, especially in the fields of engineering and information technology. Higher education establishments were asked to take 'positive steps' to increase the number of entrants with vocational qualifications, and the established universities were exhorted to move closer to the polytechnics and colleges of higher education in making provision for these students.

The third route to be recognised, that of 'access courses' leading to higher education, was new, although courses of this kind had been around since the early 1970s, with the (then) New University of Ulster among the first to enter the field (D'Arcy 1985). The primary purpose of these courses was to prepare adults, especially those with few or no formal qualifications, for entry to higher education. Most were provided by colleges of further education and some owed their origin to a government initiative in 1978 inviting selected local authorities to consider setting up 'special' preparatory courses to assist adults from minority ethnic groups in particular to qualify for training in teaching, social work and similar professions.

Their importance since that time has to be assessed in symbolic and ideological terms as much as in terms of provision and progression on the ground. Some of these courses were formally linked to particular degree schemes in local polytechnics, and places were often set aside ('guaranteed') for all those who successfully completed their access programme. This was probably the nearest one got to 'positive action' in the British system of higher education, and they were to be singled out for close attention by a Conservative government keen to expose the 'excesses' of metropolitan authorities (usually Labour controlled), especially their active promotion of equal opportunities in education and other local services.

In a now famous set of paragraphs from an official report on academic validation in public sector higher education, institutions were asked to:

> bear in mind the possible dangers involved in themselves organising and helping to organise such courses with a view to admitting students from them to their own degree courses. Arrangements of this kind can result in the formation of relationships and understandings which lead to students from the access courses being accepted for degree courses even if they lack the ability to reach degree standard. (Department of Education and Science 1985a p.70)

A similar warning was made about mature students in general:

> institutions should not accept too high a proportion of mature students and/or students lacking the normal minimum entry qualifications for degree courses which are not specifically designed for them...if too high a proportion of students is accepted for courses not designed for them they may founder and staff may be tempted to lower standards. (p.71)

The delegitimisation of these access activities in the early part of the decade and their rehabilitation following publication of the 1987 White Paper was a measure of the shift which had taken place in official policy (Parry 1989).[6] However, the reward for this recognition was the introduction in 1988 of a national regulatory framework to oversee the validation of access courses and to kitemark approved programmes. By the end of 1992 some forty 'authorised validating agencies' in England, Wales and Northern Ireland had been licensed to approve courses on behalf of the central authorities, and some 600 courses had been kitemarked by the time of the publication of the first national register of recognised access courses (Committee of Vice Chancellors and Principals and Council for National Academic Awards 1992).

While the original context for the scheme was a need to reassure an élite system, the established universities in particular, about the standards of access courses and their students, many of the features and assumptions associated with the framework have been increasingly challenged by the contemporary drive towards a mass, modular and credit-based system of post-school education and training (Davies and Parry 1993). Nevertheless, one of the chief achievements of the initiative has been to extend the number and range of regional access consortia[7] at a time of increased competition for students, and as the role of the local authorities in education has been further reduced, most notably by the removal in 1992 of the colleges of further education from local authority control.

Access courses target those adults who have benefited least from existing arrangements, and their focus on equality of opportunity has been generally at odds with the market philosophy which has informed policy and practice in other parts of the education system. The main destination for students on access courses has been full-time first degree courses and, as might be expected, their impact has been greatest in the polytechnics and colleges where 'guaranteed' places continue to be a feature of linked schemes. There is however a dearth of data on access courses and their students, but Davies (1994) has estimated there to have been some 25,000 enrolments in

1991–92 and that 9000 or more students were admitted to higher education from access courses in 1992.

The other main form of entry to higher education is not identified as a designated route but is a function of the discretion available to an institution to admit 'others', again nearly always adults, to a particular programme of study 'if fully satisfied of their capacity to benefit from it' (Department of Education and Science 1987). It was in this area that those defined in official statistics as holding 'other' and 'no formal qualifications' were likely to have been admitted – a category of admission still referred to in some quarters as 'non-standard', 'exceptional', 'alternative' or 'special'. Little is known about the students who enter this way, especially since the category of 'other' in university statistics is one which can include a wide range of qualifications, some of them at or above the level of the first degree. In the more disaggregated statistics on entry qualifications to first degree courses in the polytechnics and colleges, it is possible to identify at least four types of highest qualification relevant to this form of admission (Table 5.7): one pass at GCE A-level (a small proportion of adults who entered full-time or part-time); passes in school-leaving examinations normally taken at 16 such as the GCE O-level (an even smaller proportion); other qualifications (nearly a quarter of those aged 25 and over who entered full-time and over a third of this age group admitted part-time); and no formal qualifications (nearly one in ten of older students who entered full-time and slightly higher for those who entered part-time).

In short, more than one third of the young adults who entered first degree courses in the polytechnics and colleges, full-time and part-time, did so on the basis of 'non-standard' entry. For those aged 25 and over the proportion was larger, with more than 45 per cent admitted to full-time programmes, and over 60 per cent accepted for part-time programmes. In the Open University, where all undergraduate programmes are part-time and open entry, about one in three of all entrants had qualifications less than two GCE A-levels or their equivalents (Open University 1993).

Even less is known about the processes and procedures which inform decisions about entry for these candidates, except that they are likely to make considerable demands on the time, experience and expertise of those responsible for admissions. This is likely to be less so where 'special' admissions procedures act as a preliminary filter, as in the long-established scheme operated by the Joint Matriculation Board on behalf of the northern universities (Smithers and Griffin 1986); or where specific arrangements exist for the assessment and accreditation of experiential learning (Evans 1992). In fact, a considerable amount of work has been conducted in this area, much of it funded by the Council for National Academic Awards and linked to parallel developments in guidance and counselling, and credit accumulation and transfer.

With the exception of selective initiatives in the field of engineering and technology, such as the development of conversion courses aimed at students (young and mature) without mathematics and physics at A-level (Matterson 1990), there has been little attempt to steer demand in the direction of shortage subjects. Indeed, despite evidence of higher unemployment rates for older graduates, especially those over the age of 30 (Graham 1989), and the increased availability of access and foundation courses in subjects with high threshold knowledge requirements, most mature students continued to be attracted to subjects where entry was based on general abilities and aptitudes rather than specialist backgrounds. While business and financial studies accounted for over one third of the total mature entry to first degree and sub-degree courses in 1990, this was one of only four main subject areas (the others being education, subjects allied to medicine, and architecture) where over half of the intake was aged 21 and over (Department for Education 1992).

In order to broaden the base for entry to some programmes and so attract a larger and wider range of initial entrants, a number of institutions have successfully sought to extend the length of first degree courses to include a foundation year. At the same time, some establishments have entered into franchise and associate arrangements with local colleges of further education whereby responsibility for the teaching of certain courses, or parts of courses, is transferred to a partner institution. Whether to do with pressure on space or promotion of access (usually both), these developments have increased rapidly during the peak years of expansion since the end of the 1980s (Bird, Crawley and Sheibani 1993). Furthermore, they mark a shift away from an early notion of access based on defined routes and discrete courses to one more centrally concerned with the 'accessibility' of institutions and the suitability and flexibility of their curricula for a diverse student audience (Tight 1993, Wright 1991).

Attention has turned therefore to more strategic issues of institutional structure and curriculum organisation, with modular schemes and frameworks for credit accumulation and transfer now established in the old as well as the new universities (Harvey and Norton 1993, Davidson 1994), and a review of the academic year recently undertaken with major implications for when and how students might be admitted and assessed (Committee of Enquiry 1993). A number of institutions of higher education have embarked on radical and ambitious schemes to recast the whole of their provision in terms of more student-centred and customer-oriented modes of curriculum 'delivery'. In other establishments the response has been more segmented and uneven, with some departments determined to maintain the character and integrity of their undergraduate courses, even when demand for places is less than strong (Fulton and Ellwood 1989, Her Majesty's Inspectorate 1989).

Some of these developments, such as the introduction of accelerated degrees for mature students (existing full-time courses being reorganised to enable students to complete their studies in less than the standard period) and the accreditation of work-based learning and in-company training have been directed specifically at adults. Other changes have been addressed to strengthening participation and supporting learning for all categories of students: the introduction of integrated modular credit schemes; the recognition of intermediate and combined awards; the expansion of part-time and mixed mode provision; the provision of comprehensive advice, guidance and counselling; the coordination of access policy and activity; and the promotion of staff development and training. In a number of cases these measures were associated with efforts to 'mainstream' continuing education across an institution, reflecting a need to 'adapt to threatening change and exploit the possibilities of adultification in its various forms' (Duke 1988). And with the arrival of accessible institutions and mass conditions, a new language of 'lifelong learning' has begun to enter the mission statements and core objectives of universities (Duke 1992).

Clearly, the strategies being implemented take different forms and are at different stages of development, but a common concern for most institutions of higher education is the form to be taken by future arrangements for credit accumulation and credit transfer at national level. Within higher education, most universities and colleges have, to varying degrees, recognised or embraced the transbinary scheme established by the CNAA in 1986, but alongside this model – based on the award of credit points at certificate, diploma, degree and postgraduate levels – there exist two other credit frameworks which bear directly on access and accessibility for adults in higher education.

Both the national system of vocational qualifications instigated by the central government (Jessup 1990) and the regionally-based framework operated by 'open college networks' (Mager 1991) employ different definitions of units and credits, and they accredit learning at different levels. For those concerned with admissions in higher education, these new forms of accreditation have been a source of some confusion, and work has since begun on ways to bring these systems together within a single framework (Further Education Unit 1992). At the same time, a national task force on credit accumulation and transfer has been convened to make proposals to the various policy communities in higher education about the wider application of credit-based learning and the development of credit-based resource methodologies (Robertson 1994).

However, these and other initiatives concerned with access and accessibility in higher education will need to confront a different policy context for the sector in future years, as prefigured in the public expenditure plans for education from 1994 onwards: one based on 'consolidation' rather than expansion of full-time enrolments in higher education and one aimed instead at increasing participation in the area of further education. In these circumstances, formal opportunities for adults to qualify for higher education might be expected to be enhanced, with the funding of colleges of further education now linked directly to the recruitment, retention and achievement of students on courses which meet national targets for education and training (National Training Task Force 1992).

Included in these targets are courses which offer access to higher education, but the prospect of increased competition for places in higher education, together with reduced support from the public purse to assist with maintenance, make it less certain that demand from the 'new' majority of adult entrants will be strengthened, at least for full-time study. Whatever the size and shape of this demand over the next few years, pressure on departments and institutions to decide between the claims of younger and older students, between those conventionally certificated and those alternatively qualified, is likely to continue to be a feature of selection for admission: a process disguised rather than displaced during the most recent period of expansion.

Notes

1. The component parts of the United Kingdom are England, Wales, Scotland and Northern Ireland whereas those of Great Britain are England, Wales and Scotland. However, 'British' is the adjectival form normally applied to both territorial entities. Because there is no single governmental authority with responsibility for education throughout the country, official statistics are sometimes presented (as in this chapter) for the United Kingdom, for Great Britain, and for England. In Northern Ireland, where the age participation index is higher than for Great Britain and where participation by religion is of special significance, official statistics are complemented by the findings of quinquennial surveys of entrants to full-time degree courses carried out by academic researchers since 1973 (Cormack *et al.* 1994).

2. The concept of an 'alternative route' has been applied and interpreted in a variety of senses, educational and sociological, since it was introduced in the Crowther Report in 1959 (Central Advisory Council for Education 1959). More recent formulations have emphasised the role of further education as an 'alternative route' for school leavers to undertake A-level studies, and for adults to return to study and prepare for higher education.
3. The 'wastage' or 'non-completion' rate for full-time first degree courses in the United Kingdom has averaged about 15% (Department for Education and Office for Standards in Education 1993), although there would seem to be some variation between individual institutions (Johnes and Taylor 1990).
4. For trends by class, gender and ethnicity in access to higher education in Britain, see the special issue of the Oxford Review of Education *Access to Higher Education* edited by Halsey and Heath (1993). Included in this collection is a consideration of access and equity in Britain in an international perspective (Halsey 1993) as well as a profile of mature students on access courses (Wakeford 1993). For trends by gender, class and religion in Northern Ireland, see Cormack *et al.* (1994). See also Woodley *et al.* (1987) for an investigation of pattens of access and participation in 'qualifying' and 'non-qualifying' courses across a wide range of institutions in post-compulsory education in England and Wales.
5. The Higginson Report on the future of A-levels recommended the study of five 'leaner' and 'tougher' subjects which would broaden and enliven the upper secondary curriculum. The report also recognised that a significant proportion of A-level candidates were mature part-time students but it was the needs of full-time students in the 16 to 19 age group which were of 'primary importance' (Department of Education and Science 1988).
6. This episode also resulted in the formation of a national organisation, the Forum for Access Studies, to represent and promote access education, and it stimulated a review of the evidence relating to the progress and performance of mature and non-traditional entrants (Bourner with Hamed 1987, Brennan 1986, Davies and Yates 1987, Molloy and Carroll 1992, Smithers and Griffin 1986, Walker 1975, Woodley 1984).
7. In Wales, this expansion has been assisted by the establishment (through the Welsh Office) of a Welsh Access Unit to 'promote a specifically Welsh agenda' for access education (Elliott 1992). For a Welsh perspective on access to higher education, see Wynne (1990); and for an outline of access course developments in Northern Ireland, see Irvine (s.d.).

References

Baker, K. (1989a) *Higher Education – 25 Years On.* Speech by the Secretary of State for Education at Lancaster University, 5 January 1989.

Baker, K. (1989b) *Further Education. A new strategy.* Speech by the Secretary of State for Education at the annual conference of the Association of Colleges of Further and Higher Education in London, 15 February 1989.

Ball, C. (1989) *Aim Higher. Widening Access to Higher Education.* London: Royal Society of Arts.

Ball, C. (1990) *More Means Different. Widening Access to Higher Education.* London: Royal Society of Arts.

Ball, C. (1991) *Learning Pays. The Role of Post-Compulsory Education and Training.* London: Royal Society of Arts.

Bird, J., Crawley, G. and Sheibani, A. (1993) *Franchising and Access to Higher Education.* Bristol: University of the West of England.

Bourner, T. with Hamed, M. (1987) *Entry qualifications and degree performance*, CNAA Development Services Publication 10. London: Council for National Academic Awards.

Bourner, T. with Reynolds, A., Hamed, M. and Barnett, R. (1991) *Part-time Students and their Experience of Higher Education.* Buckingham: Society for Research in Higher Education and Open University Press.

Brennan, J. (1986) Student learning and the 'capacity to benefit': the performance of non-traditional students in public sector higher education, *Journal of Access Studies*, 1, 2, 23–32.

Browning, D. (1991) Open College Networks and Unwaged People. In K. Forrester and K. Ward (eds) *Unemployment, Education, and Training: Case Studies from North America and Europe.* Sacramento: Caddo Gap Press.

Burgess, T. and Platt, J. (1974) *Polytechnics: A Report.* London: Pitman Publishing.

Central Advisory Council for Education (1959) *15 to 18.* London: HMSO.

Committee of Enquiry (1993) *The Review of the Academic Year.* Bristol: Higher Education Funding Council for England.

Committee on Higher Education (1963) *Higher Education*, Cmnd 2154. London: HMSO.

Committee of Vice Chancellors and Principals and Council for National Academic Awards (1992) *Register of Recognised Access Courses to Higher Education.* London: CNAA.

Cormack, R., Osborne, R. and Gallagher, A. with Fisher, N. and Poland, M. (1994) Higher Education Participation of Northern Irish Students. *Higher Education Quaterly*, 48, 3, 207–226.

Council for National Academic Awards (1983) *Opportunities in higher education for mature students.* London: CNAA.

D'Arcy, F. (1985) Ten Years in Western Ulster. *Aontas: A Review of Adult Education*, 4, 2, 28–40.

Davidson, G. (1994) *Credit Accumulation and Transfer in the British Universities 1990–1993*. Canterbury: University of Kent.

Davies, P. (1994) Fourteen years on, what do we know about Access students? Some reflections on national statistical data, *Journal of Access Studies*, 9, 1, 45–60.

Davies, P. and Parry, G. (1993) *Recognising Access. An Account of the Formation and Implementation of the National Framework for the Recognition of Access Courses*. Leicester: National Institute of Adult Continuing Education.

Davies, P. and Yates, J. (1987) *The Progress and Performance of Former Access Students in Higher Education: Final Report*. London: Roehampton Institute of Higher Education.

Department for Education (1992) *Mature Students in Higher Education – Great Britain 1980 to 1990*, Statistical Bulletin 18/92. London: DFE.

Department for Education (1993) *Student Numbers in Higher Education – Great Britain 1981/82 to 1991/92*, Statistical Bulletin 17/93. London: DFE.

Department for Education and Office for Standards in Education (1993) *The Government's Expenditure Plans 1993–94 to 1995–96*, Cm 2210. London: HMSO.

Department of Education and Science (1985a) *Academic Validation in Public Sector Higher Education*, Cmnd 9501. London: HMSO.

Department of Education and Science (1985b) *The Development of Higher Education into the 1990s*, Cmnd 9524. London: HMSO.

Department of Education and Science (1987) *Higher Education. Meeting the Challenge*, Cm 114. London: HMSO.

Department of Education and Science (1988) *Advancing A Levels*. London: HMSO.

Department of Education and Science (1991) *Higher Education. A New Framework*, Cm 1541. London: HMSO.

Department of Education and Science, Department of Employment and Welsh Office (1991) *Education and Training for the 21st century*, Cm 1536. London: HMSO.

Duke, C. (1988) Adults in Higher Education: Trends and Issues in the United Kingdom. In K. Abrahamsson, K. Rubenson and M. Slowey (eds) *Adults in the Academy. International Trends in Adult and Higher Education*. Stockholm: Swedish National Board of Education.

Duke, C. (1992) *The Learning University. Towards a New Paradigm?* Buckingham: Society for Research into Higher Education and Open University Press.

Edwards, R. (1993) *Mature Women Students: Separating or Connecting Family and Education*. London: Taylor and Francis.

Elliott, K. (1992) The Wales framework for Access, *Journal of Access Studies*, 7, 1, 69–82.

Evans, N. (1992) *Experiential Learning. Assessment and Accreditation*. London: Routledge.

Fulton, O. (1991) Slouching towards a mass system: society, government and institutions in the United Kingdom, *Higher Education*, 21, 4, 589–605.

Fulton, O. and Ellwood, S. (1989) *Admissions to Higher Education. Policy and Practice.* Moorfoot: Training Agency.

Further Education Unit (1992) *A Basis for Credit? Developing a post-16 credit accumulation and transfer framework.* London: FEU.

Graham, B. (1989) *Older Graduates and Employment.* Manchester: Association of Graduate Careers Advisory Services.

Halsey, A.H. (1993) Trends in access and equity in higher education: Britain in international perspective, *Oxford Reviews Education*, 19, 2, 129–140.

Halsey, A.H. and Heath, A. (eds) (1993) Special Issue: Access to higher education, *Oxford Review of Education*, 19, 2.

Harvey, D. H. and Norton, B. (1993) *The Institution of Environmental Health Officers Survey of Credit Accumulation and Transfer.* Jordanstown: University of Ulster.

Her Majesty's Inspectorate (1989) *The Widening of Access to Higher Education.* London: Department of Education and Science.

Institute of Public Policy Research (1990) *A British 'Baccalaureat': ending the division between education and training.* London: IPPR.

Irvine, H. (s.d.) *Access Courses in Further Education Colleges in Northern Ireland.* Belfast: University of Ulster.

Jessup, G. (1990) *Outcomes: NVQs and the Emerging Model of Education and Training.* London: Falmer Press.

Johnes, J. and Taylor, J. (1990) *Performance Indicators in Higher Education.* Buckingham: Society for Research into Higher Education and Open Unversity Press.

Jones, H.A. and Williams, K.E. (1979) *Adult Students and Higher Education.* Leicester: Advisory Council for Adult and Continuing Education.

Ligget, E. (1982) The universities and mature student entry. *Adult Education*, 55, 2, 125–136.

Matterson, C. (1990) HITECC Courses in the Polytechnics and Colleges. In G. Parry (ed) *Engineering Futures. New Audiences and Arrangements for Engineering Higher Education.* London: Engineering Council.

Mager, C. (1991) *Open College Networks: A Handbook.* Leicester: NIACE.

McIntosh, N.E.S. with Woodley, A. and Griffiths, M. (1978) Access to Higher Education and Wales. In R.S. Pike, N.E.S. McIntosh and U. Dahllöf *Innovation in Access to Higher Education.* New York: International Council for Educational Development.

Molloy, S. and Carroll, V. (1992) *Progress and performance in higher education*, CNAA Project Report 34. London: CNAA.

Ministry of Education (1960) *Grants to Students*, Cmnd 1051. London: HMSO.

National Advisory Body for Local Authority Higher Education (1984) *A Strategy for Higher Education in the Late 1980s and Beyond.* London: NAB.

National Commission on Education (1993) *Learning to Succeed.* London: Heinemann.

National Institute of Adult Continuing Education (1989) *Adults in Higher Education: Policy Discussion Paper.* Leicester: NIACE.
National Institute of Adult Continuing Education (1993) *Adult Higher Education. A Vision. A Policy Discussion Paper.* Leicester: NIACE.
National Training Task Force (1992) *National Targets for Education and Training. Fact Pack.* London: National Training Task Force.
Open University (1993) *Open University Statistics 1991. Students, Staff and Finance.* Milton Keynes: Open University.
Parry, G. (1989) Marking and Mediating the Higher Education Boundary. In O. Fulton (ed) *Access and Institutional Change.* Milton Keynes: Society for Research into Higher Education and Open University Press.
Parry, G. (1993) Lifelong education and training in the United Kingdom: policies, patterns and trends. In D. Atchoarena (ed) *Lifelong education in selected industrialized countries.* Paris: International Institute for Educational Planning.
Pascall, G. and Cox, R. (1993) *Women Returning to Higher Education.* Buckingham: Society for Research into Higher Education and Open University Press.
Percy, K. (1985) Adult Learners in Higher Education. In C. Titmus (ed) *Widening the Field. Continuing Education in Higher Education.* Guildford: Society for Research into Higher Education and NFER-Nelson.
Robertson, D. (1994) *Choosing to change; extending access, choice and mobility in higher education.* London: Higher Education Quality Council.
Royal Society of Arts (1988) *Raising the Standard. Wider Access to Higher Education.* London: Royal Society of Arts.
Slowey, M. (1987) Adults in Higher Education: The situation in the United Kingdom. In H.G. Schütze (ed) *Adults in Higher Education. Policies and Practice in Great Britain and North America.* Stockholm: Almqvist and Wiksell International.
Smithers, A. (1991) *The Vocational Route into Higher Education.* Manchester: University of Manchester.
Smithers, A.G. and Griffin, A. (1986) *The Progress of Mature Students.* Manchester: Joint Matriculation Board.
Smithers, A. and Robinson, P. (1991) *Beyond Compulsory Schooling. A Numerical Picture.* London: Council for Industry and Higher Education.
Squires, G. (1981) Mature Entry. In O. Fulton (ed) *Access to Higher Education.* Guildford: Society for Research into Higher Education.
Tight, M. (1987) Access and part-time undergraduate study, *Journal of Access Studies*, 2, 1, 12–24.
Tight, M. (1991) *Higher Education: A Part-time Perspective.* Buckingham: Society for Research into Higher Education and Open University Press.
Tight, M. (1993) Access, not access courses: maintaining a broad vision. In R. Edwards, S. Sieminski and D. Zeldin (eds) *Adult Learners, Education and Training.* London: Routledge.

Trow, M. (1974) Problems in the transition from elite to mass higher education. In Organisation for Economic Cooperation and Development Policies for Higher Education. Paris: OECD.

Trow, M. (1987) Academic standards and mass higher education, *Higher Education Quarterly*, 41, 3, 268–291.

Trow, M. (1989) The Robbins Trap: British Attitudes and the Limits of Expansion, *Higher Education Quarterly*, 43, 1, 55–75.

University Grants Committee (1984) *A Strategy for Higher Education in the 1990s*. London: UGC.

Wakeford, N. (1993) Beyond Educating Rita: mature students and Access courses, *Oxford Review of Education*, 19, 2, 217–230.

Walker, P. (1975) The university performance of mature students, *Research in Education*, 14, 1–13.

Weil, S.W. (1989) Access: towards education or miseducation? Adults imagine the future. In O. Fulton (ed) *Access and Institutional Change*. Milton Keynes: Society for Research into Higher Education and Open University Press.

Woodley, A. (1981) Age Bias. In D. W. Piper (ed) *Is Higher Education Fair?* Guildford: Society for Research into Higher Education.

Woodley, A. (1984) The older the better? A study of mature student performance in British universities, *Research in Education*, 32, 35–50.

Woodley, A., Wagner, L. Slowey, M., Hamilton, M. and Fulton, O. (1987) *Choosing to learn: adults in education*. Milton Keynes: Society for Research into Higher Education and Open University Press.

Wright, P. (1991) Access or accessibility? *Journal of Access Studies*, 6, 1, 6–15.

Wynne, R. (1979) *The Adult Student and British Higher Education*. Amsterdam: European Cultural Foundation.

Wynne, R. (1990) Access to higher education – a Welsh perspective, *Journal of Access Studies*, 5, 1, 18–34.

Chapter 6

France

Pat Davies

A number of key historical events and developments have shaped the general political and constitutional context in which higher education in France operates; hence the shape of the current structure and its future development. Since the revolution of 1789, the role of the central state, *l'état*, has been to act as 'a check against the arbitrary power of sectional interests...to hold down the rapacity of local elites' (Neave 1985 p.20); thus it is essentially a benign force which protects and defends the interests of institutions and individuals. In principle, the fact that universities are national institutions under the authority and responsibility of the state, provides protection from interference and guarantees equality of provision and of opportunity for individuals. In addition, since the early nineteenth century, universities have been closely linked to the service of the state through the training of civil servants and public sector employees. This association has been reinforced by a relatively close linkage between, on the one hand, qualifications, and on the other, the terms, conditions and status of employment. Thus the role of the state and the special relationship between it and the universities has meant that the higher education system was still 'a highly centralised enterprise' (Neave 1985 p.18) in the early 1980s. In the late 1980s some modification of this position took place with the establishment, albeit with problematic and uneven implementation (Guin 1990), of state-university contracts as the basis of funding and policy development. In 1988 the scope of these contractual relationships between universities and the Ministry of Education (MEN) was broadened and in 1990 the Ministry launched the Outline Regional Plan (*Schemas régionaux d'aménagement*, SRA) as a frame-work for decentralised regional planning of all higher education and training provision, with input from industry and commerce as well as central and local government and the universities.

The Structure and Organisation of Higher Education
The institutions

As Jallade (1992) points out, higher education in France is 'fragmented' rather than 'binary' or 'unitary' as in most other European countries. The system is built on four pillars each with its own administrative arrangements: the *Grandes Ecoles*, the *Universités*, the *Instituts Universitaires de Technologie* (IUTs) and the *Sections de Technicien Supérieurs* (STS).

The *Grandes Ecoles* are the élite institutions of the system, specialising in business, administration and engineering with competitive and highly selective admissions procedures. Students are required to complete two years of *classes préparatoires aux grandes écoles* (CPGE), usually in a *lycée*, following the *baccalauréat* (the general certificate of education required for higher level study, usually referred to as the 'Bac'). In order to be admitted to the CPGE, students must have obtained good marks in the science Bac and at the end of the two years they must pass the competitive examination to enter one of the *Grandes Ecoles*.

The *universités* are in principle non-selective institutions where entry is open to all those who hold the Bac (*bacheliers*) as a legal right (with the exception of medicine and dentistry, where numbers are limited and selection takes place). Although prevented by law from screening entrants, it is frequently pointed out that unofficial screening does take place through the high drop-out during the first two years (*le premier cycle*). In 1991–2 there were 77 universities with considerable variation in the size, range of disciplines and status (Lacroix 1990): some are comprehensive, offering the full range of subjects and courses; others offer only some disciplines, especially in the larger cities where usually each institution specialises in a different range of subject areas. In principle and in law all universities are equal in status but in practice there is a hierarchy and it is argued that 'wide gaps are opening and inequalities are increasing' (Lacroix 1990).

The IUTs were created in 1966, each attached to a university but with a different legal status. They are on a par with the first cycle of university higher education and offer only a two year technological diploma (*Diplôme Universitaire de Technologie*, DUT). By 1991–92 there were 74 IUTs with 78,800 students enrolled (MEN 1992a). Admission is selective, based on marks in the Bac and during the last two years of secondary education. Since the courses are generally more vocationally oriented and often include work placements, the employment prospects for the students are generally good (Lamoure and Lamoure Rantopoulou 1992).

The *lycées*, although structurally part of the secondary sector, play an important part in the provision of higher education. They offer the CPGE and are the location of the *Sections de Techniciens Supérieurs* (STS), offering vocational courses normally of two years duration, leading to the higher technician qualification, the *Brevet de Technicien Supérieur* (BTS). Significantly for adults in particular, *lycées* in the same geographical area group together to form *Groupements d'établissements* (GRETA) for the provision of the BTS and of a wide range of preparatory and vocational courses for adults, often in the evenings and weekends.

Courses and qualifications

Figure 6.1 shows the structure of programmes and qualifications in universities.

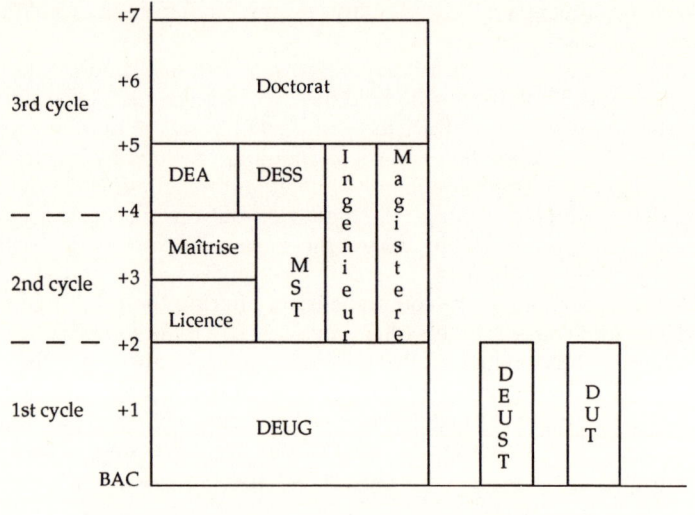

Figure 6.1 Structure of higher education programmes and qualifications

In the first cycle, the DEUST and the DUT are the more applied, vocationally oriented programmes and the DEUG provides the more general academic ones. Similarly in the second and third cycles, the MST, Ingénieur, Magistère and DESS are the more vocational/professional courses and the Maîtrise and the DEA the more academic.

An important feature of the system is the fact that these qualifications are national rather than university diplomas which, until the early 1970s were based on a national curriculum drawn up in Paris. Since then universities have increasingly been given autonomy over the content of the courses but the framework, particularly in relation to assessment, is determined at national level.

In addition, there are university diplomas at all levels, usually vocationally or professionally oriented and offered under the auspices of continuing education. While still a relatively small part of university provision, they represent a growing area of work (see table 6.2 below) and mostly for adults.

Fees and Grants: 'Formation Initiale' and 'Formation Continue'

It is important here to distinguish between two concepts of higher education: *la formation initiale* (literally, initial education and training) and *la formation continue* (literally, continuing education and training). I use the word literally here to stress that the concepts do not correspond to their UK equivalent. In order to avoid confusion therefore the French terms will be used. *La formation initiale* is the traditional form of higher education: all students are full-time (in principle if not always in practice), education is free (apart from enrolment/registration fees of approximately 800 francs per annum), grants and bursaries are available, courses might include first, second or third cycle diplomas, and students can be any age. They do not receive a mandatory grant for subsistence and although there is a system of bursaries it is relatively limited: in 1991–92, 284,510 students in higher education out of a total of 1,848,400 (just over 15%) were in receipt of some form of MEN grant (MEN 1992a). A number of benefits in the form of social security cover, medical and health services and concessions on a range of public services accrue to registered students and interviews in one university suggested that returning adults may be using the social security system in creative ways to obtain cash allowances. However, many students need to work to support themselves thus the distinction between working students (under *statut formation continue*) and students (under *statut formation initiale*) who work, is in practice somewhat blurred and is discussed further below.

La formation continue is not necessarily related to the age of the students, to the curriculum, course or level of study, mode of attendance or to the employment status of the students. It is essentially an administrative and funding concept (rather akin to the difference between full-time and part-time students in the UK) and describes the education and training which takes place within the framework of specific legislative and funding arrangements.

La formation continue in universities has its origins in 'the spirit of 1968' and the agreements between employers federations and trade unions which followed the strikes and riots. Legislation (Loi 16.7.71 – 'Loi Delors') was enacted which made the continuing education of adults an official priority (Caspar 1992). Education was seen as having dual objectives: the economic one of supplying industry and commerce with a well-qualified labour force and the social one of dealing with unemployment, inequality and the integration of young people into adult society. All companies employing more than 10 people were obliged to spend 0.8 per cent of their total wage bill on education and training. By 1 January 1993, this had risen to 1.5 per cent of which 0.2 per cent is allocated to individual paid educational leave (*congé individuel de formation*, CIF) organised through sectoral associations, 0.3 per cent relates to alternative training for young (16–25) unemployed people (*jeunes en difficulté*) and the remaining 1 per cent relates to the training plan of the company (*plan de formation*). In 1984 the legislation was extended to include small companies although at a much lower rate. From January 1993, the rate for small companies was again revised and will be increased progressively over a six year period to 75 per cent of the large company rate. In addition, people with five years work experience have the right to a day of paid leave to undertake *un bilan des competences*, literally an assessment of competence, or perhaps more accurately a skills audit or appraisal, to review their existing knowledge and skills and plan their future development. In 1992 new legislation was passed on apprenticeship, establishing the notion of a higher level apprenticeship involving university study with the certification of professional experience. In addition, alongside the sums from companies, spending by central and regional government has also increased, particularly in relation to training for the unemployed and retraining programmes in the areas of declining traditional industries.

Within this framework, students (or more usually their employers or a government programme) pay full cost fees; they are usually in employment or registered unemployed, and thus in receipt of salary (or a proportion of it) or some form of training benefit or allowance. Although most are studying for university diplomas and non award bearing courses, many are studying for undergraduate and postgraduate national awards and follow programmes identical to those followed by students in *la formation initiale* (albeit sometimes with special timetabling arrangements, for example a DEUG *au regime salarié* spread over four years instead of two). This status obliges the university to operate a separate administrative framework for the students involving reception, advice, guidance and supervision and reporting functions not provided for students in *la formation initiale*. Students studying under *formation continue* are usually referred to as trainees, (*stagiaires*), rather than students (*étudiants*), whatever their course of study.

Expansion: Implications and Consequences

The main issues and debates about the higher education system at present – reform of the curriculum of courses in the first cycle, decentralisation and contractual relationships between higher education institutions and the state (Guin 1990), new organisations for quality assurance (Staropoli 1987, Neave 1991) – are all set within the context of massive expansion, particularly in *la formation initiale*. Table 6.1 shows the extent of the expansion in recent years.

Table 6.1: Enrolments in higher education
formation initiale 1960–1 to 1991–2

Year	All HE students	IUTs	Universities and Engineering schools
1960–61	311,300	-	214,700
1970–71	854,500	24,200	637,000
1980–81	1,176,900	53,700	829,600
1989–90	1,585,600	69,900	1,074,000
1991–92	1,848,400	78,800	1,214,600

Source: MEN 1991, 1992

Further expansion is planned: '*Conduire 80% d'une generation au niveau du baccalauréat en l'an 2000*' (to have 80% of the age cohort at the level of the Bac by the year 2000) is, as Charlot (1988) has pointed out, highly symbolic since it contains the notion of crossing two quasi-mythological boundaries in the French imagination: the sacrosanct *baccalauréat* and the year 2000, an object of fear and fantasy as the beginning of a science fiction age. Although the origin of the target is often misattributed (ibid) it was first posited in 1983 and has since become firmly established in policy terms with all other reforms of curriculum and practice considered in that context. The reform of the Bac (Davies 1994), the even greater changes in the vocational training system for young people and the reform of the first two years of higher education are all designed to implement and/or to deal with the impact of this policy.

Progress towards the target has been impressive: it stood at 36.5 per cent in 1985, 54.5 per cent in 1990 (MEN 1991a) and 58.3 per cent in 1991 (slightly higher at almost 61% if education beyond the jurisdiction of the MEN is taken into account) (MEN 1992a). The concept of 'at the level of the Bac' is not the same as 'achieving the qualification' since not all those who reach the third year of the course, (*la terminale*) take the examination, and not all those who take the examination pass, although the success rate is high – almost 74 per cent provisionally for 1992 (Cressard 1994) – and rising. In 1990 when the proportion of the age group 'at the level' was 54.5 per cent, the proportion with a pass was 44.4 per cent, a success rate of 73.4 per cent. Clearly if the proportion at the level is rising and the pass rate is also rising the numbers wishing to enter higher education will rise considerably. It has been predicted (see for example Jallade 1991) that this will mean about two million students in public sector higher education in the year 2000 compared to about 1.5 million in 1988–89, an increase of approximately 33 per cent. Since many would argue that the universities were already overcrowded in 1988–89, this represents a major demand on resources, particularly buildings, equipment and staff.

The policy response to these predictions *Université 2000* (MEN 1990a) was originally to provide some higher education in all towns of more than 50,000 inhabitants by setting up university annexes. However, this was subsequently replaced by a programme of expansion in the number of IUT – 20 new ones – and a doubling of their capacity with 50,000 new places. In addition seven new universities were proposed (four in the Paris region, two in the North and one at La Rochelle) as was a new system of partnership agreements between the national, regional and local governments which 'should double' the funds pledged by central government (Henderson 1991). The seven new universities began taking students in 1991–92 and have a target of 20,000 students each by the year 2000 (Henderson 1993). In addition to this building programme, Jospin, the Minister at the time, outlined a number of plans under three headings: the development of the university community (an increase in the number of teaching and administrative posts, in the number of student grants and loans and accommodation, in libraries, theatre and cinema facilities on campus); the improvement and modernisation of the structures (the establishment of contracts and partnerships between institutions and government, a revision of management procedures, a new building programme); and the development of modern practice (the revitalisation of research, the development of new teaching methods and new courses for teachers and engineers, the improvement of relations with industry).

There has also been considerable expansion in *la formation continue* as the legislation over a number of years has generated an enormous market in the education and training of adults. Although the universities only account for a small percentage of this market as a whole (Bordage 1992), it nevertheless represents a very important additional source of students and funding for the universities which is growing significantly and likely to continue to do so given recent legislation and the general economic climate. While some universities have resisted moving towards a more vocationally oriented mission and provision, others have embraced it enthusiastically seeing it as an important part of the role of the university in the economic regeneration of the region.

Table 6.2: Enrolments in higher education *formation continue* 1988–91

	1988 %	1989 %	1990 %	1991 %	% change 1988–91
National diplomas	31.3	30.7	32.8	24.7	-5%
Institutional diplomas	8.6	8.6	9.2	17.7	+147%
Professional updating <300 hours	41.2	40.5	38.6	36.0	+5%
Non-award bearing >300 hours	3.4	3.4	3.7	2.8	-3%
General and cultural	15.5	16.8	15.7	18.8	+46%
Total %	100	100	100	100	
Total no.	343,618	354,790	384,607	412,541	+20%

Source: MEN 1990, 1991, 1992, 1993

Table 6.2 shows that in 1991 more than 400,000 people were enrolled in higher education institutions as *formation continue* students, an increase of 20 per cent over 1988. Interestingly, between 1988 and 1991, the numbers enrolled for university diplomas and for general and cultural programmes, while not the largest in terms of numbers, were the areas of most significant growth. Over the same period the total number of diplomas awarded rose by 46 per cent from nearly 17,000 in 1988 to more than 24,500 in 1991.

Admission, Participation and Progression

Admission

The most significant feature of the interface between secondary and higher education in France is the fact that the Bac taken at the end of secondary schooling constitutes the first national diploma of the higher education system and confers on its holders (*bacheliers*) the right of entry to first cycle programmes. Thus the level of higher education diplomas is usually defined in terms of the number of years of study after the Bac: the DEUG is Bac + 2, the doctorat is Bac + 7. The national targets are also described in terms of the Bac: 80 per cent of the age group at the level of the Bac by the year 2000, which, as indicated above, dominates the development of the higher education system.

The Bac is essentially a general education qualification with a compulsory core of maths, science, French and modern languages for all students. However, there are a number of *séries* which provide the opportunity to major in particular areas, and a set of technological *séries* which focus on applications of knowledge. The Bac has been recently reformed: the first students to complete the new programme will do so in the summer of 1995. Essentially the reforms are designed to provide a greater range of options and possible combinations of subjects so that students have more choice and more opportunity to pursue particular path-ways while at the same time maintaining the concept of breadth in the overall package. It is also seen as a more effective preparation for higher education. (Details of the old and new arrangements are provided in Davies 1994.)

In addition to the reform of the general and technological Bac, the *Baccalauréat Professionel* (Bac Pro) was introduced in 1986 to provide a vocational version of the qualification including a work placement of between 16 and 24 weeks over two years for those coming through the more vocational qualifications route in *lycées professionels*. The number of specialisms available has grown steadily since its introduction, and by 1993 there were 32 Bac Pros available and 69,000 students took the final examination (Cressard 1994). The overwhelming majority of students who pass the Bac Pro progress to further vocational courses: 83 per cent go on to a STS to take the BTS, 13 per cent go to a IUT and 4 per cent to a university (Jallade 1991). The Bac Pro is also significant for adults since it is usually credit based and can be taken by them within the framework of *formation continue*.

While the overwhelming majority of students of all ages enter higher education with the Bac, there are alternative routes for adults, in particular *L'examen spécial d'accès aux études universitaires* (l'ESEU) and *la validation des acquis*; these are described in detail below. In principle there are no differences between the admission regulations for students entering *la formation initiale* and those entering *la formation continue*, particularly the national diploma courses. However, there is considerably more flexibility in the university diploma courses, and on the non award bearing courses the entry requirements are either defined in terms of the target group or the prerequisite knowledge and skills (usually expressed in terms of Bac + level). The general and cultural programmes usually have no specific entry requirements.

Participation

Age on entry to higher education is not a key variable in the analysis of access and participation; such data are not produced. Instead, the rate of participation in all forms of education for all age groups (*taux de scolarisation*) and the age profile of all students enrolled in higher education at whatever level (*population universitaire par âge*) are routinely published.

Table 6.3: Age profile of student population in universities *formation initiale* 1989–90

Age	No.	%
Up to 18	108,624	9.8
19–20	303,433	27.5
21–25	429,607	38.9
26–31	149,627	13.5
32–41	84,710	7.7
42+ over	28,888	2.6
Total	**1,104,889**	**100%**

Source: MEN 1991

Table 6.3 shows that almost 63 per cent of students in *formation initiale* (at all levels) in 1989–90 were over 21. However, since many students repeat at least one year of secondary schooling, new entrants to first cycle courses tend to be older on entry than the formal structure might suggest. In addition, as pointed out above, significant proportions repeat part of the first cycle course at least once in university. Thus the age of the students is a function of their rate of progress through the system as much as of a period of time out of the system. In addition, *formation initiale* includes postgraduate courses.

Overall, women outnumber men in university courses: for 1989–90, 53.7 per cent of university students were women. However, men are in the majority in economics, science, medicine and in the IUTs; and women are in the majority in law, pharmacy, and particularly, literature and social science where they constituted 70.8 per cent in the same year (MEN 1991a).

The participation rates among different socio-economic groups has not significantly changed over time. Overall, students with parents in the professional classes (*professions libérales et cadres supérieurs*) constitute by far the largest group: 30 per cent in the universities and 47 per cent in the *grandes écoles* in 1989–90. In the same year, the IUTs had the largest proportion (20.7%) of students from the manual working classes (*ouvriers*). The higher socio-economic groups also follow longer courses: they represented 27.8 per cent in first cycle and 43.9 per cent in third cycle courses in the universities in that year; a similar pattern is found in the *écoles*, the professional training schools, where they constituted 30 per cent in the law schools and 50 per cent in the veterinary schools (MEN 1991a).

In *la formation continue* the students are counted differently in national statistics: in particular, the statistics for *la formation continue* are based on a calendar year and those for *la formation initiale* on an academic year. While there is considerable data on the funding, the numbers and distribution of students across courses, qualifications, geographical area, and sources of funding, no national data is available concerning their age, social background and so on.

Progression

The right of entry conferred by the Bac is not unproblematic. Approximately 55 per cent of those who enrol in university first cycle courses leave with no qualification (Observatoire de la vie étudiante 1990). A recent case study (Sahli 1993) illustrates this in some detail. Of 312 students enrolled in 1988 for the DEUG in humanities (*lettres modernes*) at the Université des Sciences Humaines de Strasbourg (UHSS) only 5 passed the examination at the end of year one and progressed into year two; 70 withdrew without sitting the examination; 50 failed the examination and did not re-enrol; 187 failed the examination and re-enrolled to repeat the year. Of this 187, 64 passed the examination at the second attempt; 19 withdrew; 10 failed and did not re-enrol; 94 failed and re-enrolled for a third time. Of this 94, 54 passed the examination at the third attempt; 7 withdrew; 6 failed and did not re-enrol; 27 failed and re-enrolled for a fourth time. Of this 27, 10 passed the examination; 4 withdrew; and 6 re-enrolled for the fifth time at the beginning of the 1992–3 academic year! Thus after four years only 43 per cent of the original intake had passed the year one examinations.

UHSS is not alone in this situation, and neither is humanities a special case. Although there is some dispute about the precise national figures, with some surveys indicating that this figure does not take account of approximately 26 per cent who transfer to different courses, there is nevertheless a general consensus that the drop-out rate is unacceptably high (Henderson 1990).

The reasons for this are complex. Lack of selection is clearly one aspect but this is not a question of general eligibility but of subject-specific eligibility. Since the Bac is a general education qualification it is not subject-specific and permits students to enter any course of their choice (with the exception of some *numerus clausus* subjects such as medicine) at a university. Thus there is no close link between the subject specialism in the Bac and the course of study in higher education. The high status of maths and science and the general consensus that the Bac C (the maths and physical science major) was the most demanding meant that it attracted the academically strong students and those most likely to go into selective higher education courses and institutions – CPGE, the *Grandes Ecoles* and more recently the IUTs. Because the IUTs are selective they are able to choose the strongest students and thus those with the *Bac Techno* who have had the more appropriate preparation are less likely to gain places and more likely to go into the less applied courses in the universities. Similarly those with a humanities major in the Bac may enter a science route in higher education because it appears to offer better job opportunities. There is thus considerable crossover between the major subjects studied in the preparation and those in the higher education course. This crossover is significant. Durand-Prinborgne (1988) suggest that more than 50 per cent of the places in technology courses in higher education are taken by those with the *Bac général*; only 40 per cent of those with the *Bac Techno* go on to technology courses and of those who are not admitted about 30 per cent go on to academic programmes. This is particularly important since the greatest growth in candidates for the Bac has been in the *Bac Techno* and since these students are mostly from modest social backgrounds this constitutes a new source of inequality.

While the Bac general and techno are not qualifications taken by adults, the alternative route l'ESEU (see below) designed specifically for adults presents similar problems, and once in higher education the mature students are in the same position. The whole question of retention and success rates is a major issue in the whole system for all students.

Although reform at national level has been problematic, at the local level a number of institutions have implemented strategies to address these problems. For example at Toulouse-Le Mirail an induction and guidance programme is offered in July and September for those students starting in the autumn term, with a tutorial system operated by postgraduate students for the first year and study skills/learning support workshops. From the start of the 1993–4 academic year, the first nine weeks of the first year consist of a reduced number of modules in two disciplines with the opportunity to change programme at the end of the period. These strategies emulate some of the practices developed for the support of adults in *la formation continue*, aiming primarily to offer students more guidance in their choice of subject, fitting them more closely to their strengths and aptitudes. Clearly since these are relatively recent changes, it is too early to judge their impact on retention and success rates.

Alternative Entry Routes for Adults

There are essentially two routes into higher education for adults which are alternatives to the Bac: l'ESEU (*les examens spéciaux d'accès aux études universitaires*) and accreditation of prior learning (*la validation des acquis*).

L'ESEU[1]

L'ESEU has its roots in May 1968 and the Edgar Faure bill which followed and had as one of its main purposes the promotion of access to higher education for adults (Dechy 1990a). An order (*arrêté*) of 1969 established the framework for the organisation by the universities of special entry examinations. The examinations were to involve an oral interview, designed to verify the candidates' aptitude and knowledge, and one of two sets of written papers: A for admission to humanities, social sciences, law and economics; B for science, medical and para-medical subjects, dentistry and pharmacy. Candidates had to be at least 20 years old and have been working (and paying social security contributions) for at least two years, or be at least 24 years old; those who were not French nationals but normally resident in France could obtain special exemption from the two year work requirement. In 1986 a further order modified the arrangements adding arts, languages, administration and management to strand A and technology and physical and sporting activities to strand B. In addition the students were required to take four subjects instead of three as previously; two were compulsory – French and a foreign language for strand A, French and maths for strand B. The other two subjects were to be chosen from maths, history, geography for A and physics, chemistry or natural science for B or others at the discretion of the university (full details of the curriculum and assessment arrangements are set out in Davies 1994). The other key change was that candidates were no longer required to register for all the four examinations at the same time but could choose to take them over a maximum of four years and those taken in one university could be added to in another with the approval of the *Président* of the second. An element of continuous assessment was also introduced. Thus for the first time a system of credit accumulation and transfer became possible.

At the same time there was also an extension of the conditions of enrolment: the two years work experience requirement could be replaced by a corresponding period of national service, registered unemployment, sporting activity, participation in vocational training for young unemployed, or responsibility for child care. Thus eligibility was clearly related to policies encouraging retraining and re-entry to the labour market (*reconversion* and *insertion*) and the target group clearly defined as 'returners' to education.

Successful completion entitled the students to receive a certificate, and, as well as providing entry to first cycle higher education programmes without the Bac, also conferred other rights associated with the Bac, such as access to employment and to competitive examinations particularly for work in the public sector.

The regulations set out in 1986 (which remain current at the time of writing)[1] made the system much more flexible for adults but also confirmed some key features which impact on participation. Firstly, l'ESEU is an examination for which students receive a certificate; it is not a diploma (which would oblige the minister to provide resources for a preparatory course) or a course (universities may offer the examination without any preparatory programme). This means that where courses are offered they must be self financing and full cost fees are charged. Although most students are entitled to concessionary fees through schemes for the unemployed or regional retraining programmes, such funding has fluctuated in recent years and fees for all students have generally risen. It also means that many students attempt the examination without any formal preparation, and although national statistics are not available, studies undertaken by the national working party suggest that the failure rate of such students is high (Groupe de Travail l'ESEU 1992).

Ownership is clearly vested in the universities and since the orders permitted rather than obliged universities to offer the examination, development has been somewhat patchy (Groupe de Travail l'ESEU 1992). While there is some provision in each regional education authority (*académie*), it is minimal in some and very well developed in others. The Nord-Pas de Calais region represents an example of the latter category: a preparatory programme in a wide range of subjects is offered in more than thirty venues spread across the region, on a credit accumulation and transfer basis, by the four universities operating as a consortium; together they awarded almost 22 per cent of all l'ESEU certificates in 1991.

National statistics on enrolment and performance of students are not available, although the number of certificates awarded each year is published. Recent years have seen a steady growth in the numbers with an increase of 41 per cent between 1988 and 1991 (table 6.4).

Table 6.4: L'ESEU awards 1988–91

Year	A	B	Total
1988	1957	572	2519
1989	2021	585	2606
1990	2521	943	3464
1991	2839	715	3554

A - Humanities and Social Science

B - Science

Source: MEN 1990, 1991, 1992, 1993

However, it is clear that the numbers are small compared to the number of young people awarded the Bac (in 1991, 416,300).

There are no national statistics on progression of the students following the award of the certificate. However, a number of local studies (Dechy 1990b; Dubar and Wagnon 1982; SUFOC et CRESEP 1989) suggest that between 50 and 70 per cent progress into further study in higher education. It is also clear that because the award confers the rights of the Bac, a significant proportion of students use it to progress in employment. (These local studies are explored in more detail in Davies 1994.) Thus whilst the numbers are small in a national context, the arrangements nevertheless provide an important opportunity for adults in some regions.

Accreditation of prior learning

The possibility of accrediting prior learning (*la validation des acquis*) was first established by a decree (*décret*) in 1985 which permitted a university, or a higher education institution under the supervision of the ministry of agriculture, to accredit prior learning for the purpose of admitting students to courses leading to national diplomas or to competitive entry examinations in the same university. Candidates wishing to enter first cycle courses without the Bac or a recognised equivalent had to be 20 years old and have been away from education for at least two years. Similarly, students who had failed the examinations at the end of year one of first cycle courses could not ask for that year to be accredited for entry to year two unless there had been an intervening period of three years. For candidates who fulfilled these conditions, institutions were empowered to accredit all training and education programmes offered in France, work experience in temporary and permanent employment, work based training, knowledge and skills acquired outside the education system and overseas qualifications. Students admitted in this way could be required to take complementary classes or could be exempted from some teaching; otherwise they enrolled and participated in programmes in the same way as other students.

The second stage of the development was legislation in 1992 which modified the regulations to enable all those with at least five years work experience to request accreditation of work related learning as part of the requirements of a diploma; it thus established the possibility of exemption not just from entry qualifications but from part of the diploma itself. In the parliamentary debate it was suggested to the Minister at the time, Jack Lang, that the regulations permitted exemption from the whole diploma. However, the Minister pointed out the importance of national diplomas and of maintaining their credibility and legitimacy, and that only part exemption was possible (although he did not specify a maximum); he added that it was the wish of the government to see the regulations much more widely used so that they became the rule rather than the exception. Although he did not rule out exemption from the whole diploma at some point in the future he argued that this should be achieved progressively (Flash Formation Continue 1992a).

Despite the requirement of the original order that institutions keep records of the number of students applying for and being admitted through these arrangements, no annual statistics have been published at the time of writing. However, a national survey undertaken by the MEN (Flash Formation Continue 1992b) showed that in 1990–91 there were 4283 students in first cycle courses who had been admitted this way (0.68% of all enrolments), and 7750 in second cycle courses

(2.15% of all enrolments). A total of 14,327 had been admitted in the previous five years. Clearly the legislation of 1992 had at that point not impacted on the system; numbers have certainly increased since that time. However, it is clear (Feutrie 1993) that the extent of development and the kind of procedures established varies considerably across the country with only a minority of institutions having well developed procedures. Nevertheless, some institutions have embraced the new possibilities and are admitting growing numbers of students. The employment legislation in 1992 and 1993 referred to above, which gave employees the right to one day of paid leave for an appraisal or skills audit, may also boost the demand for the accreditation of prior learning.

Access to What? The Accessibility of Higher Education

For students registered under *la formation continue* there exists a wide range of possibilities to study for university diplomas (all of which are at specified levels, often Bac +2) and for national diplomas *DEUG, Licence* and so on – sometimes full-time but frequently through blocked periods of time, evening, and/or week-end provision. However, students in *la formation initiale* may also study specially adapted programmes (*la formation aménagée*). The legislation of November 1968 (Direction of Higher Education) instructed that 'having recognised their ability, universities are to organise the reception of candidates already engaged in working life, whether or not they possess university qualifications. They are to permit them access to education or further education and to obtain the corresponding diplomas. The content of teaching, teaching methods, the means by which the studies are recognised, the calendar and the timetable are to be specially adapted' (Article 23). Mostly these adaptations relate to attendance. For example, students may take the two year course leading to a DEUG, *au régime salarié*, spread over four years, simply taking half the programme each year; sometimes the mode of attendance is different, for example in some universities students meet the tutor once a week or once a fortnight to receive assignments, reading lists and lecture notes and to submit work to be marked which they complete in their own time. Some courses in some universities are also offered on a credit accumulation basis (*unités capitalisables*) with small groups, taught in the evenings and Saturdays, assessed mostly by continuous assessment attached to each module rather than by exams at the end, and with flexibility in the length of time a student may take to complete the course. These are of course expensive models, since if the student is registered under *la formation initiale* they pay only the nominal enrolment fee paid by all students.

Most universities also offer their national diploma courses by distance learning either through written materials or through the national satellite television service (*Télé-enseignements Universitaires*). While there are usually fees for the *Télé-enseignements Universitaires*, distance learning is possible within *la formation initiale* and thus free apart from nominal enrolment fees. Although there are often criteria attached to such registration, these seem to be written widely enough to include most adults (for example the *licence à distance* may be offered to students who work more than 20 hours per week, are registered unemployed, are disabled, have childcare responsibilities, are on national service, or are retired).

In addition to individual university provision, there is a national distance learning centre, *le Centre National d'Enseignement à Distance*, (CNED) which provides a wide range of courses from sub-degree level to postgraduate level. It is funded partly by the MEN (about 30%) and partly by businesses and other ministries. It prepares students for national diplomas, and sometimes university diplomas, at the request of the universities and in partnership with them. Students have written study materials and meet in groups in regional centres with CNED tutors; special arrangements are made with companies and with universities for practical and laboratory work. Only the standard enrolment fees are payable unless the students are funded by their companies. In 1991 about 103,000 students were registered for higher education courses.

There also exists an institution unique to France: *Le Conservatoire National des Arts et Métiers* (CNAM). Founded in 1794 in the aftermath of the revolution to support the development of a national industry which would be capable of competing with England, and to improve the status and understanding of the new technologies, it was initially a centre for the collection and demonstration of machines, working models, plans and designs, and supporting books and papers. However, very soon it identified a need to do more and the first courses were established in 1796. These roots still shape the institution so that it maintains a museum of industrial technology, a library and archive, alongside its education and research activities.

At the beginning of the nineteenth century, it became a school of science applied to industry and commerce, offering classes at the end of the afternoon so that workers could attend. Based in Paris, it now has 50 regional teaching centres and 30 research laboratories, funded partly by central government, partly by regional governments, fees, research and consultancy contracts. About 100,000 students are enrolled on courses, 90 per cent of whom are registered under *la formation continue.* All courses run in the evenings and at week-ends, with a strong focus on practice, starting from and drawing on the work experience of students and tutors. Entry is open and the boast of the CNAM is that a student can enter with no qualifications and become an engineer in eight years (although this would be an extremely intensive programme for someone in employment). All programmes are based on credit accumulation and since the units of a diploma are usually almost identical in each centre, geographical mobility is possible. All levels of study are covered: pre-Bac, cycle A (up to Bac+2), cycle B (Bac+2 to Bac+4) and cycle C (Bac+5). All courses are related to industry and commerce: mostly science and engineering with relevant social sciences such as industrial psychology, sociology of work, employment law, and language for technical purposes. In cycle B there is also a course in the education and training of adults (*formation des adultes – conception et mise en oeuvre*). About 4000 diplomas are awarded each year, including about 500 engineering degrees (CNAM 1992).

The Concept of 'Adult' in Policy and Practice

The concept of 'adult' does not have strong resonance in official policy terms in France. While, as Cerych and Sabatier (1986 p.179) point out, 'democratisation of higher education has been a politically significant issue in France and indeed an underlying objective of many reforms since World War II', it has largely been addressed through the creation of the IUTs, the introduction of the 'Bac pro', the expansion of numbers, and so on, at the interface between secondary and higher education rather than in relation to returners or adults per se.

As Freynet (1991 p.78) points out 'the criterion of age would appear to be of little account. Much more important is the situation with regard to [the] working life'. In the legislation which followed the riots of May 1968 ('Direction of Higher Education' Law of November 1968 in Titmus 1979 p.252), the stated aim was that 'Higher Education must be open to former students as well as people who have not had the opportunity to pursue studies in order to allow them, according to their ability, to improve their chances of promotion or to change their occupational activity' (Article 1).

However, the provision for adults in higher education, both in terms of the curriculum and support services and the differences between the arrangements for adults in *la formation initiale* and those in *la formation continue*, has been the focus of attention of a series of working groups under the auspices of the MEN over a number of years. For example, the *Groupe de travail formation permanente* (1982) reported on the needs of adult workers as learners in terms of the curriculum, structure, teaching styles, and guidance, referring to the cultural mission of universities and the economic imperatives which required programmes aimed at social inequality (similar to existing provision but adapted to suit adults) and at coping with technological change (new needs not currently addressed). Many of the recommendations in that report found their way into the legislation of 1984 and 1985, focusing on the administration and delivery of an effective *service de formation continue*.

Much of the work of these groups has been directed at developing and promoting good practice, for example in the reception (*accueil*), information, advice and guidance services and more recently the arrangements for the accreditation of prior learning (*la validation des acquis*) and for the assessment of competence (*le bilan des competences*) (Groupe de Travail 1990). However, they have also been concerned to raise awareness in policy circles of the number and circumstances of adults in *la formation initiale*. A report in 1986 (Groupe de Travail 1986) focused on the needs of 'returners' as distinct from 'continuers', pointing out that most universities did not know how many 'returners' they had, or indeed anything about them. The report indicated the different kinds of people who may be included in that category: employed, unemployed, mothers, refugees, people with disabilities, and so on.

Four years later the group had refined their ideas about the nature of the adults they were not currently reaching through the arrangements for *formation continue* (Groupe de Travail 1990). These focused on three groups: students who work (*étudiants-salariés*) and thus are obliged to spread their studies over a longer period, often being continuers rather than returners; workers who study (*salariés-étudiants*), often in their spare time – evenings, week-ends, distance learning – possibly including the unemployed and mothers; and those looking for personal development, often retired people. The first and second of these groups either were or could be eligible for funding under *la formation continue* but were mostly not registered as such either because they lacked information about the possibilities, or did not know how to access them, or had deliberately chosen not to take advantage of them. While the arrangements for the *formation continue* carry obligations on the part of the students in terms of attendance for example, they also carry obligations on the part of the university to support and supervise in a way not provided for other students. Although fees are payable there might nevertheless be financial advantages in registration under *formation continue*, both for the students through eligibility for financial support, and for the institution from the increased income. The group pointed out the need to measure the size of the phenomenon and to ensure that students were making choices on the basis of full information rather than ignorance.

In terms of the 'size of the phenomenon', the group developed the concept of 'over age' (*hors âge*), defined as over 25 in the first cycle, over 27 in the second cycle and over 30 in the third cycle. Surveys suggested that in 1987 about 18 per cent of students in *formation initiale* – approximately 200,000 students – were *hors âge*, and further studies by members of the group in their own institutions suggested that this varied from about 15 per cent to about 30 per cent. The numbers of such students seemed to be increasing: other surveys reported indicated that some 260,000 students in higher education were also working. Most of these were studying human and social sciences or literature and languages, but more than expected were found in science programmes. While some have entered with *L'ESEU* or through *la validation des acquis*, the overwhelming majority were returners with the Bac. Little was known about these students in terms of their experience, background, success rates, motivation and difficulties since they are registered under *formation initiale* and are therefore 'non-identified' and receiving no support. The group recommended that further information be collected in order to make the case for financial support and to persuade public authorities to take into account the difficulties such students face.

Subsequent surveys undertaken in the institutions represented in the group indicated that about 40 per cent of the students who were working were in their early twenties and were 'continuers' working for reasons of economic necessity; the remaining 60 per cent were 'returners' in their early thirties with an average break in studies of 12 years, were working full time and studying to improve their employment prospects. Women were in the majority in both groups (Davies 1994).

Clearly this phenomenon of adults in *la formation initiale*, largely unacknowledged in national policy terms, is nevertheless significant in institutional and individual terms and is possibly on the increase.

Conclusion

Whilst the legislation of the late 1960s and early 1970s gave attention to the social dimension of the role of universities in the education and training of adults, this theme became weaker following the oil crisis of 1974, and through the late 1970s and 1980s the economic objectives underlying the development of policy and practice clearly became more important. The key issue in relation to adults in *formation initiale* as well as more obviously in *formation continue* became their relationship to the labour market rather than their personal and social development. It should be noted, however, that the link between higher education and the labour market is strong since there is a close connection between qualifications and access to employment, particularly in the public sector. The achievement of qualifications is thus an important mechanism in the distribution of employment prospects. Coupled with the fundamental right of entry to higher education this tends to focus policy concerns for equality towards increasing the number qualified to enter *la formation initiale* at the 'front end' and to seek the eradication of regional differences at that point. Low retention rates focus institutional and individual concerns for equality and economic efficiency on the reform of the curriculum and on guidance and academic supervision to support students through higher education, and clearly those adults in *la formation initiale* benefit from such measures alongside younger students. However, it is *la formation continue* which provides the focus of policy for adults through the provision of alternative entry routes and the development of improved accessibility by offering programmes with much greater flexibility and diversity. It has also developed models of delivery and supervision for adults which are beginning to be applied to the mainstream. The extent to which these reforms and developments can be fully extended across a mass system is not yet clear, neither has their effectiveness in dealing with the problems yet been demonstrated.

Notes

1. The status of l'ESEU was changed in August 1994: it became a national diploma, *Diplôme d'Accès aux Etudes Universitaires* (DAEU).

References

Bordage, B. (1992) Continuing University Education in France: a dichotomous system, *Higher Education Management*, 4, 1, 71–79.
Caspar, P. (1992) France. In P. Jarvis (ed) *Perspectives on Adult Education and Training in Europe*. Leicester: NIACE.
Cerych, L. and Sabatier, P. (1986) *Great Expectations and Mixed Performance. The implementation of higher education reforms in Europe*. Stoke-on-Trent: Trentham Books.
Charlot, B. (1988) 80% niveau bac: derrière le symbole, quelles politiques? *Education Permanente*, 92, 91–108.

Conservatoire National des Arts et Metiers (CNAM) (1992) *Guide de l'Elève 1992–1993*. Paris: Ministère de l'Education nationale.

Cressard, A. (1994) 52% des jeunes sont bacheliers, *Le Monde de l'éducation – Spécial Bac*, January, 9–10.

Davies, P.A. (1994) *Access and participation of adults in higher education in France*. London: City University.

Dechy, G. (1990a) *L'ESEU dans la région Nord-Pas de Calais* (unpublished).

Dechy, G. (1990b) *De la Réussite après l'ESEU – enquête sur les reçus à l'ESEU en 1987 à l'université de Valenciennes et du Hainault Cambresis* (unpublished).

Dubar, C. and Wagnon, C. (1982) *Analyse du public de l'examen spécial d'entrée à l'université dans le Nord-Pas de Calais. Rapport Final 1982*. Lille: Université de Lille I, Institut de Sociologie.

Durand-Prinborgne, C. (1988) Evolution et juridification de l'enseignement supérieur en France, *European Journal of Education*, 23, 1/2, 105–123.

Freynet, P. (1991) The Training of Adult Educators in France. In P. Jarvis and A. Chadwick (eds) *Training Adult Educators in Western Europe*. London: Routledge.

Feutrie, M. (1993) Résultats de l'enquête sur les pratiques de validation des acquis professionels mises en oeuvre par les établissements d'enseignement supérieur. In M. Feutrie (ed) *Actes des journées de travail – validation des acquis professionels*. Lille: Université des Sciences et Technologies de Lille.

Flash Formation Continue (1992a) Validation des Acquis Professionels dans l'Enseignement Supérieur, *Flash Formation Continue*, 351, 15 October, 10–16.

Flash Formation Continue (1992b) Validation des Acquis Professionels dans l'Enseignement Supérieur (2), *Flash Formation Continue*, 353, 15 November, 13–15.

Groupe de Travail l'ESEU (1992) *Rapport du groupe – les résultats de l'enquête sur l'ESEU* (unpublished).

Groupe de Travail formation permanente (1982) *Loi d'orientation – Rapport du groupe de travail au chargé de mission au cabinet du Ministre de l'Education Nationale*. Paris: Formation Permanente, Université Paris 8.

Groupe de Travail pour le développement de l'accès des adultes dans l'enseignement supérieur et notamment par le congé individuel de formation (1986) *Adultes a l'Université – développer l'accès des adultes dans l'enseignement supérieur*. Toulouse: Service Publications Université de Toulouse-Le Mirail.

Groupe de Travail sous l'égide de la Conference des Directeurs de Services Universitaires de Formation Continue et le MEN (1990) *Adultes en Formation Initiale dans l'Enseignement Supérieur – Guide pratique à l'usage des établissements d'enseignements supérieur*. Toulouse: Université de Toulouse -Le Mirail.

Guin, J. (1990) The Re-awakening of Higher Education in France, *European Journal of Education, 25*, 2, 123–145.

Henderson, E. (1990) French failure rate alarms ministers. In *Times Higher Education Supplement*, 9 November.

Henderson, E. (1991) French unveil blueprint for expansion. In *Times Higher Education Supplement*, 17 May.

Henderson, E. (1993) Magnificent seven head French growth. In *Times Higher Education Supplement*, 22 January.

Jallade, J.P. (1991) *L'enseignement supérieur en Europe. Vers une évaluation comparée des premiers cycles.* Paris: La Documentation française.

Jallade, J.P. (1992) Undergraduate HE in Europe: towards a comparative perspective, *European Journal of Education, 27*, 1/2, 121–144.

Lacroix, B. (1990) Higher Education in France, *Contemporary European Affairs*, 3, 4, 143–154.

Lamoure, J. and Lamoure Rantopoulou, J. (1992) The Vocationalisation of HE in France: continuity and change, *European Journal of Education 27*, 1/2, 45–55.

Ministère de l'Education Nationale (MEN) (1990a) *Universités 2000 Quelle Université pour demain? Assises nationale de l'enseignement supérieur, Juin 1990*. Paris: La Documentation française.

Ministère de l'Education Nationale (MEN) (1990b) *La formation continue dans les établissements d'enseignement supérieur, au cours de l'année civile 1988* (Note d'Information 90–03). Paris: MEN, Direction de l'Evaluation et de la Prospective.

Ministère de l'Education Nationale (MEN) (1991a) *Repères et Références Statistiques sur l'enseignements et la formation*. Paris: MEN, Direction de l'Evaluation et de la Prospective.

Ministère de l'Education Nationale (MEN) (1991b) *La formation continue dans les établissements d'enseignement supérieur, au cours de l'année civile 1989* (Note d'Information 91–17). Paris: MEN, Direction de l'Evaluation et de la Prospective.

Ministère de l'Education Nationale (MEN) (1992a) *L'Education nationale en chiffres 1991–1992*. Paris: MEN.

Ministère de l'Education Nationale (MEN) (1992b) *La formation continue dans les établissements d'enseignement supérieur, au cours de l'année civile 1990*. (Note d'Information 92.19). Paris: MEN, Direction de l'Evaluation et de la Prospective.

Ministère de l'Education Nationale (MEN) (1993) *La formation continue dans les établissements d'enseignement supérieur, au cours de l'année civile 1991*. (Note d'Information 93.04). Paris: MEN, Direction de l'Evaluation et de la Prospective.

Neave, G (1985) France. In B.R. Clark (ed) *The School and the University: An international perspective*. London: University of California Press.

Neave, G. (1991) The reform of French higher education, or the Ox and the Toad: a fabulous tale. In G. Neave and F.A. van Vught (eds) *Prometheus*

Bound. *The Changing Relationship between Government and Higher Education in Western Europe.* Oxford: Pergamon Press.

Observatoire de la vie étudiante (1990) *Premier Rapport du Conseil de l'Observatoire de la vie étudiante.* Paris: Observatoire de la vie étudiante.

Sahli, A.M. (1993) *La réussite en DEUG – cohorte 1988.* Strasbourg: Institut de démographie de l'Université des Sciences Humaines de Strasbourg.

Service Universitaire de Formation Continue (SUFOC) et le Centre de Recherche sur l'Emploi et la Production (CRESEP) (1989) *Que sont devenues les personnes qui ont preparé l'examen spécial d'accès aux études universitaires (ESEU) en 1986–87.* Orléans: Université d'Orléans.

Starapoli, A. (1987) The Comité National d'Evaluation: preliminary results of a French experiment, *European Journal of Education,* 22, 2, 123–131.

Titmus, C. (1979) The social role of higher education in lifelong education: the present state of French University Adult Education, *Adult Education,* 52, 4, 251–257.

Chapter 7

Germany

Pat Davies and Evelyn Reisinger

The higher education system in the Federal Republic of Germany is based on cooperation between the federal government (*Bund*) and the respective states and city states (*Länder*). While the federal authorities provide the legal framework, the *Länder* provide detailed legislation. All institutions of higher education – except colleges of the armed forces, church-run colleges and other private institutions of higher education – are *Länder* facilities supervised and funded mainly by the *Länder* ministries of education. The laws of the individual *Länder* must comply with federal legislation, but certain aspects vary to such an extent that it would be possible to speak of sixteen different (higher) education systems.

The Institutions of Higher Education

The institutions of higher education (*Hochschulen*)[1] in Germany are public corporations with the right to self-government, basically non-competitive and 'include all institutions (public and private) as defined in the higher education act of the *Land* concerned' (Federal Ministry of Education and Science 1992 p.66).

This covers:

- *Universitäten/Hochschulen* (universities), including colleges specialising in medicine, veterinary medicine, theology, administrative sciences and sports sciences
- *Technische Universitäten/Hochschulen* (technical universities)
- *Gesamthochschulen* (comprehensive universities), including the Open University (*FernUniversität-Gesamthochschule*) in Hagen, which combine the characteristics of *Universitäten* and *Fachhochschulen*
- *Kunsthochschulen* and *Musikhochschulen* (colleges of art and colleges of music)

- *Pädagogische Hochschulen* (colleges of education)
- *Fachhochschulen* (originally schools of engineering and other technical subjects, now mainly offering courses in engineering and technology-related subjects, business management and social work), which offer practice-orientated degree courses and applied research
- *Fachhochschulen für Öffentliche Verwaltung* (colleges of public administration).

In addition there are a number of special institutions outside the responsibility of the *Länder*:

- *Bundeswehrhochschulen* (colleges of the Armed Forces)
- Non-state-funded universities: church-run institutions and private institutions of higher education.

In 1991 there were a total of 315 institutions of higher education in Germany, of which 114 were *Fachhochschulen*, 99 were universities (including one comprehensive university) and 62 were private institutions (Federal Ministry of Education and Science 1992).

Higher Education Courses and Qualifications

There are essentially two types of higher education degree programmes: *Fachhochschul-Diplom* and the University *Diplom*/degrees (for further details see van Resandt 1991).

The *Fachhochschul* degree:

- has a 'standard time' for completion of four years (eight semesters)
- includes (depending on the *Land*) one or two semesters of practical training
- has a high level of contact time
- is a tightly structured programme in which attendance is monitored
- is vocationally/professionally oriented.

The University degree:

- has a 'standard time' for completion of five to six years, according to subject; an average student takes about seven years
- is not limited by a set time allowed for completion (although there is a time limit for the student grant)
- has more loosely structured courses

- has open access to lectures
- has less monitoring of attendance.

In addition there are differences in entry requirements and in the currency and status of a degree from the two different institutions.

At the moment there is a trend amongst new entrants to choose *Fachhochschulen*. This is due to the current economic climate, in which shorter, more practice-oriented courses seem to offer better job prospects, as well as to the fact that industry is keen on graduates from *Fachhochschulen* (Gloger and Scherer 1992, Wissenschaftsrat 1991).

Funding and Student Support

Institutions of higher education (except private ones) do not charge course fees. Resources and funding are provided by the Länder, the federal government and, to some extent (especially for research) by third parties. (For details of public expenditure on higher education see BMBW 1992b.) The federation is responsible for student (and pupil) support under the Federal Education Assistance Act (*Bundesausbildungsförderungsgesetz* (BAföG) 1971). This federal financial support for students is means-tested and from 1983–1990 it was granted to those in higher education in the form of a loan. In 1990 it was changed to a 50 per cent grant and 50 per cent interest-free loan through an amendment to the law. Since this change the number of pupils and students in the 'old *Länder*'[2] who receive *BAföG* has risen: from 328,000 in 1990 to 420,000 in 1991. In the new *Länder* approximately 180,000 pupils and students receive *BAföG* (Harenberg 1992). The length of the period for which financial assistance is granted is determined by the specific regulations regarding the 'standard study time' (*Regelstudienzeit*) and thus varies depending on the type of course. As few students complete their courses within the 'standard study time', support is usually granted for one or two semesters longer. With some exceptions, laid down in the Federal Education Assistance Act, students who are over 30 when they start their course are not eligible for support (BMBW 1991).

Expansion

The expansion of the higher education system started in the 1960s, due to labour market needs as well as a political demand for equal opportunities and mass education. The 1970s saw an increase in buildings and equipment, student numbers and the provision of financial assistance to students and parents through *BAföG* (Karpen

1988). In 1977 the *Länder* and federal governments stressed their commitment to opening up *Hochschulen*, despite the high number of school-leavers, with a decree to open up the higher education system, the so-called *Öffnungsbeschluß* (Führ 1989). This decision was based on forecasts that student numbers would decrease due to a fall in the birth rate. However, student numbers continued to rise throughout the 1980s as a consequence of an increase in participation and in the average study time of seven years (see for example Canibol and Krumrey 1992). The percentage of German school-leavers with higher education entrance qualifications who actually go into higher education from school has dropped from 90 per cent in the early 1970s to just under 80 per cent (BMBW 1992a, HIS 1992). This may be due to the relative decline of importance of the *Abitur* as the 'king's way' (*Königsweg*) into higher education once a more diverse secondary education system had created a more diverse body of school-leavers (Karpen 1988). However, the drop has been offset by the increasing number of people holding such qualifications. Table 7.1 shows the scale of expansion both in the number of new entrants and in the total student population in recent years in the old *Länder* and the impact of unification on the size of the system.

Table 7.1: Entrants and student population in higher education 1970–91

Year	Old Länder				Old and New Länder			
	New entrants		Students		New entrants		Students	
	1000	%[1]	1000	%[2]	1000	%[1]	1000	%[2]
1970	125.7	15.4	510.5	9.5				
1980	195.0	19.1	1044.2	15.9				
1990	278.2	32.2	1585.2	22.0	317.7	29.6	1717.4	19.6
1991	271.2	33.7	1647.0	24.3	307.9	31.0	1782.7	21.3
% increase 1979–91	115.8%	118.8%	222.6%	164.4%				

[1] Percentage of 19–21 age cohort
[2] Percentage of 19–26 age cohort
Source: Federal Ministry of Education and Science 1992

With changes in the labour market and a tighter public expenditure policy in the 1980s and 1990s, buildings, staff and study places were not increased in line with the rise in student numbers. In 1991 over

1.7 million students had to share just 900,000 study places (*Der Spiegel* 50/1991). The teacher–student ratio in the old *Länder* increased from 1:10 (1:16 at *Fachhochschulen*) in 1977 to 1:16 (1:39 at *Fachhochschulen*) in 1991–92; and in the new *Länder* the overall ratio is 1:20 (Harenberg 1992). The number of students is still increasing – 1,800,000 in the academic year 1992–93 despite the drop in new entrants in 1991. This situation has led to widespread dissatisfaction amongst students and teachers in higher education, industry and the public, and has sparked a debate in the national and foreign press (see *Der Spiegel* 50/91 and 16/93, Gardner 1993, Gow 1991), in the government and in the agencies and bodies engaged in higher education.

Participation

Consideration of recent studies and statistics about higher education in Germany must take into account the significantly different conditions in the area of the former GDR and at the same time provide information on the 'new' unified Germany. Figures are given separately for the east (the new *Länder*) and the west (the old *Länder*), as statements about the Federal Republic as a whole 'would in most cases lead to a distortion of reality' (HIS 1992 p.3). In addition, while statistics distinguish between German and foreign students (including the children of migrant workers, *Bildungsinländer*), no figures are available on ethnic group participation.

Age

In 1991, the percentage of the 19 to under 26 age group enrolled in higher education was 24.3 per cent for the old *Länder* before reunification, 9.1 per cent for the new *Länder*, and 21.3 per cent for Germany after reunification (BMBW statistics do not include figures for students over 26). The low level of participation in the new *Länder* must be seen in the context of admission restrictions imposed by the former government (HIS 1992). The percentage of the 19–21 year old age group who were new entrants in 1991 was 33.7 per cent in the west, 19.2 per cent in the east, and 31.0 per cent in both areas combined (BMBW 1992a).

Due to the length of study time and later entrance into higher education, German students as a whole tend to lead 'adult' lives: in 1991, 7 per cent of students in the old *Länder* were married, 23 per cent lived in a stable relationship, 6 per cent had children. In the new *Länder*, 13 per cent were married, 26 per cent lived in a stable relationship, and 11 per cent had children. Thirty-five per cent of students in the west (though only 8% in the east) were aged 26 or over. In the summer semester of 1991, 66 per cent of all students in the west and 23 per cent in the east were in some form of paid employment (HIS 1992).

Gender

The percentage of female students in higher education in the old *Länder* rose from 30.2 per cent in 1972 to 38.3 per cent in 1990. In the winter semester 1991–92 the percentage of female students in Germany was 38.7 per cent rising to 44.3 per cent in the new *Länder* (Bundesministerium für Frauen und Jugend 1992).

However, participation varies strongly according to subject. Women are under-represented in engineering and the technical and natural sciences and over-represented, for instance, in language studies and teaching degrees, especially in the old *Länder*; in the new *Länder* women participated to a much greater extent in technical subjects (HIS 1993). Furthermore, the percentage falls as the level of qualification rises: in the west, women constitute 28 per cent of doctorate awards and 10 per cent of 'habilitations' (a post-doctoral qualification for those wishing to follow an academic teaching career); in the east, 36 per cent of doctorate and 13 per cent of 'habilitations' (Bundesministerium für Frauen und Jugend 1992).

Social background

There are clearly difficulties in comparing data relating to the old and new *Länder*, since for the latter the data are somewhat unreliable. In addition, definitions of 'lower' and 'higher' social backgrounds are not neutral concepts but rather are applied in the context of political ideologies. Despite these caveats, Figure 7.1 shows that the participation in the former GDR was lower in all social groups, including among the children of workers (7.7% compared to 11.8%). This is seen as a 'clear indication that access to studies in the ex-GDR was socially highly selective' (HIS 1992 p.10).

Changes in the pattern of participation over time in the former GDR cannot readily be evaluated since 'no sufficiently reliable data exist' (HIS 1992 p.10). In the west, the participation rate for children of workers rose slowly from a very low level between 1985 and 1989; in 1990, however, it rose by 36 per cent (from 8.7% to 11.8% overall). This is seen partly as a result of the change in the *BAföG* system at that time from loan to part grant/part interest free loan.

Germany

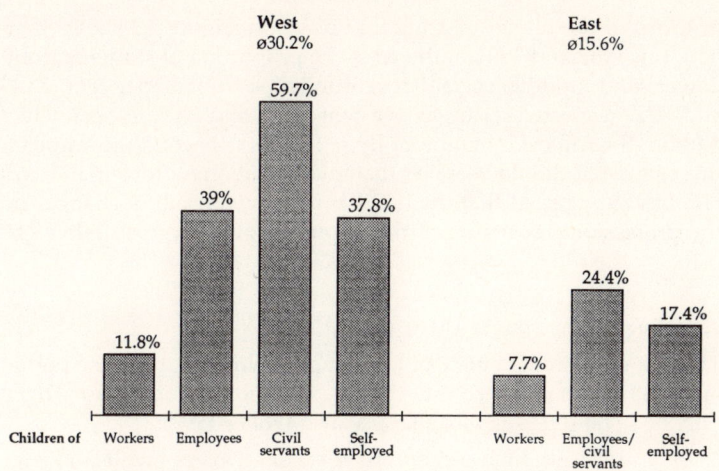

Note: These figures represent the number of entrants into higher education as a percentage of the corresponding age cohort in the same social group, 1990

Source: HIS 1992

Figure 7.1: Social background of entrants – 1990

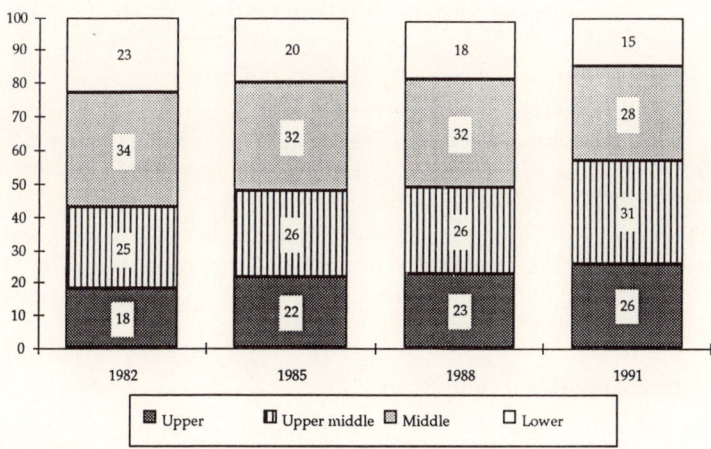

Note: The term 'lower' social background refers to students with parents who are workers, employees or lower- or middle-ranking civil servants. 'Middle' social background means that parents are in lower or middle management, higher-ranking civil servants, 'small-scale self-employed persons or members of the liberal professions with low incomes' (HIS 1992 p.10)

Source: HIS 1992

Figure 7.2: Social background of student population in higher education, 1982–91 (old Länder)

In terms of the higher education population, Figure 7.2 shows that between 1982 and 1991 in the west the proportion of students from 'lower' and 'middle' social backgrounds fell from 57 per cent (23% and 34% respectively) to 43 per cent (15% and 28% respectively). Although a full examination of these figures is beyond the scope of this chapter, it should be noted that interpretation is problematic and HIS have suggested that the fall is primarily a 'result of changes in the professional structure of the population as a whole' (HIS 1992 p.10).

Targeting
There is no national policy of targeting specific groups of the population as far as entrance into higher education is concerned. There may be several reasons for this (see also Wolter 1990):

- the already high percentage of school-leavers – male and female – with entrance qualifications
- the current number of students and the precarious financial situation which has been made worse by reunification
- a 'targeting through the system' through the establishment of *Fachhochschulen*, which draw more students from 'working class' backgrounds than from universities (Karpen 1988)
- the relative homogeneity of the population
- the long tradition of the Humboldt humanist educational ideal, whose supporters are strongly in favour of general (as opposed to vocational) education as a precondition for higher education studies.

There are however a great number of charitable trusts with various political or religious links that provide financial support for eligible students from particular groups.

Admission: Rights and Restrictions

Access and admission to higher education in Germany are to a considerable extent determined by the constitution: Article 12, 3 of the Basic Law guarantees Germans 'the right freely to choose their trade, occupation, or profession, their place of work and their place of training', and according to the 1976 Framework Act for Higher Education, every German citizen with the necessary higher education entrance qualification has a legal right to higher education and therefore to a study place if available. *Hochschulen* are thus legally obliged to take as many students as possible (Karpen 1988). Five year interim arrangements regarding the legal details of admission restrictions have been made for the new *Länder* to bring them into line with the west.

Until recently, school leavers with higher education entrance qualifications were able to study any subject at any institution, provided that they fulfilled all the relevant requirements. With the increase in the last three decades in numbers of school leavers holding higher education entrance qualifications this has changed, and in subjects where demand exceeds the available study places, admission is restricted through the so-called *numerus clausus*. Such restrictions may apply nationwide, as for instance in medicine, or to certain *Länder* or even individual *Hochschulen*.

Study places for restricted subjects are allocated in complex procedures through the Central Office of Admission (*Zentralstelle für die Vergabe von Studienplätzen, ZVS*) in Dortmund. If prospective students do not agree with the decision of the *ZVS* they can take legal action. The criteria for distribution include achievement (measured by the average grade of the entrance qualification exam), aptitude (measured by the average grade and a test), waiting time and, in some cases, interviews carried out by the institution. There are quota for specific groups of applicants, for example those who may face 'unusual, in particular social, hardship' if not admitted, and for foreign and stateless students. Exactly what constitutes 'social hardship' is not defined in the Framework Act.

Traditionally, institutions of higher education play no part in the selection of their students except in courses where there are aptitude tests. However, in 1991–92 teachers at *Hochschulen* suggested that their institutions have more decision-making power in the selection process in order to restrict access. This was a reaction to the growing number of school leavers with higher education entrance qualifications and the fear of some that the high number of students might 'devalue' higher education degrees. As an experiment, *Hochschulen* were allowed to allocate approximately 15 per cent of study places in economics and information technology courses in the winter semester 1992–93 (Harenberg 1992). The impact of this policy is not yet clear.

Entry Qualifications: The 'First Educational Route'

In Germany there are basically two types of pathway into higher education: the traditional 'first educational route' (*Erster Bildungsweg*), and two 'alternative' routes, the so-called 'second' and 'third educational route' (*Zweiter* and *Dritter Bildungsweg*). The most common route is via a higher education entrance qualification, gained through a final exam (*Abitur*) at a general or vocational upper level secondary education school (including private schools). As Table 7.2 shows, over 90 per cent of new entrants (in the old *Länder*) gain their higher education entrance qualification via this 'first educational route' (BMBW 1992a). The alternative routes – chosen by only a small number of students, but nevertheless a current political issue – are discussed in more detail below.

In the 'first route' there are three types of higher entrance qualifica-

Table 7.2: Entrants to higher education, 1990 (old *Länder*)

Entry route	German students		Foreign students*	
	No	%	No	%
'First route'	197,914	92.7	17,167	92.8
'Second route'	5,124	2.4	204	1.1
'Third route'	10,462	4.9	1,129	6.1
Total	213,500	100	18,500	100

* including children of migrant workers, who were educated in Germany (*Bildungsinländer*)

Source: BMBW 1992

tions – general, subject specific and vocational – and the different types of *Hochschulen* have different requirements for admission (Bund-Länder-Kommission für Bildungsplanung und Forschungsförderung und Bundesanstalt für Arbeit 1992, Führ 1989, van Resandt 1991).

The general entry qualification, *Allgemeine Hochschulreife*, commonly referred to as the *Abitur* is normally gained in a *Gymnasium* (grammar school) and gives access to all types of higher education. The subject specific qualification, *Fachgebundene Hochschulreife*, gives access to all types of institution but only courses in related subjects. The vocational qualification, *Fachhochschulreife*, gives access to vocationally oriented courses in *Fachhochschulen* or the *Gesamthochschule*.

In addition to the entry qualifications, applicants for art-related courses and sports courses must also pass an aptitude test. Applicants with proof of above-average artistic talent but without an entrance qualification can gain admission by passing a special entrance exam. *Fachhochschulen* usually require a period of work experience besides the entrance qualification. In individual cases, people with disabilities who do not hold traditional entrance qualifications may gain admission to *Fachhochschulen* through rehabilitation schemes.

Alternative Entry: The Second and Third Educational Routes

In the context of alternative routes into higher education, the specific group of adults who decide to become students are defined as adults 'who have work experience but no traditional entry qualifications' (Teichler 1990 p.34) 'Mature entrants' as defined by the OECD are 'adult students with work experiences' who hold no traditional higher education entrance qualifications (Kluge *et al.* 1990 p.9). However, these definitions are narrowed down in practice since the criteria for what is considered to be 'work experience' in the context of access are quite specific. Although regulations vary considerably in the individual *Länder* (see below), 'work experience' generally means work in a job that requires vocational training and qualifications, and the minimum age is usually specified as 24 or 25 (KMK 1992). 'Vocationally qualified mature entrants' would therefore be a more appropriate term, but for reasons of convenience the German term *Berufserfahrene* is used (literally, 'people with work experience', but also used in the specific context of alternative educational routes; see for example Kluge *et al.* 1990). It will be used here to refer to (future) full-time or part-time adult students in higher education who are vocationally qualified, have work experience and do not have traditional higher education entrance qualifications.

Berufserfahrene can enter higher education via the 'second educational route' or the 'third educational route'. Definitions of the 'second' and the 'third' educational routes have changed over the years and are somewhat blurred because the routes themselves have gradually changed and developed. The broad distinction between the two paths is that the 'second route' follows the syllabus of the grammar schools and is mainly offered at two 'classic' institutions of adult education: the *Kolleg* and the evening grammar school (*Abendgymnasium*). It normally takes two to three years to complete and leads to the *Abitur* qualification, thus conferring the right to study a subject of their choice and the right to a certain level of pay and conditions in employment, particularly in the public sector. On the other hand, the 'third route' takes into account the professional experience of the future student and is based on cooperation between institutions of adult education and institutions of higher education. It is shorter than the 'second route' and confers eligibility to study specific subjects rather than a general right of entry. There are also more variations between *Länder* in this route. In reality, the border between the two routes is blurred because alternative entry to higher education is regulated by two different fields of legislation: school legislation and higher education legislation. Whereas all procedures under higher education legislation belong to the 'third route', some of the examinations under school legislation are part of 'the second route' and some part of the 'third route'. This causes a problem, especially with examinations which lead to a *general* higher education entrance qualification, since even if they are intended for *Berufserfahrene*, they tend to imitate the traditional *Abitur* and are therefore less geared towards working adults than they should be ideally (Wolter 1990).

The 'second route'

The 'second route' mirrors the first route in that it consists of programmes leading to the *Abitur* (the general or subject-specific version). The difference is its location: the programmes are offered in *Kolleg*, daytime adult colleges; *Abendgymnasium* evening grammar schools; or *Volkshochschulen*, adult centres (including distance learning provision).

The 'second educational route' is undoubtedly an important route for a small number of adults (see Table 7.2): in 1990, 2.4 per cent of new entrants (German nationals) and 1.1 per cent of new entrants (foreign nationals, including *Bildungsinländer*) gained their entrance qualification at evening grammar schools or *Kollegs* in the Western *Länder* (Federal Ministry of Education and Science 1992). It is complementary to, rather than in competition with, the 'third educational route' but has been criticised on a number of grounds. Since it imitates the grammar school model it strengthens the monopoly of the *Abitur* while neither meeting the needs nor taking into account the experience and skills of vocationally qualified working adults.

While the *Abitur* in the 'first route' is usually examined internally (set and marked by teachers), within the 'second route' some *Länder* have external examinations and these tend to have lower pass rates.

In addition, the inflexibility in the length of the preparatory course (two or three years minimum) creates later difficulties in employment opportunities. By the time adults have completed their higher education studies (four years minimum in a *Fachhochschule* and five or six years in a university) they are likely to be too old for many posts in the public sector which usually have an age limit for entry of 32 or 35.

The 'third route'

Under school legislation there are a number of special provisions limited to vocational courses and qualifications leading to *Fachhochscule* entrance in specific subjects. Two warrant reference here. The 'Exam for the Specially Competent in Employment' (*Prüfung für den Hochschulzugang von besonders befähigten Berüfstätigen*) is for those have special 'talent' and 'personality' and have acquired, through work, the knowledge necessary for their future studies. Preparation for the examination is offered at some adult education centres. The exam was introduced in the time of the Weimar Republic and newly regulated most recently in 1987. It has been criticised on grounds similar to those used in relation to the 'second route' – that it strengthens the *Abitur*, and also that it creates the notion of the 'special personality' which an adult without traditional entrance qualification supposedly needs in order to succeed in higher education (Kluge *et al*. 1990, Wolter 1990). As applicants have no formal assessment before they are admitted to the examination, it is not quite clear how they can prove their 'special competence' – except by passing the examination itself. However, only a very small number of adults enter higher education that way – 0.3 per cent of new entrants of German nationality, 0.5 per cent of new entrants of foreign nationality (including *Bildungsinländer*) in 1990 (Federal Ministry of Education and Science 1992) – and in the current debate on access it is not highly significant for that reason. A notable exception is in Bremen, where measures such as preparation at adult education centres and credit for family care have increased the number of successful applicants.

Hamburg and Niedersachsen did not adopt this examination but instead introduced their own arrangements: Hamburg under higher education legislation (see below), and Niedersachsen a subject-specific entrance exam, the so-called 'Z-Exam' (*Befähigungsprüfung zum Hochschulstudium ohne Reifezeugnis*, or *Z-Prüfung*) was introduced in 1971. The notion of 'time credit' is significant here since the regulations normally require work experience before the examination can be attempted. Time credit allows time spent on family care and/or bringing up children to count as work experience for these purposes. The *Z-Prüfung* is subject-specific and takes into account the skills and work experiences of the applicants; preparation for the exam is institutionalised and takes place at adult education institutions in co-operation with *Hochschulen*. The examination boards consist of one teacher from a school offering the *Abitur* exam, one from a *Hochschule* and one from an adult education institution.

The *Z-Prüfung* plays an important part in the debate on the 'third route' because the Federal Ministry of Education and Science and the Niedersachsen Ministry of Education commissioned the University of Oldenburg to carry out research on this model at the beginning of the 1980s – the only collection of data on the progress and experiences of *Berufserfahrene* available to date that goes beyond merely quantitative analysis (KMK 1992). The research provides arguments in favour of higher education entrance for *Berufserfahrene* in the present discussion on opening up the system. It disproves fears that student numbers may soar and quality standards will fall. According to the research, *Berufserfahrene* are equally successful and more determined than their 'traditional' colleagues, whether or not their courses are related to their former work. These results are important in a context where the notion of 'maturity' and 'ability to study' gained through 'general education' has such a strong tradition. As far as equal opportunities are concerned, this model is especially attractive for women (Wolter 1990, Reibstein 1990).

Within the higher education regulations there is considerable variation between the *Länder* although in general the forms of examinations and interviews do not imitate the *Abitur* but are tailored, to varying degrees, to the needs and aspirations of vocationally qualified adults with work experience (*Berufserfahrene*). It is notable that more opportunities exist in the *Länder* under SPD control (see Reisinger and Davies 1994 for further details). While in most *Länder*, the 'third route' offers access to most higher education institutions, in some, admission from the 'third route' is restricted to *Fachhochschulen* or Colleges of Education.

There are two types of alternative model within this framework. First, there are 'trial studies' (*Probestudium*) where entrants are provisionally registered for one to four semesters; if these are successfully completed the students can fully register and obtain credit for the provisional time. Second, there are various types of entry examinations – the aptitude test (*Eignungsprüfung*), the classification test (*Einstufungsprüfung*) – or interviews/'advisory talk' (*Beratungsgespräch*) the aptitude interview (*Eignungsgespräch*).

To be eligible for all these arrangements, applicants must be of a minimum age and must have vocational qualifications and several years of work experience. Time for family care and/or the rearing of children is credited as work experience in five *Länder*. In Bremen and Hamburg there are special possibilities for master craftsmen or technicians (*Meister*) and people with equivalent vocational qualifications.

Regulations vary considerably in a number of ways, for example in the degree to which examinations differ from the traditional general *Abitur* and in the conditions for admission (age, years of work experience/family care, qualifications, additional vocational continuing education, residence in the respective *Land*). The similarity lies in the fact that most regulations place considerable emphasis on the part of the examination/interview that deals with the subject the applicant wishes to study; that work experience and 'key qualifications' are taken into account; and that examination boards consist of representatives of *Hochschulen*, of different types of educational institutions and/or of industry, and of vocational education and training authorities.

The whole concept of the 'third route' is strongly linked to the notion that general and vocational education and training should be of equal status and that work-based learning – the acquisition of 'key qualifications' – is an essential element of the 'ability to study.' It is in fact a condition of admission, and as such a restrictive factor: for example, unskilled workers are excluded. It is also important to note that these regulations and opportunities do not confer the same rights as the *Abitur* in other contexts, such as public sector employment. However, the issue of skills and vocational qualifications is important in an education system where general, that is, academic, education leading to the *Abitur* has traditionally been the key to higher education and has been regarded as superior to vocational training (Wolter 1990).

Alternative Higher Education Provision

In general, the higher education system in Germany is geared towards full-time students. This has led to the paradoxical situation whereby a great many students – 'traditional' students as well as *Berufserfahrene* – are in employment and studying part-time in full-time courses, having to adjust course timetables to work commitments and vice versa, which often adds a number of semesters to their studies.

The Science Council has acknowledged that a concept which is exclusively based on full-time courses is far from today's reality of student life and has therefore demanded new forms of courses enabling students to combine employment and/or childcare with study, and has recommended that alternative routes and part-time and evening preparatory courses are kept open or extended where necessary (Wissenschaftsrat 1991, 1993).

Institutions offering courses designed for *Berufserfahrene* who do not wish to give up work at present include

- The Open University (*FernUniversität/Gesamthochschule*) at Hagen (with study centres in a number of towns all over Germany) offers modularised distance learning programmes, including a part-time extended version

- *Fachhochschulen* offering 'evening study courses parallel to work' (*berufsbegleitende Abendstudiengänge*)
- *Fachhochschulen* offering 'work-integrating' courses (*berufsintegrierendes Studium*) with part-time, evening and Saturday courses
- *Fachhochschulen* offering courses combined with vocational training at companies.

All these programmes are designed for business management studies and engineering. Exceptions are social studies courses for employed people at one Protestant and one Catholic *Fachhochschule*.

In addition, there are a number of institutions which focus exclusively on employed people:

- *Hochschulen* for Working Adults in Baden-Württemberg, Sachsen and Schleswig-Holstein, which are state-recognised private *Fachhochschulen* offering distance studies, decentralised seminars at their study centres and flexible study time for working students
- *Hochschule für Wirtschaft und Politik* (history and politics) in Hamburg where students can choose between full-time studies and a 'courses parallel to work' model (*berufsbegleitendes Studium*) with evening and weekend classes and classes during educational leave. This institution also has a tradition of allowing a 60 per cent quota for students without the traditional qualifications (Epskamp 1990).

To date, the majority of part-time courses are offered for economics-, science- and technology-related courses and are not available in the universities. However, in its recent statement concerning higher education policy, the Science Council suggested the introduction of such courses including humanities and the use of distance learning modules (Wissenschaftsrat 1993).

Policy Debates and Developments

The recent and current policy debates relating to widening access for adults are underpinned by two key factors: the economic climate and traditional concepts of the ability to study.

Although there are differences between institutions, on average German students spend an average of seven years in higher education (theoretically there is no time limit) and graduate aged 27.9 years. This feature, coupled with the increase in entrants and unification has meant an enormous increase in costs at a time of economic recession.

Hence, much of the debate has focused on shortening study, and increasing the use of *numerus clausus* (Harenberg 1992).

Access to higher education has traditionally been based on the concept of the 'ability to study', acquired through a grammar school providing academic knowledge and the education of the 'personality'. This process culminated in the *Abitur*, the *Reifeprüfung*, or 'maturity examination'. Although these traditions have been weakened by mass education, and by the development of the vocational schools and the *Fachhochschulen*, the distinction between general/academic and vocational education, and consequently, careers, remains clear in terms of status and financial rewards (Scholz 1993).

Despite the strength of these factors, both the dominating force of the *Abitur* and the resulting discrimination of vocational education and training have been questioned. Social democrats and the trade unions, as the representatives of the 'working class', have had equal educational opportunities and therefore the equivalence of vocational and academic education on their agenda since the 1920s; they have published a number of statements on the issue and have worked on the implementation of their demands. Other institutions such as the Federal Institute for Vocational Education and Training (*Bundesinstitut für Berufsbildung*) and individual *Länder*, in particular Niedersachsen and other *Länder* under non-conservative governments, have held the same views (Fehrenbach 1990).

But it was support from industry and commerce that put the final pressure for change on the federal and *Länder* governments. This happened for a particular reason: the changing technological environment and the challenge of EC competition were seen to require an increasing number of highly qualified workers and professionals, and industry and commerce were concerned about the lack of skilled workers. Thus labour market demands have finally sparked a public debate on the issue. The Association of German Chambers of Industry and Commerce (*Deutscher Industrie- und Handelstag*) demanded in a paper in 1990 that measures be taken to put the idea of equivalence of vocational training into practice (*Deutscher Industrie- und Handelstag* 1990). Industry argues that vocational qualifications in the 'dual system' have reached unprecedentedly high standards, equalling the *Abitur*, and should therefore open up the same educational opportunities as the *Abitur*. This view is supported by studies on access to higher education, where a 'functional' approach to qualification replaces the concepts of 'maturity' (Deutscher Industrie- und Handelstag 1990, Schmidt 1991, Wolter 1993). Industry and commerce hope that by making higher education more accessible to *Berufserfahrene*, vocational training will lose its so-called 'dead end quality' (*Sackgassencharakter*, a term used to illustrate the fact that vocational qualifications alone do not provide access to higher education) and will therefore become more attractive. The objective is seen in terms of raising the status of vocational qualifications and therefore recruiting higher numbers to the vocational route rather than admitting more people into the academic route.

There is now a basic consensus amongst the decision-making bodies and the parties consulted on the issue that higher education must be opened for *Berufserfahrene* and that the Higher Education Framework Act has to be amended accordingly in order to guarantee nationwide implementation (KMK 1993).

The Social Democrats introduced to parliament a draft for an amendment to the national legislation, stating that vocationally qualified people with 'special professional qualifications' should be 'provisionally' admitted to higher education courses for up to four semesters and should gain final admission if they completed this period successfully. Several reasons were given for the amendment: first, that access without traditional entrance qualifications will promote the equality of general/academic and vocational education, and, as a consequence promote equal opportunities 'in the sense of equal access to tertiary education'; second, that motivations for taking up higher education studies and learning opportunities have changed; and third, that the new regulations are more suitable to the changing requirements of the European single market (GEW 1992).

While there is widespread consensus about the need for change, there are nevertheless concerns, particularly among the unions in higher education and among Rectors, that in the current economic climate such changes cannot be introduced without loss of quality. It is also not clear how such policies could be implemented on a national basis since there are also several contradictions in the theory and practice of opening access which will need to be addressed in the development of such policies. First, while the new policy is intended to raise the status of vocational education and training and thus attract more students with a vocational background, it is at the same time hoped that there will be only few students taking this chance because the system is already full. Second, although industry and commerce lament the lack of skilled workers, they still award higher salaries and status to graduates than to people with vocational qualifications gained in the 'dual system'. The same holds true for employees in the civil service, where chances of promotion are linked with qualifications and degrees (Canibol and Krumrey 1992, Gloger and Scherer 1992). Third, the policy of raising the status of vocational education and training through access for *Berufserfahrene* may in itself be contradictory because it might further stress the importance of academic and higher education (GEW 1992).

Notes

1 The term *Hochschulen* is used in the generic sense to refer to all institutions of higher education. *Fachhochschulen* are referred to as such, in order to distinguish them from *Universitäten/Hochschulen*, which offer doctoral degrees. The latter are referred to as 'universities'.

2 The term 'old *Länder*' is used here to denote that part of Germany which, before unification in October 1990, formed the Federal Republic (West Germany); the 'new *Länder*' is that which previously constituted the GDR (East Germany).

References

Bundesminister für Bildung und Wissenschaft (BMBW) (1991) *Neues BAfög 91–92* (The new Federal Education Assistance Act) Bonn: BMBW.

Bundesminister für Bildung und Wissenschaft (BMBW) (1992a) Grund- und Strukturdaten 1992–93 (Basic and Structural Data, German edition) Bonn: BMBW.

Bundesminister für Bildung und Wissenschaft (BMBW) (1992b) *Zahlenbarometer. Ein bildungsstatistischen Überblikk* (Numerical Barometer. Some educational statistics). Bonn: BMBW.

Bundesministerium für Frauen und Jugend (1992) *Frauen in der Bundesrepublik Deutschland* (Women in the Federal Republic of Germany). Bonn: Bundesministerium für Frauen und Jugend.

Bund-Länder-Kommission für Bildungsplanung und Forschungsförderung und Bundesanstalt für Arbeit (1992) *Studien- und Berufswahl 1992–92* (Choosing courses in higher education and professions). Bad Honnef: Verlag Karl Heinrich Bock.

Canibol, H. and Krumrey, H. (1992) Studium für Maurer. In *Wirtschaftswoche*, *18*, 24 April, 40–48.

Deutscher Industrie- und Handelstag (1990) *Hochschulzugang für Absolventen des Dualen Systems. 11 Thesen für eine größere Durchlässigkeit der Bildungsebene* (Access to higher education for people who have qualified in the 'dual system'. 11 propositions for a greater interchangeability in education). In Bundesinstitut für Berufsbildung (BIBB) (1992) *Gleichwertigkeit beruflicher und allgemeiner Bildung. Hochschulzugang für Berufserfahrene. Stellungnahmen und Vorschläge zur Verwirklichung* (Equivalence of vocational and general education. Access to higher education for *Berufserfahrene*. Statements and suggestions for implementation). Berlin and Bonn: BIBB.

Epskamp, H. (1990) *Der Verzicht auf den Zweiten Bildungsweg: Das Konzept der Hochschule für Wirtschaft und Politik* (Renouncing the 'second educational route': the programme of the University for Economics and Politics). In Kluge *et al.* (eds) 261–275.

Federal Ministry of Education and Science (1992) *Basic and Structural Data 1992–93*. Bonn: Federal Ministry of Education and Science.

Fehrenbach, G. (1990) *Berufliche Qualifikation und Hochschulzugang -Bildungspolitische Entwicklung und Perspektiven aus gewerkschaftlicher Sicht* (Vocational qualification and access to higher education – development of education policies and prospects from a trade union point of view). In Kluge *et al.* 291–303.

Führ, C. (1989) *Schools and Institutions of Higher Education in the Federal Republic of Germany*. Bonn: Inter Nationes.

Gardner, M. (1993) Germans limit study time. *Times Higher Education Supplement*, 2 July.

Gewerkschaft Erziehung und Wissenschaft (GEW) (ed) (1992) *Hochschulzugang für Berufstätige – Anhörung zur 4. HRG-Novelle, 11. November 1992* (Access to higher education for working adults – plenary on the 4th amendment to the Framework Act for Higher Education, 11th November. Frankfurt: GEW.

Gloger, A. und Scherer, H. (1992) Heimliche Stars (Secret stars). *Wirtschaftswoche*, 16, 4 April, 56–58.

Gow, D. (1991) A head start threatened. *The Guardian*, 30 June.

Harenberg, B. (ed) (1992) *Aktuell 93. Das Lexikon der Gegenwart*. (Encyclopedia 1993). Dortmund: Harenberg Lexikon-Verlag.

Hochschul-Informations-System (HIS) GMBH (1992) Schnitzer, K. *et al. Social Conditions of Students in Germany. Summary of the 13th Social Survey of the Deutsches Studentenwerk in 1991*. Hannover: HIS.

Hochschul-Informations-System (HIS), Kurzinformation A10/92 (1992) Lewin, K. *et al. Deutsche Studienanfänger im Wintersemester 1991/92: Studienwahl und ihre Begleitumstände* (German entrants into higher education in the winter semester 1991/92: choice of courses and motives for choice). Hannover: HIS.

Hochschul-Informations-System (HIS), Kurzinformation A3/93 (1993) Minks, K. and Bathke, G. *Berufliche Integration und Weiterbildung von Ingenieurinnen der neuen Länder* (Professional integration and continuing education of women engineers in the new *Länder*). Hannover: HIS.

Karpen, U. (1988) *Access to Higher Education in the Federal Republic of Germany with texts from the Federal Higher Education Framing Law and Cases*. Frankfurt am Main: Peter Lang.

Kluge, N. *et al.* (1990) *Die Reform des Hochschulzugangs und die Gleichwertigkeit der beruflichen Bildung* (The reform of access to higher education and the equivalence of vocational education). In N. Kluge, *et al.* (eds), 7–22.

Kluge, N., Scholz, W. and Wolter, A. (eds) (1990) *Vom Lehrling zum Akademiker* (From Apprentice to Graduate). Oldenburg: Bibliotheks-und Informationssystem der Universität Oldenburg.

Reibstein, E. (1990) *Hochschulzugang ohne Abitur: Eine besondere Chance für Frauen?* (Access to higher education without *Abitur*: special opportunities for women?). In N. Kluge *et al.* (eds), 205–228.

Reisinger, E and Davies, P (1994) *The access and participation of adults in higher education in Germany*. London: City University.

Schmidt, H. (1991) *Gleichwertigkeit beruflicher und allgemeiner Bildung – Voraussetzung für die Erhöhung der Attraktivität beruflicher Bildungsgänge* (Equivalence of vocational and general education – precondition for an increased attractiveness of vocational courses). BIBB, 19–21.

Scholz, W.-D. (1993) *Wege in ein Hochschulstudium für Berufstätige ohne Abitur in der Bundesrepublik Deutschland* (Paths to Higher Education for Working Adults without *Abitur* in the FRG). Oldenburg: Bibliotheks- und Informationssystem der Universität Oldenburg.

Sekretariat der Ständigen Konferenz der Kultusminister der Länder in der Bundesrepublik Deutschland (KMK) (1992) *Zugang zu den Hochschulen für beruflich qualifizierte Bewerber ohne schulische Hochschulzugangsberechtigung. Übersicht über die Möglichkeiten des nachträglichen Erwerbs einer Hochschulzugangsberechtigung. Stand: Juni 1992* (Access to higher education for vocationally qualified applicants without higher education entrance qualifications. Survey of the possibilities of gaining a higher education entrance qualification, as of June 1992). Bonn: KMK.

Sekretariat der Ständigen Konferenz der Kultusminister der Länder in der Bundesrepublik Deutschland (KMK) (1993) *Pressemitteilung. 264. Plenarsitzung der Ständigen Konferenz der Kultusminister und -senatoren der Länder in der Bundesrepublik Deutschland am Juli 1993 in Hamburg* (Press release. 264th plenary of the Standing Conference of the Ministers and Senators of Culture of the *Länder* in the FRG on 1–2 July 1993 in Hamburg). Bonn: KMK.

Der Spiegel (1993) 19 April, 80–101.

Der Spiegel (1993) Willkommen im Labyrinth (Welcome to the labyrinth). 16, 19 April, 80–101.

Der Spiegel (1991) *Bald knallt's* (Explosion expected). 9 December, 36–59.

Teichler, U. (1990) Hochschulzugang für Berufserfahrene – Erfahrungen und Zukunftsperspektiven (Access to higher education for *Berufserfahrene* – experiences and prospects). In N. Kluge *et al.* (eds) 23–48.

van Resandt, A. (ed) (1991) *Commission of European Communities: A Guide to Higher Education Systems and Qualifications in the European Community*. The Hague: Office for Official Publications of the European Community.

Wissenschaftsrat (1991) *Empfehlungen zur Entwicklung der Fachhochschulen in den 90er Jahren* (Recommendations for the Development of the Fachhochschulen in the 90s). Köln: Wissenschaftsrat.

Wissenschaftsrat (1993) *10 Thesen zur Hochschulpolitik* (10 Propositions on Higher Education Policy). Berlin: Wissenschaftsrat.

Wolter, A. (1990) Die symbolische Macht höherer Bildung – Der Dritte Bildungsweg zwischen Gymnasialmonopol und beruflicher Öffnung (The symbolic force of the grammar school tradition in education – the 'third educational route' between the monopoly of the grammar school and opening access for the vocationally qualified). In N. Kluge *et al.* (eds), 49–115.

Wolter, A. (1993) Hochschulzugang und Studierfähigkeit von qualifizierten Berufstätigen – Modelle und Erfahrungen (Access and ability to study of qualified working adults – models and experiences). In W. Kramer and W. Schlaffke (eds) (1994), *Studierfähigkeit qualifizierter Berufspraktiker*. Köln: Deutscher Instituts-Verlag GmbH, p.76–97.

Chapter 8

Italy

Stella Parker

The Structure and Organisation of Higher Education in Italy

The providers

The majority of higher education in Italy takes place within state recognised universities (*università*), 45 of which are funded by the state and 5 of which are private. There are two other types of institutions at university level, namely the five *politecnichi* and the seven *istituti universitari* (Marinucci 1993). The differences between the three types reflect the range of provision offered by each – a *università* has a broad range of faculties, limited only by its size and the number of professors. A *politecnico* has faculties of engineering and architecture only, and an *istituto universitari* has just one faculty or one specialised course, such as that for medical technicians. Between them, these institutions have a total of over 1,300,000 enrolments, which is 96 per cent of the student population (Marinucci 1993).

In addition to these three types there are several other organisations which offer higher education in Italy: academies of fine arts; *Istituti Superiori di Educazione Fisica* (institutes of physical education); higher vocational training, run by the regional governments; military academies; and some private institutions, not recognised by the state.

Admissions

Entry to Italian universities is open to all who possess the Upper Secondary School leaving diploma – *Diploma di Maturità* (or its foreign equivalent). It is the only qualification that enables candidates to be considered for entry to first or second level studies in Italian universities. This is laid down in legislation and universities are obliged to adhere to these regulations; in other words, access to university education is permitted by only one route which requires central government sanction. Admission is not regulated nor coordi-

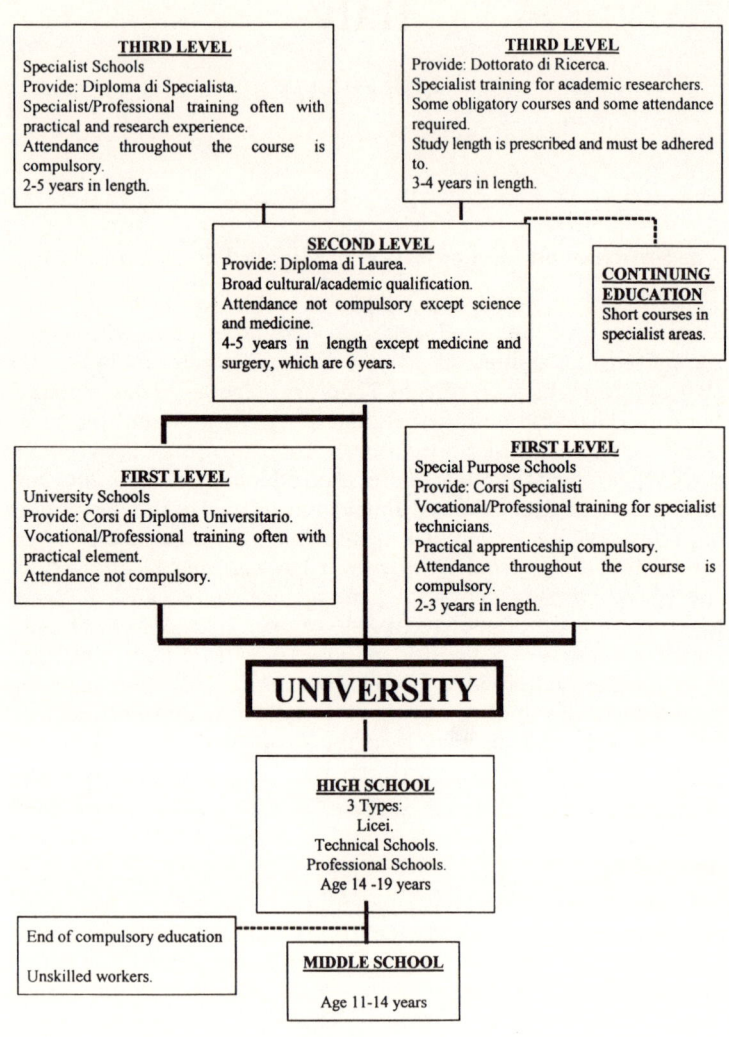

Figure 8.1: The formal education system in Italy

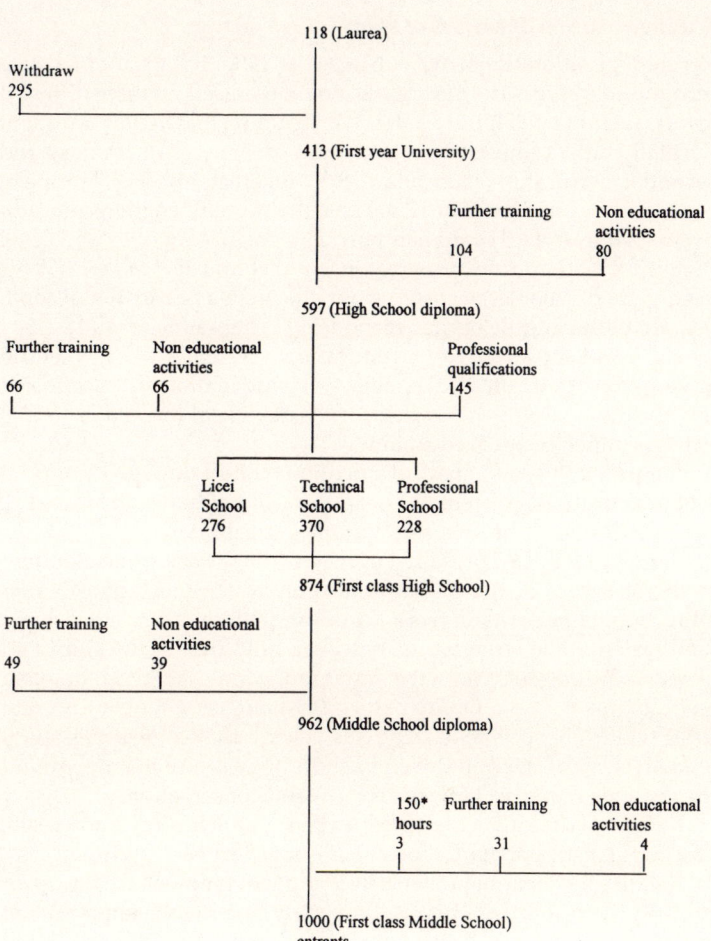

* Explanation in text
Source: Angelli (1992)

Figure 8.2: A fictitious cohort through the formal Italian educational system in 1990–91

nated in any way; a university must accept all suitably qualified applicants.

The organisation of courses of study

Recent legislation (Reform Act No. 341 of 1990) has meant that state recognised university education is now organised on three different levels, as shown in Figure 8.1. It is worth noting that in Italy a student normally enters university after a total of 13 years of primary and secondary education (see Figure 8.2), whereas in other European countries and in America, 12 years is the normal length of pre-university education. The Italian curricula for first and second level higher education are run partly in parallel and not in series. This arrangement enables transfer from the first level to the second, usually in the middle of the second level programme of study.

Figure 8.1 shows the formal educational system which has central government sanction and is able to award nationally recognised qualifications. Any system which exists outside of this is non-formal – that is, much of adult education.

Figure 8.2 shows the path of a fictitious cohort through the formal Italian educational system; the proportion of graduates, at around 12 per cent, is one of the lowest in Europe (Angelli 1992).

Figures 8.1 and 8.2 provide a framework for a basic understanding of the structure of the Italian education system, including higher education. Because it follows a European pattern, its framework is a familiar one. The structure is, however, only part of the story and gives no indication of how the system functions. Although in many respects this is also a familiar story, there are certain operative features which are specific to Italy. It is beyond the scope of this study to analyse all of these in detail; in short, they centre mainly around the tensions that exist between reform and conservation.

Reform of the Italian higher education system has, for many years, had popular support; but reforms have only ever been partly successful because the locus of power is in central government. Government controls the resources – that is, university finance, the appointment of personnel and also course curricula. Because they are appointed by central government, the professors are in reality civil servants and thus answerable to government. This status encourages academic staff at all levels to be acutely knowledgeable about the fine details of educational legislation, and many of the discussions with academics for this study were couched in terms of legislative requirements rather than curriculum requirements – a new experience for the author. Prestige for faculties is measured in terms of professors, students and resources, and these are at the behest of central government. In order these are: medicine, the sciences (including mathematics), engineering, law, literature and philosophy, economics and business, architecture, and political sciences (Martinelli 1992). Faculties control conditions of work, teaching methods, choice of colleagues and so on. In other words, faculties have a certain amount of autonomy but are unable to generate their own changes in curricula or staffing levels because these require government sanction, as do many other changes. So a tension exists between the popular movement for change (in which many academics are involved) and those in central authority (government and professors) whose lead-weighted bureaucracy stifles innovation and thus maintains the status quo (Clark 1977).

Provision for Adults

In Italy, anyone over the age of sixteen is permitted by law to work and is regarded as an adult. Only 20 per cent of the Italian adult population has a high school certificate (Angelli 1992) and Table 8.1 indicates how this compares unfavourably with other European countries. In Italy, this low achieving majority is the target for educational provision designated as 'adult education', and such provision includes all non-university educational programmes, both vocational and non-vocational. Adult education signifies marginality, ranging from the remedial to the adult liberal. However there are many other providers, not designated as adult educators, but which offer educational opportunities for adults; for example, higher education provides opportunities specifically for adults but in professional and academic disciplines only.

The providers

In contrast to the centrally controlled and inflexible system of higher education, Italian adult education is decentralised, flexible and mainly uncoordinated. There are no laws governing the provision of adult education except for legislation of 1991 which stated that universities should promote continuing education but without involving any expense of public funds (Torsello 1993). In spite of the lack of a legislative framework, some adult/continuing education does receive state support; for example certain courses which are either at a basic training-for-work level or at the level of higher vocational training (see Figures 8.1 and 8.2). Where such courses lead towards a state-recognised qualification, they are classified as 'formal'. Other examples of formal provision are the school diploma courses, held in lower and upper secondary schools, and specifically for adult returners. All other adult provision is non-formal because it does not lead to qualifications recognised by the state. It is organised through political groups, trades unions, religious bodies, voluntary and private organisations.

Table 8.1: Educational level of the population (25–64 age range), in some EEC countries (percentages of total population, 1989 data)

	France	Germany	Italy	United Kingdom
Elementary school education with no final qualification	24	-	44	-
Secondary school education	26	22	30	35
High school education	33	61	20	48
Non-university higher education	7	7	-	6
University education	7	10	6	9
Other types	3	0	0	1
Total	100.0	100.0	100.0	100.0

Source: Angelli 1992

Courses of study

Provision which is non-formal can be either vocational or non-vocational. Vocational training opportunities are available for people with experience or qualifications, and because some of these opportunities are under regional control, there exists a framework in which to describe them. This vocational training is distinctly oriented towards the labour market, and can lead towards qualifications which, although they do not have national recognition, nonetheless do have currency in the labour market. In contrast, non-vocational programmes have no links with the labour market, are beyond the boundaries of accountability to central control and are designated as non formal. Programmes for adults in Italy can be divided into three categories: courses for personal development, for updating and for returners.

Courses for personal fulfilment and enrichment

In the case of non-formal provision which is not organised through regional government but may receive some government aid, it is difficult to obtain an accurate picture of participation. There is some evidence that significant numbers of participants are engaged in programmes such as the University of the Third Age. Turrini (1987) estimates that such institutions number at least 106 and have 20,000 associates, whilst Lichtner (1992) believes that these and other programmes are expanding. In some cases universities are involved in these activities. Monno and Moramarco (1988 p.19) describe an adult education programme in Southern Italy, the aim of which was to train executives by means of courses which had a 'cultural' and not 'vocational' purpose. The point these authors make is that the divide between the vocational and non-vocational is often blurred in Italian adult education. Orefice describes an action research community based programme in Southern Italy, which aimed to promote an 'educative community' (Orefice 1988 p.58) by intervening in local agencies such as trades unions, health services, regional government and co-operatives. This programme was facilitated by academics from the University of Pescara working with teachers, adult educators and others drawn from the participating groups. Federighi *et al.* (1988) describe other examples of adult education initiatives being undertaken by universities, such as the creation of an adult education programmes in the Molise region and general education for adults in Basilitica (Susi); University of the Third Age in Orvieto (del Corno); the mass media and adult education in Sardinia (Fabio); and finally, Federighi's description of the role of the public library in the education of adults.

Courses for training and up-dating

Vocational training is organised by the regions, with or without the assistance of state funds. It covers a range of levels from basic, initial training programmes for young people to higher postgraduate levels. Universities do not play any part in these regional, basic, initial programmes, nor in any form of on-the-job training or retraining (Villa and Marchetti 1991). They can, however, offer post-experience training for diploma holders or graduates, or for people with some work experience. The content of these courses is technological, specialist and/or managerial.

Higher education also has a role in training under special State legislation programmes. These training programmes, organised locally but accountable to the central state, enable people (mostly young people) to become engaged in certain occupations such as the retail trade, technical occupations, the paramedical professions and others. In addition to this training, higher education offers postgraduate courses, mainly two or three years in length, of which the majority are in the scientific and medical fields (Bussi 1992). They lead to qualifications which are specifically vocational.

The continuing education that occurs within universities in Italy is not delivered through units or departments of continuing education. Recent changes in the law (1990) concerning the training of school teachers have meant that some teachers are now returning to university for the purpose of up-dating their skills (de Natale 1993) by engagement with a body of knowledge related to adult and continuing education offered as an option within 'pedagogy'. Other opportunities for in-service teacher training are available in centres which have been set up by the Ministry of Education; university academics may be involved in the delivery of these programmes. Finally, some short courses, conferences and seminars are available through universities for doctors, scientists, lawyers and engineers.

In addition to the programmes outlined above there are others which are organised entirely by private companies and take place either within the company or in private institutions. There is little data available on the scope of in-company programmes, but there is some evidence that this type of training is becoming more important, particularly in the area of management training (Villa and Marchetti 1991).

Courses for adult returners

There are opportunities for adults to re-enter education, and Italy's '150 hour' courses provide an interesting example of this type of educational opportunity. These courses originated in demands from the unions for 150 hours of paid educational leave with the aim of improving the education of workers with few qualifications (Newport 1979, Risk and Crossman 1979). The curricula of these courses have been adapted to suit local needs and in some cases universities have been partners in their development and teaching. The topics covered include basic literacy, health education (for example, alcohol abuse) and social and political issues. In some cases, for example in the Veneto region, educational centres have been set up to promote and develop worker involvement in the study of complex social issues (Albarea 1985). Many of the 150 hour courses are for adult returners who wish to return to study to take the lower secondary school certificate. These classes are held mostly in secondary schools and attract relatively large numbers of adult students, for example 55,000 for the year 1990–91, although numbers have been dropping over the past few years (Lichtner 1992).

For adults who left school with no qualifications but who wish to enter university late as 'returners', it is necessary to obtain an upper secondary school *Diploma di Maturità*. The state provides adult evening classes in high schools covering upper secondary school curricula, as do private institutions. These courses are especially accelerated, but students need to be highly motivated. Many drop out (Meghani 1989) and their failure rate is over 50 per cent (Monasta 1993). This poor success rate, coupled with the recognition that the high school diploma curriculum is inappropriate for experienced and motivated adults, has prompted the University of Florence to design a university entrance diploma curriculum for adult returners and this is recognised as equivalent to the *Diploma di Maturità* curriculum (Monasta 1993). However,in spite of studying a different curriculum, adult students are required to take the same examination as school children at the end of their upper secondary schooling.

For adults who possess the *Diploma di Maturità* and who wish to take up their university studies later in life, there is no difficulty, and there are examples of those who do this. Included in their numbers are some adult students returning to study alongside their children, some who enter a completely different field later in life (such as a 60 year old qualified engineer retraining as a pharmacologist) and some who take up the status of *fuori corso*. This status enables them to attenuate the length of their university studies as long as they re-register within 8 years of completing their last course of undergraduate study.

Policy issues and developments

Since the second world war, European preoccupations with the equality of educational opportunity have shifted in focus from issues concerning the accessibility of secondary education to issues concerning that of tertiary education, be it further or higher (Halsey 1993). Italy has been no exception to this, the trend having its origins in the country's postwar economic miracle. This laid the foundations for a major evaluation of beliefs and attitudes in society, as the country's labour force changed from being mainly agricultural to being mainly occupied in the industrial and service sectors. These occupational changes took place alongside structural changes whereby millions of families moved from the countryside to the cities and from Southern to Northern Italy (Martinelli 1992). Consequently, the traditional values of agricultural peasant communities gave way to those of urban industrialisation. Education of all kinds, and higher education in particular, came to be regarded as a valuable tool for enabling social mobility.

Expansion and responses

In Italy in the late 1960s these changes gave rise to a sudden and unanticipated escalation in university enrolments by young people in search of upward mobility. Enrolments increased from 41,000 in 1969 to 89,000 in 1971 (de Francesco 1978), at first without any response from the State. The resulting chaos and overcrowding in the universities led to several years of student protest and unrest. This unrest occurred not only within the universities: at this time there was an intense and widespread ideological debate carried out at all levels within society (Moscati 1991). As a result, the government eventually changed the laws controlling admission to universities. For the first time all students with a high school diploma (the *Diploma di Maturità*) from technical and professional schools were able to enter university; previously only *Licei* diplomates had been eligible. In addition, such students became eligible for entrance to all faculties, including law and medicine, which previously had been restricted to *Licei* diplomates only. As well as permitting greater flexibility in student choice of curriculum, the law also put an end to the recruitment of professors according to the old rules, in an attempt to break the academic oligarchy.

Since the late 1960s then, the Italian higher education system has been accessible to many, but this has not been sufficient to satisfy demands for equality of opportunity. Those who have commentated on access over the last two decades (Scott 1991) have concluded that equality of opportunity to higher education cannot be ensured simply by opening wider the traditional entrances. Other entry routes need to be designed, as do flexible modes of admission and participation, and the barriers between vocational and non-vocational and between further and higher need to be eliminated. In addition to this, higher education curricula need to be reformed so that the requirements of a mass system are served well. These issues and others concerning public accountability, wastage and quality assurance provide an agenda for Italian higher education in the 1990s, and the pressures for change continue to gather force (Luzatto 1988, Moscati 1985, Simone 1993). The inside observations made by these university academics, and their continued calls for reform, indicate the difficulties ahead as Italian higher education continues to move towards establishing equality of opportunity. A study of access to and participation in Italian higher education provide examples of these difficulties.

The spirit of state legislation in the late 1960s was to increase educational opportunity by extending university access, but it was done piece-meal and had the opposite effect to its intention. The legislation did not allow sufficient time for the system to adjust, nor did it enable an increase in the human resources required for a high quality system, and universities thereby became degraded. Table 8.2 illustrates this point with respect to the influx of student numbers which occurred without a corresponding increase in terms of teaching staff.

Table 8.2: Staff: student ratios in Italian universities

	1960/61	1970/71	1980/81	1986/87
Total student numbers (000)	268	682	1048	1130
Numbers of faculty	37,396	50,394	43,270	51,081
Staff: student ratio*	1:7	1:13	1:24	1:22

Source: Martinelli 1992

* NB drop-out rates will distort these figures to some extent

This has had a deleterious effect on the morale of academic staff (Bompard 1994) and has given rise in some cases to overcrowded lecture halls and organisational chaos, and has exposed academics to the brunt of student dissatisfaction. Until recently, universities did not have sufficient institutional autonomy to alleviate these problems. However, in response to the problems, recent changes in legislation (Act 245 1990) have allowed a certain increase in the numbers of university teaching staff although some of the staff interviewed in this study regarded this as too little, too late. These changes have not yet provided the relief needed in some of the larger universities, where the only source of respite to the overcrowded facilities has been non-attendance on the part of the students. The 1990 legislation has also given universities a sufficient amount of autonomy to deal with over-crowding in their own ways and the University of Venice has taken advantage of this freedom by introducing a system of financial penalties (based on examination results) aimed at weeding out unsatisfactory students or those who show no determination to graduate (Bompard 1993). Prior to this legislation, individual academics have always engineered their own solutions and a common response undertaken by those who take their jobs seriously has been to work at home as much as possible, going into the university only when absolutely necessary. This appears to be recognised as acceptable practice, because telephone enquiries to Italian academics usually produce (unsolicited) the home telephone number. Absenteeism is a characteristic of another group of academics, possibly as many as 60 to 70 per cent of them (Bompard 1994), who do other things, such as practice their professions (for example, medicine or the law) or work for the government in parallel to their academic duties.

Central government control of university education is supposed to ensure uniformity of quality and provision, but this is difficult to achieve when admissions to universities are neither regulated nor coordinated. The growth and consequent overcrowding of some Italian universities is a result of the popularity and prestige of these institutions in the eyes of students who make their choice with no guidance or information other than hearsay. This has led to the development of very large universities, such as Rome (over 170,000 students) and Milan (over 120,000 students), and some very small ones, such as Reggio Calabria (4,000 students) and Casino (3,500 students) (Edizione 1989). In some universities, such as Rome, the overcrowding problem is particularly serious as most of the students are concentrated in one institution. The problem is less pressing in Milan, where there are five different academic loci, but even there conditions are difficult. These different working conditions mean that the nature of academic work varies greatly from one university to another and even within the same university between the popular overcrowded faculties and the less popular ones. This heterogeneity has its genesis in the very legislation which was designed to ensure uniformity. The more recent legislation (Act 245 1990) aims to relieve the overcrowding by splitting the very large institutions and encouraging enrolments at the smaller ones. The outcome of these reforms is awaited with interest. Little seems to have happened so far, and there are some who consider that little is likely to happen in the near future. More radical measures, such as staff development for the introduction of new teaching methods, extending and staggering the teaching day and the streamlining of enrolment procedures would require the operation of complex and cumbersome state machinery, and even if these changes were to occur (which seems unlikely at present), years would pass before any effects became apparent.

Accessibility

Unfettered student choice cannot increase the participation of young people from lower social groups unless accompanied by curriculum reforms needed to increase opportunity. For example, it has long been recognised that differences in university participation originate in the differences between school curricula (de Francesco and Trivellato 1978). The *Licei* are specifically concerned with university preparation, and the technical and professional schools with the education of technicians and other operative personnel. In recent years, just over half of university students (55%) graduated from technical and professional secondary schools and the remainder from *Liceis* (Moscati 1991) which educate just one fifth of upper secondary pupils (Angelli 1992). University teaching staff openly admit that *Licei* diplomates are better prepared for study than students from other schools, and it is these staff who are responsible for allowing progression from one year to the next. The selection that they impose within universities is very severe and is one of the reasons why only about 12 per cent of students graduate. De Francesco and Trivellato (1978) have shown that the greatest number of drop outs are students from lower economic and social groups, who tend to become more scarce from the second year onwards and form only about one quarter of the graduates (MacGregor and Bompard 1993). Various authors have pointed out that these inequalities could be solved either by preparing all entrants in the same way by standardising the school curricula or, alternatively, by changing the nature of university curricula to accommodate the needs of the majority. Neither of these has happened, but they have been the subject of much debate over many years (Luzatto 1988, Simone 1993).

The expansion of Italian higher education has not been accompanied by an increase in the variety of higher education institutions – that is, higher level vocational or technical universities. This is very unusual; in many other European countries some alternative state controlled system has generally been developed alongside traditional universities, enabling access for groups generally unrepresented (Hore 1993). Wherever this has happened, whether these alternative curricula are offered in the same or different institutions, they represent the comprehensivisation of higher education via a technical /vocational route. There now exist within Italian universities the beginnings of such programmes. In 1992, new, shorter *Laurea* (*Laurea breve*) were introduced, with the aim of attracting students who are either unwilling or unable to spend five years or more on their studies. These new courses are supposed to be vocational and applied and they exist side by side with the four to five year *Laurea*, so that there is opportunity for students to cross the divide between the applied and the academic after two years of study. However, there is the possibility that these new courses could be still-born; they may suffer from 'academic drift', particularly as they will be taught by the same academics who teach the *Laurea* and who see their role as that of transmitting theoretical knowledge.

The role of Italian universities is based in a tradition that has been to provide a route for the few to the traditional high status occupations such as law, medicine and engineering and this is reflected in the traditionalism of their courses, which are academic and non-vocational. An alternative and more diverse range of post-school options, geared somewhat more closely to the needs of the economy is offered by means of the first level university diplomas and the courses for special purposes (Bussi 1992). These diplomas cover such areas as computer science and fine arts; the special purpose schools prepare for professions such as physiotherapy, nursing, librarianship. However, relatively small numbers enrol on these courses – two per cent of all higher education enrolments in 1984–1985 (Ribolzi 1987) – and there is some evidence to suggest that even the minor outflows from this type of programme is decreasing, whilst the outflow of trained personnel from the private sector is increasing (Bussi 1992). So where the state has not provided formal routes towards recognised qualification for a wide diversity of needs, a gap has opened up. It would appear from Table 8.3 that there is emerging in Italy a private sector which is filling this gap by offering a wider range of vocational provision than is provided by the state. Some of these private organisations award their own qualifications (Catalano *et al.* 1992). The growth in this non-formal, private sector is taking place at the same time as decreases in the formal, state sector, the evidence being the fall in the proportion of graduates from traditional university degrees over this period.

Table 8.3: Graduates 1982–1987

	1982	1985	1987
First level of which:	31,587	32,262	37,362
University Diploma	4233	3533	3784
Special purpose schools	2081	1805	2045
Private Institutions	6017	10,419	13,542
Vocational Training (*)	19,144	15,539	15,451
Others	112	966	2540
Second Level	70,244	68,855	74,085
Third Level	11,806	14,456	14,333
Total	**113,637**	**115,663**	**125 780**
First Level	27.8	27.9	29.7
Second Level	61.8	59.5	58.9
Third Level	10.4	12.6	11.4
Total	**100.0%**	**100.0%**	**100.0%**

(*) Estimates

Source: Bussi 1992

All Italian university first degrees are organised on a traditional model which is based on the expectation of full-time attendance and completion within a prescribed period (de Francesco 1978). In spite of this, the reality is that much of the Italian university system is used by groups of adults who are part-time students, only 10 per cent of whom complete their degree within the minimum period of four or five years (OECD 1985). They have insufficient income to support their costs and have to take up employment concurrently with their studies. Most university staff who were interviewed for this study stated that significant numbers of their students are in employment, although evidence suggests that the number who work concurrently declined from 50 per cent in 1977 to 32 per cent a decade later (Bussi 1992). This situation can operate, first because *Laurea* students are not required to attend every course of study, and secondly because some students can register as 'non-attenders' and turn up only to take the examinations. In addition, some students may prolong their degree (to a limited extent), using university facilities only intermittently. Ribolzi (1987) estimates that 25 per cent of students are in reality part-timers. However, the system makes no concessions to part-timers who are unable to attend lectures because of other commitments; they simply miss lectures but must pass their examinations if they wish to return the following year. Some students spend most of the second decade of their lives engaged in both part-time study and employment, and although this is bound to be difficult, it does seem to promote employment after graduation. In an inquiry into the link between university education and work, Anolli *et al.* (1992) state that students who had work experience during their university years find full-time employment more easily and quickly than those who did not work.

Government financial support for the growth of Italian universities has been the subject of recent legislation, but this is unlikely to ease immediately the financial difficulties of students from lower income backgrounds. Students and/or their families are expected to pay fees (which are relatively low – a few hundred pounds per year), buy their own books and pay for their living costs (Catalano *et al.* 1992). These authors point out that the low fee level means that each student is subsidised, irrespective of parental and other income. Hence taxpayers from lower social economic groups subsidise the education of the successful university students, who are drawn mostly from the wealthier classes. They suggest that some of the costs incurred would be distributed more equitably if student loans were introduced together with an increase in tuition fees (for which there would be exemption for low income groups). These new measures would help towards the costs of the reform of the system as well as encouraging students to choose their degree more carefully.

The increase in numbers of Italian universities over the past thirty years has not meant equality of opportunity, because more of these establishments are in the richer urban regions than in the poorer rural regions. The majority of higher education takes place in cities: it increased from 41 establishments in 29 cities in the 1960s to the present number of 62 in 48 cities (Moscati 1991). As a result the student population in, for example, the southern regions of Italy must travel long distances or live away from home if they choose to participate in higher education. The proximity of a university can determine whether or not a student enrols (Clancy 1991), particularly if he or she has limited resources, whether of time or of money. So even though the Italian educational system has expanded, it has done so without plans to expand educational opportunity to areas of social and economic deprivation.

There have been some initiatives to increase the participation in the education of groups traditionally under-represented in Italian education, for example, women. In the late 1970s and early 1980s, some universities used the 150 hour provision to organise courses for working women in collaboration with their unions, or for women returners to the *scuola media*. Later, women's centres were set up and in Milan the 'Free University for Women' grew directly out of '150 hour' courses. None of these initiatives is part of the formal, state system but there have been some university-level initiatives in teacher training to cater for the educational needs of women (Lichtner 1992). The proportion of female entrants to universities has been directly related to the participation of females in upper secondary schools, where enrolment of girls reached a peak of 57 per cent in the mid 1980s (Ribolzi 1987). In 1981, women constituted 44 per cent of university enrolment and by 1988 this had increased to 47.4 per cent. The distribution of women by subject group has not changed significantly over the years, the majority being found in humanities (where they represent 81.5% of all graduates) and scientific disciplines (where they represent 55.7% of total graduates). In the traditional male preserve of medicine, female graduates rose from 29 per cent in 1981 to 38 per cent in 1988 and in engineering over the same period of time, enrolments rose from 14 per cent to 17 per cent (Bussi 1992). Bussi considers that the increases in these disciplines represent a switch by women from the public sector services (where the number of jobs has decreased) to the more available employment in the professions. Graduates in humanities are the most likely to be unemployed, and, as we have seen, women are well represented in these disciplines which, incidentally, also have a high drop-out rate (de Francesco 1978).

Problems of Articulation

The accessibility of Italian higher education for groups who do not have traditional entry qualifications has been restricted by a lack of articulation between first degree and other providers at different levels, and inhibited by the divide between formal and non-formal. Where articulation does exist, it is always between agencies of formal provision, for example the vertical articulation between the upper secondary school and universities, and intra-university articulation between diplomas and *Laureas* (lateral) and between *Laureas* and doctorates (vertical) (Catalano *et al.* 1992).

In addition, the system is characterised by a lack of flexibility in modes of attendance and an absence of any system of credit accumulation and transfer. For example, if students wish to change to another degree course, they are unable to make a lateral transfer; they have to go back to the beginning of the new degree of their choice. About 10 per cent of all graduates obtain their degree in a discipline different to the one in which they enrolled, with social and political subjects having the highest rate of change (21%) and scientific ones having the lowest at 11 per cent (Bussi 1992). This suggests that students have little guidance in their initial choice of study. There are no opportunities either for the accreditation of experiential learning, work-based or otherwise. Even returning school teachers who upgrade their initial non-university qualifications by means of the educational options available in the *Laureas* cannot gain any credit or exemption for previous experience. There is no formal credit system available for a wide range of higher level occupational skills, even though there is a demand for them, particularly in the area of management development programmes (Villa and Marchetti 1991). There are public sector management programmes for government officials, and the private sector provides for its own needs, but in neither case is a formal management qualification available. In some cases, Italian executives are sent abroad to gain a high level management qualification because of the rarity of such courses on home ground. Finally, there are few opportunities for distance learning at university level although there have been some experiments in teacher education (Osbat 1980), and the University of Parma has been considering distance learning for one of its science courses (Colombo 1993).

Although lacking in articulation with other providers, Italian higher education does have links within some communities, as shown by the examples given above with respect to adult education. But these and any other connections are marginal to the university mainstream and, because of the legislative divide between the formal and the non-formal, it is currently impossible for an adult with a non-traditional educational background to enter the Italian university system, unless s/he passes the school leaving diploma. There is no opportunity to cross this divide nor to carry credit from non-formal to formal education. Non-formal adult education, which could provide fertile ground for adults who wish to advance their knowledge for its own sake (and this is the stated aim of Italian universities) is beyond the pale of legislation and thus cannot at present generate access routes.

Conclusion

Italian higher education is, in theory, freely accessible to all who possess the correct entry qualifications. This makes entry to the system clear, simple and straightforward, and avoids the expenditure of time and other resources on selection. It is non-discriminatory, and students from non-traditional backgrounds are not hampered by their ignorance of entry procedures because there are none. These are the good points, but as this study has shown, there are bad points too. The system exhibits all the problems inherent in the transition from an élite to a mass one as identified by Trow (1974), and few of the solutions. The first problem has been the rate of growth: Italian universities expanded student intake so quickly that they had neither the chance nor the means to adjust. Second, these large institutions developed on such a scale that neither they nor the system as a whole could be managed by the old methods, which have remained unchanged. Finally, no measures have been developed to encourage or accommodate the changed student profile. In short the expansion of the Italian universities has been simply an expansion of the older elite system, and is the source of many difficulties to those who work and study in it, and of much discontent.

It is surprising that this state of affairs could remain and be tolerated for so long. Angelli (1992) suggests as a reason that society as a whole is indifferent to these issues, but Trow (1974) points out that Italians do have expectations about education. In Italy, according to Trow, a university education is perceived by students and their families as a guaranteed route to securing an élite post. Indeed, these rather atavistic expectations have been the source of considerable discontent and have given rise to the popular movements for reform and fuelled much of the educational legislation discussed above. Ribolzi (1987) states that much of the student discontent has been defused because the difficulties of university life have the effect of dampening aspirations. But in spite of this, discontent remains, and the calls for reform continue as the experience of university life becomes more and more restive.

It is not difficult to identify what needs to be done in order to reform the universities and to extend participation in post compulsory education in Italy; what does seem to be difficult is how to do it. Clark (1983), in his international analysis of the higher educational systems of developed countries, argues that higher education is subject to influence and control from three agents – the state, the academic oligarchy and the market. Taking the state first, if change in Italian higher education is to come about, it would require first of all a change in the relationship between universities and the state. The state would need to change the laws that determine the organisational structures of universities to give the university more autonomy. This would allow them full control over the management of their own resources and the determination of their own curricula. The state would require universities and a variety of tertiary institutions to be answerable for the expenditure of public funds and to demonstrate the achievement of high quality provision. The universities would be required to become more efficient, but any changes required would need to be monitored so that they do not disadvantage the less privileged.

These and other changes (such as the reform of the system of financial support to students, the reform of the secondary curricula) need to be part of a coherent plan rather than the piecemeal changes of the past. A system for analysing needs and formulating policies based on satisfying these needs is required as well as some mechanism for monitoring the effects of change (OECD 1985).

Second, the academic oligarchy (the professors in particular) would need to tackle seriously the issues concerned with teaching and learning. They would need to structure better student learning opportunities, and one way forward would be to improve articulation between secondary school and university curricula. Unrestricted student entry would be controlled; students would receive advice and guidance on courses of study and be permitted to pursue a course of study only if it was consistency with the previous secondary curricula. This would necessitate an increase in the variety of university curricula (a differential degree structure with more short opportunities) and in modes of study (part-time, sandwich etc.). Different routes of university entry would need to be designed to articulate in some way with non-formal education.

The third of Clark's factors is the 'market', which includes the students and employers. There is evidence that students are participating increasingly in vocationally oriented courses which are shorter in length than university studies. These should be further encouraged. With respect to employers, Italian universities have very low levels of collaboration with industry and commerce which work increasingly with private providers. Locally generated training requires some form of formal recognition so that it could be used as credit to progress to higher education. These measures would go some way towards increasing and/or undermining participation in Italian higher education, but would also give rise to a complete reform.

Simone (1993) puts the blame for current problems on the universities. His thesis is that Italian universities have perpetrated three betrayals. The first is to the state, which pours resources into a system dominated by confusion and disorganisation; the second is that there is little or no generation of new knowledge by means of research; and the third is that there is poor transmission of knowledge to the students. He concludes that the intellectual life of Italian society is declining and that this will affect the country badly in many ways. His suggestions for wide-ranging reform echo much of what has been said above and include details of measures intended for the control of student entry and the working conditions of academic staff. The crux of Simone's argument for the whole-scale reform of Italian universities to make them fairer and more efficient corresponds with the requirements needed to broaden access and participation. Whether or not this will happen remains to be seen.

References

Albarea, R. (1985) I corsi per adulti delle 150 ore in tre complessi urbani della provincia di Venezia: opinioni a confronto, *Educazione Permanante*. Veneto: Giunta Regionale del Veneto.

Angelli, F. (ed) (1992) *Italy Today. Social Picture and Trends*. Roma: Centro Studi Investimenti Sociali.

Anolli, L., Ciceri, R. and Denti, I. (1992) *L' Incrocio fra Università e Lavoro*. Milano: Universita degli Studi di Milano.

Bompard, P. (1993) Venice floats 'fees to please' idea, *The Times Higher Educational Supplement*, 30 April.

Bompard, P. (1994) Faulty Ivory Towers, *The Times Higher Education Supplement*, 28 January.

Bussi, F. (1992) *From higher education to Employment. Volume 111: Finland, France, Italy, Japan, Netherlands, Norway*. Paris: OECD.

Catalano, G., Silvestre. P. and Todeschini. P. (1992) Financing higher education in Italy, *Higher Education Policy*, 5, 2, 37–43.

Clancy, P. (1991) Patterns of access to higher education in the Republic of Ireland. In G. Neave and F. van Vught (eds) *Prometheus Bound. The*

Changing Relationship Between Government and Higher Education in Western Europe. Exeter: BPCC Wheatons Ltd.

Clark, B. (1977) *Academic Power in Italy.* Chicago: Chicago University Press.

Clark, B. (1983) *Higher Education Systems. Academic organisation in cross-national perspectives.* California: University of California Press.

Colombo, P. (1993) personal communication.

Edizione, F. (ed) (1989) *Vadecum.* Strasbourg: Council of Europe.

Federighi et al. (1988) *World Perspective Case Studies on Educational Programmes for Adults: Italy.* Battle Creek, Michigan: Kellogg Foundation.

Federighi, P. (1991) The Organisation of agencies for adult education in Italy. In P. Jarvis and A. Chadwick (eds) *Training adult educators in Western Europe.* London: Routledge.

de Francesco, C. (1978) The growth and crisis of Italian Higher Education during the 1960s and 1970s, *Higher Education,* 7, 2, 193–212.

de Francesco, C. and Trivellato, P. (1978) *La Laurea e il posto.* Bologna: Il Mulino.

Halsey, A.H. (1993) Trends in Access and Equity in Higher Education: Britain in international perspective, *Oxford Review of Education,* 19, 2, 129–140.

Hore, T. (1993) Nontraditional Students: Third-age and Part-time. In B.R. Clark and G. Neave (eds) *The Encyclopaedia of Higher Education.* Oxford: Pergamon Press.

Lichtner, M. (1992) Italy. In P. Jarvis (ed) *Perspectives on Adult Education and Training in Europe.* Leicester: NIACE.

Luzatto, G.(1988) The debate on the university and the reform proposals in Italy, *European Journal of Education,* 23, 3, 237–47.

Macgregor, K. and Bompard, P. (1993) Short degrees to help labour market, *The Times Higher Educational Supplement,* 26 March.

Marinucci, C. (ed) (1993) *Higher Education in Italy A Guide for Foreigners 1993.* Italian Ministry for Universities and Scientific and Technological Research Higher Education in Italy. Roma: Istituto Poligafico e Zecca dello Stato.

Martinelli, I. (1992) Italy. In B.R. Clark and G. Neave (eds) *The Encyclopaedia of Higher Education.* Oxford: Pergamon Press.

Meghani, S. (1989) Technical and Vocational Education in Italy: The State and the Regions, *European Journal of Education,* 24, 2, 159–165.

Monasta, A. (1993) personal communication.

Monno, S. and Moramarco, S. (1988) Cultural action and the training of executives. The 'case' of the Altamura Cultural Service Centre (Bari). In *Education and Training of Adults for participation in Working Life and in the Community. Report of the International Seminar.* Bari: University of Bari.

Moscati, R.(1985) Reflections on Higher Education and the Polity in Italy, *European Journal of Education,* 20, 3, 127–139.

Moscati, R. (1991) Italy. In G. Neave and F. van Vught (eds) *Prometheus Bound. The Changing Relationship Between Government and Higher Education in Western Europe*. Exeter: BPCC Wheatons Ltd.

de Natale, L. (1993) personal communication.

Newport, A. (1979) A Comparative Study of Provision Made in Recurrent Education for Workers, with Special Reference to the '150 hours' in Italy, *Comparative Education, 15*, 3, 269–75.

OECD, (1985) Educational Reforms in Italy. In *Reviews of National Policies for Education*. Paris: OECD.

Orefice, P. (1988) A ten-year experimentation of participatory action research in Southern Italy (Naples). In *Education and Training of Adults for participation in Working Life and in the Community. Report of the International Seminar*. Bari: University of Bari.

Osbat, L. (1980) *The Provision of Distance Learning in Italy*. Berlin: European Centre for the Development of Vocational Training (CEDEFOP).

Ribolzi, L. (1987) Interfaces between secondary and higher education in Italy, *Higher Education in Europe, 12*, 2, 50–53.

Risk, M. and Crossman, R. (1979) The right to continuing education and the Italian initiative, *Adult Education 5*, 2, 244–50.

Scott, P. (1991) Access: An Overview. In T. Schuller (ed) *The Future of Higher Education*. Milton Keynes: Society for Research into Higher Education and Open University Press.

Simone, R. (1993) *L'Universita dei tre tradimentà*. Bari: Laterza et Figli.

Torsello, C. (1993) *Language Training for Professionals*. Paper presented at the EUCEN Conference, Barcelona, May 1993 (unpublished).

Trow, M. (1974) Problems in the transition from elite to mass higher education. In *Policies for Higher Education from the Conference on Further Structures of Post Secondary Education*. Paris: OECD.

Turrini, O. (1987) *Le Universita della Terza Eta*. Roma: Edizioni Lavoro.

Villa, P. and Marchetti, A. (1991) *Continuing training in firms and trainer development in Italy*. Berlin: The European Centre for the Development of Vocational Training (CEDEFOP).

Chapter 9

The Netherlands

Anna Spackman and Marleen Owen

The intimate relationship between higher education and fiscal policies has long been recognised in the Netherlands; for, according to tradition, when honoured by William the Silent in 1575 for the heroic defence of their city against the Spaniards, the citizens of Leiden chose the establishment of a university in preference to exemption from certain taxes. Now, in common with those of its European neighbours, the Dutch education system is attempting to produce a more highly qualified and trained population, whilst being very conscious of the cost of the enterprise. Figures published in 1989 (Kouwenaar and Stannard 1989) show that the proportion of the workforce with higher education increased between 1960 and 1985 from 4.4 per cent to 17.3 per cent of which 1.6 per cent and 4.4 per cent respectively were university educated. This sustained growth has been accompanied by a decline in higher education expenditure as a percentage of the national budget from 5.4 per cent in 1970 to 3.5 per cent in 1985. Nevertheless, predictions suggest that 1960 population training levels will be inverted by the year 2000, with about 66 per cent having gained qualifications at or above upper secondary level in contrast to about 20 per cent in 1960.

The last 15 years have seen a major overhaul of the education system affected by immigration, demographic changes, technical change, female participation, internationalisation and market forces, as well as ideological and economic concerns of improving quality, decentralisation of power from central government, economy of scale, policies for women and immigrant groups and the integration of the education system. Reform is continuing: 1993–94 sees the implementation of the Higher Education and Research Act and the new Secondary Education Act, which join legislation approved in 1992 – the Adult Education Framework Act, the Adult General Secondary Education Act and the Vocational Courses Act. These are being introduced within a policy which has as declared priorities:

- the improvement of teachers' pay and working conditions to raise the profession's status and encourage recruitment
- the reorganisation of secondary curricula
- a 'social innovation' policy using education to ease existing social problems
- cooperation between primary and special education
- the education of immigrants
- the limitation of 'the right to learn' to a first qualification at an appropriate level before the age of 27.

Whilst governmental control over the education system is extensive despite developments in decentralisation, provision of education is met by both state and private institutions. Since 1917 a constitutional right has existed allowing the establishment of educational provision according to religious and other principles to be equally funded with public authority education. Such compartmentalisation along religious and political lines is considerable in Dutch life, especially in education, and about 70 per cent of school pupils are educated privately. Three universities, the Free University of Amsterdam (Reformed Protestant), the University of Nijmegen and that of Tilburg (Catholic) are private and the other stream of the higher education sector, the *hogescholen*, will remain private under new legislation.

In a densely populated country – 15 million inhabitants in an area of 41,500 kilometres – there is one school to every square kilometre (Donkers 1993). With a decline in school leavers which is set to continue until the year 2000 (the birthrate having dropped by 25% since the end of the 1960s) and a shift away from agriculture and industry to the service sector, education and training are being increasingly geared towards employment. There are three areas of concern: female participation in employment (50.6% in 1988), the level of basic adult education amongst the unemployed, and the need to integrate an immigrant population – six per cent at present – amongst whom unemployment is high, despite the fact that 37 per cent have professional qualifications. Such considerations, as well as the need for 10,000 primary school teachers during the next decade to meet a birthrate rise ending 15 years of falling school rolls, have influenced the allocation of government finance and planning in both school and adult education.

The Structure of Higher Education

The implementation of the Higher Education and Research Act, replacing the Open University Act (1984), the Higher Vocational Education Act (1986) and the University Education Act (1986), affects the 13 universities, the Open University with its distance learning arrangements and some 83 *hogescholen*. The fact that the Act deals collectively with all these institutions marks the formal recognition of their equal footing, since under the new provisions, institutions will operate within the same framework, although the binary divide with regard to function is maintained.

The universities (excepting the Open University) will continue to carry out research and to provide education with a prominent academic component. Those of Leiden, Groningen, Amsterdam, Utrecht, Nijmegen, Tilburg, Rotterdam and Limburg, and the Free University of Amsterdam offer this in six of the eight recently identified sectors of university education – language and culture, law, economics, behavioural and social sciences, health sciences and natural sciences; three – Delft, Eindhoven and Twente – will continue to specialise in technology, and one – Wageningen – in agriculture. In addition, there are a number of institutions such as seven theological higher educational institutions, the Netherlands School of Business at Nijenrode and the Humanist University of Utrecht, which are independent but recognised by the *Ministerie van Onderwijs en Wetenschappen* (MOW), the Ministry of Education and Science.

The *hogescholen*, offering *hoger beroepsonderwijs*, variously translated as 'higher vocational education' in government publications and 'higher professional education' by the institutions themselves, offer programmes in agriculture, health care, the fine and performing arts, social work and community education, teacher training, technology and commerce and administration. The range offered by each institution varies, although all provide practical, professional training with only non-government funded research being carried out. Until 1985, the *hogescholen* came under the Secondary Education Act.

The developments of the last 25 years in higher education have been affected, as elsewhere, by the desire to meet increased participation within financial restrictions, resulting in budgetary cuts, programme restructure, institutional reorganisation and retrenchment and alterations in student funding. This has been accompanied by government policy to increase institutional autonomy, although funding is dependent on research and teaching quality and 'mission' achievement. One area in which central control is maintained, and is to be increased, is access to higher education. Admission depends upon achieving the appropriate secondary school diploma in the state examinations, giving the right to entry (with some restrictions) to universities and, from August 1994, to most *hogescholen*.

The Size of the System

The size of individual institutions varies: the University of Amsterdam is the largest university with about 25,000 students (1990) and the University of Limburg the smallest with 5000. The *hogescholen* vary from small institutions of about 300 students, mainly denominational training colleges, to very large institutions with thousands as the result of merger.

Table 9.1: Enrolments in higher education 1980–90

	Full-time			Part-time		
	M	W	All	M	W	All
Universities						
1980	92,712	42,588	135,300	3,061	974	4,035
1987	94,894	61,557	156,451	7,126	5,084	12,210
1990	86,216	65,393	151,609	7,712	6,801	14,513
Change						
1980–90	−7%	+54%	+12%	+152%	+598%	+260%
Hogescholen						
1980	77,192	54,747	131,939	36,568	42,170	78,738
1987	87,047	73,297	160,344	30,130	27,668	57,798
1990	103,092	90,640	193,732	26,924	26,034	52,958
Change						
1980–90	+34%	+66%	+47%	−26%	−38%	−33%

Source: Central Bureau for Statistics 1991 and 1992

Table 9.1 shows the number of enrolments between 1980 and 1990 and illustrates the scale of the expansion which has taken place in the period, particularly in the participation of women and in part-time university enrolments.

Higher Education Courses and Qualifications

Since 1982 with the introduction of the Two Tier Act, university students follow a four year, full-time undergraduate programme in most subjects for which five years' grant (reduced from six in 1991) is provided by the state and for which there is a six-year registration period. The first or *propaedeutic* year allows transfer, re-orientation or termination and can operate as a form of selection as students cannot proceed if they fail to pass within two years. If students do not graduate within the registration period, they can become 'auditors' with all regular student rights but with no study finance and at a higher fee. Students graduate either with a *doctoraal* qualification (drs before name), or *ingenieur* (ir) in engineering, and *meester* (mr) in law, all considered to be at international Master degree level.

The *hogescholen* courses also normally last for four full-time years and include practical training for up to a year during the third year, an emphasis necessitating the development of close ties with industry and other providers. *Hogescholen* students use the title *baccalaureus* (bc after name), although technology and agricultural students use *ingenieur* (ing): these are considered to be at international Bachelor degree level according to government publications or Master according to *hogescholen* publications. Professional qualifications in both sections may also be awarded at graduation.

Since 1986, as part of the process of institutional equalisation and horizontal mobility, *hogescholen* students passing *propaedeuse* examinations can transfer to the first year of a university course. Although transfer can occur at the end of second year, this is discouraged. Despite the formal recognition of equal footing in recent legislation, the detailed and distinct nomenclature, which will remain, is a confirmation of the continued kudos of a university degree, also reinforced by higher salaries. It is further reflected in the increasing number of students with a *hogescholen* diploma, ostensibly a higher education qualification, entering universities to upgrade their qualifications by a further two years' study.

Entry Qualifications and Routes

The distinction between intellectual and vocational training carried out by different kinds of institutions reflects earlier ideas of social class divisions, also seen in the secondary school system established in the late 1960s. Since 1968 children have proceeded at the age of 12, from primary education to different types of secondary school via a transitional class originally designed to facilitate transfer between schools. The six-year secondary education at an *atheneum*, *lyceum* or *gymnasium* provides pre-university education, *Voorbereidend Wetenschappelijk Onderwijs* (VWO), also a recognised qualification for *hogescholen*. All pupils in this route take a mixture of internally designed and national examinations in seven or more subjects. The five-year secondary education leading to the senior general secondary education diploma, *Hoger Algemeen Voortgezet Onderwijs* (HAVO), consists of six or seven subjects and ensures entry to the *hogescholen* but not to university. The four-year course results in a junior secondary education diploma, *Middelbaar Algemeen Voortgezet Onderwijs* (MAVO), which may be upgraded to HAVO. It can also lead onto a senior vocational education diploma, *Middelbaar Beroepsonderwijs* (MBO) after a further three or four years' study between the age of 16 and 20, based on an examination in six or seven subjects which is mainly internally assessed and includes compulsory work experience. This MBO diploma is a recognised *hogescholen* entry qualification and can also be taken after a four-year pre-secondary vocational education, *Voorbereidend Beroepsonderwijs* (VBO).

The four streams of VWO, HAVO, MAVO and VBO (until August 1992 this was known as junior secondary vocational, LBO) aim at horizontal mobility after the transitional year and vertical mobility after the completion of one stream. Despite this selective procedure, there is a drop-out rate although completion and continuation have improved. For example, in 1968, 45 per cent of MAVO pupils left without the qualification in comparison with only 3 per cent in 1992; similarly, of the 1992 HAVO leavers only 10 per cent left without the qualification in comparison with 40 per cent in 1968. Vertical mobility has been more successful, but costly, and the new Secondary Education Act introduces a core curriculum of 15 subjects with national attainment targets for all. From 1995–96 proposals to improve the transition from secondary to tertiary education or to employment will be introduced. For the former, four new study areas – environment and technology, environment and health, economics and society, culture and society – will relate more closely to those of higher education. In vocational education a new qualification structure will be produced from the existing apprenticeship system and vocational secondary education.

With the exception of the *colloquium doctum*, which is discussed in more detail below, the VWO programme was, until 1986, the sole university entrance qualification, enabling a student to be admitted to any university programme, although some subjects have legal requirements, such as Greek and Latin for theology, which if not gained as part of a VWO qualification must be met by additional tests either before entry or before the *propaedeuse* examination. In 1990, 70 per cent of first year students entered with VWO qualifications,

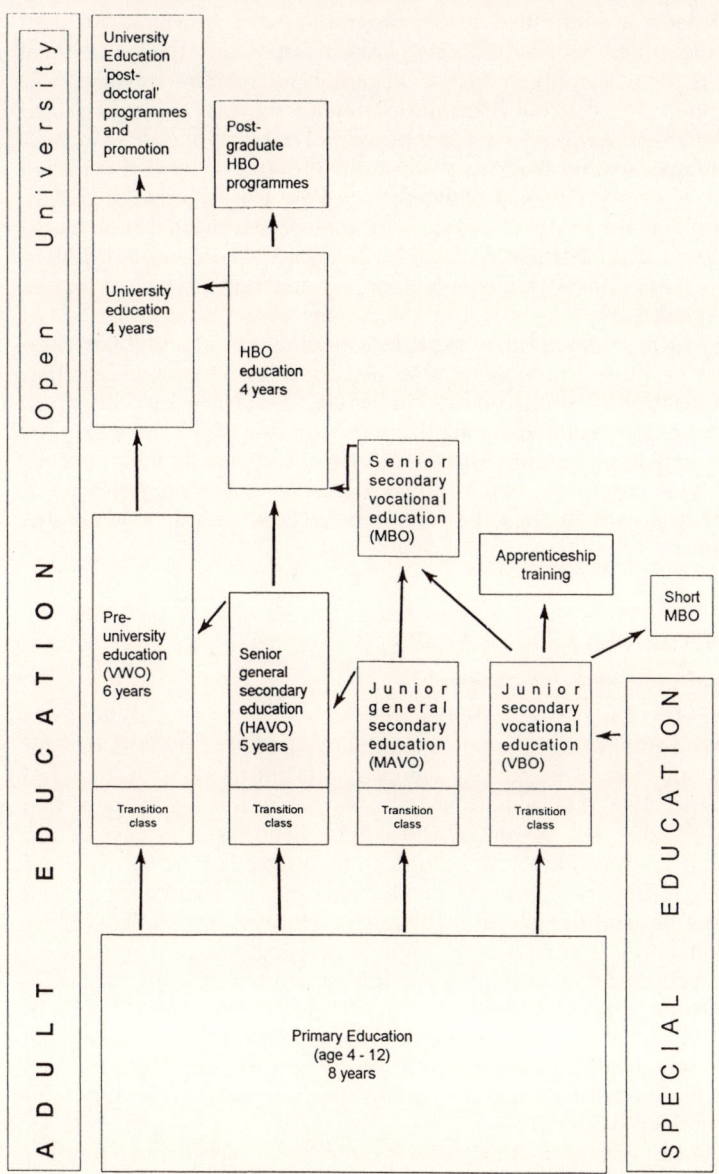

Source: Maassen *et al.* 1993

Figure 9.1: The Dutch education system

having applied through the Bureau of Registration and Placing. Students are admitted to the programme and university of their choice unless a *numerus clausus* has been imposed by the government to regulate the labour market in certain occupations or capacity is limited. The first bill (1966) proposing a temporary *numerus clausus* for medicine was rejected as it prevented freedom of choice. In 1972, a temporary bill was accepted on the grounds of limited capacity; subsequently (1985) prolonged, it is now closely associated with employment prospects, often with unexpected results, such as the current dire shortage of dentists. If quotas are imposed, a lottery procedure (in part dependent on examination grades) is implemented.

The *hogescholen* have operated without a central admissions system, each institution being able to select its own students. The harmonisation of admission rules in the 1992 Act is meeting with mixed reactions, one opinion being that it is depriving the *hogescholen* of the capacity to target individual or groups of students. It will, however, provide more information, since at present statistics are difficult to obtain as each faculty collects its own and is not permitted to divulge them.

Alternative Routes for Adults
Adults and adult education
The age of majority is 18, the school leaving age, 16 and, whilst in 1989 adult education was 'a readily available facility intended for anyone above compulsory school age' (Ministry of Education and Science 1989 p.1), a more recent government document states that 'adult education means all the activities and facilities designed to provide education and training for adults (that is, persons of 18 and over)' (Ministry of Education and Science 1992 p.13). In common with other parts of the educational system, education for adults is being changed both to reflect and reinforce the trend towards vocational education, the main activity of adult participants. During the last 20 years there has been an increase of participants from 10 to 12 per cent in 1971 to 20 per cent since 1985 with significant rises in vocational education, adult basic education and private training, balanced by a decline in participation in general adult secondary education and liberal adult education.

Adult education, in its widest sense, can be applied to a number of processes occurring after compulsory schooling, irrespective of age and setting. In practice, recent legislation covers four major areas, concerned with developing competences and gaining qualifications:

adult basic education, non-formal education and development work, short courses of vocational education, and adult general secondary education. Intended to provide a framework for achieving qualifications and skills within recognisable routes whilst being responsive to local conditions and demands, the Adult Education Framework Act differentiates between planning at national and regional level. Whilst the government allocates budgets, indicating priority areas, implementation is the responsibility of local authorities. It seems probable that this situation will result in increasing competition for resources and an attempt to generate more income from such sources as student fees.

Adult basic education has been a priority since 1987 and is concerned with numeracy, literacy, social and cultural skills, as well as introductory vocational courses and courses for immigrants. Participation has increased from 30,000 in 1981 to 115,000 in 1991; two-thirds are women, half are younger than 35 and 50 per cent are from ethnic minorities including immigrants from Turkey, Morocco, Surinam and the Dutch Antilles as well as second generation immigrants who suffered set-backs at school.

To achieve its broader social objectives, non-formal education takes place through voluntary organisations such as trade unions, churches and political parties and since 1988 has been the responsibility of the MOW. The provision is diverse, numerically unquantifiable and offered in such subsidised institutions as folk universities, local educational and creativity centres, music schools, residential colleges and many community and neighbourhood centres.

Vocational training is provided by schemes such as the part-time secondary vocational education which allows adults to acquire an MBO certificate. Participation in this programme has grown significantly from 33,000 in 1979 to 53,000 in 1987. In addition there is day release for apprentices, and since the mid 1980s when the upper age limit of 16–27 for the apprenticeship scheme was removed, numbers have doubled to 138,000.

General secondary education for adults

Opportunities for older students to gain academic qualifications are supported by the government through adult general secondary education provided at the day/evening schools. The divide between academic and vocational continues with MAVO, HAVO and VWO provided under the Adult General Secondary Education Act (VAVO) and the MBO courses under the Vocational Courses Act, although all are funded by the MOW. Until 1975, the schools offered only evening classes, but day classes were added to accommodate women who wished to improve their limited education. This emancipatory 'Mother MAVO', not always resulting in qualifications, was important in encouraging female participation and is now often used by immigrants. Since 1978, unlike ordinary school diploma programmes, certificates may be obtained for individual subjects and accumulated to complete MAVO, HAVO or VWO diplomas. In contrast to young school pupils, adults studying for VWO require only six subjects, the seventh being untested 'life experience'. The courses are state subsidised, although students pay a contribution to non-subsidised costs, as well as examination and course fees, financial help being available from the Ministry or the local authority. Normally a HAVO course lasts three years and a VWO course four, but accelerated courses are offered, and for every course there are prior educational requirements. Whilst it is possible to accumulate qualifications from a low initial basis, the provision is increasingly being used by secondary school 'drop-outs'. Drop-out rates from the day/evening classes are high and, from a peak in 1982, total registration has declined by 25 per cent to 90,000 in 1988, and further, to 87,817 in 1990–91. The most dramatic fall has been in MAVO, which traditionally attracts women in the 30–40 age range, whilst the age range 25–30 is hardly represented in HAVO and VWO, (the main groups being 18–25 and 30–50). These changes may show increasing moves away from personal development towards career-orientated programmes supported institutionally by condensed courses, efficient flow-through and economy of scale. Significantly the new Secondary Education Act has not been framed with any consideration of the needs of adults.

Since September 1992 there have been 78 day/evening schools (previously 84 and to be reduced further to 45–50), which will become part of the Regional Training Centres (ROCs), although smaller branches (up to 125 are anticipated) may be established where and whenever a regional council decides. The ROCs will accommodate adult basic and general secondary education, day-release courses for apprentices, secondary vocational education and training for job-seekers and are an important development in government plans towards a single Vocational Education Act dealing with adult education and training. Whilst recognising advantages, there is a fear that, with the increased emphasis on basic education and vocational training, the academic work of the institutions will be reduced.

Colloquium doctum

In the British sense, access courses do not exist and indeed a description of one was met by the indignant response, 'That is not fair!' However, both universities and *hogescholen* operate their own entrance procedures for students aged over 21 without standard qualifications. The university *colloquium doctum* was developed in the nineteenth century from rural students' desire to study theology – how different would have been the fate of Jude the Obscure if he had been Dutch. Once quite literally a chat with a professor to assess aptitude, it is now an entrance examination regulated by law which all universities must implement, although certain subjects can be exempted. Required by law since 1921, the qualifying age has been reduced from 30 to 25 in 1981 and further to 21 in 1986, a move towards social equity, enabling, although not encouraging, greater participation. It is open to all over 21 who possess some form of educational qualifications, such as a higher vocational diploma gained, for example, in the armed forces or the civil service, but which is not recognised for university admission. The *colloquium doctum* is an individual and subject-specific admissions procedure, based upon equivalences and deficiencies, and students with MAVO and HAVO diplomas can enter by this procedure. Each application, which must be for a specific course at a specific university, is assessed by a faculty committee to determine which entrance examinations should be taken to supplement deficiencies in the chosen subject. A maximum number of subjects, varying from faculty to faculty, is imposed and tests set by the faculties are based closely upon (at times are) the written VWO examinations, resits being allowed at faculty discretion. To prepare for the examinations students may study privately, do a correspondence course or enrol at an institute or school. The University of Utrecht has its own arrangements for students with deficiencies, the James Boswell Institute, providing courses of between six weeks and a year.

Application rates have declined since 1986 as the *colloquium doctum* is no longer obligatory for transferring *hogescholen* diploma students. In 1979 11.8 per cent of all university students entered with a *colloquium doctum* (Karstanje 1981); in 1991–92, 2.4 per cent (4027) of all registered university students (165,791) had entered by this method. Among the 1991 intake they constituted 1.9 per cent (536) of all entrants (27,932) and of these, nearly 75 per cent (401) were aged between 19 and 29. Whilst among those under 35 years old the proportion of men and women was similar, among those aged over 35 there were 61 women to 35 men. These figures may include students registered for single courses and foreign students, as well as full degrees. Predictably, the intake varies from subject to subject, agriculture and technology having few entrants by this method, and from university to university. In 1991–92, the University of Amsterdam had 1130 *colloquium doctum* students, 4.6 per cent of its registered total of 24,466; Leiden had 582, (3.3% of 17,855); and the Free University, 325 (2.8% of 11,732). Between them, Delft, Eindhoven, Twente and Wageningen had 60 among 30,736 registered students, less than 0.2 per cent. From September 1993, each university's *colloquium doctum* will apply only to that university, replacing a number of reciprocal arrangements. This restriction, due in part to the perception that certain university tests are easier than others, illustrates how an enabling facility has been tightened by reference to 'standards'. The lottery for certain subjects where numbers are limited will affect the *colloquium doctum* student who is not awarded his or her preferred university and who is directed to another at which the qualification will be invalid. Other changes are being implemented: for example, the requirement for adequate general knowledge is being dropped and the requirement for 'knowledge' of the Dutch language is increased to 'mastery', although no further test is required if the candidate is satisfactory at interview. Nevertheless, the *colloquium doctum* does provide an alternative admission, especially for the humanities and social sciences and for part-time degree students.

Hogescholen routes

A further variation on the route to university is via the *hogescholen*. Since 1986, (although an experimental stage existed earlier) *hogescholen* students who pass the *propaedeuse* examination can enter a university course, although no credit is given for the *hogescholen* year, as the qualifying HAVO diploma is a year shorter than the VWO qualifying time. This route, which theoretically enables a student to gain university entrance with a VBO followed by a MBO certificate plus the *propaedeuse* diploma, is seen as a 'back door' route, an opportunity for lower income students with non-VWO qualifications. However, it has not been successful, as many of the 'switching' students drop out. More favoured is the entrance of *hogescholen* diploma students to a university degree course, normally in a related subject. This accumulation brings a more prestigious qualification and in six years a student who has spent a year less at school can achieve a degree by the HAVO–HBO diploma route. This has been successful – in 1991 8003 of 39,235 entrants had such a diploma – and welcomed by the universities because of the quality of students. However, it is likely to decline because of the restriction of the student grant to five years. The government is discouraging *stapelen*, the accumulation of diplomas, by supporting the payment of only one higher education qualification.

Because of institutional diversity and professional considerations, the *hogescholen* have selected students with a wider range of qualifications, and since 1985, entrance assessments have been operated for students over 21. One interesting scheme is that run by the *hogeschool* at Haarlem in the Social Work sector, providing only part-time courses for adults and available in a further 19 towns in the north. The specific didactic requirements of adults are recognised, including the opportunity to do a follow-through MBO and HBO in the same institution. As the courses are built on life and work experience, all HBO students must be over 21 years of age and work a minimum of 20 hours a week in a relevant occupation, paid or voluntary, and they can participate in a pre-entry test provided that they have at least two years relevant work experience and have a specified diploma, certificate or degree in addition to the general requirements. In contrast at the Catholic Hogeschool at Tilburg, the general entrance test for those over 21 years of age and without recognised qualifications is an interview, to prove suitability for the course and possession of sufficient general knowledge and knowledge of Dutch. In addition, some subjects, including social work, have a national entry exam for non-standard students.

Another recent development has been *Hoger Onderwijs voor Ouderen*, (Higher Education for Older Adults) or HOVO, for those over 50, provided by various universities and *hogescholen*. Rotterdam, for example, has had 1114 *cursist*, 'course takers', registered for programmes consisting of 10 to 12 weekly meetings of two-and-a-half hours, and 2921 attending lecturers since its inceptions in 1988. In 1992–93, 383 *cursist* registered for 15 certificated courses and 1067 attended lectures. *Cursist* do not need entry qualifications, although many have diplomas or degrees. They study primarily for interest but 10 have enrolled subsequently for degrees. For those qualified with VWO, HBO diplomas or university degrees, it is possible to join a special 50+ programme in philosophy, which must be completed within two years and which can be credited for subsequent degree work.

At present the government has no plans to relax the standard entry requirements, although accreditation of work-based and experiential learning is being considered and VAVO students require only six VWO subjects, with the internally examined part adapted to the age and experience of older students. It is claimed that the different means of gaining qualifications are increasing, but an interviewed official stated that 'if you have the entry ticket, you get in, no problem. That is not going to change, not at all'. Currently there are indications that the standard of the 'entry ticket' (VWO, HAVO and MBO diplomas) will be raised so that admission to higher education will become more limited.

Policy Relating to Adults and Higher Education

Encouragement and a consideration of the needs of older students have played no part in the formulation of higher education policy during recent changes. Indeed, progressive alterations to the grants and loans system can be seen to penalise such students, for the expectation is that pupils proceed from secondary to tertiary education without a break. Reforms to the secondary school syllabus, with the addition of better careers and subject guidance, are being made partly to reduce the drop-out rate from the *propaedeuse* year. Although efforts have and are being made to increase participation of female students and of those from immigrant groups, similar efforts are not being made to attract older students. The ethos of life-long vocational training, in-service training, up-dating of job qualifications and the acquiring of basic skills are seen to be the more appropriate outlet for adult educational aspirations.

Training and the consideration of labour market demands mark changes to higher education during the last 25 years. Since the late 1970s, government policy has been to support open access to higher education, increasing efficiency and making the universities in particular responsive to market-orientated aims. This has been effected by top-down reforms: by reorganising the *hogescholen* (reduced from 348 to 85 between 1983 and 1987), increasing their autonomy and improving their status; by 'internally democratising' university government through the addition of non-professorial and external representatives and by increasing institutional autonomy; by stimulating the efficiency of graduate production through reduced registration times for undergraduate programmes, reduced programme length and alterations to student grants and loans. All these reforms have been accompanied by severe cuts in budgets.

These earlier 'corrective' policies have, more recently, given way to 'facilitative' policies (Maassen, Goedegebuure and Westerheijden 1993, van Vught 1991), in which the introduction of quality controls, performance indicators, separate research, teaching and mission budgets have been introduced to improve the ability of institutions to respond to societal changes. Reduced government control and increased institutional autonomy over courses and personnel have been implemented to aid this process.

These developments were discussed through a number of ministerial policy documents, especially the consultative *Hoger Onderwijs en Onderzoek Plan* (HOOP) (1987) and a further white paper of the same name in 1992. In each, the greater emphasis on market-responsive education is shown clearly. The first HOOP had as its aims:

> to ensure that individuals have access to higher education regardless of social background or financial resources, but only on the basis of academic aptitude as expressed in formal qualifications; to respect the individual's freedom to enter the university or HBO institute and the course programme, of his or her choice; to meet society's demands for higher education, both quantitatively and qualitatively. (Kouwenaar and Stannard 1989 p.11)

The 1992 HOOP stated that:

> no contradiction exists between the value of education for the labour market and the importance of personal development...because education which does not prepare for vocational occupation does not really offer any personal development...it is also true that education is more than just a preparation for the labour market. (Ministry of Education and Science 1992 p.3)

Changes to an emphasis on quality, accountability, efficiency, institutional performance and management are to be seen against the continual discussion of the financing of education and the responsibility of the government to provide funded tertiary education. In 1991 the upper age limit for eligibility for financial support was reduced from 30 to 27, particularly affecting older part-time *hogescholen* students studying to improve their employability. Fees are rising: in 1993–94, Dfl 2050 (full-time), Dfl 1550 (part-time); in 1994–95, Dfl 2150 and Dfl 1625 and in 1995–96 Dfl 2250, and Dfl 1700 respectively. Consideration is also being given to abolishing the basic grant for all and introducing an income-related grant for the most needy and loans for others. An intention to achieve improvement in school teaching conditions by a budget re-allocation from higher education may result in higher fees for older students.

Whilst older students have no influence on policy, students as individuals are envisaged as playing an increasing role in institutional planning through their choice of course, based on qualitative information, which will encourage 'consumer satisfaction' to be considered in course development. Under the new Act, all courses will be registered by a central government bureau and consultation of the register will be encouraged, as will consultation of quality reports on teaching and research. There is little doubt that the ethos of the market-place, as well as its language, is all-pervasive.

Alternative, Accessible Programmes in Higher Education
The Open University

The third component of the Higher Education and Research Act is the Open University, widely regarded as the most appropriate route for adults who desire academic qualifications. Started in 1984, it offers both university and *hogescholen* diplomas to those over 18 who do not wish to or cannot attend regular classes. No qualifications are required as it is intended as an accessible second chance route ideally to be combined with employment. Its 'four freedoms', expressed in the 1984 Open University Act, are freedom of access, of compiling an individual study programme, of studying when and where wished and of proceeding at an individual pace. Seen as cheaper and as reducing pressure on existing institutions, a founding principle was to encourage innovation in course and teaching methods. Distance learning packages, structured into modules consisting of 100 study hours (equalling three study points), provide degree or certificate programmes or combinations from both university and *hogescholen* programmes. The guided self-study, essentially a correspondence course, is delivered through written and audio-visual materials, although not regular television and radio programmes because of individual pacing requirements. Flexibility is essential to meet employment demands and, if the course is for a particular job, structured courses are offered with compulsory elements. Advice and tutoring can be obtained from 18 centres throughout the country and fees vary according to previous education, those with higher education paying more, although means-tested grants are available.

Although designed as a corrective mechanism for unqualified students, the Open University has been used predominantly by students with higher qualifications taking short courses: in 1992, from a total enrolment of 57,028 (21,649 women), 88.9 per cent had a higher education qualification or were qualified to enter higher education. As yet, there are no graduates, and, in its original terms, the Open University has not been a success, but it has developed a recognised strength in short courses. Similarly, its innovative effect has not been extensive, except perhaps upon those regular university staff who cooperated to provide course material. Indeed, the opposite can be seen in the recent move to establish faculties instead of interdisciplinary teams at the University's headquarters at Heerlen.

Part-time provision

Commitment to concurrent higher education and employment can also be seen in the development of part-time courses and evening classes in the universities. Regular university part-time study is recent (early 1980s), brought about by the prospect of increasing competition from the Open University and the reduction of registration time to six years which resulted in pressure on students in employment. In 1991, the 13 universities offered 36 courses taught in both full and part-time mode: in 1993–94 42 will be offered, with one, labour market studies at Groningen, part-time only. However, part-time provision at Wageningen ceased in 1992 because of lack of funding and interest. The most widely offered part-time course is in law, which nearly 50 per cent of part-time students were studying in 1986, with 28 per cent in behavioural or social sciences. The sector is growing: by 1988 it had increased by 300 per cent over 1979 to 13,000 and had risen by a further 1500 in 1990 (see Table 9.1). Most students are over 25 and one in three has completed a higher vocational course. In addition, some universities offer the opportunity to follow lecture courses, either for interest or as 'refresher' courses. The *à la carte* students of the Faculties of Arts and of Religion and Philosophy at Leiden are not allowed to sit tests, whilst those attending the 'open lectures' at the University of Amsterdam may. Fees depend on the number of courses taken and whether they are examined.

Hogescholen part-time enrolment, often for professional reasons, has always been higher, although there has been a recent decline – from 72,599 in 1985 to 52,958 in 1990 (see Table 9.1). In 1986, a quarter of the pre-diploma total of 200,000 was studying part-time, nearly half being registered in education, whilst registration was high in behavioural and social studies. In contrast, the male-dominated subjects were almost all full-time: engineering had only 10 per cent of its students part-time and agriculture had none. In 1991, 418 courses were offered both on a full and part-time basis and 183 part-time only: in 1993–94, 462 will be full- and part-time and 165 part-time only, mainly in teaching. Part-time courses are popular with those from lower income groups, women, immigrants and older students, and in 1991 about 38,500 of the 53,000 part-time students were over 27, with women in the majority. Part-time diploma courses normally take five or six years to complete but students with jobs can complete in four years, with different teaching methods and examinations to take account of their work experience. This group is older, on average aged 25–40, and will be affected by the increase in fees and lack of grants.

Modularisation is being stimulated. For example, at the University of Amsterdam, arts courses have been modularised since 1991 and merit seven points a unit, six units being taken in a year. At the

University of Groningen there is centrally organised modularisation and at the University of Utrecht some faculties are modularised. The *hogescholen* run modular programmes, which are continuously assessed, and many courses in the day/evening schools are modular. These developments have met with mixed reactions: students have a greater say in study methods and programmes thus making education more flexible and relevant, but demands upon staff for guidance and advice increase. Modules have been tried experimentally in 23 per cent of schools for the more academic programmes, but are more common in vocational secondary education.

In general, discussions on the evaluation of distance learning, accreditation of prior learning and accreditation, seen as part of the internationalising of education, are occurring, but, given the current drop-out rate in higher education, the need for counselling for such students is seen as the priority to prevent failure. Credit transfer in higher education exists for students who wish to transfer between the Open University and other institutions and from *hogescholen* to a university degree, the new Act determining that a study point equals 40 hours with first degrees having 168 points, 42 for the *propaedeutic* year. It appears that the few university students transferring to *hogescholen* (mainly from the technical universities) can bargain for credit recognition.

Resources and Funding

Public spending on education is high: in 1988 it was 6.8 per cent of the Gross Domestic Product, 28.8 per cent of the education budget being spent on higher education, the highest among OECD countries (OECD 1992). The funding of the two streams of academic and vocational higher education has been subject to change and simplification, although the block grant funding, conditional upon operating within government plans and regulations, remains different between the universities and the *hogescholen*. The universities receive *per capita* grants for students whilst the *hogescholen* are funded to encourage completion, receiving 1.35 years for any student who leaves without a diploma and 4.5 years for a graduate.

The cost of higher education student grants (Dfl 2500 million in 1991) has become of major concern. In 1986, the Student Grants and Loans Act was intended to make full-time students over 18 years old in secondary and tertiary education more independent, whilst enabling anyone capable to receive education. A basic grant, including an element for fees, was available to all, with means-tested supplementary grants and interest-bearing loans. Eligibility for finance ceased at 30 years of age although older students qualified if they started before that age and studied without interruption or alteration. Since 1991, changes to reduce expenditure by Dfl 700 million by 1995 have been introduced: the basic grant was frozen at August 1991 level (Dfl 570 a month for students away from the parental home), and only available for five years with an upper age limit of 27. Additional finance in the form of a loan (to be paid off over 15 years), a supplementary grant for low income students and a reduced price travel card became available but higher tuition fees were also introduced. Further changes were announced in May 1993: study registration is to be reduced to five years and the possibility of making grants income and performance related and of restricting the use of the travel card are mooted. As part-time students receive no funding (abolished in 1991), the increasing fees are a particular blow to them, and those over 27 are further hit by the encouragement being given to institutions to set higher fees for older students. Differential fees are being set: 1993–94 fees for 'auditors' are Dfl 2730 at the Free University of Amsterdam and Dfl 2870 at the University of Amsterdam with examination only fees of Dfl 1120 and Dfl 1180 respectively.

Conclusion

Whilst the future for adults in higher education seems increasingly uncertain, there is nevertheless a growing demand for adult education arising from an ageing work force needing retraining. Whilst recent changes are encouraging more responsiveness to societal needs, the Dutch higher education institutions have not in the past responded adequately to the demands for continuing education as can be seen by the amount of corporate education and training supplied by private establishments (Hake 1992). The Open University is perhaps the exception, although the government stress on market-orientation and internationalism may result in others following suit.

There is little research in this field. Whilst pioneering work has been done in such areas as the theory of andragogy and its rise and fall as a university discipline (see Van Gent 1992), participation in adult education, the effectiveness of institutions and curriculum development (see Cramer and Houtkoop 1990 and their suggestions for further research) and in adult education history (Van Gent 1987), there is little on adult participation in tertiary education. Fieldwork in the Netherlands for a research project from which this chapter comes showed that information and statistics relating to non-standard students are limited. Further work is required to investigate more closely the intake of second chance students, their backgrounds, motivation and success especially in the changing world of contracting government finance and institutional competition. In particular, the impact of recent legislation on accessibility and participation by adults requires careful monitoring.

Note

This chapter arises from a UFC/SHEFC-funded research project, 'Policy Frameworks for Access in three European Educational Systems (Denmark, the Netherlands and Scotland)' carried out in 1992–93. Particular thanks are due to Dr B. Hake of the University of Leiden for his support in this work.

References

Central Bureau for Statistics (1991) and (1992) *Zakboek Onderwijsstatistieken.* 's-Gravenhage: CBS.

Cramer, G. and Houtkoop, W. (1990) *Investing in Human Resources.* Utrecht: RVE Adviescentrum Volwasseneneducatie.

Donkers, B. (1993) Going to school in Holland, *Holland Horizon 5,* 3, 12–15.

Hake, B.J. (1992) *The Emergent Learning Force: some critical notes on continuing education and adult learners.* Paper delivered at the EUCEN conference, Leiden (unpublished).

Karstanje, P. (1981) Selection for Higher Education in the Netherlands, *European Journal of Education 16,* 2, 197–208.

Kouwenaar, K. and Stannard, J. (1989) *Higher Education in the Netherlands.* Zoetermeer: Netherlands Organisation for International Co-operation in Higher Education.

Maassen, P.A.M., Goedegebuure, L.C.J. and Westerheijden, D.F. (1993) Social and political considerations for the changing higher education structure in the Netherlands. In C. Gellert (ed) *Higher Education in Europe.* London: Jessica Kingsley Publishers.

Ministry of Education and Science (1989) *Newsletter 23E.* Zoetermeer: Ministerie van Onderwijs en Wetenschappen.

Ministry of Education and Science (1992) *Education policy in the Netherlands: 1990–1992.* Zoetermeer: Ministerie van Onderwijs en Wetenschappen.

Ministry of Education and Science (1992) *Hoger Onderwijs en Onderzoek Plan 1992.* Zoetermeer: Ministerie van Onderwijs en Wetenschappen.

OECD (1992) *Education at a Glance. OECD Indicators.* Paris: OECD.

van Gent, F.A. (1987) Government and voluntary organisations in the Netherlands: two hundred years of adult education and information (1784–1984), *International Journal of Lifelong Education* 6, 4, 279–294.
van Gent, B. (1992) The Netherlands. In P. Jarvis (ed) *Perspectives on Adult Education and Training in Europe*. Leicester: NIACE.
van Vught, F.A. (1991) The Netherlands: From Corrective to Facilitative Governmental Policies. In G. Neave and F.A. van Vught (eds) *Prometheus Bound. The Changing Relationship between Government and Higher Education in Western Europe*. Oxford: Pergamon Press.

Chapter 10

Scotland

Michael Osborne and Jim Gallacher

The importance of encouraging the participation of adult students in higher education has been a major theme in educational policy in Scotland in recent years. The effects of this can be seen in national initiatives such as the Scottish Wider Access Programme (SWAP) and the Scottish credit accumulation and transfer network (SCOTCAT). This chapter will explore the reasons for the emergence of these policies, the developments in provision to which they have led, and their consequences in encouraging adult participation.

Relevant Aspects of Scottish Educational System

Higher education provision in Scotland is the preserve of three main types of institution: universities, colleges of education and further education colleges. At undergraduate level the main function of universities is to offer three year general degrees and four year honours degrees, although opportunities are increasingly provided for students to exit with certificates or diplomas if they do not wish to, or are unable to, complete their degree studies. The colleges of education are relatively small institutions offering a range of provision, notably teacher training, and a number have amalgamated with universities since the early 1990s. The universities and these colleges together represent the higher education section, but some higher education provision is found within the further education sector. The major function of the further education colleges is the provision of post-16 vocational education, mainly through Scottish Vocational Education Council (SCOTVEC) qualifications, and included in this is a growing range of Higher National Certificate (HNC) and Higher National Diploma (HND) courses, which, as well as providing vocational qualifications, also parallel years one and two of certain university courses. An important focus of recent access initiatives has been to provide new routes into and through this provision. Figure

10.1 shows the various routes into higher education, the provision therein and the providers.

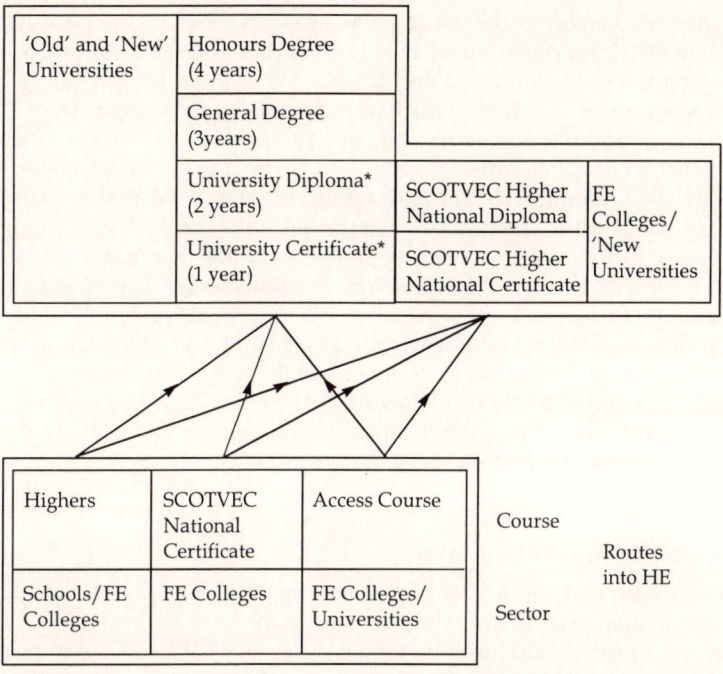

* Possible exit points – students at universities are admitted to degree programmes (a minimum of three years full-time study)

—— An unusual route, particularly to 'old' universities

Figure 10.1: Routes into higher education and higher education provision

The reference to 'new' universities is a reflection of one of two major legislative changes in the 1990s that have affected the whole of the post-compulsory sector. Prior to 1992 there were eight publicly funded universities in Scotland (Aberdeen, Dundee, Edinburgh, Glasgow, Heriot-Watt, St. Andrews, Stirling and Strathclyde) funded by the Universities Funding Council (UFC) which in turn was responsible to the Secretary of State for Education and Science in London.

Other higher education institutions in Scotland, the central institutions (CIs) (equivalent to polytechnics in England) and colleges of education, were funded directly through the Scottish Office in Edinburgh by the Secretary of State for Scotland.

The distinction between universities, polytechnics and colleges, generally known as the 'binary line', was described by the government in its 1991 White Paper, 'Higher Education – A New Framework' (Department of Education and Science 1991), as an obstacle to the progression of its policies, which were designed to help 'secure record numbers and participation in higher education'. Legislation in 1992 abolished the binary line by setting up a new framework for higher education through the creation of a single funding agent for the whole sector, the Scottish Higher Education Funding Council (SHEFC), and the extension of degree awarding powers and the title of university to those central institutions which met certain criteria. The effect has been to create four new universities, Glasgow Caledonian, Napier, Paisley and Robert Gordon's, from four existing CIs. Other CIs and colleges of education have either not met the criteria and retain their old titles (although they are now funded by SHEFC), or have amalgamated with existing universities. This parallels similar developments in England and Wales.

Routes to Higher Education

The traditional route into higher education is through 'Highers', examinations which are administered by the Scottish Examination Board (SEB) and are taken by school pupils normally at 17. A minimum of three and more often four or more Higher subjects must be passed in order to secure entry to university courses. Depending on which university degree applicants wish to enter, the subjects and grades required will vary. As a general rule the grades required will increase in proportion to demand for available places, rather than in relation to the academic demands of the degree. Many pupils stay at school for a further year, taking the Certificate of Sixth Year Studies (CSYS) before proceeding to university.

However, these qualifications may not be maintained as the structure of compulsory (up to age 16) and post-compulsory (up to age 18) school education has been the subject of extensive review by the Howie Committee which reported in 1992 (Scottish Office Education Department (SOED) 1992a), recommending the creation of separate academic and vocational routes for pupils from age 14 upwards. Although the SOED have not accepted all the recommendations of the committee, the Secretary of State for Scotland announced in

March 1994 that significant reforms in upper secondary education will be introduced in 1997–98 (SOED 1994a). The most significant changes will be that whilst Highers will be maintained, content will be drawn from both current SCOTVEC and SEB provision and that a new two year 'Advanced Higher' will be developed, incorporating and replacing CSYS. It is likely that pupils intending to enter universities from this time will be largely encouraged to by-pass Highers examinations at age 17 and instead take a diet of 'Advanced Highers' at 18, making this age the norm for admission.

At present, adult students may use the traditional Highers route as a mechanism for gaining entry to higher education, normally by taking part-time courses in schools (either in the evening or in the day, often alongside school pupils) or full-time or part-time courses in further education colleges. Commonly, adults, particularly those studying Highers on a part-time basis in the evening because of work commitments, are made offers of entry to university courses on the basis of achieving less than the 'going rate' for entry through traditional routes.

The further education sector offers a range of other educational provision, much of which is of relevance to adult students: in particular, full-time Access courses under the auspices of the Scottish Wider Access Programme (SWAP) (Scottish Education Department (SED) 1988). In addition there is a range of vocational qualifications, mainly provided under the auspices of SCOTVEC, ranging from National Certificate (NC) programmes (pre-HE) to Higher National Certificate (HNC) and Higher National Diplomas (HND). In turn students can use each of these vocational qualifications as a means of progression to a related higher level vocational programme or to a degree programmes. Acceptance on a degree programme and the stage of the degree to which applicants with vocational qualifications are admitted is at the discretion of each university. The development of the SCOTCAT network, and of articulation arrangements (which we discuss below), are designed to create frameworks which will assist these processes of transfer. However, it remains that in a number of cases universities may not recognise the HNC/D as equivalent to the first or second year of degree level study, and students transferring from an FE college to a university may not obtain full credit for their earlier course.

The older universities also offer other potential programmes of preparation for and articulation with degree structures via the tradition of liberal adult education courses. The extent of such offerings and its associated government funding has recently been summarised by SHEFC (1993 annex 3) and takes the form of short courses in a range of disciplines with open access to members of the community.

Historically this provision has most easily fitted into the internationally understood category of 'lifelong learning', and has not been associated with accreditation or certification. However, with the onset of new funding mechanisms for continuing education which carry with them requirements for quantifiable performance indicators, the universities which offer liberal adult programmes are devising mechanisms by which such provision can be credit-rated against existing Access and undergraduate courses. It is therefore likely that within the next two years, many existing structures will offer credit points that can be accumulated towards a qualification and *de facto* adult access to higher education will have been increased to a considerable extent.

The university contribution to adult participation would not be complete, however, without a consideration of the Open University. This distance education institution operates throughout the UK offering all levels of university courses. Although centrally organised from England, it has a major base in Scotland and a Scottish director in Edinburgh. Through the use of radio and television, open learning materials, personal tutorials and summer schools, it offers, according to 1991 figures (SOED 1992b), modular undergraduate programmes to some 11,000 students in Scotland alone. For entry to its Foundation Courses no qualifications are required, although demand frequently outstrips supply leading to waiting lists for places.

Although further and higher education provide important routes through which adults gain access to higher level programmes, other sectors provide mechanisms for entry. A notable contribution is that made by schools where there has been a long tradition of 'in-filling' adult students into all levels of courses associated with various SEB examinations. According to recent statistics, in 1990, 340 of the 424 Scottish secondary schools made available study opportunities to adult students (SOED 1992c); almost one fifth of the courses on which adults study were at SEB Higher level.

The complete extent of relevant education provision for adults is detailed in two recent publications (Munn, Tett and Arney 1993, SOED 1992b) which provide examples from other sectors. For instance, the Community Education Service in Strathclyde Region which is responsible for a range of provision including adult basic education, youth work, community development and in some cases adult educational guidance, together with other providers facilitates the 'Local Collaborative Programme' initiative in which courses are made available in the community based on locally identified needs. The Workers Educational Association (WEA) programme 'Learning for Earning' is another example. The WEA is an organisation which has its origins in developing adult education provision in cooperation with the labour movement and is now a major provider to a wide range of groups such as women, the unemployed and adults living in areas of economic and social disadvantage. The course quoted is aimed at unemployed people over 25 seeks to give a 'taste' of education, to develop confidence and to explore opportunities for progression to further and higher education. It is but one of the many initiatives in the non-formal and informal sectors of education that leads to initial participation, a key factor in encouraging further participation (Macpherson 1989).

Adult Participation

For the purposes of entry to higher education in Scotland, the age of 21 delineates the 'adult' from other entrants; although by no means an 'official' cut-off point, it is the age at which the Scottish Universities Council on Entrance (SUCE) and the SOED make their distinctions. According to recent provisional SOED statistics there were over 11,000 full-time and over 17,000 part-time entrants to higher education aged 21 and over in 1991-92. These figures represent age participation indices per 1000 of the Scottish population aged 21 and over of 3.1 and 4.6 respectively.

Table 10.1: Entrants to higher education courses, 1985-1991, aged 21 and over

	Full-time			Part-time		
	No. 21+	21+ as % of all Entrants	Age Participation Index**	No. 21+	21+ as % of all Entrants	Age Paricipation Index**
1985	6052	20.4	1.7	13718	54.3	3.8
1986	6449	25.0	1.8	15555	61.4	4.3
1987	6977	26.1	1.9	15269	60.5	4.2
1988	7378	27.2	2.0	15190	62.7	4.1
1989	8354	27.2	2.3	15346	62.1	4.1
1990	9358	28.9	2.5	15273	63.2	4.1
1991*	11614	31.4	3.1	17142	70.0	4.6

Source: SOED 1992c and 1994b

** Age Participation Index (per 1000 of population in Scotland)

* Provisional data

More detailed data (Table 10.1) show that the 1991–92 figures are the culmination of a steady increase in adult entry to full-time courses from 1985 onwards. Entry to part-time study, whilst increasing over the same period, does so less markedly (albeit from a higher base) and through two stepped increases in 1986 and 1991. Table 10.2 provides further information regarding the sectors which full-time and part-time students were entering in 1991.

Table 10.2: Entrants to higher education courses, 1991, full-time and part-time by age and sector

	First Degree			Other Advanced Courses (scotvec)		
	Age 21+	All ages	21+ as % of all entrants	Age 21+	All ages	21+ As % of all entrants
Full-time						
Universities	3920	16228	24.2			
Central Institutions	1673	7373	22.7	970	2486	39
Scottish Agricultural College	17	74	23	124	302	41.1
FE Colleges	32	201	15.9	4048	8638	46.9
Colleges of Education	594	1447	44.1	236	237	99.6
Part-time						
Universities	646	669	96.6	0	0	0
Central Institutions	1449	1548	91.5	2411	3603	66.9
Scottish Agricultural Colleges	0	0	0	0	0	0
FE Colleges	96	427	22.5	12471	18154	68.7
Colleges of Education	0	0	0	0	0	0

Source: SOED 1994b

Within full-time provision it is very evident that whilst adult entrants are approximately equally distributed across first degree and other advanced courses (mostly HNCs and HNDs), proportionally they have a much greater representation in the latter category. So whilst just under a quarter (24.2%) of entrants to full-time university first degree programmes are 21 or over, almost a half (46.9%) of those entering full-time higher level SCOTVEC programmes in further education colleges can be categorised in this way.

Absolute numbers in part-time first degree programmes are low, but almost all of these participants are adults (81.8%). Entrants to other advanced courses, largely within further education colleges, make the most significant single contribution to the part-time mature entry to higher education courses. Of all part-time mature entrants, 87.2 per cent are on HNCs or HNDs, representing just over two-thirds (68.4%) of all those students of any age admitted to such courses.

Less detail is available in relation to the entry routes that adults take in order to access higher education, though some detailed figures on participation by entry route can be gathered from SUCE data for the years 1990–91 and 1991–92 as shown in Table 10.3. It should be noted that the SUCE data is inconsistent with that of SOED both in terms of total and adult entrants to the eight 'old' Scottish universities.

Table 10.3: Qualifications of entrants with UK non-standard qualifications (as defined by SUCE) to the 8 'old' universities in 1990 and 1991

Qualification	Number of entrants through 'non-standard routes'	
	1990 Entry	1991 Entry
SCOTVEC NC Modules	58	77
SCOTVEC HNC/HND	309	372
BTEC NC/ND*	57	68
BTEC HNC/HND*	129	70
Scottish Access Course	260	364
Other UK Access Course	31	51
Partially Completed UK Degree (including OU credits)	182	169
Other UK Qualifications	72	80
No Formal Qualification	44	93
Total Non-Standard Entry	1142	1344
Total Entrants over 21	2314	2556
Total Entrants (UK & Overseas)	13521	14541

Source: SUCE (1991 & 1992a)

** BTEC is the Business and Technician Education Council which provides parallel qualifications in England and Wales to those of SCOTVEC in Scotland

SUCE use the term 'non-standard' here to include all adult students not using Scottish Highers or other equivalent UK qualifications (GCE 'A' levels) as the principal qualification to gain entry. Some of the qualifications included as non-standard are beyond that normally required to access the initial levels of university study, such as Open University credits and partially completed UK degrees. Each category of non-standard entry includes some students aged under 21, although the majority are likely to be over 21. The data shows that within these universities 'non-standard' entrants represent relatively small but significant proportions of total admissions, 8.4 per cent in 1990 and 9.2 per cent in 1991. The principal categories of 'non-standard' entry are clearly Scottish HNC/HND, Scottish Access Courses, and partially completed degrees. All Access entrants, both Scottish and English, when combined provide the greatest contribution within the 'non-standard' typology with 2.2 per cent in 1990 and 2.9 per cent in 1991.

This data should also be viewed in relation to SUCE figures for the total adult entry for these years of 17.1 per cent in 1990 and 17.6 per cent in 1991. This implies that at least 8.7 per cent in 1990 and at least 8.4 per cent in 1991 of all entrants were adults holding traditional qualifications. An alternative interpretation of this data is that in 1990 and 1991 respectively, at least 50.6 per cent and 47.4 per cent of adult entrants possessed traditional qualifications.

Development of Policy

During the late 1980s, widening access to higher education and encouraging the participation of adult students became a major theme of educational policy within Scotland. In developing these policies Scotland has differed from many other countries in the extent to which nationally coordinated and funded initiatives have been established; however the factors which have contributed to this emphasis on access are similar to those which have been influential in England.

First there has been the emphasis on the need to increase participation in higher education for reasons associated with the economic development of the country. The need to establish closer links between the educational system and the processes of economic development had been a theme of educational policy debate and a concern of successive governments since the 1970s. This was clearly enunciated by the then Prime Minister James Callaghan in 1976 (Centre for Contemporary Cultural Studies 1981), and by the second half of the 1980s there was growing concern that the higher education system was unsuited to plans for economic growth and compared badly with international competitors in this respect. This was summed up by the Council for Industry and Higher Education:

> At present the UK's plans for the development of highly educated people are at odds with its ambitions for renewal and growth. The UK must change its higher education system from one geared to a small minority to a more open system which brings many more people to a generally higher level of education than they attain now… (quoted in Pearson *et al.* 1989 p.1)

These concerns have led to the growing recognition of the need to widen access to higher education and move towards a mass rather than an élite system of higher education. Thus the White Paper published in 1987 (DES 1987) emphasised the importance of widening access to vocationally relevant education, and recognised Access courses as the third route into higher education; the first route was A levels, or the Scottish Certificate of Education Highers, and the second route was vocational qualifications. This concern with widening access to higher education and changing the nature of the system continued to be the theme of a number of reports and Department of Employment funded development projects (Ball 1990, Pearson *et al.* 1989). It was also strongly emphasised in the 1991 White Paper on higher education (DES 1991) and the separate Scottish White Paper on further education (Scottish Office 1991) which began by emphasising the importance of a well-trained and educated workforce for the development of a modern economy, and went on to recognise the importance of aims such as greater participation, vocational qualifications providing a route to higher education as well as a preparation for employment, and the creation of more opportunities for the existing workforce to raise skill levels through education and training.

The second, and closely related, factor which contributed to the growing emphasis on adult participation during the 1980s was concern about the implications of the demographic trends, which produced predictions that by the mid-1990s the number of school leavers in Scotland would have fallen by some 40 per cent (SOED 1993). On this basis it was argued that if the numbers entering higher education were to be maintained and increased, then new groups of potential students would need to be identified. It became clear during the late 1980s and early 1990s that the more pessimistic forecasts about the implications of this demographic downturn were ill-founded. This reflected the fact that the relative decline in the birthrate had been lower in professional and middle class families, who still provide about two thirds of the entrants to higher education, and that the percentages of children staying on at school and obtaining qualifications for entry to higher education also increased during the 1980s, particularly in Scotland, where both of these percentages figures were higher than in England (McPherson et al. 1991). As a result, the Age Participation Index (API) and the numbers entering higher education continued to increase. Nevertheless these concerns over the implications of demographic decline were a significant factor in influencing both national and some institutional policy, particularly in discipline areas where recruitment has traditionally been more difficult, such as science and engineering. A number of institutions thus began to place greater emphasis on policies to widen access associated with these fears about their traditional student base. The impact of these demographic factors has also contributed to the continuing recognition that if higher education is to be expanded, and the proportion of graduates in British society to be significantly increased, then new student groups must be successfully targeted (Pearson et al. 1989).

The third set of factors which have helped establish widening access as an important issue in the policy debate are concerns over social justice, and the idea of providing 'second chances' for groups who gained relatively little from education at school level. The idea of using education as a means of promoting greater equality, or at least equality of opportunity, is of course a well established theme in both educational policy and research. However, the recognition of the failure of the educational system for many people has led to a growing interest in the possibility of adult education as an alternative means of tackling these problems. These approaches became well established in community based adult education initiatives and were a central concern for many adult educators (Lovett 1975, Thompson 1980). While Access courses of the kind developed in England were not established in Scotland during the 1970s or early 1980s, they did become the model for an initiative taken by Strathclyde Regional Council (SRC) in 1987 to establish a consortium linking further education colleges and higher education institutions in developing and providing Access courses. This initiative must be seen within the context of the Regional Council's social policies, developed by a large authority controlled by the Labour Party, responsible for an area with some of the highest levels of social and economic deprivation in Britain (SRC 1983). It was also to provide the basis for the national Scottish Wider Access Programme (SWAP) established in 1988, and the idea of targeting Access courses towards under-represented groups has continued to be an important aspect of this programme. The 'social justice' arguments in favour of widening access to higher education also derived from the tradition that the Scottish system of higher education is a 'democratic' one, accessible to the local community. This can be seen in the strong tradition of part-time education in the Scottish universities in the 19th century (Anderson 1983) and in the 'myth' of a Scottish educational system which provided opportunities for students of ability regardless of social origin (Gray *et al.* 1983). Gray *et al.* argue that this 'myth' has had continued influence in shaping Scottish educational policy, and it is certainly the case that the Scottish universities (particularly in the west of Scotland), and the other institutions of higher education, as largely non-residential institutions drawing the vast majority of their students from an area within travelling distance, see themselves as institutions with strong links to, and responsibilities towards, the local community. The higher education institutions have therefore been positive about supporting initiatives which they see as encouraging participation from people who would otherwise be unlikely to gain access to higher education.

While the initiatives to develop access provision have been more 'top-down' in Scotland than in England (Gallacher and Osborne 1991) and there has been less of a practitioner-led 'Access course movement' of the kind described by Brennan (1989), social justice arguments have nevertheless been influential with many of the staff responsible for the development of Access courses in the colleges and institutions of higher education.

The idea of widening access to higher education for adults students has therefore become a well established aspect of educational policy in Scotland in the 1980s and early 1990s, although the reasons for this reflect a number of different concerns among those who have advocated it and have been responsible for developing provision, and this is reflected in the initiatives which have been taken. However, a number of major national initiatives have been taken which have had a significant impact on the educational system.

National Initiatives Designed to Widen Access to Higher Education

The Scottish Wider Access Programme (SWAP)

While the importance of educational provision for adults was well established in Scotland, and although there was a tradition that higher education should be accessible, there was relatively little formal Access provision until the late 1980s. The Government sponsored Scottish Tertiary Education Advisory Council (STEAC) in its report published in 1985 had argued the case for measures to involve more adults in higher education (STEAC 1985). However it was only in 1988, following the 1987 White Paper, that the Scottish Wider

Access Programme (SWAP) was launched as a major national initiative to help promote the rapid growth of access to vocationally relevant higher education throughout the country, and to ensure that this growth would take place within a nationally agreed framework. The importance of the need for education and industry to work together in widening participation in education and training to encourage economic development, particularly at a time of demographic decline, was also emphasised by the Scottish Office in 1988 (Jordinson 1990). While the government was largely influenced by the need to promote economic growth and concerns about demographic patterns, the success of SWAP owed much to the support of the major regional authorities, such as Strathclyde, within which, as we have argued above, social policies associated with tackling economic and social deprivation were more central.

The letter from the Scottish Education Department (SED) which announced the establishment of SWAP, invited regional councils and higher education institutions to collaborate 'with other education authorities and higher education institutions in the area in submitting a bid for development funding support for the operation of a consortium to promote wider access to vocationally relevant higher education' (SED 1988). The proposed consortia were seen as important elements within the national framework which the SED wished to establish, and four were initially set up; West, South East, Mid and North Scotland (Jordinson 1990). Subsequently the Mid Scotland consortium has ceased to exist as a separate entity, with parts being absorbed into the neighbouring consortia. A central task for the consortia has been to encourage collaboration between further education, higher education and industry; indeed the SED stated in its 1988 letter that 'a pre-condition of support to any consortium would be that it brought together education authority and higher education interests; an added advantage would be if there was evidence of employer support' (SED 1988). The consortia took on responsibility for developing new Access courses, negotiating guaranteed places in higher education for Access course students, developing guidance and counselling services, staff development, links with employers and marketing of Access opportunities. In marketing the courses and recruiting students, a number of target groups were identified: women entering science, engineering and technology, ethnic minorities, the physically disabled, and the socially and economically disadvantaged (SOED 1993). These consortia quickly became established as important elements in educational provision in Scotland with a central place within national policy.

To support SWAP, initial funding of £1m was made available by the SED and the then Manpower Services Commission (MSC) for the period 1988–91. This has since been extended by the now retitled Scottish Office Education Department (SOED), and while the Training Education and Employment Division of the Department of Employment (TEED), the successor to the MSC, has not continued any financial support, the regional councils have augmented the consortia budgets.

The decision to establish SWAP as a national framework for the development of Access provision marks a clear difference from Access course development in England during the 1980s, where there was little in the way of central planning or support at a national level. The most obvious reason for the Scottish initiative was the desire to achieve rapid growth in participation rates in line with government policy while ensuring that the system could be kept under close scrutiny and regulation. However, this can also be seen to fit well with the Scottish educational tradition of a strong national system. Thus the Scottish Highers are and have been a national examination system, administered initially through the SED and more recently through the Scottish Examinations Board. This strong national system has been seen as important in helping maintain the democratic tradition in education, with its concern to promote equality of opportunity within society. There were therefore strong historical forces encouraging the integration of Access into this national system.

A major priority within SWAP was the development and establishment of full-time Access courses, with bursaries for students and a guarantee of entry to higher education. This clearly involved a major commitment of resources on the part of the Regional Councils which were responsible for running the courses and providing the bursaries for the students; this commitment can be seen to be related to the Scottish tradition of providing a well supported public education system as a route to opportunity, referred to above.

Since their introduction, SWAP Access courses have enrolled increasing numbers each year (Table 10.4).

Over the period 1989 to 1992 numbers in certain 'vocationally relevant' disciplines, particularly science and engineering, the original *raison d'ère* of SWAP, have begun to flatten whilst simultaneously recruitment to arts and social sciences has increased substantially. This perhaps reflects a variety of factors: general difficulties in recruitment of mature students to subjects such as mathematics and science; reductions in targets within higher education in vocational disciplines such as teacher training; and previously unmet demand from adults in the area of arts and social science.

Table 10.4: Enrolments by subject to SWAP courses, 1989-92

	1989-90	1990-91	1991-92	1992-93
Science & Engineering	276	413	630	626
Business & Administration	44	71	172	333
Art & Social Sciences	95	194	127	529
Education	0	230	209	213
Nursing	1	129	190	299
Other/Unspecified	334	65	260	103
Total Entrants	**750**	**1103**	**1588**	**2103**

Source: SOED 1993

Based on students intended destinations, progression rates into higher education were 43 per cent in 1989-90, 48 per cent in 1990-91 and 47 per cent in 1991-92 (SOED 1993). However, students also proceed to other courses of an advanced nature such as HNCs and HNDs in further education colleges or to nursing training, so that overall progression rates are approximately 70 per cent.

SCOTVEC qualifications

The development of SWAP was also supported by the growing importance of the Scottish Vocational Education Council (SCOTVEC), the national body responsible for the development, validation and award of vocational qualifications in Scotland. It established a new National Certificate (NC) for non-advanced vocational courses in 1985, aimed initially at students in the 16-18 age group who were not proceeding with Scottish Examinations Board O-grades or Highers and who would be studying towards a vocational qualification, possibly as part of an apprenticeship or training. The certificate is based on 40 hour modules involving 'criterion referenced assessment' rather than the traditional 'norm referenced assessment'. For each module, a module descriptor specifying learning outcomes, methods of assessment and content is developed nationally by SCOTVEC. They cover a very wide range of subjects, including many which would not normally be thought of as vocational education: there are now over 3000 module descriptors and these cover topics as diverse as pig keeping, calculus and philosophy.

Advocates of this approach have argued that these modules are particularly suited to the needs of adult students and indeed now widely used by them, because, while providing a route to a nationally recognised qualification, they are flexible, provide the opportunity for a student centred and participatory approach to learning, and have an assessment system which is more positive for adult returners than traditional norm referenced examination based systems. However, it has also been criticised on the basis that the learning styles associated with the assessment of the various learning outcomes for the modules do not encourage students to integrate learning within and between modules. A number of staff, particularly in higher education, have also been critical of the absence of examinations in courses which are designed to prepare students for entry to higher education, where such forms of assessment are still widely used.

SCOTVEC has also been involved in a major restructuring of its provision at higher education level, where it is responsible for the development and validation of Higher National Certificates (HNCs) and Higher National Diplomas (HNDs). New ranges of units are being developed at this level which are based on similar principles to the National Certificate Modules. These frameworks are also designed to provide flexible routes to vocational qualifications in higher education, although the idea of a 'vocational' qualification is being interpreted very widely with, for example, an HNC in social sciences now available. There is also considerable emphasis on the provision of articulated routes from the HNCs or HNDs into degree courses in the universities, and this is seen as an increasingly important way of widening access, through providing greater flexibility within the system.

The development of a framework of Scottish Vocational Qualifications (SVQs) has also involved a major role for SCOTVEC. These awards are now being made available in further and higher education and private training organisations. They are competence-based qualifications, specific to a particular occupation, which can be mapped onto existing qualifications, particularly those of SCOTVEC (which accredits SVQs), or can be gained in a variety of modes, such as through the accreditation of work-based learning (AWBL). The SVQs exist at levels one to five across a range of occupational sectors, although the higher levels of four and five have yet to be developed in a number of disciplines.

It is likely that SVQs will have relevance for employed adults wishing to access higher education on a part-time basis, but of particular significance may be the development of general SVQs (GSVQs) which have been piloted in various institutions since 1992. The GSVQs are not as occupationally specific as SVQs, but are intended to prepare students for entry into both work and higher education. They are designated as level three awards and consist of selected groups of modules from the National Certificate provision of SCOTVEC, which again is the accrediting body. Since full-time

Access programmes are almost exclusively based on groups of SCOTVEC National Certificate modules which are almost identical to gSVQ groupings, there is a likelihood that they will come to be defined in terms of gSVQs.

At present, particularly in the older universities, there are some reservations about the quality of gSVQ awards. The Scottish Council on University Entrance (SUCE) has suggested that they 'should be treated with caution' and advised that in prospectuses they might simply say that 'holders of (pilot) gSVQs will be considered sympathetically on their individual merits' (SUCE 1993). Similarly the higher level SVQs at four and five which might justify admission to the second year and above of university awards are so new in their concept that they too have yet to be fully accepted as vehicles for entry. Here reservations may be various: typically selectors in universities argue that competency-based qualifications lack the underpinning knowledge component required to cope with 'academic' courses, and that formative assessment procedures (often without formal examinations) further disadvantage candidates.

The SCOTCAT Scheme

The third major national development which has been important in widening access for adults to higher education has been the establishment, in 1991, of the Scottish Credit Accumulation and Transfer (SCOTCAT) Scheme which involves a formal agreement between all the major institutions of higher education in Scotland to recognise a similar framework for building credit towards a degree. The framework adopted has been based on the idea of four levels of study to complete an undergraduate honours degree, equivalent to the traditional four year Scottish honours degree. Students need to acquire 120 credit points at each of these four levels, and awards are available as follows:

Level	Points	Award
1	120	Certificate
2	120	Diploma
3	120	Degree
4	120	Honours degree

The system is designed to encourage flexibility and the principle on which it is based is that credit can be gained from a variety of sources. As well as the student current programme of study, this can include prior certificated learning, including work based learning.

The idea of a SCOTCAT Scheme has been to establish a framework within which all institutions will work and which will facilitate the transfer of credit between institutions, although the receiving institution retains the discretion regarding the credit which will be awarded. It is also providing a framework for staff development, and encouraging further policy initiatives which will embed these principles more firmly within the system, particularly in the 'new' universities (Sharp 1991).

Institutional Access Initiatives

In addition to the national initiatives there have been a significant number of institutional initiatives designed to widen access and increase flexibility within the higher education system. In parallel to Access Courses being developed through the SWAP consortia, the universities themselves have greatly expanded their in-house provision during the same period. This provision dates from 1979, and was initially mainly in the arts and social sciences (Dalgarno and Hart 1987). Recent developments extended this provision across the range of disciplines, although arts and social sciences still predominate. The courses are offered in seven of the 12 universities, and are organised by Centres for Continuing Education, or their equivalent. They are exclusively part-time, often in the evening, and no financial support is available to students. Unlike the programmes based in further education, the content of courses is completely at the discretion of the universities who have academic autonomy. Mutual recognition of university Access courses has been organised under the auspices of SUCE. Intake to these courses has increased from 466 in 1989–90 to 891 in 1992–93 (UACE(S) 1993).

Access Courses offered through the medium of distance teaching are largely the preserve of the University of Aberdeen, and are offered at a number of centres in four of the northern areas of Scotland with the most sparse and isolated populations: Highlands, Western Isles, Orkney and Shetland. The course offered in each location is a re-packaged version of the University's own in-house provision, using audio tapes of lectures and a course materials workbook. On a weekly basis staff and students engage in workshop sessions using interactive audio-conferencing equipment supported by an electronic writing system. The demand for the provision since it was set up in 1990 is a pointer to the potential within these regions: during 1993–94 over 100 students registered for the programme, well over the funded target. Demand for this provision may increase should the plans for a University of the Highland and Islands, operating through an electronically linked network of small sites, come to fruition.

The extent of Access provision in the 'old' universities can be gathered from the number of 'full-time equivalents' funded by SHEFC: 650 for 1993–4. Assuming recruitment to target, this suggests around 1300 enrolments, since one FTE is typically two part-time students. Progression rates of students from these courses are not readily available, although some examples from 1992 (SUCE 1992b) are illustrative: the University of Aberdeen reported that since 1984 the pass rate had never fallen below 92 per cent'; the University of Dundee noted that from an intake of 70 students, 30 took the final examination and 28 passed; the University of Glasgow stated that 65 per cent usually complete the course and 60–65 per cent of completers gain places in higher education.

One institution, the University of Stirling, offers its own course at other locations as part of its outreach provision. More prevalent forms of collaboration with further education colleges are those whereby a number of universities make substantive teaching contributions, sometimes as much as a day per week throughout the year, to full-time SWAP Access programmes. The reasoning behind this commitment has been outlined by Johnstone *et al*. (1992) who suggest that students absorb something of the general culture of a university and thus pre-empt problems of culture stress; more specifically they become acquainted with the staff of their future departments and with relevant faculties. However, there is as yet no empirical evidence of a link between university input to such courses and student progression or performance.

A number of other efforts to combat disadvantage in access to higher education exist; an imported example is the Summer School. The longest standing pre-university summer school programme is that within Strathclyde Region which dates from 1985 as part of the Drumchapel/Easterhouse Initiative, these being two areas of Glasgow described as Areas of Priority Treatment (APTs) with high levels of social deprivation, poverty, unemployment and poor housing. The scheme was initially focused on schools in these socially deprived areas and sought to provide opportunities for pupils to access the University of Glasgow. Latterly it has been extended to 30 schools within APTs and to all of the higher education institutions in Strathclyde region. It is important that the scheme now also recruits adults, mostly those who have already completed a SWAP Access programme during the preceding year. Thus it acts as a 'top-up' for those students who have either not yet met the preconditions for university entry or who wish to gain experience of university study prior to entry. The tuition is of ten weeks duration (180 hours) running from late June to early September. Students take four courses in a variety of academic subjects, reflecting their intended undergraduate destination, as well as courses in written English and an orientation to 'universities and their ways'. Success in a given subject is determined by performance in attempting work drawn from the corresponding first year of undergraduate study, and this assessment usually involves a tutor in charge of that first university year. The programme predominantly recruits students who wish to access higher education courses in science and engineering, these being the disciplines in which there is greatest availability at this late time in the admissions cycle. Figures for 1991 show that one third of 216 participants were adults, and that 138 of all recruits proceeded to higher education (Dunn 1991).

Similar courses are now run in a number of other Scottish universities, including Edinburgh, Dundee and Aberdeen and Glasgow Caledonian. The Summer School for Access at the University of Aberdeen is an example of the institution's particular role in Scotland in providing educational opportunities for geographically isolated communities. In order to identify appropriate candidates the University has set up special partnership arrangements with schools and further education colleges in Orkney, Shetland, Western Isles, Grampian and Highland regions. According to Cudworth (1994) registrations for the programme have increased from 57 in 1991 to 166 in 1993. Furthermore, he reports that approximately one third of the most recent cohort were adults and suggests that this age mix is a positive catalyst in building interaction, confidence and commitment in the class as a whole, through peer tutoring and self-help groups. The net result of the course which is offered as a discrete ten week block, covering a full range of academic disciplines, is 90 per cent progression to higher education, mainly to degree programmes at the University of Aberdeen.

Articulation arrangements whereby students can progress from a non-degree course such as an HNC or HND into a degree programme are a further means through which additional attempts are now being made to widen access to higher education. While there has been a long history of students using HNCs or HNDs to gain admission to degree programmes, this often involved loss of time for the students as they have been required to enter year one of the degree. The aim of articulation agreements is to ensure that students can progress directly into the subsequent year of study without loss of time. This often involves the HNC/HND programmes being written with progression to certain degree programmes as a clear aim, and it may in certain circumstances involve additional bridging material.

These arrangements are now being established between an increasing number of courses particularly as a result of agreements of collaboration between some of the universities and the further education colleges. There are a number of reasons why these arrangements have been seen to be of importance in widening access. The first and most important one is that they offer clearly established progression routes which provide 'second chances' for adults who, for a variety of reasons, have not progressed from school into higher education. This includes students who have been attending further education colleges on a part-time basis as part of a vocational training, as well as adult returners. Secondly, they are being used as a means of providing routes to higher education for students in areas which are remote from existing established universities. An example is the link between Lews Castle College on the island of Lewis in the Outer Hebrides and a number of higher education institutions on the mainland. Glasgow Caledonian University has been particularly active in developing these links and has now established three levels of partnership with selected FE colleges, which range from associate college through affiliate college to college of Glasgow Caledonian University. These relationships between further and higher education are still at a relatively early stage of development and there has as yet been no systematic research to investigate the nature of these relationships and their consequences for the institutions, staff and students involved. However, a small study is currently being undertaken by the Higher Education Quality Council, and a three year longitudinal study is about to be undertaken by staff at Glasgow Caledonian University.

Institutional Initiatives to Increase Flexibility

Part-time degrees have been an important means of providing opportunities for adults who would otherwise be excluded because of work or domestic commitments. This is a long established tradition in Scottish higher education (Anderson 1983), although research into provision in the late 1980s (Gallacher et al. 1989) indicated that part-time provision was more firmly established in the CIs and colleges of education. The universities, while providing a substantial number of opportunities for part-time study did not have a share of student numbers proportionate to their share of degree courses. This reflects important differences in tradition between the sectors. Both the CIs and colleges of education have had a strong vocational element in their courses, encouraging them to focus on the needs of particular occupational groups many of whom are adults already in employment. The 'old' Scottish universities have in contrast traditionally provided mainly for 17–18 year old school leavers, taking full-time faculty based degrees chosen from a very wide range of available subjects. Little priority has been given until recently to the development of special provision for part-time students which would encourage large numbers of adult participants (Gallacher *et al.* 1989). However, several 'old' universities have now developed a major programme of part-time degree provision and it seems likely that this will continue to be an area of significant growth.

Associated with part-time degree provision is the issue of distance learning. We have referred above to the role of the Open University. However, a number of other institutions are becoming increasingly involved in this area of work. Most notably the University of Aberdeen makes provision for a wide area of the Highlands and Islands and is making increasing use of new forms of telecommunications in the process. There is also a proposal to establish a new University of the Highlands and Islands, in which distance learning using modern methods of telecommunications would have a key role. Some of the existing 'campus-based' universities are also showing an increasing interest in becoming 'dual mode' universities, in which appropriate courses will be offered in a distance learning mode.

The development of opportunities for work based learning also represents an important initiative designed to increase flexibility of access to higher education for employed adults, particularly to part-time study. While developments of this kind are still not widespread throughout the Scottish higher education system, significant progress is now being made to design schemes that maximise the potential of adult workers through the use of Accreditation of Prior Experiential Learning (APEL) and the Accreditation of Work-Based Learning (AWBL). In particular, the 'Developing Employment-based Access to Learning' (DEAL) Project has brought together Glasgow Caledonian University, Napier University and the University of Stirling in a major national project (Sharp *et al.* 1993). This project builds upon earlier work in the three institutions (Marshall and Mill 1993, Osborne *et al.* 1993) and has resulted in significant further progress in developing Access courses, Diplomas and parts of degree programmes based in the workplace. Further work is now being undertaken through the DEAL Project to investigate the possibilities of providing work-based learning routes in the small and medium sized enterprise (SME) sector. Research programmes to analyse the effectiveness of this provision are also now planned.

The development of semesters to replace the traditional term structure, and the associated change to a modular form of provision, has now been introduced, or is in the process of being introduced in an increasing number of universities in Scotland. One of the major arguments in favour of these changes has been that the movement towards modularity, combined with the development of CATS, will increase flexibility through making it easier for students to construct degree programmes which reflect their experience, interest and needs. However, critics of these developments have argued that a major pressure for change has been the desire to create more cost effective structures, which will allow the possibility of introducing 'a third semester' and will enable the system to process more students more rapidly. Nonetheless, such a structure would be particularly advantageous to adult students on part-time programmes for whom the present lack of provision during 22 weeks of the year is both a disincentive and an impediment to rapid progress through their degree. The move towards this reorganisation of provision has received further impetus from the Irvine Committee Report which recommended that all Scottish higher education institutions should aim to move to a common semester structure for the beginning of the 1995–96 academic year (Irvine 1993). The University of Stirling has also recently received special project funding from SHEFC for the introduction of a third semester which will provide part-time and visiting students with the opportunity to take a range of modules during the summer. This will run for the first time during 1994. Developments of this kind open the way for the more rapid completion of degrees than the traditional structures have allowed.

The Impact of These Policies and Initiatives

Access courses have gained the greatest prominence as a route to higher education for adults in recent years despite the fact that they represent only a small percentage of all entrants. However, in absolute terms approximately 1000 Access course students are entering higher education on an annual basis, and this number is increasing from one year to another. More importantly, however, these is some evidence, particularly within SWAP programmes, that the courses are having some success in attracting those types of students historically under-represented in higher education. Gallacher *et al.* (1992) surveyed 459 students on all Access Courses in the largest SWAP consortia during 1990–91, gathering information in relation to gender, parental status, educational disadvantage, employment status, social class and ethnicity. According to their findings women represented 57 per cent of all students in their sample, and typically 'Access courses appear to be a stage in the re-entry to the labour force after the early years of childbearing or following the breakdown of a marriage.' They pointed out that 'many of these women appear to have been working in low paid part-time work as a first step in that re-entry' and that 'for men the pattern is different and appears to be one of using Access to establish careers prior to marriage' (p.3). Within the sample 15 per cent were identified as single parents, and this subset were attracted disproportionately into courses associated with caring such as nursing and primary education. There was also considerable evidence that Access courses were having success in making provision for students who have been disadvantaged in their earlier educational experience, since some 60 per cent of the sample left school at the minimum age. They also found that 'relatively high proportions of students...come from working class homes when measured by father's occupation (64%)' and that 'the majority of students were also in manual (54%) or routine non-manual (28%) occupations before entering their Access courses' (p.5). Clearly these are relatively high proportions from their social class groups, particularly when viewed in the context of the backgrounds of typical recruits to higher education in the UK (Smithers and Robinson 1989).

Munn, Johnstone and Lowden (1993) also provided interesting information on the age profile of SWAP students: just over 50 per cent of the 1991–92 cohort (1588) were aged under 30, indicating that these programmes are attracting significant numbers who, rather than being returners to study, are, as Woodley *et al.* (1987) have suggested in other studies of mature students, studying slowly with relatively small gaps between periods of academic study.

Conclusion

Widening access to higher education has been a major theme of policy in Scotland in recent years. This has contributed to increased numbers of adult students, increased participation of groups traditionally under-represented, and initiatives designed to increase flexibility within the higher education system.

However, recent developments in national policy have cast some doubts over the continuing commitment to these initiatives. First the government have made it clear that they wish now to enter a period of what they have termed 'consolidation' rather than continued growth. This is associated with wider cuts in public spending plans and has resulted in the capping of student numbers. The SOED has also indicated that it does not plan to continue to provide financial support for SWAP beyond 1994, although it has encouraged the institutions to establish a national forum to ensure that issues associated with widening access are actively pursued. In particular the following items have been identified as ones which should be addressed within such a forum:

targeting of wider access programmes upon under-represented groups and keeping targeting priorities under review; working to ensure that the multiplicity of access routes does not set one age, social or gender group of students at a disadvantage; extension of provision to people in areas remote from local further and higher education institutions; diversification of types of provision to accommodate part-time and full-time students. (SOED 1993 pp.20–21)

The onus for further development of this work has now been placed on the institutions of further and higher education. However whilst many institutions, and staff within them, are committed to widening access, the current funding climate is one which will discourage expansion and make it difficult to continue to pursue policies of this kind.

Further uncertainty also exists in the university sector. While the Funding Council (SHEFC 1993) recognises the value of part-time flexible provision and confirms its 'general concern to maintain, and where possible increase, breadth, diversity and ease of access in Scottish higher education', it is far from certain that it regards the funding of sub-degree level courses to be within its remit. Thus the subsidies that underpin the provision which facilitates the participation of a half of all Access entrants is by no means assured. However it seems likely that this review of funding methods will lead to pressure on universities to accredit a wider range of part-time provision, including the traditional adult liberal education courses which may help create additional flexible routes into and through the higher education system.

There is clearly continuing support at the level of national policy for a range of measures which are designed to increase flexibility through the development of part-time provision, CATS, work-based learning and the introduction of a semester and module based system. In this respect it seems likely that significant change will continue to be an important feature of the Scottish education system in the coming years, and that in the longer term the trend towards a more open, accessible and flexible system will continue.

References

Anderson, R. (1983) *Education and opportunity in Victorian Scotland: schools and universities.* Oxford: Clarendon Press.

Ball, C. (1990) *More Means Different: widening access to higher education.* London: RSA/Industry Matters.

Brennan, J. (1989) Access courses. In O. Fulton (ed) *Access and Institutional Change.* Milton Keynes: Society for Research in Higher Education and Open University Press.

Centre for Contemporary Cultural Studies (1981) *Unpopular Education.* London: Hutchison.

Cudworth, C. (1994) *Summer School for Access – Report on the 1993 course.* Aberdeen: University of Aberdeen.

Dalgarno, M. and Hart, L. (1987) Access courses to higher education. In R. Jordinson (ed) *Access by mature students to higher education.* Edinburgh: Scottish Institute of Adult and Continuing Education.

Department of Education and Science (1987) *Meeting the challenge.* Cm 114. London: HMSO.

Department of Education and Science (1991) *Higher Education – A New Framework.* Cm 1541. London: HMSO.

Dunn, W. (1991) *Pre-University Summer School – 1991 – Report from Director.* Glasgow: University of Glasgow.

Gallacher, J., Leahy, J., Sharp, N. and Young, A. (1989) *Part-Time Degree Provision in Scotland: Courses and Students 1987–88.* Glasgow: Glasgow College.

Gallacher, J. and Osborne, M.J. (1991) Differing national models of Access provision: a comparison between Scotland and England. *Journal of Access Studies,* 6, 2, 147–164.

Gallacher, J., Scott, G. and White, A. (1992) *Access Courses Monitoring and Evaluation Report, 1990–91. Summary of Report.* Glasgow: West of Scotland SWAP.

Gray, J., McPherson, A.F. and Raffe, D. (1983) *Reconstructions of Secondary Education: theory, myth and practice since the war.* London: Routledge & Kegan Paul.

Irvine, J.M. (1993) *Review of the Academic Year, Final Report of the Scottish Advisory Group on the Academic Year.* Edinburgh: Scottish Higher Education Funding Council and Committee of Scottish Higher Education Principals.

Johnstone, R., Cope, P. and Osborne, M.J. (1992) Recruiting mature adults into concurrent initial teacher training – the Stirling Access to teaching scheme. *Scottish Journal of Adult Education,* 11, 1, 44–51.

Jordinson, R. (1990) Access to higher education in Scotland: an overview. *Journal of Access Studies,* 5, 1, 72–88.

Lovett, T. (1975) *Adult education, Community development and the Working Class.* London: Ward Lock Educational.

McPherson, A., Munn, P. and Raffe, D. (1991) *Aiming for a College Education: a strategy for Scotland.* Glasgow: BP Exploration.

Macpherson, I. (1989) *Attracting New Students to Adult Education; the learner's point of view.* Edinburgh: Scottish Institute of Adult and Continuing Education.

Marshall, I. and Mill, M. (1993) Using student-driven learning contracts – higher education. In J. Stephenson and M. Laycock (eds) *Using Learning Contracts in Higher Education*. London: Kogan Page/Higher Education for Capability.

Munn, P., Johnstone, M. and Lowden, K. (1993) *Students' Views on SWAP (The Scottish Wider Access Programme)*. Interchange, No 17. Edinburgh: SOED.

Munn, P., Tett, L. and Arney, N. (1993) *Negotiating the Labyrinth –progression opportunities for adult learners*. Edinburgh: SCRE.

Osborne, M.J., Yule, W., Dockrell, R. and Carmichael, J. (1993) *Accreditation of In-house Courses and Accreditation of Prior Experiential Learning – some case studies*. Stirling: Stirling University and Glasgow Caledonian University.

Pearson, R., Pike, G., Gordon, A. & Weyman, C. (1989) *How many graduates in the 21st Century? The choice is yours*. Summary of IMS Report 177. Brighton: Institute of Manpower Studies.

Scottish Education Department (1988) *Scottish Wider Access Programme*. Letter from Secretary of State for Scotland, 22 April.

Scottish Higher Education Funding Council (SHEFC) (1993) *Funding of continuing education*. Consultative Paper 10/93 December.

Scottish Office (1991) *Access and Opportunity*. Cm 1530. Edinburgh: HMSO

Scottish Office Education Department (1992a) *Upper Secondary Education in Scotland* (The Howie Report). Edinburgh: HMSO.

Scottish Office Education Department (1992b) *The Education of Adults in Scotland*. Edinburgh: SOED.

Scottish Office Education Department (1992c) *Adults in Schools and Colleges*. Statistical Bulletin K1/1992/2. Edinburgh: SOED.

Scottish Office Education Department (1993) *Review of the Scottish Wider Access Programme*. Edinburgh: SOED.

Scottish Office Education Department (1994a) *Higher Still – Opportunity for All*. Edinburgh: HMSO.

Scottish Office Education Department (1994b) *Adult Participation in School, Colleges and Universities – Provisional Data for 1991*. Edinburgh: SOED.

Scottish Tertiary Education Advisory Council (1985) *Future Strategy for Higher Education in Scotland*. Edinburgh: HMSO.

Scottish Universities Council on Entry (1991) *SUCE Report for 1990–91*. St. Andrews: SUCE.

Scottish Universities Council on Entry (1992a) *SUCE Report for 1991–92*. St. Andrews: SUCE.

Scottish Universities Council on Entry (1992b) *Access Courses Database 1992*. St. Andrews: SUCE.

Scottish Universities Council on Entry (1993) *Letter to Secretaries/Registrars of the eight older Scottish Universities – General Scottish Vocational Qualifications (GSVQs) and General National Vocational Qualifications (GNVQs)*. 10 June.

Sharp, N. (1991) *Changing Patterns in Higher Education: a guide to the development of credit accumulation and transfer in Scotland*. The Scottish Central Institutions Committee for Educational Development, Teaching and Learning in Higher Education, Series 5, No. 4.

Sharp, N., Whittaker, R., Osborne, M.J., Dockrell, R., Land, R. and Reeve, F. (1993) *The DEAL Project – an Interim Report*. Glasgow: Glasgow Caledonian University/University of Stirling/Napier University.

Smithers, A. and Robinson, P. (1989) *Increasing Participation in Higher Education*. London: BP Educational Services.

Strathclyde Regional Council (1983) *Social Strategy for the Eighties*. Glasgow: SRC.

Thompson, J. (1980) *Adult Education for a Change*. London: Hutchison.

Universities Association for Continuing Education (Scotland) (1993) *Access Working Group Report*. Stirling: UACE(S).

Woodley, A., Wagner, L., Slowey, M., Hamilton, M. and Fulton, O. (1987) *Choosing to Learn: Adults in Education*. London: SRHE/OU.

Chapter 11

Spain

Michael Osborne

In Spain, responsibility for all forms of pre-university education is distributed between the State and the Autonomous Communities with the constitution listing 32 areas where the state has exclusive responsibility and 22 areas where Autonomous Communities may have administrative powers. For instance, the State retains responsibility for basic legislation, the regulation of the validity of certificates and degrees, the organisation of the system's levels, of its subject material and its duration, of minimum subject matter, of the prerequisites for passing from one level to another, the minimum requirements for educational institutions and general planning. Other responsibilities, notably the administration of the educational system, staffing matters and where appropriate the organisation of education in languages other than Castillian Spanish have been devolved to seven of the Autonomous Communities: Andalusia, the Canary Islands, Catalunya, Galicia, the Basque Country, Navarra and Galicia. However, in the other Autonomous Communities educational management is still the responsibility of the national Ministry of Education and Science (MEC).

At university level, the Reform of Higher Education Act, *Ley de Reforma Universitaria* (BOE 1983), defines the powers allocated to the State, the Autonomous Communities and the universities themselves. This law gave universities academic freedom for teaching and research as well as limited self-government, though the basic structure of programmes of study remains within the control of the state. Further comprehensive details of the structure of the education system can be found in a number of publications: prior to and after the reforms of 1970 can be found in OECD (1972); useful more recent summaries of the system for readers in English are those of Holmes (1983), McNair (1984), OECD (1986) and DES (1989). The Ministry of Education's report to the 42nd International Conference in Education in Geneva (MEC 1990a) provides details of structures prior to and after the reforms of 1990. A very comprehensive statistical summary

Reforms in Secondary Education

Possibilities for access to higher education for adults in Spain are largely determined by the structure of the educational system and its regulations and the ways in which these are implemented at national, regional and local levels. The present structure was defined by the *Ley General de Educación y Financiación de la Enseñanza Obligatoria* (LGE) of 1970 (BOE 1970), and was amended in the early 1980s (BOE 1983, BOE 1985). It is, however, being radically changed following the introduction of the *Ley Orgánica de Ordenación General del Sistema Educativo* (LOGSE) of 1990 (BOE 1990). LOGSE is being gradually implemented over a ten year period and affects all levels of education from pre-school to pre-university, including technical training, *Formación Profesional*. The structures as defined by the LGE and the LOGSE are shown in Figures 11.1a and 11.1b, and although the changes incorporated within LOGSE may not have profound direct effects on access to higher education for adults, a number of its directives are likely to lead indirectly to greater participation at higher levels than previously.

Of particular note in the 1990 reform is that compulsory school education has been extended by two years to the age of 16, thus matching the minimum age for employment. Within the secondary element of this compulsory provision there is included, in addition to a common academic core and options, an integrated basic vocational training which according to the Ministry of Education and Science (MEC 1990a p.99) 'must be substantiated in a general technological education for all pupils, in the form of a specific area comprising training in different techniques and the introduction of diverse and optional educational contents allowing for occupational experiences or activities.'

For those pupils who achieve the objectives of compulsory education a Certificate of Secondary Education is to be awarded; this certificate will provide access to a new two year Baccalaureate and the Intermediate Specific Vocational Training. The new Baccalaureate aims to prepare pupils for University, for Higher Level Specific Vocational Training and for the labour market. It replaces the existing *Bachillerato Unificado y Polivalente* (BUP) and the *Curso de Orientación a Universidad (COU)*. Essentially this new post-16 qualification differs from the BUP in as much as its terminal outcome is not simply university entry. It will consist of four main modes: arts, human and social sciences, natural and health sciences, and technology, each of which will give access to specified university courses as well as particular modes of Higher Level Specific Vocational Training (level three professional modules). Additionally, baccalaureate schools will also offer the optional subjects required as basic Vocational Training for the modes of Higher Level Specific Vocational Training.

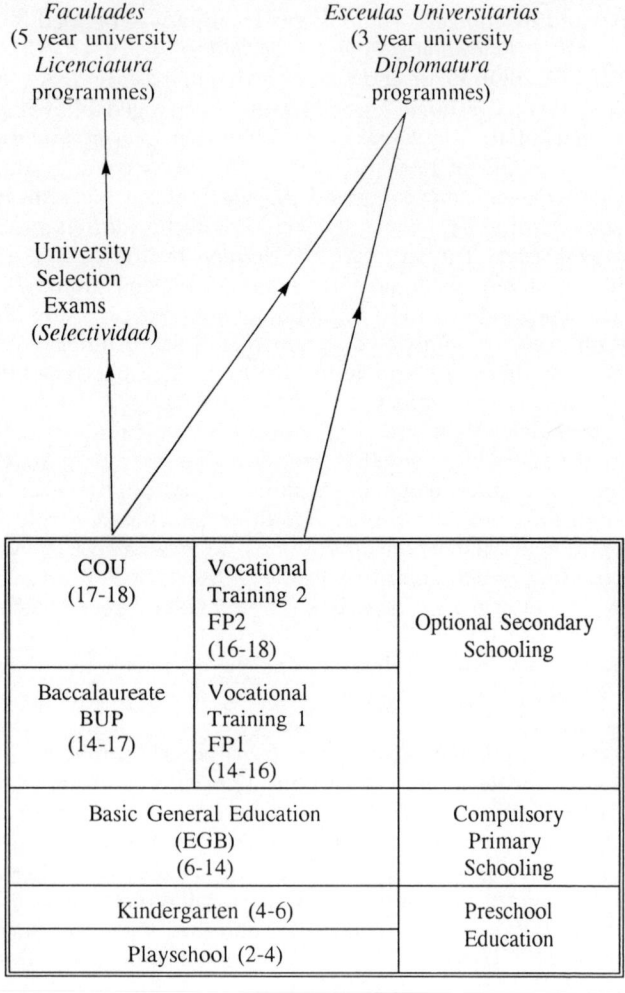

Figure 11.1a Education system, LGE, 1970

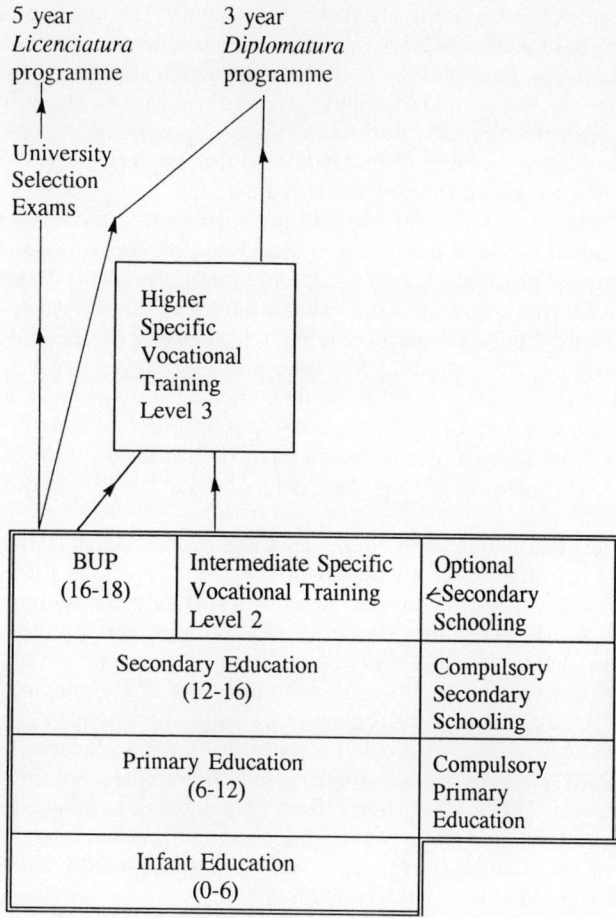

Figure 11.1b Education system, LOGSE, 1990

The new Intermediate Specific Vocational Training (level two professional modules) is a route parallel to that of the new Baccalaureate and is also to be placed in post-compulsory secondary education within a variety of public and private vocational education centres, *centros de formación professional industrial*. Specific vocational training had already been reorganised as Professional Modules at levels two and three in anticipation of the implementation of LOGSE, and are being tried out extensively throughout Spain. For instance, in the province of Asturias, 20 centres are offering collectively 14 modules at each level. Four of these modules at level two are being offered by distance learning, and are being targeted exclusively at adults and those in work (Escuela Asturiana 1993). Approximately 80 per cent of teaching is carried out in designated teaching centres and 20 per cent is work-based training in companies.

These levels of vocational training correspond, of course, to the equivalent levels of qualification as defined by the European Community in Directive 85/368/CE. It will eventually replace the existing technical training, *Formación Professional de Primero y Segundo Grado* (FP-1 and FP-2), presently offered within these centres, and will provide a further route of access to the new Higher Level Specific Vocational Training. In both the new and old systems of vocational training a variety of branches, corresponding to families of professions, exist; details of the structures of both systems, including the various branches are comprehensively described by Ibáñez Aramayo (1992).

The justification of the new structures for vocational training are detailed in the government's *Plan de Reforma Formación Professional* (MEC 1992). These include the creation of specific programmes which more nearly meet the 'dynamic requirements' for qualifications within the job market and the grounding of training within the context of social and economic planning both at regional and local level. Under the present regime of vocational training FP-2 can be used to gain direct access to university study within *Escuelas Universitarias* (University Schools offering only the first level of university education, *Diplomatura*, normally a professional training). Indeed, *Escuelas Universitarias* are obliged to reserve up to 30 per cent of the places on each course for those who have successfully completed FP-2. Until FP-2 is phased out (1997–1998), it will also provide a route of access to Higher Level Specific Vocational Training. This in turn will provide access to *Escuelas Universitarias* in certain circumstances which are regulated by Ministerial Order (BOE 1989) and are delineated by Ibáñez Aramayo (pp.155–157). For example, the professional module of infant education provides access to first level university courses in nursing, social work, primary education or tourism.

The Structure of Higher Education

In 1991–92 there were 36 public universities and five private universities mainly controlled by the Catholic Church in Spain. This provision is in the process of being supplemented, albeit marginally, by the creation of further private institutions, some of which will be controlled by business and commerce, and which will offer a broader range of disciplines than the traditionally academic ones, such as business studies and information technology. In addition, in each region there are a number of both public and private university colleges, *Colegios Universitarios*, which are associated with specific universities and which offer only the first cycle of university education *Diplomatura*. Within each university there exist faculties, *Facultdades*, and higher technical schools, *Escuelas Technicas Superiores*, and university schools, *Escuelas Universitarias*. Whilst the university schools can offer only the qualification of the first cycle of university education, the three-year *Diplomado* (normally in a vocational areas such as primary teacher training, nursing and business studies), faculties and higher technical schools offer all three cycles of university study leading to the *Licentiado* or its equivalent (historically five to six years, but in transition to four years) and *Doctor* (two further years) as shown in Figure 11.2. Progression from *Diplomatura* to the second cycle *Licenciatura* for those studying in university schools is possible providing that they successfully complete a bridging course, *Curso Adaptación*, though increasingly this requirement is beginning to disappear.

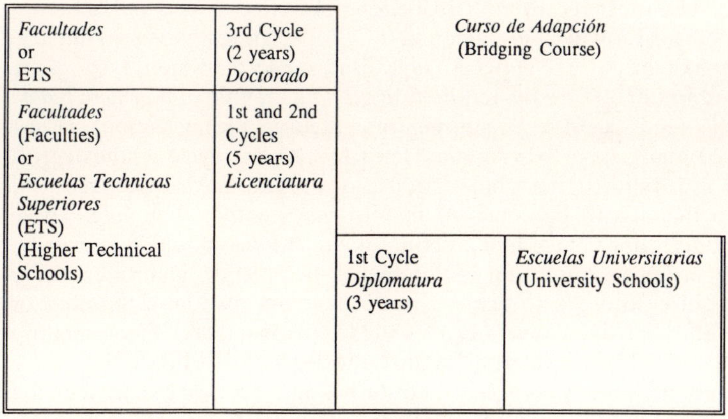

Facultades or ETS	3rd Cycle (2 years) Doctorado		*Curso de Adapción* (Bridging Course)
Facultades (Faculties) or Escuelas Technicas Superiores (ETS) (Higher Technical Schools)	1st and 2nd Cycles (5 years) Licenciatura		
		1st Cycle Diplomatura (3 years)	*Escuelas Universitarias* (University Schools)

Figure 11.2: Structure of the university system

This model has resulted from and is still subject to ongoing modifications that date back to legislation in the early 1980s. At that time, orders to ensure coherence and homogeneity in provision, degrees being formally recognised by the state and validated throughout the country, were established by the *Ley de Reforma Universitaria* (1983). It was this same law that also created general guidelines for the curriculum which have been substantiated over a number of years by Royal Decrees redefining very specifically, course by course and subject by subject, the minimum content of each higher education qualification in each institution. It is these decrees that also have instructed that the formal period of time required to achieve certain degrees should be reduced.

For any given discipline, there is a strictly prescribed core content (*materias troncales*) that is determined by the state and which is then supplemented by further compulsory and optional material set out by individual institutions; the total amount of content (measured in credits) is further regulated within certain maxima for the whole qualification and for each cycle. A more significant modification still in the process of being introduced is that the minimum time required to achieve the *Licenciatura* (or its equivalent) has been reduced to four years. The *Diplomatura*, however, has kept its three year duration in the reforms, although bridging courses will be phased out, allowing free transition to the second cycle.

The most recent and final prescribing decree was published in 1992 for Industrial Engineering (BOE 1992) and serves as an illustration of the balance between centralised and local influence. 167 of the minimum 300 credits required to achieve the title of *Ingeniero Industrial* (equivalent to *Licentiado*) are defined in the legislation; at least 120 credits have to be devoted to each of the two cycles of the degree. The duration of the whole engineering programme has been reduced so that it can be achieved in four years rather than five. These prescriptions of content and duration of studies should, however, be regarded as minimum requirements. In practice, institutions may require students to achieve more than the mandated number of credits; at the University of Oviedo, for instance, 375 credits are included in the Industrial Engineering degree. Also, in practice, many students already complete their studies over a period greater than the defined minimum; such extensions are likely to become more common, but can be easily facilitated in a credit-based system.

Access and Participation

Entry to university education for school leavers is at present dependent on successful completion of the three-year BUP, followed by the one-year COU and, in the case of entry to most faculties and higher technical schools, the grade obtained in a university entrance examination, *Preuba de Acceso de la Universidad*, more commonly known as *Selectividad*, which is offered by each university. The *Selectividad* is normally offered on two occasions, in June and September, and consists of a series of tests in four optional discipline areas according to the faculty to which entry is sought. The administration of the *Selectividad* is a substantial undertaking for each university. An example of the extent of the organisation of entry tests can be found in the University of Granada's record of academic courses for 1992–93 (University of Granada 1993). The University organised 22 tribunals relating to tests taken in 15 separate geographical locations in Andalusia, Spanish enclaves in North Africa (Cueta and Melilla) and Morocco. Over 8000 students completed the tests offered in June. Although under the reforms of LOGSE, COU, which is linked closely to *Selectividad* and jointly supervised by universities, will disappear, some form of selective test for university entry will almost certainly still exist at individual institutions' discretion, particularly when courses are over subscribed. So whilst the possession of the *Bachillerato* alone should in theory secure admission, restrictions will exist.

At present there are a series of priorities that universities are instructed to follow in relation to recruitment; for instance, those who complete *Selectividad* in June will have priority over those who complete in September (MEC 1990b). Even under the present system, however, the regulations are overlaid by institutional practices to restrict entry to certain popular subjects; for instance, in Madrid, there is limited entry into all higher technical schools offering architecture (Royal Institute of British Architects 1991).

According to the most recent figures from the Ministry of Education and Science (MAC 1993), almost 1.3 million students were enrolled in either the first or second cycle of university education in 1992–93.It is estimated that this figure will rise to almost 1.38 million in 1993–94, almost double the equivalent figure of 1982–83.

A number of factors have contributed to this expansion of students in higher education which has been continuous since the late 1970s. First, during the period since then there has been a concomitant increase in the population of 14–18-year-olds as a result of high birth rates in the 1960s and 1970s. Second, more of this age cohort have stayed at school or entered vocational training; for instance, during the period 1978 to 1987 almost 50,000 extra pupils per year took BUPL and LOU (a 35% increase over this timespan) and 25,000 extra per year took a post-compulsory vocational training course (a 66% increase in the same time). Third, there has been a recognition by government, particularly since Spain's entry to the European Community, of the need to increase its supply of well-trained workers, especially in technical areas, and of the scarcity of employment possibilities for young untrained people.

The expansion of educational opportunities has been described as 'more spectacular than in any other OECD country' (OECD 1986 p.12) and been driven by government policy, backed by regular budgetary increases for education.

Although still lower that most countries in the European Community (4.41% of GNP in 1990), by 1991 the percentage spent on education had increased to 145 per cent of its 1985 level. For the individual school-pupil or university student such increases have been manifested most obviously in funding devoted to means-tested scholarships; a 9.5-fold increase for the whole of the education sector during the period 1982–90, and a 4.4-fold increase in the post-compulsory sector. Clearly this policy of the socialist government has been a key factor in encouraging participation.

The vast majority (96.7%) of students attend public universities according to the 1993–94 estimates. In total over 30 per cent of the population of school-leaving age attends university courses, although the proportion that complete their studies is low. For instance, in 1986 from a total population of over 850,000 students only 90,000 graduated, of whom 55 per cent obtained a *Licentiado*, 38 per cent with a *Diplomado* from a university school and the rest as architects and advanced engineers (MEC 1990a).

Critics of this expansion are not, however, impressed by the increase in funding. For instance, Garcia de Leon (1993) reports that whilst there was a 56 per cent increase in students from 1975 to 1985, there was only a concomitant 39 per cent increase in professors and that 'a professor will normally have between 300 and 500 students during the entire school year without the help of an assistant'. She continues that 'in short, the Spanish universities are crowded' and 'easily accessible'.

The age profile of students within universities reveals that there is a greater concentration of those up to the age of 22: 61.2 per cent in 1987–88 according to Ministry of Education statistics (MEC 1990a). It is perhaps more helpful, however, if the age participation bands shown below in Table 11.1 are used, since these bands provide a dividing line for the age of 25 which has some significance (as will be detailed later) as the point at which alternative mechanisms of entry become available to adults.

Table 11.1: Enrolment in higher education 1987–88

Age Band	Numbers Enrolled	% of All Enrollees
18 – 24	735 465	75.9
25 – 28	118 570	12.2
29 and over	115 4731	1.9
All	**969 508**	**100**

Source: MEC 1990a.

This data shows that just over 12 per cent of the higher education population in 1987–88 was aged 25 or over, and that almost 12 per cent were 29 or over. The data from which the information in Table 11.1 derives also shows that 6.9 per cent of the total Spanish population aged 25 and 2.9 per cent aged 29 were enrolled in higher education in that year. However, it should be noted that the 6.9 per cent here represents both new and continuing students; many enrollees continue their studies over a much longer period that the minimum three or five years required to complete the first or second cycle.

Access to higher education should be viewed not only in the context of the substantial numbers of the school-leaving age cohort presently entering university, but at the same time the very much greater proportion of the adult population who have not even reached the final level of compulsory schooling. As Flecha (1992) points out, the 10.8 million Spanish adults who in 1981 had not reached this level may very well rise to almost 16 million in the year 2000 as the reforms of LOGSE extend compulsory schooling to the age of 16. Furthermore he reports that by the year 2000, the reform anticipates 80 per cent of the school population staying at school until 18, making this the effective norm. Even with the minimum school leaving age of 16, Flecha notes that about 50 per cent of adults will be 'without the compulsory level of education'. Consequently there will develop concurrently higher proportions of well qualified young people and, potentially, of progressively less qualified adults.

It is not surprising then that much of education for adults in Spain concentrates on basic education and vocational training (and sociocultural awareness), rather than access to higher education. This is reflected in the White Book on the Education of Adults, *Libro Blanco Educación de Adultos*, published by the Ministry of Education (MEC 1986) and, most importantly, with respect to adult basic education in

LOGSE. Flecha (MEC 1986p.196) has enumerated some pertinent objectives in relation to this law:

- prolongation of basic education for adults (art.52)
- extension of adult education to secondary non-compulsory education (art.53)
- priority for most needy people (art.51)
- centres specifically for adults, open to the community (art.54)
- inclusion of socio-cultural awareness and occupational training (art.51.2, 53 and 54.1)
- coordination with universities, local government and non-governmental organisations, principally associations without financial gain (art.54.3)
- specific methodology adapted to adults (art.51.4 and 52.1)
- specialisation of teachers of adults (art. 54.2 and 54.3).

The emphasis on adult education included in LOGSE is also reflected in laws passed within the Autonomous Communities. For instance, Díaz Medina (1992) describes the arrangements in Andalucía which included the setting up of a Commission for the Education of Adults in the region as a whole and in each of its provinces, and the establishment of Centres of Adult Education. This reflects the need to deal with the high proportion of the population of the region that have not completed compulsory schooling, and of the even greater concern for its proportion of total illiterates. According to Gracia Navarro and López Eisman (1985), the average rate of illiteracy in Andalusia was 11.8 per cent in 1981 compared to 6.6 per cent in Spain overall. They also report that all eight Andalusian provinces were among the twelve Spanish provinces in which illiteracy ran highest. Furthermore the university system within Andalucia has also responded to LOGSE by recognising the issue of specialist training for adult educators. For example, for the first time in 1993, the University of Granada offered a post-experience course for teachers and other graduates entitled, *Curso de Experto Universitario en Educación de Adultos*.

Access for Adults

Whilst access routes to higher education do not predominate within adult education provision, opportunities and mechanisms for entry to university do exist. These take four principal forms.

(1) Tests for access to university for those over 25, *Las preubas de acceso a la universidad para mayores de 25 años*, and related courses of preparation.
(2) The National University of Distance Education, *Universidad Nacional de Educación a Distancia* (UNED).
(3) Adult Education Schools.
(4) Vocational Training (*Formación Profesional*).

The LGE of 1970 established the possibility of entry to university study for adults over the age of 25 who had not pursued Baccalaureate level studies. The outline of a regime of tests to be offered by each university on a biannual basis, and of a subsequent 'Course of Orientation and Initiation' was laid down in a government order of 1971 (BOE 1971). Subsequently amendments to this order were made in 1981 and 1982 (BOE 1981 and BOE 1982 respectively). The 1981 amendment reduced the testing system to an annual one because experience had shown that this could meet demand. The 1982 amendment allowed those who passed the 'Access Test' of one university to transfer to another university including UNED, if a place in their elected subject was not available in their local university. Universities, however, whilst being obliged to offer entry tests, do not have to offer preparatory programmes for them, an important caveat which maybe reflected in this mechanism's value as a mode of access.

At each institution the testing regime has some similarities; two examples from the Universities of Oviedo and Granada typify systems of assessment that are set in place. At Oviedo, candidates are required initially to present their curriculum vitae in which they are asked to include, according to guidelines provided by the University, 'all the merits that, from the judgement of the candidate, they wish to be taken into account'. Second, in order to determine that they possess 'a basic education and the capacity for balanced reasoning' candidates take a series of four tests in the following areas: psychometrics and reasoning; general knowledge; a written commentary on a text in Spanish; a dictionary translation of a text in a chosen foreign language.

At Granada (and other universities in Andalusia) there is a two-stage testing procedure consisting of a 'General Test', *Preuba Común*, which must be passed in order to qualify to take the 'Specific Test', *Preuba Especifica*. The 'General Test' consists of three components: a multiple choice test containing 100 questions covering the general history of Spain (15 questions), basic world and Spanish geography (15), the Spanish language (10), world and Spanish culture, literature and art (10), basic mathematics (10), general science (30), and national and international events (10); a dictionary translation of a text in chosen foreign language (French, English, German or Italian); and a written commentary on a text in Spanish. Those who successfully complete the 'General Test' then qualify to take the 'Specific Test' in one of four areas (each of which corresponds to the equivalent subject areas in COU and *Selectividad*): science and technology, natural and health science, social science or humanities. Each of the four areas offers three one-and-a-half hour tests, all of which are taken on a single day. For instance, a candidate taking the 'Specific Test' in the area of science and technology would take tests in mathematics, chemistry or technical drawing and physics over a period of five-and-a-half hours with two half-hour breaks. Successful completion of the 'Specific Test' requires an achievement of an average of a least 50 per cent over its three components. It is possible for candidates who do not successfully complete the tests to repeat them, and those who fail the 'Specific Test' have the option of repeating it in the following year without re-taking the 'General Test'.

In the case of both Oviedo and Granada, an obligatory Course of Orientation and Initiation, *Curso de Orientación e Iniciación*, then follows for those who successfully complete the 'Access Test'. In the case of Oviedo, a three-month short course is offered in which it is mandatory for students to take mathematics and Spanish language. Additionally, they opt for an introduction to the subjects offered in the faculty or school they have elected to enter. At the end of the course, a further test is taken, 'of an orientative character, but in no case selective for entry to the University', and a Certificate of Attendance, *Certificado de Asistencia*, is awarded which can be used to gain entry to the corresponding University centre of study. At Granada, and other universities in Andalusia, the Course of Orientation and Initiation, is of a shorter duration, perhaps reflecting the more demanding 'Access Test', and is held during the month of June only. It consists of two phases: a General Module, *Módulo Común* of 15 hours duration and a Specific Module, *Módulo Específico*, of six hours. In the General Module, all students are introduced to the skills required to study successfully at University and in the Specific Module they are inducted into the structures and content of courses offered within their elected faculty or school. Students are not tested after this course, but must attend to receive the Certificate which is required to obtain admission to a degree programme. Because there is a common system of assessment for adults throughout the region, students who pass the test and obtain the Certificate of Orientation and Initiation can obtain entry to any of the pertinent universities in the Andalusian Autonomous Community that offer their chosen course of study providing they can justify with appropriate documentation their reasons for transfer.

Whilst there exists a clear mechanism for entry for adults through an 'Access Test', it appears in the case of the aforementioned universities that it contributes a small proportion of entrants, and is subject to a very high failure rate. Some statistics (Table 11.2) show that in the University of Oviedo over the past three years, the overall pass rate has been no greater than 25 per cent, and for women has not been greater than 16 per cent.

Table 11.2: Entrants and passes on the 'Access Test', Preuba de Acesso, University of Oviedo 1990–92

	Entrants			Passed		
	Total	Men	Women	Total	Men	Women
1990	230	100	130	20	12	8
1991	223	116	107	56	39	17
1992	397	178	219	71	35	36

Source: Vicerrectorado de Estudiantes y Extensión Universitaria, Universidad de Oviedo (personal communication 1993)

The contribution that entry through this route makes to the overall intake can be gathered from further data for 1993 (Table 11.3) showing the total numbers of students taking and passing *Selectividad* in the four options at the June and September sittings of the examination in Oviedo.

It can be seen clearly that the number of entrants to the University on the basis of *Selectividad* (mainly school leavers, but possibly some adults) at 5542 (June and September) dwarfs the 71 entrants through the 'Access Test'. Furthermore the proportions that successfully complete the tests of *Selectividad* (83% in June and 51% September) are far greater than the percentage that pass the 'Access Test' (18% in 1992–93) and there appears to be little difference in the performance of men and women. The numbers quoted for entry through the 'Access Test' become proportionally smaller when considered in relation to the total entry to the University. Admission to certain faculties and schools can be achieved without *Selectividad* or through *Formación Profesional* Grade 2, and a sense of the scale of the system can be gathered from its total enrolment (in all years) in 1992–93 of 37008 (Universidad de Oviedo 1993). The reasons for the low numbers progressing to the University through the 'Access Test' route have not been clearly identified, but clearly the absence of a course of

Table 11.3: Entrants and passes, in the Selectividad,
University of Oviedo, June & September 1993

	June 1993					
	Entrants			Passed		
	Total	Men	Women	Total	Men	Women
Total	5292	2174	3118	4394	1820	2574
Option A	2101	1249	852	1727	1044	683
Option B	1127	272	855	883	210	673
Option C	1257	436	821	1069	366	703
Option D	807	217	590	715	200	515

	September 1993					
	Entrants			Passed		
	Total	Men	Women	Total	Men	Women
Total	2247	1021	1226	1148	522	626
Option A	886	545	341	405	257	148
Option B	487	135	352	192	58	134
Option C	571	251	320	353	152	201
Option D	303	90	213	198	55	143

Source: Vicerrectorado de Estudiantes y Extensión Universitaria, Universidad de Oviedo (personal communication 1993)

Table 11.4: Provision for the 'Access Test Preparation': 'Preparación preuba de acceso a la Universidad para mayores de 25 años' 1992–93

Site	Number of Courses	Number of Students	Number of Staff
Granada	10	595	5
Ceuta	1	66	11
Almeria	7	349	35
Jaen	1	83	14
Melilla	2	52	16

Source: Universidad de Granada 1993

preparation within the University could be a major contributory factor, since the test itself appears not unduly demanding.

At Granada, whilst similarly low pass rates are achieved by prospective adult students who take the 'Access Test', this may be less due to lack of preparation than to the stringency of the entry examinations. Indeed the University organises a comprehensive set of courses throughout the provinces of Granada and in the Spanish enclaves of Cueta and Melilla in North Africa, for which it takes responsibility. The extent of this provision in 1992–93 is shown in Table 11.4.

The provision, which has been in existence for five years, was initially brought into existence as part of in-service training for administrative and secretarial staff within the University who wished to seek promotion, and later was opened to members of the general public. It is not mandatory to follow the course of preparation in order to take the 'Access Test', and indeed, whilst in 1992–93 a total of 1145 students were enrolled in the course, 2748 persons registered and 2292 took this 'General Test'. Complete data for this test, and for the 'Specific Test' is shown in Table 11.5.

Table 11.5: Data for the 'Access Test', Preuba de Acceso, University of Granada

	Registered	Taken	Passed
General Test	2748	2292	1446
Specific Test (all options)	1899	1724	295

Source: Universidad de Granada 1993

The fact that only 295 (17%) passed the 'Specific Test' has been the subject of considerable debate within the local community, mainly because it is a lower proportion of success than in previous years when 50 per cent pass rates were the norm. A newspaper report in Granada (*Ideal* 1993) relayed the frustrations of students, and the responses of the Director of the Institute of Educational Sciences, Maria Luz Uliarte responsible for organising the examinations. The major point of contention has been that in each of the Andalusian universities in 1992–93, the 'Access Test' had been changed making it in structure similar to COU. The perception of students interviewed was that the test was the same as COU, but Luz Uliarte commented that it was similar in form, but not in level. She justified the high number of failures in relation to examinations from previous years by saying that until 1992–93 the level required had been very low and that 'it is not the same to have to show your skills in three subjects, as they have had to do this year, as getting through an interview as they did up until now'. Clearly it appears that the testing system is the major factor that explains the low pass rate, and the regime seems to have had even greater effect in the other Andalusian Universities of Cordoba and Malaga where only ten and nine students, respectively passed.

The Distance Learning University

Whilst the Access Test Preparation Course, *Curso de Acceso*, may not be a significant feature within traditional Universities, it is obligatory for those wishing to take the Access Test for admission to the *Universidad Nacional de Educación a Distancia* (UNED). This University was established by the government in 1972 to supply university courses through distance learning, starting its operations in the following year. According to recent statistics (Farjas Abadia and Madrigal Collazo 1990), students are registered in 50 Spanish provinces as well as overseas; total enrolments in 1987–88 numbered 83,121 and in 1988–89 numbered 99,226. These figures represent those studying on a variety of courses from the access to doctorate level, omitting certain continuing education and professional updating courses. The extent of the provision that is taken up by the *Curso de Acceso* can be determined from Table 11.6, which shows data for the most recent two years available, and for purposes of comparison 1980–81.

Table 11.6: Numbers in faculties and Access course, UNED

	1980–81	1987–88	1988–89
Numbers in Faculties	31060	63315	74388
Numbers on *Curso de Acceso*	10761	19806	24838

Source: Farjas Abadia and Madrigal Collazo 1990

Clearly the Access provision of UNED represents a substantial element of its activity and has increased dramatically during the 1980s in line with its almost two-and-a-half fold increase in all forms of undergraduate activity. The proportions of students on the 'Access Course' is reflected to a substantial degree in the numbers of those on undergraduate programmes who have entered the system with this qualification. Table 11.7 shows the qualifications held on entry by those on undergraduate programmes in UNED for the years 1987–88 and 1988–89.

Table 11.7: Numbers in Faculties by initial qualification, UNED

Type of Qualification	1987/88		1988/89	
	No.	%	No.	%
Pre-University	14092	16.95	16006	16.13
Transfers	8608	10.35	10689	10.77
Primary Teachers	3197	3.84	3193	3.21
Secondary Teachers	10336	12.43	11240	11.32
Diplomates	6270	7.54	7007	7.06
Licentiates	6612	7.95	7874	7.93
Convalidated Qualifications	726	0.87	767	0.77
Others	957	1.15	1488	1.49
Access Course	9778	11.76	11395	11.48
No Information	2739	3.30	4728	4.76
Total	63315	100	99226	100

Source: Farjas Abadia and Madrigal Collazo 1990.

These figures show that the Access route is second only to traditional pre-university entry qualifications as a mechanism for entry to UNED, and is the mode of entry for over 11 per cent of undergraduate entrants. It would not be wise, however, to compare directly the figure of 19,806 on the Access Programme in 1987–88 (shown in Table 11.6) with the 11,395 undergraduates holding this qualification in the following year (shown in Table 11.7) as this later figure is distributed over students at all stages of the University's programmes. In fact only 2835 of this number represented new entrants to the system. Furthermore some of this number will have been transfers from other universities (UNED 1993a), since UNED regulations allow the admission of students who have completed the Access Test at another university, if that university does not offer a suitable regime of teaching at undergraduate level. Students have to be able to justify such transfers, which can occur without their having completed the first year at their original university (the usual norm for any inter-university transfer). So whilst in absolute terms the numbers studying on the 'Access Course' at UNED, and those entering its courses from such studies, are high in comparison to the traditional universities, the progression rates (of the order of 15%) are of the same magnitude as those at the other universities previously considered, perhaps reflecting a demanding examination regime.

The 'Access Test' at UNED is one of five examinations held over two separate days at the end of May and in mid June; a further set of examinations is offered over two consecutive days in mid September to provide re-sit opportunities and to cater for those unable to take the earlier examination. The five subjects offered are as follows: Spanish language, basic mathematics (or specific mathematics if the subsequent course demands it), a foreign language, one from history of the contemporary world, philosophy, literature, history of art or biology, and a subject related directly to the student's intended undergraduate degree such as 'Fundamentals of Technology' if they wish to progress into Industrial Engineering or 'Basic Legal Concepts' for Law. In order to successfully complete the 'Access Test' as a whole, each of the individual components must be passed and a total score of 50 per cent or more obtained; when particular subjects are failed, these alone are repeated in the September test.

The preparatory course itself lasts one year, is offered at distance with the aid of regular seminars, telephone tutorials, audio cassette material and radio programmes, the details of which are found in a comprehensive course guide (UNED 1993b) and a Guide to Audiovisual Materials (UNED 1993c); a commentary on this provision has been made by Marzo (1993). Standard texts are recommended for all courses, and in order that students get feedback on their progress, each subject sets evaluation tests (typically five during the year); these do not contribute to students' grades and are not obligatory, being used solely as a means of self-evaluation.

Thus UNED offers an Access Course that is delivered and tested in exactly the same way throughout Spain. For many students, in the absence of a preparatory course at a local university or because of geographical isolation, it represents the most viable way of gaining entry to university, although not, it would appear, a route without difficulties. From UNED students can then obtain transfers to another university, subject to being able to justify their request to the receiving institution and having completed the first course at UNED (equivalent to one full-time year). Although figures for transfer out of UNED are not available, it would appear that transfer in represents a more significant occurrence: over 10 per cent of its entry in both 1987–88 and 1988–89 (Table 11.7). Once in the University, students, almost all of whom follow one of the 14 Licientiado programmes, typically take eight years to complete the five year programme (Ramos Corrada 1993). The majority of students are in the 25–44 age band (81.2% according to 1988–89 statistics), though a sizeable proportion lie in the 20–24 band (12.9%). The significance of these figures is that, although for the purpose of mature access regulations to all universities 25 is the delineating age, a number of students in UNED and other institutions are admitted between the ages of 20 and 24, an age considered to be adult by many definitions. The entry qualification that such students typically hold is COU and *Selectividad* or FP-2 (or its equivalent) which may have been gained whilst in formal schooling or later through some form of continuing education. Since COU and *Selectividad* has an unlimited shelf-life, clearly this will be a mode of entry for some of the adult population.

Other Routes for Adults

Obtaining COU and *Selectividad* when beyond the traditional school leaving age is not an easy matter. It is possible to obtain post-secondary qualifications through the auspices of the National Institute for Distance Secondary Education (INBAD) (Flecha 1990), though the extent to which this facilitates university entry is difficult to determine. Another possibility is through Official Adult Education Schools which have been in existence since the early 1970s and where according to Flecha (1992 p.194) there are more than 70,000 learners. These schools were in fact set up under the terms of the LGE in 1970 which determined that life-long education, *Educación Permanente*, for adults should be available. According to an official report (MEC 1990a), in practice, only basic education for adults has been developed, though the Act contains other possibilities (art. 44) for studies and courses for advancement and updating. Flecha also describes state-independent 'Popular Schools', 'Peasant Schools' and 'Popular Universities', all of which came into existence as or after the Franco dictatorship came to an end. All of these institutions focus on one or more of the main types of adult education activity in Spain and have a broader remit than the official schools: in addition to basic education, provision related to socio-cultural awareness, and to a lesser degree vocational training is offered. This perhaps reflects the prevailing concept of adult education as described by a number of authors, including Quintana Cabanas (1993), who describes a number of examples of initiatives throughout Spain in these fields. Many novel developments are taking place which indicate priorities not necessarily prevalent in other countries; for instance, Peiró i Gregori (1991 and 1992) describes schemes such as the Parents' School, *Escuela de Padres*, a project whereby education programmes are provided for the parents of educationally disadvantaged children.

Adult Education Schools do not in general offer teaching that prepares mature students for university entry such a development is envisaged, however: through LOGSE's provisions adult education is to be extended to the secondary non-compulsory sector and therefore may become more significant in this field in the future.

Finally, vocational training as a means of access to high education for adults is likely to become an increasingly viable route. Whether it be under the old, experimental or planned regimes of *Formación Profesional* adults are able to attend Vocational Training Schools and obtain qualifications that can provide access to a corresponding *Diplomado* in an *Escuela Universitaria*. Both present and past legislation has recognised that the particular circumstances of adults may not make it feasible for them to attend such schools. Therefore certain elements of flexibility have been written into structures. First, opportunities are provided to study both FP-1 and FP-2 at evening classes, providing students are over 18 or over 16 and in work. Second, the assessments to obtain these qualifications can be obtained without attendance at the Vocational Schools at all, simply by taking the tests. Age limits again apply: over 18 for FP-1 and 'adults' for FP-2. To obtain FP-2 by this mechanism an adult candidate has to complete successfully all of the examinations corresponding to its three areas ('General Training' including a foreign language, technical and practical knowledge, and 'Business Training' including business organisation, economics and administration) in one sitting.

Further flexibility has been written into the new experimental level two and level three vocational qualifications by allowing entry through taking a test. At level two, a two part test, consisting of general and professionally specific components, is offered to those over 17 irrespective of their previous educational qualifications; at level three a similar regime exists for those over 20. These tests are designed to be equivalent in level to those offered at the end of compulsory schooling and at the end of the Baccalaureate respectively.

So in moving from the old system to the new, there has been a shift from 'assessment on demand' to 'access on demand', but both occur on the basis of very traditional testing. The regime of testing for entry to level three Professional Modules serves as an illustration of this: firstly there is a general test which assesses 'capacities of comprehension, analysis, synthesis, evaluation, problem solving, calculations and reasoning'; and second, a 'specific test...tries to assess basic knowledge of the business world, economics and of a foreign language' (Ibáñez Aramayo, 1992 p.60).

In addition to certification obtained through Vocational Training Centres, occupational training, *La Formación Occupacional*, also occurs within the workplace itself with Certificates of Competence, *Certificaciones de Profesionalidad*, being validated by the National Institute of Employment, *Instituto Nacional de Empleo* (INEM), an autonomous organisation responsible to the Ministry of Labour and Social Security. LOGSE had contemplated the establishment of systems of equivalences between occupational training courses and the new Modules of Professional Training, but according to Ibáñez Aramayo (1992 p.158), as of 1992 such possibilities have not yet been established. Nonetheless the Plan for the Reform of Vocational Training does specify that 'the adult population that possess professional competence...will be able "to realise" their professional practice in centres of work as training credits towards the corresponding award' (MEC 1992 p.72). Consequently, in theory if not yet in practice, opportunities exist for those in work to embark on a route towards higher education, based on the accreditation of work-based competencies. Furthermore the same plan suggests that 'distance education constitutes one of the forms of teaching most suitable and accessible to the adult population' (MEC 1992 p.73), and reports that the Ministry of Education has designed distance learning material for trialling within certain professional areas.

Conclusion

The characteristic that defines a prospective entrant to higher education as an adult is simply age, with 25 as the effective minimum for university courses. However, the age of 20 is also an important point of delineation since it is at this age that entry to the highest level of vocational training can be gained through a special test; and subsequently this qualification can lead on to the *Diplomatura* and later the *Licentiatura*, given the increasing elements of flexibility that have been built into articulation.

It may therefore be concluded that a variety of routes to higher education exist for people characterised as adults. However, these routes are very much tied into a centralised system of planning at national, regional or provincial level. Furthermore, courses through which access is gained are either similar to those taken by school pupils, albeit in a flexible fashion (at work, in the evenings, at distance) or are variants of traditional pre-university qualifications (eg. the university 'Access Courses'). Consequently there is little adaption of the curricula of pre-entry courses and related testing regimes to meet the particular needs of adult learners. The absence of a customised provision is perhaps a reflection of the lack of expertise previously identified in an OECD survey which stated that 'there appears to be a lack of professionalism in the field of adult education, associated with the absence of applied research inquiries into adult learning needs and problems' (OECD 1986 p.44). There is now a recognition of the need for a specific teaching methodology adapted to adults and for specialist teacher training within the terms of

LOGSE, but this is an initiative largely directed to basic education. Without the recognition that particular methods are applicable for all forms of adult education, there is a likelihood that mechanisms for entry, particularly the University Access Tests will continue to be very selective and, as is the case with the three universities sampled, will continue to lead to low progression rates. At present whilst such mechanisms may maintain parity of quality with traditional routes, they select on the basis of limited criteria, principally the ability to pass unseen time-constrained tests. It might be argued, however, that because this form of assessment is a reflection of the regime of undergraduate programmes themselves, preparation via such routes may be necessary to ensure subsequent success. Nonetheless, there is some irony in the selective nature of the Access routes for adults, given that the 'standard' routes of *Selectividad* for school leavers is hardly a barrier to entry at all and according to Garcia de Leon (1993 p.78) 'should more fittingly be called *distribution examinations*, for they distribute the applicants among different univerisites, according to the admission grades which the latter require', the level of which 'is not high'.

Expansion of the higher education system has been continious for more than a decade, and has been assisted by a demographic upturn following the baby boom of the 1960s and early 1970s. However, this supply of school leavers will not be maintained since there has been a subsequent downturn in births which is reflected in basic general education (6–14 year olds) where numbers peaked at 5.6 million in 1985, but had reduced to 4.9 million by 1990. According to Bruton (1994) this downturn is the greater than all other countries of the European Union, and is most marked in the urban centres, where there exists the greatest concentration of universities. In order to maintain their share of the diminishing market of students, universities are likely to have to offer a more attractive range of courses, moving away from simply a diet of traditional academic degrees to programmes in subjects such as information technology and business studies which are presently very scarce. In addition, there will be increasing pressure to provide courses with a European dimension as students and employers become aware of the demands of the single market.

References

Boletin Official del Estado (1970) *Ley General de Educación y Financiamiento de le Reforma Educativa*. 21, 4 August. Madrid: Boletin Official del Estado.

Boletin Official del Estado (1971) *Orden de 26 de mayo de 1971 por la que se regula el acceso a los estudios universitarios de los mayores de veinticinco años.* 131, 8816. Madrid: Boletin Official del Estado.

Boletin Official del Estado (1981) *Orden de 24 de febrero de 1981 por la que se modifica el articulo 2.1. de la Orden de 26 mayo de 1971 que regula el acceso a los estudios universitarios de los mayores de veinticinco años.* 57, 1066. Madrid: Boletin Official del Estado.

Boletin Official del Estado (1982) *Orden de 7 de abril de 1982 por la que se regula el acceso a los estudios universitarios de los mayores de veinticinco años.* 93, 9875–6. Madrid: Boletin Official del Estado.

Boletin Official del Estado (1983) *Ley Reforma Universitaria.* Madrid: Boletin Official del Estado.

Boletin Official del Estado (1985) *Ley Orgánica de Derecho a la Educación.* Madrid: Boletin Official del Estado.

Boletin Official del Estado (1989) *Orden de 5 de junio de 1989, por la que se determinan los titulos a expedir a los alumnos que finalizan Módulos Profesionales.* Madrid: Boletin Official del Estado.

Boletin Official del Estado (1990) *Ley de Ordenación General del Sistema Educativo.* 4 October, 238, 28927–28942. Madrid: Boletin Official de Estado.

Boletin Official del Estado (1992) *Real Decreto 921/1992, de 17 de julio, por el que se establece el titulo universitario oficial de Ingeniero Industrial la aprobación de las directrices generales propias de los planes de estudios conducentes a la obtención de aquel.* Madrid: Boletin Official del Estado.

Bruton, K. (1994) *The Business Culture in Spain.* London: Butterworth Heineman.

Department of Education and Science (1989) *Selected National Educational Systems II.* London: Department of Education and Science.

Díaz Medina, R. (1992) La Educación de Adultos. Marco Legal. In A. Romero Lopez, *La Educaión de Adultos – Aspectos Curriculares y Metodológics*, 43–50. Granada: Universidad de Granada.

Escuela Asturiana (1992) *Edición Especial. Los Módulos Profesionales*, VII. 62, April.

Farjas Abadia, A. and Madrigal Collazo, C. (1990) *Datos Estadisticos de la UNED Curso 1987–88 y 1988–89.* Madrid: UNED.

Flecha, R. (1990) Spanish Society and Adult Education. *International Journal of Lifelong Learning*, 9, 2, 99–108.

Flecha, R. (1992) Spain. In P. Jarvis (ed) *Perspectives on Adult Education and Training in Europe.* Leicester: National Institute for Adult Continuing Education.

Garcia de Leon, M.A. (1993) Academic Women in Spain: An Elite Subject to Discrimination. In *Higher Education in Europe*, 18, 4, 78–92.

Gracia Navarro, M. and López Eisman, J.L. (1985) Adult Education in Andalusia. *Prospects*, 15, 3, 400–406.

Holmes, B. (ed) (1983) *International Handbook of Education Systems, Vol 1 Europe and Canada.* Chichester: John Wiley.

Ibáñez Aramayo, J. (1992) *La Nueva Formación Profesional*. Madrid: Fundación Universidad-Empresa.
Ideal (1993) *Sólo 295 mayores de 25 años entrarán en la Universidad*. Granada, June 1993.
Marzo, A. (1993) La educación a distancia (II) – Radio y Educación, *Herramientas*, 64–66.
McNair, J. M. (1984) *Education for a changing Spain*. Manchester: Manchester University Press.
Ministerio de Educación y Ciencia (1986) *La Educación de Adultos, un libro abierto*. Madrid: Ministerio de Educación y Ciencia.
Ministerio de Educación y Ciencia (1989) *Libro Blanco para la Reforma de la Enseñanza. Propuesta para debate*. Madrid: Ministerio de Educación y Ciencia.
Ministerio de Educación y Ciencia (1990a) *Development of Education – National report on Spain*. International Conference in Education, 42nd Meeting, Geneva.
Ministerio de Educación y Ciencia (1990b) *Estudios en España – II Nivel Universitario*. Madrid: Ministerio de Educación y Ciencia.
Ministerio de Educación y Ciencia (1992) *Plan de Reforma de la Formación Profesional*. Madrid: Ministerio de Educación y Ciencia.
Ministerio de Educación y Ciencia (1993) *Curso Escolar 1993–94 – Datos y Cifras*. Madrid: Ministerio de Educación y Ciencia.
Organisation for Economic Co-operation and Development (1972) *Classification of Educational Systems*. Paris: Organisation for Economic Co-operation and Development.
Organisation for Economic Co-operation and Development (1986) *Reviews of National Policies for Education – Spain*. Paris: Organisation for Economic Co-operation and Development.
Peiró i Gregori, S. (1991) Educación de los Adultos in Iniciativas Sociales. In D. García Hoz *Iniciativas Sociales en Educación Informal*. Madrid: Rialt Ediciones.
Peiró i Gregori, S. (1992) *Educación de Adultos y Desarrollo Comunitario*. Granada: Seminario de Pedagogia Social.
Quintana Cabanas, J.M. (1993) Experiencias en Educación de Adultos. In J.A. Ortega Carrillo, *La Educación de Adultos Hoy – Ponencias del I Congreso Internacional de Educación de Adultos*. Granada: Fundación Educación y Futuro.
Ramos Corrada (1993) personal communication.
Revuelta, J. M. (ed) (1993) *Anuario el Pais*. Madrid: Prisa.
Royal Institute of British Architects (1991) *Architectural Practice in Europe: Spain*. London: Royal Institute of British Architects.
Universidad Nacional de Educación a Distancia (1993a) *Información General*. Madrid: Universidad Nacional de Educación a Distancia.

Universidad Nacional de Educación a Distancia (1993b) *Guia del Curso 1993–94 – Curso de Acceso*. Madrid: Universidad Nacional de Educación a Distancia.

Universidad Nacional de Educación a Distancia (1993c) *Guia de los Medios Audiovisuales*. Madrid: Universidad Nacional de Educación a Distancia.

Universidad de Granada (1993) *Memoria del Curso Académico 1992–93*. Granada: Universidad de Granada.

Universidad de Oviedo (1993) *Normas e Información de Interés para Estudiantes de 3o de B.U.P., C.O.U., F.P.2 y Universidad*. Oviedo: Universidad de Oviedo.

Chapter 12

Themes and Trends

Pat Davies

This book has attempted to look at policy and practice in relation to adults in a number of countries at the macro, meso and micro level and as such is an ambitious undertaking. However, as was made clear in the introduction, it was not the intention to provide analyses and classifications but rather to promote understanding through exploring empirical questions, and to test and illuminate the developing models in the field of comparative studies of higher education.

The preceding chapters have provided details and examples of 'what is happening and what is being done' (Gellert 1993 p.241) in relation to adults in higher education. What picture do they present of the way in which adults have been affected by some of the changes identified by others and set out in the introduction to this volume?

Expansion

It is quite clear that the expansion of the early 1980s identified by others continued in the late 1980s and into the 1990s. The demographic trends of falling numbers of school leavers were offset by increasing numbers of young people gaining secondary qualifications which enabled them to enter higher education, and above all by the increasing participation of women which has been marked in all the countries represented here. The demographic trend also provided opportunities for adults to increase their participation, and although the data for age on entry is not always readily available the age profile of students has undoubtedly risen. This is not necessarily a result of policies targeted at adults indeed such policies are the exception rather than the rule and where they exist are relatively marginal in terms of total numbers. Rather it is a function of a number of interrelated factors: the increasing time taken by many students to complete their programmes of study – partly because of failure and repetition of courses, partly due to the need to work to support themselves; and an increase in numbers pursuing second and third cycle courses as the economic situation has led to both a reduction in employment opportunities as an alternative to continuing study, and to an increase in credentialism.

In countries with selective systems, in particular the UK and Australia among those represented here, there has been a tension between the recruitment of adults and the recruitment of school leavers since in the main the status of institutions is linked to their reputation with young students, and an institutional profile which demonstrates a high proportion of adults in undergraduate programmes is often associated with lower status. Whilst adults have been welcomed during periods of expansion, young people constitute the priority for most universities and adults may find their opportunities restricted if the continued expansion is constrained.

Efficiency

The increase in costs arising from expansion and the reduction in available resources arising from economic recession has created the pressure for greater efficiency in higher education. In all cases, this has meant higher productivity and reducing the unit of resource so that funding has not kept pace with the expansion of student numbers. It has also led to pressure to improve the throughput of students: a reduction in drop-out and in the length of time taken to complete study programmes. In general there have been three approaches: the first is financial, through for example limiting the time for which grants are available, as in Denmark; the second is through increased selection, a point which will be explored in greater detail later; and the third is an increase in guidance, advice and counselling, as for example in France, in order to better match the students' preparation and competence with their programmes of study. While such developments are often couched in the language of industry – productivity, efficiency and so on – they are often overdue in educational terms, since there is nothing necessarily educationally or socially desirable in students taking five years to complete a two year diploma course.

There has also been increased pressure on financial support for students and, as predicted by the CERI report (1987), a general shift towards fees and/or loans for all students, as for example in Australia and UK. Others, Denmark for example, have set a time limit on grants or, as in Austria, have limited eligibility for support by age. In addition, programmes aimed at those in work increasingly are not free: in the UK part-time versions of courses have fees; in Denmark those in work are now expected to contribute 20 per cent of the cost; and in the Netherlands differential fees are being introduced with upper age limits for financial support. Thus increasingly there are differential costs associated with studying, often the same programme, according to employment status and hence usually age. Higher education is shifting from being free for those qualified to benefit irrespective of age, to a service which must be paid for in varying extent according to age and means.

Horizontal Diversity

Horizontal diversity – the existence of different types of higher education institutions and courses (Rasmussen 1992) – is well established in some of the countries represented in the volume (Belgium, Denmark, Netherlands, France, Germany), fuelled, as Gellert (1993 p.240) pointed out, by the 'manpower requirement approach' and the 'social demand approach' to managing growth and by economic developments and needs. In these countries it is also clear that the growth in student numbers has been greatest in the non-university institutions (although in the Netherlands there are some signs that this trend has now reversed). However, in some the development has been relatively recent: Austria, for example, established *Fachhochschulen* only in the late 1980s and is thus still a relatively small sector. In others, Spain for example, there is differentiation within the university sector; in Italy such differentiation has not taken place in the public sector: rather a growing private sector has met the demand for different kinds of provision. In the UK and Australia, the policy has operated in the opposite direction: binary systems have been unified, so that previously differentiated institutions now have at least the same title and funding framework (although it should be noted that they are still frequently differentiated by provision and mission). While there has clearly been a financial motive in these developments and, some would argue, motives relating to control and direction, it has also represented an attempt to equalise the status of the 'vocational/professional' and the 'academic' institutions and to facilitate movement between them. Undoubtedly, the status of the non-university sector is usually lower (with some notable exceptions such as the *Grandes Ecoles* in France) and since most are associated with particular professional areas – engineering, business and administration, social work, teaching, nursing – they generally recruit higher proportions of those studying alongside work and this has a disproportionate effect on adults. In addition, the problem of movement between them often discriminates against adults since graduates of the non-university sector are frequently unable or find it difficult to move into the university sector. However, there are early signs in some countries, Germany, the Netherlands and Spain for example, of an easing of the regulations surrounding such movement at least partly to increase the attractiveness of the vocational route by opening up progression from it to the university sector at higher levels.

Halsey (1992 p.15) points out that although institutional differentiation promotes expansion, it is also socially controlled 'so that élite universities...remain the cultural possession of traditionally advantaged groups'. While data on social class and socio-economic background of students is neither readily available nor easily aggregated, and thus fraught with difficulty, it is clear that the non-university sector frequently recruits higher proportions of disadvantaged groups, as is the case in the IUTs in France and the former polytechnics in England and Wales. Although this may insulate the élite institutions, it is also clear that in some cases it provides better employment prospects in a shorter time, for example in Germany, than the university sector. In a period of high unemployment, with no indication that this will change in the near future, institutions which offer better employment prospects are increasingly in demand and the fact that courses are often shorter is also an advantage for many adults who do not have time on their side. Increased demand may bring increased status, if the differential employment prospects are sustained.

Institutions are also increasingly differentiated by the extent to which they are they local, national or international in terms of their client groups. In many countries, universities have recruited primarily from their neighbouring community, and this seems to have been given additional emphasis; the link between the local or regional economy and the university is often becoming stronger or being stressed as a policy objective. In France, for example, the contractual arrangements between government and university involve attention to relations with the regional development plan; in Britain, universities are being encouraged to work more closely with the local Training and Enterprise Councils (TECs). This also involves attention to the needs of adults in the locality, particularly their training needs in relation to employment.

Alongside this shift to a more local focus for the activities of universities, there is also a shift to a more international focus and institutions are increasingly differentiated by the degree to which they are involved in international exchanges, collaborative research activities, or recruit from beyond the national boundaries, and the extent to which they are seen as international centres of excellence in particular fields.

Vertical Diversity

Rasmussen (1992) notes an increase in vertical diversity – the increase in courses of differing lengths, with different exit points – and Gellert (1993) notes the development of new modes of teaching and learning, more transparent curricula and more practical approaches to learning. In several of the countries represented in this volume, for example Italy, Denmark and Spain, there are explicit attempts to shorten the length of existing courses and/or to introduce new shorter courses. In Britain, there is considerable encouragement for the two year vocational diploma and a pilot scheme offering the usual three year degree over an 'accelerated' two year period. In many countries the growth in the shorter courses has been more rapid than the longer courses. All these measures should, given adequate financial support, be beneficial to adults, who often either prefer to or need to re-enter the labour market as quickly as possibly.

At the same time as this acceleration at the front-end of higher education, there is a parallel movement to extend the length of studies particularly for those already in the labour market: the growth of *formation continue* and *régimes salariés* in France and the special funding arrangements which accompany it, the growth of part-time programmes of study in England, Scotland and the Netherlands are obvious examples. These more flexible programmes over a longer period are primarily to accommodate those who work alongside their studies and thus have developed first in work-related or professional fields.

It is interesting to note that those systems which are most selective at the front end, notably UK and Australia, are also those which seem to be at the forefront of the development of modularisation and credit accumulation and transfer schemes. In all systems, however, it is clear that flexibility is greater at second level or postgraduate level than at the first cycle or diploma level. Again, although there are often financial savings in public expenditure terms in such flexible schemes, through differential funding regimes, these developments have undoubtedly provided new and additional learning opportunities for adults.

In addition to the greater flexibility in the timing and pace of study, there are two other trends which have grown considerably in recent years: open or distance learning and work-based learning. Technological development, frequently supported in Europe by EU funding, has obviously boosted distance learning and made possible modes of study previously unavailable. This has happened in large countries such as Australia enabling people in remote areas to be reached, but also in small countries such as Austria which also has potential learners for whom attendance at university on a regular basis is not possible. Sometimes this is based at national or regional centres designated by government, sometimes individual universities develop their own arrangements, and sometimes, as in France, both have been developed. It should be noted however, that most distance learning systems require the same entry qualifications as the conventional university programmes – only in the Netherlands and UK is entry totally open. In most cases distance education techniques and materials have had an impact on teaching and learning in the traditional classroom, sometimes by osmosis and sometimes by intent. In all cases, the majority of students on such courses are adults and in some they are defined exclusively as adults, often who are in some way disadvantaged and unable to attend conventional classes either by virtue of the distance, personal circumstances such as disability, or domestic responsibility.

There has also been an increase in the recognition of the value of work-based learning at a number of levels. In some countries – England, Scotland, France, for example – there has been a growth in the recognition of work-based learning as equivalent to formal qualifications for entry to both first cycle, first degree programmes and perhaps more frequently to second cycle, postgraduate programmes especially the more professional or technological fields. The use of the workplace as a source of learning within higher education courses has also increased, through either *alternance* or sandwich type courses or through programmes focusing on professional activities in the work place.

A university is thus increasingly becoming an activity rather than a physical location for many students, particularly for adult learners. Given the cost of buildings, plant and equipment, it seems likely, again for financial reasons if none other, that this trend will increase. It remains to be seen whether or for how long such modes of learning will stay on the margins of the traditional university.

Autonomy and Admissions

Goedegebuure *et al.* (1994) point out that there has been a trend towards deregulation and decentralisation of higher education decision-making from central government and thus a shift to greater institutional autonomy. However, there is a danger of confusing greater responsibility with greater autonomy, which although closely related are not the same. The difference is perhaps highlighted in the matter of admissions.

In general, admissions regulations are still firmly in the hands of the state, often written into the constitution as rights or freedoms which it is the duty of the state to protect and promote. However, although all but UK and Australia of the countries represented here have systems which are open to all those with the appropriate qualifications, there is considerable evidence of increasing selection, and only Italy and Belgium remain totally non-selective. In Denmark for example *numerus clausus* has been extended from dentistry and midwifery to medicine, architecture and library qualifications; in France, the IUTs are selective; in Germany the use of *numerus clausus* is spreading and some institutions have been given permission to reserve a quota of places for selected students; in Austria the introduction of *numerus clausus* is under discussion. Despite the fact, as de Weert (1994) points out, manpower planning techniques have largely failed to match the output of graduates with the needs of the economy and have often been dysfunctional by creating surpluses in those subjects areas not restricted, the high cost of some disciplines, particularly medicine, dentistry and veterinary science have continued to provide a justification for limits to the number of students recruited.

In parallel to this increase in selectivity, there is an increase in the decentralisation of decision making. Thus for example, in Denmark, institutions have been given the responsibility for managing admissions as part of an attempt to address the question of mismatch between the secondary experience or qualification and the university programme. In France there is an increase in the attention being paid to guidance and counselling at entry and some universities have introduced a period of orientation at the start of the diploma course with the opportunity to change course at the end of the period. In the UK, where traditionally institutions have complete autonomy over which students are recruited and considerable discretion over their distribution across subject areas, central government now uses the funding mechanism with increasing rigour to control the numbers in each subject category. Thus while institutions have increasing responsibility for admissions they do not necessarily have increased autonomy.

Alternative Entry

Gellert (1993 p.17) suggests that functional modifications in higher education, the 'emergence of new tasks and purposes', have created the 'need to open up restrictive tertiary structures in favour of better participation opportunities for larger segments of society'. As indicated above, higher education institutions have clearly become more accessible through greater diversity in both their structures and their provision. However, there has also been an increase in the diversity of routes in to higher education for adults. While most countries have had, for a considerable time, arrangements for adults to take the traditional secondary school qualification for example in Germany the *Abendgymnasium* and *Kolleg* have provided preparation for the *Abitur* for adults, these have generally replicated the school experience with few concessions to adult learners. In particular, because of the length of time required to replicate the school curriculum in the evenings, it has not always been a sensible option, especially where there are age restrictions on certain types of employment or on the eligibility for grants. For these reasons, a number of alternatives have also been developed. Frequently established originally as an examination, for example *l'ESEU* in France or HF in Denmark, increasingly this has been followed up with the establishment of a preparation course, geared to the needs and learning styles of adults. Frequently too, although the qualification may be national, the preparation course and the assessment is owned by the university and may explain why some universities have used it to establish some institutional influence over recruitment and to attract adults and non-traditional students. However, it has also been problematic in some cases with little or no mutual recognition of the examination thus it has functioned to exclude as well as to admit.

The other more recent development has been the use of the accreditation of prior learning to admit adults without the traditional entry qualifications. Sometimes this is dealt with informally, and this is often the case in the UK through the use of interviews; sometimes it is more formal, often in collaboration with employers, increasingly the case in the UK; or through the formal recognition of the equivalence of vocational qualifications, as in Germany. In France, legislation has created the right to request *la validation des acquis* – usually knowledge, skills and competences acquired at work – for both entry to and exemption from parts of a diploma course. The diversity of such arrangements is greatest at present in those systems where institutions have control over selection (the UK and Australia for example) or where regional government has control or influence over the process (Australia and Germany) so that, paradoxically, some of the apparently most closed systems are in practice the most open to non-traditional students. Since these measures are increasingly related to work experience and used to access professional courses, it seems likely that they will continue to increase and given the variation in work experience which will be presented, they are also likely to become more diversified.

At present these arrangements are still relatively marginal in terms of the numbers of students who are able to gain access via such means. In general, the proportion of students entering the first level of higher education seems to be between 2.5 per cent and 10 per cent, with the exception of Denmark where 16 per cent gain entry with the HF. However, it seems likely that the figure may be higher in some countries where informal processes are not recorded in the statistics. It also seems likely that some of these routes, particularly the accreditation of work-based learning, are often used to access second level or postgraduate studies and statistics are not routinely published which would reveal this trend since it is generally assumed that the first level qualification has been used. Nevertheless, even though the figures are relatively small, such alternatives are important for significant numbers of adults and where the data is available it suggests that they are of particular importance for women, people from lower socio-economic backgrounds and other under-represented groups. However, while there is some reason to believe that the alternative routes are meeting, at least in part, the demands of social justice and equity, there is no evidence to suggest that they are changing the traditional patterns of participation in different subject areas, for example the gender patterns in teaching and engineering remain strong. Hence it could be argued that such routes serve to protect the traditions of the élite professions while giving the impression of equality of opportunity.

Concept of Adult

The definition of adult is not consistent across the countries included in this volume, and indeed it is clear that the definition varies within countries depending on the context. In some countries, Italy for example, adults are not present in the policy debates surrounding higher education. In the UK, to be 21 or over on entry to first degree programmes is to be a young adult, and 25 or over a mature adult. In Denmark the 'normal' age on entry is 20 or 21 and in Belgium and France practitioners tend to work with a definition which distinguishes between level: 23 or over in first cycle, 25 or 26 and over in second, and 29 or 30 and over in third cycle programmes. In Australia, the most common is 25 and over, although this varies between institutions. It is also clear that students in some countries are older, simply because it takes longer to prepare for, or successfully obtain, entry and longer to progress through the system. A simple statistical aggregation of data according to age, even if it were readily available, would not explain the relevance of the concept in policy terms.

The significance is revealed in other kinds of definition, in particular those which reflect the gap between leaving school and entering higher education, the relationship between the student as learner and the student as worker, and issues related to social equity. Hence there appear to be three types of adult who have significance in policy and practice. First, 'deferrers' who may be similar to the traditional student who has progressed directly from school, except that they have either taken extra time to obtain the usual entry qualification, or have taken time out for a variety of reasons before entering higher education. Second, there are the 'second chancers', those who did not obtain the traditional entry qualifications at school, often for reasons associated with some form of disadvantage. Third there are the 'returners', those who have re-entered the system to update or upgrade the level of their qualifications. Only in Australia of the countries represented here has the government set a clear objective in terms of equity, focusing in particular on the 'second chancers'. The general trend of policy in others is away from a concern with equal opportunities in terms of class, gender, or ethnicity, although arguably such concerns were always fragile and often absent, and towards a concern with the needs of society in economic terms focusing on the 'returners'. Thus the concept of adult has moved away from a consideration of the whole person, with cultural and social needs to one of an economic being with work related needs; the 'second chancer' has moved to the wings and the centre stage is now occupied by current and future workers capable of sustaining or regenerating economic competitiveness.

As Goedegebuure *et al.* (1994 p.346) point out 'social equity and cultural enrichment' have been factors in the expansion of higher education but the more fundamental reason is to be found in the global economic restructuring which increases the need for people skilled in applied science and technology and in social and administrative sciences for more efficient management. The shifting concept of adult in this context highlights this imperative and also reveals an underlying tension since science and technology courses are the most expensive and, despite much of the rhetoric and a number of special arrangements, much of the expansion, certainly in terms of adult participation, does not seem to have taken place in these areas.

Conclusion

It is clear that the environment of higher education is increasingly turbulent and that change has been rapid and widespread. In almost all the countries considered in this volume there has been a spate of legislation reforming and reshaping of the system in recent years. In addition there has been an increase in the number of stakeholders in higher education as the needs of the economy as a whole, the needs of the local region, the needs of a more heterogeneous student body and diverse sources of funding have been added to the traditional role and function of the sector.

An increase in 'the market' as a mechanism for regulating and managing higher education has set up tensions in the system and has particularly affected provision for adults making the world of work significant as a source of prior and higher learning and making the system more flexible in its approach to teaching and learning. Despite this overall spread of the ideology of the market and policies to increase market forces on higher education, the influence of political control has been important for adults. Where socialist or left of centre parties have political control, there has been more intervention on the part of disadvantaged groups and adults in the name of equal opportunities and social justice. While this may only operate at the margins and be small in absolute terms it is nevertheless important for significant numbers of people.

It is interesting that, while the market has tended to push institutions into a competitive relationship, technology, both its potential and its cost, has encouraged cooperation – between universities in some cases and between universities and other institutions in others – particularly in the field of distance education. Similar considerations lie behind a new form of internationalism in higher education, so that in Austria, students can study with the British or German distance learning universities and in Belgium with the Open University of the Netherlands.

The sense of crisis which the enormous expansion and the spate of legislation in recent years have generated is pervasive. However, as Neave (1984 p.111–112) pointed out, crisis is a 'tactic of negotiation that serves to regulate the speed of change coming from without to a pace that academics may assimilate within...part of the politics of incremental change'. While some might argue that it supports resistance to change rather than promoting its assimilation, there is no doubt that a considerable struggle is taking place for control of the mission and function of higher education and that adults are at the centre of that struggle. Most of these developments are too recent to permit an analysis of the outcomes, but it will be interesting to examine the data in the year 2000 to ascertain the impact on participation.

References

Centre for Educational Research and Innovation (CERI) (1987) *Adults in Higher Education*. Paris: OECD.

Gellert, C. (ed) (1993) *Higher Education in Europe*. London: Jessica Kingsley Publishers.

Goedegebuure, L., Kaiser, F., Maassen, P., Meek, L., van Vught, F., and de Weert, E. (eds) (1994) *Higher Education Policy. An International Comparative Perspective*. Oxford: Pergamon Press.

Halsey, A.H. (1992) An International Comparison of Access to Higher Education. In D.Phillips (ed) *Lessons of Cross-national Comparison in Education*. Wallingford: Triangle Books.

Neave, G. (1984) On the Road to Silicon Valley? The Changing Relationship between Higher Education and Government in Western Europe. *European Journal of Education, 19*, 2, 111–129.

Rasmussen, T.K. (1992) Equality. In B. Marchione and M. Giuberti (eds) *Proceedings of the Conference on Access to Higher Education in Europe, Parma 13–16 October 1992*. Parma: Università degli Studi di Parma.

de Weert, E. (1994) *Access to Higher Education and Labour Market Needs. An international review of policy instruments*. Paper presented at the European East/West Convention on Access to Higher Education, March 1994, Berlin (unpublished).

The Contributors

Pat Davies is Director of the Continuing Education Research Unit at City University. She has been involved in research in the field of adult access and participation in higher education for a number of years and has published widely in the field, including *Recognising Access* (with Gareth Parry). She was assistant editor, and subsequently joint editor for three years, of the *Journal of Access Studies*.

Roseanne Benn is Lecturer and Access Coordinator at the University of Exeter. She has worked in this field since 1978 as a practitioner and researcher and has been closely involved in the development of policy and practice at local, regional and national level. She is involved in a number of research projects and has published widely on the political and historical aspects of widening access to higher education.

Etienne Bourgeois is Assistant Professor in the Unit for Research in Continuing Education and Organisations in the Faculty of Education at the Université Catholique de Louvain in Belgium. He has published widely, in French and English, in the field of university decision-making in relation to the education of adults. His current teaching and research interests focus on international comparisons of adult access, participation and achievement in higher education and on the development of instruments for assessing change in adult learners.

Anthony Cooke is Senior Lecturer in Continuing Education at the University of Dundee and has served as Secretary of the Universities Council for Adult and Continuing Education (Scotland) and as editor of the Scottish Journal of Adult Education. He has published in the field of the history of adult education and has research interests in international perspectives on access issues.

Jim Gallacher is a Reader in Continuing Education at Glasgow Caledonian University. He has undertaken research and published on a number of topics associated with access to higher education in Scotland including part-time degrees, Access Courses, and the performance of students with non-traditional qualifications. He also has research interests in work-based learning, credit accumulation and transfer and the use of computer assisted learning for adults.

Jean-Luc Guyot is a Research Assistant in the Unit for Research on Continuing Education and Organisations at the Université Catholique de Louvain, Belgium. He is currently working on the project 'Belgium-UK Comparative Study of University Access Policies'.

Michael Osborne is Assistant Director of the Division of Educational Policy and Development at the University of Stirling with responsibility for continuing education and access. He has previously worked in a range of further and higher education institutions and has published extensively in the field of access to higher education, particularly in the areas of science, mathematics and technology. His other research interests include environmental education and work-based learning.

Marleen Owen is Research Assistant in the Department of Continuing Education at the University of Dundee, working with Anthony Cooke and Anna Spackman on the project 'Policy Frameworks for Access in three European Education Systems'. She also teaches Dutch and German.

Stella Parker is Professor and Head of the Department of Continuing Education at City University and previously worked in a range of institutions in the post-compulsory sector of education. Her research interests include the staff development and organisational responses that are required for and result from widening access to higher education and associated quality assurance issues. Her publications include materials and study guides for teaching and learning and papers on access and change, particularly in the field of science education.

Gareth Parry teaches at the Institute of Education, University of London. He was formerly Senior Lecturer and Director of the Continuing Education Research Centre at the University of Warwick. He was founding editor of the *Journal of Access Studies* and has published widely in the field of access and continuing education, including two books: *Recognising Access* (with Pat Davies) and *Access and Alternative Futures for Higher Education* (edited with Clive Wake).

Glen Postle is Director of the Office of Preparatory and Continuing Studies at the University of Southern Queensland. He was seconded for two and a half years until April 1994 to the Queensland Department of Education as Coordinator of the Open Access Support Centre for the state of Queensland.

Evelyn Reisinger is a tutor in German and was also the Research Assistant for the project 'Access and participation for adults in German Higher Education', in the Continuing Education Research Unit at City University.

Anna Spackman is Lecturer in Access Studies in the Centre for Continuing Education at the University of Dundee and has been involved in the planning and presentation of the Centre's return to study programme since 1988. She has been involved for several years in researching access to higher education for adults in a number of European countries.

Subject Index

References in italic indicate figures or tables.
Abbreviations:
Aus. = Australia
Aust. = Austria
Bel. = Belgium
Den. = Denmark
Eng. = England, Wales and Northern Ireland
Fra. = France
Ger. = Germany
Ita. = Italy
Neth. = Netherlands
Sco. = Scotland
Spa. = Spain

A-level examinations, Eng. 118, *119*, 120, *120–1*, 121, 128
Abendgymnasium 169, 170
Aberdeen University 241, 245
'ability to study' concept, Ger. 175
Abitur 168, 169, 170, 175
Aborigines 17, 18, 25
academic staff, Ita. 184–5, 199
academic tradition, Den. 90
accelerated degrees, Eng. 126

'access and equity' policy, Aus. 7–8, 19–20, 22
access and equity units, Aus. 32–3
access courses: Aus. 22–3, 30–*1*; Eng. 122–4, 125, 128; Sco. 227, 233, 234, 235–8, *238*, 241–3, 246–7; Spa. *266, 267, 268, 269,* 270–1
access tests, Spa. 263–8, *265, 266, 267,* 269–70
'access' theme 1, 3, 4
accessible programmes: Aus. 26–30; Aust. 55–8; Bel. 76–80; Den. 95–7; Eng. 108, 125–7; Fra. 150–2; Ger. 173–4; Ita. 185–9, *186,* 195; Neth. 213, 218–20; Sco. 227–9, 244–6; Spa. 268, 273
accreditation of prior learning 283, 285; Aus. 24, 95; Bel. 75, 78; Den. 95; Eng. 124–5; Fra. 149–50; Ita. 197; Neth. 215; Sco. 245; Spa. 273
admissions procedures 283–4; Aus. 9–11, *9, 10*; Aust. 40–2, *41*; Bel. 65–6, *65*; Den. 86–7, *86*; Eng. 106–7, 109–10; Fra. 142–3; Ger. 166–9, *168*; Ita. 181–4, 190, 192; Neth. 205–6,

207–10, *209*; Sco. *225,* 226–9; Spa. 259
'adult' concept 286–7; Aus. 13–17, *14, 15*; Bel. 70–1; Den. 88; Eng. 107–8, 109, 110; Fra. 152–4; Ger. 169; Ita. 185; Neth. 210; Spa. 273
adult education colleges: Aust. 45–7, 50–3; Den. 90, 93, 94, 95, 99; Ger. 170; Spa. 271
Adult Education Framework Act, Neth. 211
'Advanced Highers' proposals 227
advanced study degrees, Bel. 64–5
age, and participation: Aus. *13*; Aust. 41, *41*; Eng. 104, *104*; Fra. 143, *143*; Ger. 163–4; Sco. 247; Spa. 260–1, *261*
Agrégation degrees 64
'alternative route' concept, Eng. 107, 128
Andalucía, basic adult education 262
aptitude tests, Ger. 172
Australia (Aus.) 6–37, 280
admissions procedures 9–11, *9, 10,* 284, 285
alternative accessible programmes 26–30, 282
alternative entry routes 22–5

concept of adult
   13–17, *14*, *15*, 286,
   287
influence of
   institutions 21–2
institutional
   arrangements
   32–3
participation
   patterns 12–13, *13*
policy relating to
   adults 17–21
research 33–4
resources and
   funding 30–2, 279
size of system 11–12,
   11, *12*
Austria (Aust.) 38–60
   admission and
      participation
      40–2, *41*, 284
   alternative accessible
      programmes
      55–8, 282, 288
   alternative entry
      routes 45–54, *49*,
      50
   policy relating to
      adults 42–5
   research 58–9
   structure and
      organisation 38,
      39–40, 279, 280
AVU (formal adult
   education courses),
   Den. 94, 95

baccalauréat (Bac), Fra.
   135, *136*, 139–40,
   142, 145
Baccalaureate, Spa.
   253–4

*Bachillerato Unificado y
   Polivalente* (BUP)
   253, *254*, *255*, 259
BAföG
   (*Bundesausbildungs-
   förderungsgesetz*)
   161
*Befähigungsprüfung
   zum Hochschul-
   studium ohne
   Reifezeugnis* 171–2
Belgium (Bel.) 61–83
   admissions
      procedures 65–6,
      65, 284
   alternative accessible
      programmes
      76–80, 288
   alternative entry
      routes 74–5
   concept of adult
      70–1, 286
   participation
      patterns 67–9, *68*,
      69
   policy relating to
      adults 71–4
   research 82
   resources and
      funding 81–2
   size of system 66, *67*
   structure and
      organisation
      61–5, *62*, *63*, 280
Beratungsgespräch 172
Berufserfahrene 169, 172
Berufsreifeprüfüng 47
*Brevet de Technicien
   Superieur* (BTS) 136
bridging admissions
   policy, Bel. 74–5
BTEC qualifications
   107, *119*, *120–1*,
   121–2

*Bundesausbildungsförder-
   ungsgesetz* (BAföG)
   161
BUP (*Bachillerato
   Unificado y
   Polivalente*) 253,
   254, *255*, 259
Business and
   Technology
   Education
   Council *see* BTEC

CAEs (Colleges of
   Advanced
   Education), Aus. 7,
   16
Candidature degrees,
   Bel. *63*, 64, *65*, 66,
   68, 74–5, 78, 80
Centre for Distance
   Education
   proposal, Aust.
   53–4
*Centre National
   d'Enseignement à
   Distance* (CNED)
   151
Certificate of Sixth
   Year Studies
   (CSYS), Sco. 226,
   227
*classes préparatoires aux
   grandes écoles*
   (CPEG) 135, 136
classification tests,
   Ger. 172
CNAM (*Conservatoire
   National des Arts et
   Métiers*) 151–2
CNED (*Centre National
   d'Enseignement à
   Distance*) 151
Colegios Universitarios
   257

collaboration between institutions, Sco. 243–4
colleges of adult education *see* adult education colleges
Colleges of Advanced Education (CAEs), Aus. 7, 16
colleges of education, Sco. 224
colleges of further education *see* further education colleges
colleges of higher education, Eng. 102–3, 117
colloquium doctum 208, 213–14
Commonwealth government influence, Aus. 6, 7–8, 15–16, 17–20
communications technology, Aus. 28, 29, 35
comparative approaches 2
'competencies' development, Aus. 21
complementary degrees, Bel. 63, 64
Conservatoire National des Arts et Métiers (CNAM) 151–2
consortia for SWAP 236
Continuing Education Units, Aus. 31–2, 33
COU (*Curso de Orientación a Universidad*) 253, 254, 259, 267, 271

counselling 279
CPGE (*classes préparatoires aux grandes écoles*) 135, 136
credit accumulation and transfers: Aus. 29–30; Aust. 55; Bel. 74–5, 78–80; Den. 95; Eng. 125, 126–7; Fra. 147, 152; Ita. 197; Neth. 220; Sco. 224, 227, 228, 240–1, 243
crossover between subjects, Fra. 145
CSYS (Certificate of Sixth Year Studies), Sco. 226, 227
Curso Adaptación 257, 257
Curso de Acceso (access test) 266, 267, 268, 269, 270–1
Curso de Orientación a Universidad see COU
Curso de Orientación e Iniciación 264

DEA *see Diplôme d'études approfondies*
DEAL (Developing Employment-based Access to Learning) project 245
de-centralised programmes, Bel. 76
DECs (distance education centres), Aus. 26–8
'deferrers' 287

demographic trends, Sco. 233–4
Denmark 84–101
  admissions procedures 86–7, 86, 284
  alternative accessible programmes 95–7, 282
  alternative entry routes 93–5, 285, 286
  concept of adult 88, 286
  participation 88–9
  policy relating to adults 89–93
  research 99–100
  resources and funding 97–8
  structure and organisation 84–6, 279, 280
descriptive approaches 2–3
DEUG (*Diplôme d'études universitaires Générales*) 136, 137, 139, 150
DEUST (*Diplôme d'études universitaires scientifiques et tôchniques*) 136, 137
Diploma di Maturità 181, 188–9, 190
Diplomado 257
Diplomatura 257, 258
Diplôme d'études approfondies (DEA): Bel. 64–5; Fra. 136, 137
Diplôme d'études complémentaires 64

Diplôme d'études universitaires Générales (DEUG) 136, 137, 139, 150
Diplôme d'études universitaires scientifiques et techniques (DEUST) 136, 137
Diplôme universitaire de technologie (DUT) 135, *136*, 137
disabled students: Aus. 17; Den. 89
distance education 282–3; Aus. 26–9, 31, 32, 33; Aust. 53–4, 55–7; Bel. 77; Den. 96; Eng. *see* Open University; Fra. 151; Ger. 173–4; Ita. 197; Neth. 218; Sco. 228, 241, 245; Spa. 268–71, *268*, *269*, 273
distance education centres (DECs), Aus. 26–8
Doctorado, Spa. 257
Doctorat degrees, Bel. 64
Dritter bildungsweg see 'Third educational route'
drop-out rates: Den. 98; Fra. 144–6; Ita. 193; Neth. 212; Spa. 279
Drumchapel/Easterhouse Initiative 242–3
Dundee University 242
Dutch Open University 76, 218, 221

economic factors, Ger. 174–5
Education Reform 92 – A Danish Open Market in Higher Education 91
educational level, Italian population compared 185, *186*
efficiency in higher education 279–80
Eignungsgespräch 172
Eignungsprüfung 172
Einstufungsprüfung 172
employee organisations, Aus. 21
employers, influence: Aus. 21; Bel. 73
'enclaves', Aus. 25, 33
England, Wales and Northern Ireland (Eng.) 102–33
  numbers, patterns and policies 110–19, *111*, *112*, *113*, *115*, 279, 280, 281
  pathways, programmes and credits 120–7, *119*, *120–1*, 282, 283, 284, 285, 288
  trends, terms and territories 103–10, *104*, 286
  entry routes alternatives for adults 284–6; Aus. 22–5; Aust. 45–54, *49*, *50*; Bel. 74–5; Den. 93–5; Eng. 107, *119*, *120–1*, 121–4, 127; Fra. 143, 146–50, *148*; Ger. 167–73, *168*; Ita. 197, 198; Neth. 210–16; Sco. 227–9, 231–2, *231*, 233; Spa. 262–8, *265*, *266*, 267
standard *see* admission procedures
equal opportunities provision 287; Aus. 17–20, 21; Aust. 43–5; Bel. 71–4; Den. 88, 89, 91, 92; Ger. 166; Ita. 190, 195, 196; Sco. 234, 242–3
Erster Bildungsweg see 'first educational route'
Escuelas Technicas Superiores 257
Escuelas Universitarias 256, 257
ESEU, L' (*L'examen spécial d'accès aux études universitaires*) 143, 146–8, *148*
ethnic minorities, participation rates: Aus. 17, 18, 25; Aust. 43–4; Den. 89; Eng. 115, 116, 128; Neth. 211
evening course provision, Bel. 76
'Exam for the Specially Competent in Employment', Ger. 171
examen spécial d'accès aux études universitaires

(L'ESEU) 143,
146–8, *148*
expansion of higher
education
provision 4, 278–9,
288; Aus. 11–12, *11*,
12; Bel. 66, *67*; Den.
85; Eng. 103–4; Fra.
139–42, *139*, *141*;
Ger. 161–3, *162*; Ita.
189–92, *191*; Neth.
203, *206*, 206; Sco.
229–30, *229*; Spa.
259–60, 274
experience *see*
accreditation of
prior learning
external diversity *see*
horizontal diversity
external studies
departments, Aus.
26–9

*Fachgebundene
Hochschulreife* 168
Fachhochschul-Diplom
degrees, Ger. 160
Fachhochschulen: Aust.
40, 42–3, 44–5, 55,
59; Ger. 160, 161,
174
Fachhochschulreife 168
'facilitative' policies,
Neth. 216
Faculdades 257, *257*
Fair Chance for All, A
17–18, 25
Federal Education
Assistance Act,
Ger. 161
federal *Matura*
courses, Aust. 45–7
financial support to
students 279–80;
Bel. 73, 82; Den. 98;
Eng. 108–9; Ger.
161; Ita. 195; Neth.
217, 220–1
'first educational
route', Ger. 167–9,
168
first-level degrees, Bel.
63, 64
flexibility 282
see also credit
accumulation
and transfer;
modularisation;
part-time study
folkeoplysning, Den.
89–90, 91
foreign study centres,
Aust. 55–7
Formación Occupacional
272–3
Formación Profesional
272
Formal Adult
Education Act,
Den. 88
formal adult
education (AVU)
courses, Den. 94, 95
'formal' courses, Ita.
183, 184, 185–6,
197–8
formation aménagée 150
formation continue
137–9, 141–2, *141*,
144, 150, 153, 155
formation initiale 137,
139, *139*, 143, *143*,
150–1, 153–4, 155
Forum for Access
Studies, Eng. 128
foundation years; Aus.
34–5; Eng. 125
Framework Act for
Higher Education,
Ger. 166

France (Fra.) 134–58
admissions
procedures
142–3, 284
alternative accessible
programmes
150–2, 282
alternative entry
routes 146–50,
148, 279, 283, 285
concept of adult
152–4, 286
expansion 139–42,
139, *141*
participation 143–4,
143, 281
progression 144–6
resources and
funding 137–9
structure and
organisation
135–7, *136*, 280
'free' students, Bel. 79
full-time study,
part-time
compared: Aus. *14*;
Eng. 108–9, *112*,
119, *120*; Sco.
230–1, *230*
funding *see* resources
funding councils; Eng.
103, 117; Sco. 225,
226, 227
Further and Higher
Education Act,
Eng. 103
further education
colleges: Eng.
118–19, 120, 123,
125, 127; Sco. 224,
227, 243–4
Further Training Act,
Den. 99

gender, and
  participation rates:
  Aus. 13, 14, 15;
  Aust. 43, 49–50, 49,
  50; Bel. 68; Den. 89;
  Eng. 113, 113, 115,
  116, 128; Fra. 144;
  Ger. 164; Ita. 196;
  Neth. 211; Spa. 265,
  266
General National
  Vocational
  Qualifications
  (GNVQs) 118
general Scottish
  Vocational
  Qualifications
  (gSVQs) 239–40
Germany (Ger.) 159–80
  admissions
    procedures
    166–9, 168, 284
  alternative accessible
    programmes
    173–4, 288
  alternative entry
    routes 169–73, 285
  expansion 161–3, 162
  participation 163–6,
    165
  policy relating to
    adults 174–6
  resources and
    funding 161
  structure and
    organisation
    159–63, 162, 280,
    281
Glasgow Caledonian
  University 243,
  244, 245
Glasgow University
  242–3
GNVQs (General
  National
  Vocational
  Qualifications) 118
government
  involvement: Aus.
  6–8, 15–17, 17–21;
  Bel. 72–3; Den.
  91–2; Eng. 116–17,
  118–19; Fra. 134,
  138; Ita. 184–5,
  191–2, 199; Neth.
  204, 216–18; Sco.
  232–3
Graduate Consortium,
  Aus. 28
Granada, University
  of 259, 262, 263–4,
  266, 267, 267
Grandes Écoles 135
*Groupements
  d'établissements*
  (GRETA) 136
Grundtvig, N.F.S.
  89–90
GSVQs (General
  Scottish Vocational
  Qualifications)
  239–40

Haarlem *hogeschol*
  scheme 215
Hagen, University of
  55–6, 57, 173–4
Hamburg, *Hochschule
  für Wirtschaft und
  Politik* 171, 174
Harder, Bertel 91
HAVO (*Hoger
  Algemeen Voortgezet
  Onderwijs*) 208, 209,
  211, 212, 214, 216
HBO (higher
  professional
  education), Neth.
  209, 215
HECS (Higher
  Education
  Contribution
  Scheme), Aus. 31
HF (*Hojere
  Forberedelseseksamen*)
  86, 86, 88, 90, 93–4,
  285, 286
HHX (*Hojere
  handelseksamen*) 86,
  86
Higginson Report 128
*Higher Education: A
  Policy Statement*,
  Aus. 7–8
Higher Education and
  Research Act,
  Neth. 205, 218
higher education
  colleges, Eng.
  102–3, 117
Higher Education
  Contribution
  Scheme (HECS),
  Aus. 31
Higher Preparatory
  Examination *see*
  HF
'Highers'
  examinations, Sco.
  225, 226, 227
Highlands and
  Islands, proposed
  university 245
HNC/HND
  qualifications *see*
  BTEC
  qualifications;
  SCOTVEC
  qualifications
Hochschulen, Ger.
  159–60, 177
  for working adults
  174

Hoger Algemeen Voortgezet Onderwijs see HAVO
Hoger Onderwijs en Onderzoek Plan (HOOP) 217
Hoger Ondewijs voor Ouderen (HOVO) 215
hogescholen, Neth. 205, 206, 207, 210, 214–16, 219, 220
Hojere Forberedelseseksamen see HF
Hojere handelseksamen (HHX) 86, *86*
Hojere teckniskeksamen (HTX), Den. 86, *86*
home location, and participation, Aus. 15, *15*
HOOP (*Hoger Onderwijs en Onderzoek Plan*) 217
'horizontal diversity' 4, 85, 280–1
'*hors âge*' concept, Fra. 154
HOVO (*Hoger Ondewijs voor Ouderen*) 215
Howie Committee 226
HTX *see Hojere teckniskeksamen*

IFF (Institute for Interdisciplinary Research and Continuing Education), Aust. 58–9

INBAD (National Institute for Distance Secondary Education), Spa. 271
Industrial Engineering degree, Spa. 258
INEM (*Instituto Nacional de Empleo*) 272
Institute for Interdisciplinary Research and Continuing Education (IFF), Aust. 58–9
Instituto Nacional de Empleo (INEM) 272
institutional influence: Aus. 21–2, 32–3; Bel. 73–4; Sco. 241–6
'institutional profiles', Aus. 7–8
Instituts Universitaires de Technologie (IUTs) 135
Intermediate Specific Vocational Training, Spa. 253, 255
internationalism 288; Aus. 56–7; Bel. 76
interviews, Ger. 172
Italy 181–202
  expansion 189–92, *191*
  policy relating to adults 189–96, *191*, *194*, 286
  problems of articulation 197–8
  provision for adults 185–9, *186*

structure and organisation 181–5, *182*, *183*, 282
IUTs (*Instituts Universitaires de Technologie*) 135

Jysk Aabent Universitet (Open University of Jutland) 88, 96–7

Kolleg 169, 170
Koori people 25

labour market trends: Aust. 42–3; Den. 92; Fra. 155; Ger. 175; Neth. 216–17
Laurea courses 193
level of study, and participation, Eng. 111, *111*, 112
Ley de Reforma Universitaria 258
Ley General de Educación y Financiación de la Enseñanza Obligatoria see LGE
Ley Orgánica de Ordenación General del Sistema Educativo see LOGSE
LGE (*Ley General de Educación y Financiación de la Ensenanza Obligatoria*) 253, 254, 271
Libro Blanco Educación de Adultos 261

Licei schools, Ita. 192–3
Licence degree, Bel. 63, 64, 74, 75, 78
Licence speciale 64
Licenciatura 257, 258
Licentiado 257, 257
local authority policies, Eng. 115
Local Collaborative Programme, Sco. 228
LOGSE (*Ley Orgánica de Ordenación General del Sistema Educativo*) 253, 255, 261–2
Louvain, Catholic University of 69, 70, 76
lycées 136

Margareten *Volkshochschule* 50–1, 52
market factors 288; Ita. 199–200; Neth. 218
mass higher education, Eng. 103–4, 118–19
Matura examination, Aust. 39, 40, 42, 45–7, 59
MAVO (*Middelbaar Algemeen Voortgezet Onderwijs*) 208, 209, 211, 212
MBO (senior secondary vocational education), Neth. 211, 214, 215, 216
Middelbaar Algemeen Voortgezet Onderwijs see MAVO
Ministry of Education and Research, Den. 91, 92
modularisation: Bel. 78–80; Den. 95–6; Eng. 125, 126; Neth. 219–20; Sco. 245–6
Modules of Professional Training, Spa. 272–3
Monash Orientation Scheme for Aborigines 25
Mons, University of 77
multi-media courses, Bel. 77

Namur, University of 77
Napier University 245
National Advisory Board for Local Authority Education (NAB) 114, 116, 117
National Institute for Distance Secondary Education (INBAD) 271
Netherlands (Neth.) 203–23
alternative accessible programmes 218–20
alternative entry routes 210–16
courses and qualifications 207, 282
entry qualifications and routes 207–10, *209*, 283
policy relating to adults 216–18
resources and funding 220–1
size of system 206, *206*
structure and organisation 205–6, 280, 281
'new' v. 'old' universities, Eng. 102, 106
Newcastle (Aus.), University of 22, 23
Niedersachsen, entry exam 171–2
'non-formal' courses, Ita. 186, 197–8
'non-standard' entry qualifications: Eng. 119, *120–1*, 124; Sco. 231–2, *231*
non-university sector 6–8, 12, *12*; 280–1; Aust. 39–40, 42; Bel. 61, *62*, 67, *68*, 69, 74; Den. 84–5; Eng. 102–3; Fra. 135; Ger. 159–60; Ita. 181; Neth. 205, 206, *206*, 207; Sco. 224; Spa. 255–6
Northern Ireland *see* England, Wales and Northern Ireland
numerus clausus 284; Den. 87, 92; Ger. 167, 175; Neth. 210

occupational status, and 'adult' concept 70
Office of Aboriginal and Torres Strait Islander Education (OATSIE) 25
'old' v. 'new' universities, Eng. 102, 106
open admissions policy, Bel. 75
'open college networks', Eng. 126
Open Education Act, Den. 88, 90–1, 95, 96, 97, 99
Open Foundation Course, University of Newcastle, Aus. 22, 23
Open Institute of the Technical University of Vienna 57
open learning *see* distance education
Open Learning Agency, Aus. 28
Open Learning Network, Queensland 27–8
Open University, British 109–10, 113–14, *115*, 124, 228
  courses in Aust. 56–7
Open University Act, Neth. 218
Open University of Hagen 55–6, 57, 173–4
Open University of Jutland 88, 96–7
Open University of the Netherlands 76, 218, 221
Open University project, Bel. 71–2, 77
organisation *see* structure of higher education
orientation and initiation courses, Spa. 263, 264
Ottakring *Volkshochschule* 51, 52
Outline Regional Plan, Fra. 134
'over age' concept, Fra. 154
overcrowding of universities, Ita. 190–2, *191*
Oviedo, University of 263, 264, 265, *265*, *266*

part-time study 282; Aus. *14*; Eng. 108, 109, 111, *112*, *119*, *121*; Ita. 195; Neth. 219–20; Sco. 230, *230*, 231, 235, 244–5
participation patterns 3, 4, 278; Aus. 11, 12, *13*, *14*, *15*; Aust. 40–2, *41*; Bel. 67–9, *68*, *69*; Den. 88–9; Eng. 104–5, *104*, 110–14, *111*, *112*, *113*, *115*; Fra. 143–4, *144*; Ger. 163–6, *165*; Ita. 186–7, 196, 199; Neth. 211, 213; Sco. 224, 229–32,
229, *230*, 231, 246; Spa. 260–1, *261*
partnership arrangements, Sco. 242, 243, 244
passerelles programme, Bel. 74
pedagogical arrangements, Bel. 80
personal development courses, Ita. 186–7
Plan de Reforma Formación Professional 256
policy towards adults: Aus. 17–21; Aust. 42–5; Bel. 71–4; Den. 89–93; Eng. 114–19; Fra. 138, 139–41; Ger. 174–6; Neth. 203–4, 216–18; Sco. 232–5
polytechnics, Eng. 102, 111, *112*, 117
'popular enlightenment', Den. 89–90, 91
positive action strategies, Aus. 25
preparatory courses *see* access courses
preubas de acceso 263–8, *265*, *266*, *267*, *268*, *269*
prior learning *see* accreditation of prior learning
private sector institutions, Ita. 194, *194*
Probestudium 172
Prüfung für den Hochschulzugang von besonders

befühigten Berüfsätigen 171

qualification updating, Aus. 26, 31

recognition of prior experience *see* accreditation of prior learning
Reform Act on Higher Education, Den. 98
Regional Training Centres (ROCs), Neth. 212
research: Aus. 33–4; Aust. 51, 58–9; Bel. 82; Den. 99–100; Ger. 172; Neth. 221–2
resources 279; Aus. 7, 30–2; Bel. 81–2; Den. 97–8; Eng. 103, 115, 117; Ger. 161; Ita. 195; Neth. 205, 220–1; Spa. 260
'returning' students 70, 107, 153, 188–9, 287
Robbins Report 116
ROCs (Regional Training Centres), Neth. 212

Sackgassencharakter 175–6
schemas régionaux d'aménagement (SRA) 134
SCOTCAT (Scottish credit accumulation and transfer network) 224, 227, 240–1
Scotland (Sco.) 224–51
 adult participation 229–32, *229*, *230*, *231*, 286
 impact of policies and initiatives 246–7
 institutional initiatives 241–6, 282, 288
 national access initiatives 235–41, *238*, 283, 285
 policy development 232–5
 relevant aspects of system 224–6, *225*, 279, 280, 284
 routes to higher education 226–9
Scottish credit accumulation and transfer network *see* SCOTCAT
Scottish Higher Education Funding Council (SHEFC) 226, 227
Scottish Vocational Education Council *see* SCOTVEC
Scottish Vocational Qualifications (SVQs) 239–40
Scottish Wider Access Programme *see* SWAP
SCOTVEC (Scottish Vocational Education Council) 224, *225*, 227, 238–40
screening procedures *see* selection
'second chancers' 287
'second educational route', Ger. 168, *168*, 169–70
second-level degrees, Bel. *63*, 64
secondary education reforms, Spa. 253–6, *254*, *255*
Sections de Technicien Superiéurs (STS) 135, 136
selection, and admissions regulations 279, 282, 284, 285; Aus. 9–11, 20; Den. 87, 92; Eng. 106–7, 109–10; Ger. 167, 175; Neth. 210; Sco. 226; Spa. 259
Selectividad 259, 265–7, *266*, 271
SHEFC (Scottish Higher Education Funding Council) 226, 227
size of higher education: Aus. 11–12, *11*, *12*; Aust. 40–1, *41*; Bel. 66, *67*; Den. 85; Eng. 104–5, *104*; Fra. 139–42, *139*, *141*; Ger. 161–3, *162*; Ita. 189–92; Neth. 206, *206*; Sco. 229–30, *229*; Spa. 259–60
social background of students 281; Aus. 17–19; Aust. 42, 43, 44; Bel. *68*, 69, *69*, 73; Den. 88–9; Eng. 128; Fra. 144; Ger.

164–6, *165*; Ita.
195–6; Sco. 242–3,
247
'social justice'
concerns, Sco.
234–5
Southern Queensland,
University of 22–3,
25
Spain (Spa.) 252–77
access and
participation
259–62, *261*
access for adults
262–8, *265*, *266*,
267
distance learning
university
268–71, *268*, *269*
other routes for
adults 271–3
reforms in secondary
education 253–6,
254, *255*
structure 256–8, *257*,
280, 281, 282
staff-student ratios,
Ita. 190–1, *191*
state/territory
government
influence, Aus. 6, 8,
20–1
Stirling University
242, 245
*Strasbourg, Université
des Sciences
Humaines de* 144–5
Strathclyde region
228, 234, 242–3
structure of higher
education: Aus.
6–9; Aust. 39–40;
Bel. 61–5, *62*, *63*;
Den. 84–6; Eng.
102–3, 105–6; Fra.

135–42, *136*, *139*,
141; Ger. 159–61;
Ita. 181–5, *182*, *183*;
Neth. 205–10, *206*,
209; Sco. 224–9,
225; Spa. 256–8, *257*
STS (*Sections de
Technicien
Supérieurs*) 135, 136
Student Grants and
Loans Act, Neth.
220–1
student services units,
Aus. 32, 33
Studentereksamen, Den.
86, 86, 87, 90, 93
*Studienberechtigung-
sprüfung* 40, 42,
47–53, *49*, *50*, 51
evaluation 51–3
examples 50–1
subject crossover, Fra.
145
summer school
programme, Sco.
242–3
SWAP (Scottish Wider
Access
Programme) 224,
227, 234, 235–8,
238, 246–7

TAFE colleges
(technical and
further education
institutions), 6, 8–9,
12, *12*, 20–1, 24,
29–30
targeting of specific
groups *see* equal
opportunities
provision
technical and further
education

institutions, Aus.
see TAFE colleges
Technical University
of Denmark 96
*Télé-enseignements
Universitaires* 151
'third educational
route', Ger. 168,
168, 169–70, 171–3
third-level degrees,
Bel. *63*, 64–5
Tilburg, Catholic
Hogeschool at 215
'time credit' system,
Ger. 171
time off for study, Bel.
73
Torres Strait Islanders
17, 18, 25
'trial studies'
(*Probestudium*) 172

UHSS (*Université des
Sciences Humaines
de Strasbourg*)
144–5
Ulster, University of
122
under-represented
groups *see* equal
opportunities
provision
UNED (*Universidad
Nacional de
Educación a
Distancia* 268–71,
268, 269
University
Diplom/degree,
Ger. 160–1
University Funding
Council (UFC) 225

University Grants
  Committee (UGC)
  116, 117
University of the
  Third Age, Ita. 187
university sector: Aus.
  6–8, 12, *12*; Aust.
  39; Bel. 61–5, *62*, *63*,
  67, 69, *69*; Den.
  84–5; Eng. 102–3,
  106; Fra. 135; Ger.
  159–60; Ita. 181;
  Neth. 205, 206, *206*,
  207; Sco. 224; Spa.
  256–7
updating courses, Ita.
  187–8

validation des acquis, la
  143, 149–50
VBO (*Voorbereidend
  Beroepsonderwijs*)
  208, *209*, 214
'vertical diversity' 4,
  85, 282–3
vocational training:
  Aus. 6, 8–9, 12, *12*,
  20–1, 24, 29–30;
  Aust. 39–40, 42–3,
  54, 57–8; Bel. 61, 71,
  75; Den. 85, 90, 96;
  Eng. 118, 121–2,
  126; Fra. 142; Ger.
  173, 175–6; Ita. 185,
  186, 187–8, 193–4,
  199–200; Neth. 205,
  211; Sco. 224, 227,
  233, 239–40; Spa.
  253, 254, 255–6,
  272–3
Volkshochschulen, Ger.
  170
Volkshochschulen, Aus.
  Matura courses 45–7

*Studienberechtigung-
  sprüfung* courses
  50–3
*Voorbereidend
  Beroepsonderwijs see*
  VBO
*Voorbereidend
  Wetenschappelijk
  Onderwijs see* VWO
voucher system, Den.
  98
VUCs (adult
  education
  colleges), Den. 90,
  93, 94, 95, 99
VWO (*Voorbereidend
  Wetenschappelijk
  Onderwijs*) 208, *209*,
  211, 212, 214, 216

Wales *see* England,
  Wales and
  Northern Ireland
WEA (Workers
  Educational
  Association) 228–9
weekend course
  provision, Bel. 76
Welsh Access Unit 128
Wollongong,
  University of 28
women, participation
  rates *see* gender
work-based
  learning 282, 283
  see also accreditation
  of prior learning
Workers Educational
  Association (WEA)
  228–9

Z-Prüfung ('Z-exam')
  171–2

*Zweiter Bildungsweg
  see* 'second
  educational route'

Author Index

Albarea, R. 188
Anderson, D. 22, 30, 33, 34–5
Anderson, R. 235, 244
Angelli, F. 183, 184, 185, 186, 192, 198
Anolli, L. 195
Arney, N. 228
Australian Bureau of Statistics 11
Australian Education Council Mayer Committee 21
Australian Education Council Review Committee 21

Bache, P. 85, 86, 98
Baker, K. 119
Ball, C. 107, 117, 233
Barwood, B. 25
Bird, J. 125
BMBW (Bundesminister für Bildung und Wissenschaft) 161, 162, 163, 168
BMUK (Bundesministerium für Unterricht und Kunst) 38, 41, 42, 43, 44, 45, 57
BMWF (Bundesministerium für Wissenschaft und Forschung) 38, 40, 41, 42, 43, 44, 45, 49, 50, 51, 52, 57
BOE (Boletin Official del Estado) 252, 253, 256, 258, 263
Bompard, P. 191, 193
Bordage, B. 141
Bourgeois, E. 2, 71, 76, 82
Bourner, T. 108, 128
Bredo, O. 88, 99
Brennan, J. 128, 235
Broadfoot, P. 2
Browning, D. 115
Bruton, K. 274
Bundesminister für Bildung und Wissenschaft see BMBW
Bundesministerium für Frauen und Jugend 164
Bundesministerium für Unterricht und Kunst see BMUK
Bundesministerium für Wissenschaft und Forschung see BMWF
Bund-Länder-Kommission für Bildungsplanung und Forschungsförderung und Bundesanstalt für Arbeit 168
Burgess, T. 106
Bussi, F. 187, 193, 194, 195, 196, 197

Canibol, H. 162, 176
Carroll, V. 128
Caspar, P. 138
Castles I. 8, 11, 12, 13, 14, 15
Catalano, G. 194, 195, 197
Central Advisory Council for Education 128
Central Bureau for Statistics 206
Centre de Recherche sur l'Emploi et la Production (CRESEP) 148
Centre for Contemporary Cultural Studies 232
CERI (Centre for Educational Research and Innovation) 3, 279
Cerych, L. 152
Charlot, B. 139
Clancy, P. 196
Clark, B. 185, 199
CNAA (Council for National Academic Awards) 106, 123
CNAM (Conservatoire National des Arts et Metiers) 152
Collins, J. 23
Colombo, P. 197
Committee of Enquiry, Higher Education Funding Council 125
Committee of Vice Chancellors and Principals 123
Committee on Higher Education 116
Committee on the Future of Tertiary

Education in
  Australia 7
Commonwealth
  Tertiary Education
  Commission
  (CTEC) 7, 15–16
Conservatoire
  National des Arts
  et Metiers (CNAM)
  152
Council for Academic
  Awards (CNAA)
  106, 123
Cox, R. 107
Cramer, G. 221
Crawley, G. 125
CRESEP (Centre de
  Recherche sur
  l'Emploi et la
  Production) 148
Cressard, A. 140, 142
Crossman, R. 188
CTEC
  (Commonwealth
  Tertiary Education
  Commission) 7,
  15–16
Cudworth, C. 243
Currie, J. 16

Dal, L. 68
Dalgarno, M. 241
Danish Research and
  Development
  Centre for Adult
  Education
  (DRDCAE) 99
D'Arcy, F. 122
Davidson, G. 125
Davies, P. 123, 128,
  140, 142, 147, 148,
  154, 172
Dechy, G. 146, 148

DEET (Department of
  Employment,
  Education and
  Training) Aus.
  17–18, 27, 29
Department for
  Education, Eng.
  104, 111, 112, 113,
  115, 119, 121, 125,
  128
Department of
  Education and
  Science (DES), Eng.
  and Sco. 103, 104,
  116, 117, 118, 122,
  124, 128, 226, 233,
  252
Department of
  Employment, Eng.
  118
Department of
  Employment,
  Education and
  Training (DEET),
  Aus. 17–8, 27, 29
Der Spiegel 163
DES *see* Department of
  Education and
  Science
Deutscher Industrie-
  und Handelstag
  175
Díaz Medina, R. 262
Donkers, B. 204
DRDCAE (Danish
  Research and
  Development
  Centre for Adult
  Education) 99
Dubar, C. 148
Duke, C. 126
Dunn, W. 243
Durand-Prinborgne,
  C. 145

Edizione, F. 192
Edwards, R. 107
Elliott, K. 128
Ellwood, S. 121, 126
Employment and
  Skills Formation
  Council Australia
  21
Epskamp, H. 174
Escuela Asturiana 256
Evans, N. 124

Farjas Abadia, A. 268,
  269
Federal Ministry of
  Education and
  Arts, Aust. 42
Federal Ministry of
  Education and
  Science, Ger. 159,
  160, 162, 170, 171
Federighi, P. 187
Fehrenbach, G. 175
Feldner, E. 46, 47
Feutrie, M. 150
Flash Formation
  Continue 149
Flecha, R. 261, 271
Foersom, T. 88, 99
Fondation
  Universitaire 67, 68
Francesco, C. de 190,
  192, 193, 194, 196
Fransen, J. 77
Freynet, P. 152
Führ, C. 162, 168
Fulton, O. 114, 121, 126
Further Education
  Unit 126

Gallacher, J. 235, 244,
  245, 246

Garcia de Leon, M.A. 260, 274
Gardner, M. 163
Gellert, C. 1, 3, 278, 280, 282, 285
Gent, B. van 221
Gent, F.A. van 221
GEW (Gewerkschaft Erziehung und Wissenschaft) 176
Gloger, A. 161, 176
Goedegebuure, L. 1, 3, 216, 283, 287
Gow, D. 163
Gracia Navarro, M. 262
Graham, B. 125
Granada, universidad de 259, 266, 267
Gray, J. 235
Griffin, A. 124, 128
Groupe de travail formation permanente 153
Groupe de travail l'ESEU 147, 148
Groupes de travail 153
Guin, J. 134, 139
Guyot, J.L. 68, 76, 82

Hake, B.J. 221
Halsey, A.H. 3, 4, 128, 189, 281
Hamed, M. 128
Harenberg, B. 161, 163, 167, 175
Hart, L. 241
Harvey, D.H. 125
Healy, G. 19, 28
Heath, A. 128
Heinz, G. 47
Henderson, E. 140, 145
Her Majesty's Inspectorate 126

Higher Education Funding Council, Committee of Enquiry 125
HIS (Hochschul-Informations-System) 162, 163, 164, 165, 166
Holmes, B. 252
Hore, T. 15, 16, 26, 33, 193
Houtkoop, W. 221

Ibáñez Aramayo, J. 256, 272, 273
Ideal 267
IFF (Institut für interdisziplinäre Forschung und Fortbildung) 59
Institute of Public Policy Research 118
Irvine H. 128
Irvine, J.M. 246

Jacobsen, B. 99
Jallade, J.P. 2, 4, 135, 140, 142
Jessup, G. 126
Johnes, J. 128
Johnstone, R. 242, 247
Jones, H.A. 110
Jordinson, R. 236

Karpen, U. 161, 162, 166, 167
Karstanje, P. 213
Kluge, N. 169, 171
KMK (Sekretariat der Ständigen Konferenz der Kultusminister der Länder in der Bundesrepublik Deutschland) 169, 172, 176
Kouwenaar, K. 203, 217
Krumrey, H. 162, 176

Lacroix, B. 135
Lamoure J. 135
Lamoure Rantopoulou, J. 135
Laursen, P. 89, 99
Lichtner, M. 187, 188, 196
Liénard, G. 68, 69
Liggett, E. 109
López Eisman, J.L. 262
Lovett, T. 234
Lowden, 247
Luzatto, G. 190, 193

Maassen, P.A.M. 209, 216
MacGregor, K. 193
Macpherson, I. 229
Madrigal Collazo, C. 268, 269
Mager, C. 126
Marchand, L. 70
Marchetti, A. 187, 188, 197
Marinucci, C. 181
Maroy, C. 71
Marshall, I. 245
Martinelli, I. 185, 189, 191
Marzo, A. 270
Matterson, C. 125
McIntosh, N.E.S. 110
McNair, J.M. 252
McPherson, A. 234

MEC (Ministerio de Educación y Ciencia) 252, 253, 256, 259, 260, 261, 262, 271, 273
Meek, L. 2
Meghani, S. 189
MEN (Ministère de l'Education Nationale), Fra. 135, 137, 139, 140, 141, 143, 144, 148
Mill, M. 245
Ministère de l'Education, Bel. 67
Ministère de l'Education Nationale, Fra. *see* MEN
Ministère de l'Enseignement supérieur de la Communauté française de Belgique 79
Ministerió de Educacion y Ciencia, Spa. *see* MEC
Ministry of Culture, Den. 94
Ministry of Education, Eng. 108
Ministry of Education and Research, Den. 84, 86, 88, 89, 91, 93, 94, 95, 96, 97, 99, 100
Ministry of Education and Science, Neth. 210, 217
Molloy, S. 128
Monasta, A. 189
Monno, S. 187
Moramarco, S. 187

Moscati, R. 190, 192, 196
Munn, P. 228, 247

Natale, L. de 188
National Advisory Body for Local Authority Higher Education 116
National Board of Employment, Education and Training (NBEET) 7, 29, 30
National Commission on Education 107
National Institute of Adult Continuing Education 118
National Training Task Force 127
NBEET (National Board of Employment, Education and Training) 7, 29, 30
Neave, G. 86, 134, 139, 288
Newport, A. 188
Nielsen, J.L. 84, 85, 89
Norton, B. 125

Observatoire de la vie étudiante 144
OECD (Organisation for Economic Co-operation and Development) 41, 42, 44, 47, 67, 68, 92, 195, 199, 220, 252, 260, 273
Office for Standards in Education 128

Open University 114, 115, 124
Orefice, P. 187
Osbat, L. 197
Osborn, M. 2
Osborne, M.J. 235, 245
Oviedo, Universidad de 265, 266

Palank, F. 55, 56
Parry, G. 17, 117, 123
Pascall, G. 107
Pearson, R. 233, 234
Peiró i Gregori, S. 271
Percy, K. 110
Platt, J. 106

Quintana Cabanas, J.M. 271

Ramos Corrada, 270
Rasmussen, T.K. 4, 85, 89, 92, 280, 282
Reibstein, E. 172
Reisinger, E. 172
Resandt, A. van 160, 168
Revuelta, J.M. 253
Ribolzi, L. 194, 195, 196, 198
Risk, M. 188
Robertson, D. 127
Robinson, P. 108, 247
Royal Instutute of British Architects 259
Royal Society of Arts 117
Ryan, S. 16

Index

Sabatier, P. 152
Sahli, A.M. 144
Saint George, P. de 76, 82
Scherer, H. 161, 176
Schmidt, H. 175
Scholz, W-D. 175
Scott, P. 190
Scottish Education Department (SED) 227, 236
Scottish Higher Education Funding Council (SHEFC) 227, 248
Scottish Office 233
Scottish Office Education Department *see* SOED
Scottish Tertiary Education Advisory Council (STEAC) 235
Scottish Universities Council on Entry (SUCE) 231, 240, 242
SED (Scottish Education Department) 227, 236
Sekretariat der Ständigen Konferenz der Kultusminister der Länder in der Bundesrepublik Deutschland (KMK) 169, 172, 176
Service Universitaire de Formation Continue (SUFOC) 148

Sharp, N. 241, 245
SHEFC (Scottish Higher Education Funding Council) 227, 248
Sheibani, A. 125
Simone, R. 190, 193, 200
Slowey, M. 110
Smart, D. 7
Smith, 108
Smithers, A. 121, 124, 128, 247
SOED (Scottish Office Education Department) 226, 227, 228, 229, 230, 233, 236, 238, 248
Squires, G. 110
SRC (Strathclyde Regional Council) 234
Stannard, J. 203, 217
Staropoli, A. 139
STEAC (Scottish Tertiary Education Advisory Council) 235
Stirling University 246
Strathclyde Regional Council (SRC) 234
SUCE (Scottish Universities Council on Entry) 231, 240, 242
SUFOC (Service Universitaire de Formation Continue) 148

Task Force on Human Resources, Education, Training and Youth 1
Taylor, J. 128
Teichler, U. 169
Tett, L. 228
Thaning, K. 89
Thompson, J. 234
Tight, M. 108, 125
Titmus, C. 152
Torsello, C. 185
Toyne, P. 16
Trivellato, P. 192, 193
Trow, M. 4, 104, 118, 198
Turrini, O. 187

UACE(S) (Universities Association for Continuing Education (Scotland)) 241
UNED (Universidad Nacional de Educación a Distancia) 269, 270
Universidad de Granada 259, 266, 267
Universidad de Oviedo 265, 266
Universidad Nacional de Educacion a Distancia (UNED) 269, 270
Universities Association for Continuing Education (Scotland) (UACE(S)) 241
University Grants Committee 116

Villa, P. 187, 188, 197
Vught, F.A. van 216

Wagnon, C. 148
Wake, C. 17
Wakeford, N. 128
Walker, P. 128
Waterschoot, V. 77
Webb, T. 84, 85, 89
Weert, E. de 4, 284
Weil, S.W. 107
Welsh Office 118
West, L.H.T. 11, 15, 16, 26, 33
Westerheijden, D.F. 216
Williams, K.E. 110
Wissenschaftsrat 161, 173, 174
Wolter, A. 166, 170, 171, 172, 173, 175
Woodley, A. 110, 128, 247
Wright, P. 4, 125
Wynne, R. 110, 128

Yates, J. 128